The Genesis of the GATT

This book is part of a wider project on the economic logic behind the General Agreement on Tariffs and Trade (GATT). This volume asks: What does the historical record indicate about the aims and objectives of the framers of the GATT? Where did the provisions of the GATT come from and how did they evolve through various international meetings and drafts? To what extent does the historical record provide support for one or more of the economic rationales for the GATT? This book examines the motivations and contributions of the two main framers of the GATT, the United States and the United Kingdom, as well as the smaller role of other countries. The framers desired a commercial agreement on trade practices as well as negotiated reductions in trade barriers. Both were sought as a way to expand international trade to promote world prosperity, restrict the use of discriminatory policies to reduce conflict over trade, and thereby establish economic foundations for maintaining world peace.

Douglas A. Irwin is Robert E. Maxwell Professor of Arts and Sciences in the Economics Department at Dartmouth College. He is author of *Free Trade under Fire* (2002) and *Against the Tide: An Intellectual History of Free Trade* (1996).

Petros C. Mavroidis is Edwin Parker Professor of Law at Columbia Law School, New York, and Professor of Law at the University of Neuchâtel. He is chief reporter of the American Law Institute for the project "Principle of International Trade: The WTO" and Research Fellow at the Centre for Economic Policy Research.

Alan O. Sykes is James and Patricia Kowal Professor of Law at Stanford Law School. A leading expert on the application of economics to legal problems, Sykes has focused his research on international economic relations.

The Genesis of the GATT

Douglas A. Irwin
Dartmouth College

Petros C. Mavroidis
Columbia Law School

Alan O. Sykes
Stanford Law School

The American Law Institute

CAMBRIDGE UNIVERSITY PRESS
Cambridge, New York, Melbourne, Madrid, Cape Town, Singapore,
São Paulo, Delhi, Dubai, Tokyo, Mexico City

Cambridge University Press
The Edinburgh Building, Cambridge CB2 8RU, UK

Published in the United States of America by Cambridge University Press, New York

www.cambridge.org
Information on this title: www.cambridge.org/9780521142069

© The American Law Institute 2008

This publication is in copyright. Subject to statutory exception
and to the provisions of relevant collective licensing agreements,
no reproduction of any part may take place without the written
permission of Cambridge University Press.

First published 2008
Reprinted 2009
First papreback edition 2009

A catalogue record for this publication is available from the British Library

Library of Congress Cataloging in Publication Data

Irwin, Douglas A., 1962–
The genesis of the GATT / Douglas A. Irwin, Petros C. Mavroidis, Alan O. Sykes.
  p. cm. – (American Law Institute reporters' studies on WTO law)
ISBN 978-0-521-51561-0 (hardback)
  1. General Agreement on Tariffs and Trade (Organization) – History. 2. Foreign trade
regulation – History. 3. Tariff – Law and legislation – History. I. Mavroidis, Petros C.
II. Sykes, A. O. III. Title. IV. Series.
K4609.5.I79 2008
343'.0870261–dc22   2008015269

ISBN 978-0-521-51561-0 Hardback
ISBN 978-0-521-14206-9 Paperback

Cambridge University Press has no responsibility for the persistence or
accuracy of URLs for external or third-party internet websites referred to in
this publication, and does not guarantee that any content on such websites is,
or will remain, accurate or appropriate. Information regarding prices, travel
timetables, and other factual information given in this work is correct at
the time of first printing but Cambridge University Press does not guarantee
the accuracy of such information thereafter.

Contents

Executive Summary	*page* ix
Preface	xi
Foreword	xiii

Introduction		1
1	**The Creation of the GATT**	5
	1.1 After the First World War	5
	1.2 The Atlantic Charter and Article VII Negotiations	12
	1.3 The Structure of Anglo-American Negotiations	22
	1.4 The 1942 Meade Draft for Commercial Union	27
	1.5 The Washington Seminar, September–October 1943	37
	1.6 Years of Deadlock and Delay, January 1944–September 1945	43
	1.7 The British Loan Negotiations, Washington, September–October 1945	65
	1.8 Moving Toward the GATT	72
	1.9 First Preparatory Meeting, London, October–November 1946	77
	1.10 Toward Geneva, December 1946–April 1947	80
	1.11 Second Preparatory Meeting, Geneva, Switzerland, April–October 1947	84
	1.12 Conclusion	95
2	**The Negotiation of the GATT**	98
	2.1 London Calling: the London Draft	104
	2.1.1 The Mandate	104
	2.1.2 Institutional Issues	106
	2.1.3 The Output	108
	2.1.4 An Assessment	109

2.2	Atlantic Crossing: the New York Conference (1947)		111
	2.2.1	The Mandate	111
	2.2.2	Institutional Issues	112
	2.2.3	The Output	113
	2.2.4	An Assessment	113
2.3	GATT Finalized: the Geneva Conference (1947)		114
	2.3.1	The Mandate	114
	2.3.2	Institutional Issues	115
	2.3.3	The Output	116
	2.3.4	An Assessment	119
2.4	The Havana Conference (1947–1948)		120
	2.4.1	The Mandate	120
	2.4.2	Institutional Issues	120
	2.4.3	The Output	121
	2.4.2	An Assessment	122
2.5	The Review Session of 1954–1955		122
	2.5.1	The Mandate	122
	2.5.2	Institutional Issues	122
	2.5.3	The Output	123
	2.5.4	An Assessment	123
2.6	Development Enters the GATT: Negotiating Part IV (1965)		124
	2.6.1	The Mandate	124
	2.6.2	Institutional Issues	126
	2.6.3	The Output	126
	2.6.4	An Assessment	132
2.7	The Evolution of the GATT Provisions		133
	2.7.1	MFN	133
	2.7.2	Tariff Reduction	135
	2.7.3	Internal Taxes (Domestic Regulation)	138
	2.7.4	Transit	143
	2.7.5	Antidumping and Countervailing Duties	144
	2.7.6	Tariff Valuation	146
	2.7.7	Customs Formalities	147
	2.7.8	Marks of Origin	149
	2.7.9	Publication and Administration of Trade Regulations	150
	2.7.10	Quantitative Restrictions	151
	2.7.11	Balance of Payments	153
	2.7.12	Exchange Restrictions	155
	2.7.13	Subsidies	156
	2.7.14	State Trading	159
	2.7.15	Safeguards	161

Contents vii

	2.7.16 General Exceptions	162
	2.7.17 Consultations – Dispute Settlement	165
	2.7.18 Preferential Arrangements	167
	2.7.19 Institutional Provisions	168
	2.7.20 Boycotts	169
	2.7.21 Information, Statistics, and Trade Terminology	170
2.8	Property Rights on the GATT	171

3 The Rationales for the GATT 176
   3.1 Economic Theory and Trade Agreements 177
   3.2 Commitments and Trade Agreements 184
   3.3 Foreign Policy Motivations for Trade Agreements 188
   3.4 Concluding Assessments 197

Conclusion 201

Annex A – Documents Relating to the Negotiations 203
  1 General Provisions for Inclusion in Trade Agreements (1941) 203
  2 A Proposal for an International Commercial Union (1942) 213
  3 Anglo-American Discussions under Article VII: Commercial Policy (1943) 222
  4 Proposed Multilateral Commercial Convention on Commercial Policy: Summary of Significant Provisions (1944) 239
  5 Excerpts from "Proposals for Expansion of World Trade and Employment" (1945) 244
  6 Preparations for Preliminary Meeting on Trade and Employment (1946) 261
  7 U.S. Delegation Report on First Preparatory Meeting for an International Conference on Trade and Employment (1946) 270
  8 U.S. Report on the Geneva GATT Negotiations (1947) 277

Annex B – Negotiating Committees and Subcommittees 285
  1 London Conference 285
  2 New York Conference 287
  3 The Geneva Conference 288
  4 The Havana Conference 291
  5 The Review Session 293
  6 The Negotiation of Part IV of the GATT 295

References 297
Index 307

Executive Summary

This book examines the rationales for concluding the General Agreement on Tariffs and Trade (GATT) in 1947. We do this mainly by evaluating the historical record, that is, the various phases of the negotiation of the GATT, and also the views, positions, and ambitions of the key negotiating partners. Our goal is not to provide a detailed account of the negotiating history of each and every GATT provision. However, we study the negotiating history of the most representative GATT provisions and, based on this discussion, aim to advance our understanding of the common intent of the GATT negotiators. This volume sets the stage for subsequent American Law Institute (ALI) volumes that will examine the role of economic theory in interpreting the GATT.

Our book consists of three parts: the first examines the diplomatic origins of the GATT in terms of the post-war economic planning by officials in the United States and the United Kingdom; the second studies the evolution of the provisions of the GATT text from the primary negotiating documents to their modern content; finally, the third advances some preliminary thoughts on the historic validity of the various economic- and international-relations explanations for the GATT.

Although we refer to existing historical accounts, we also rely extensively on *primary* historical sources. The first part uses official memoranda of important bilateral and multilateral discussions as well as the diaries and memoirs of participants. The second is based on the various negotiating documents from the London (1946), the New York (1947), the Geneva (1947), and the Havana (1948) conferences, as well as the Review Session (1955) and the negotiation of Part IV of the GATT on trade and development (1965).

We seek to put the negotiation of the GATT in its historical context. We focus on the particular and time-specific economic problems that confronted policymakers in the mid-1940s, as well as how state interests – and even personalities – played a role in shaping the GATT. In comparison to modern-day trade delegations, the small composition of national delegates 60 years ago is remarkable. Back then, a handful of remarkable personalities participated directly or indirectly in the negotiation of the GATT: Will Clayton and Harry Hawkins from the United States; James Meade, Lionel Robbins, and John Maynard Keynes from the United Kingdom; Norman Robertson from Canada; and Alexandre Kojève from France. These remarkable personalities produced a text dealing with highly complicated issues that has managed to withstand the test of time for more than 60 years now. We hope our work sheds new light on some of the possible reasons for this success.

Preface

This book is the first in a series sponsored by the American Law Institute (ALI) on the foundations of world trade law as found in the General Agreement on Tariffs and Trade (GATT) and other agreements dealing with trade in goods under the auspices of the World Trade Organization (WTO). The project is entitled Principles of World Trade Law and aims at illustrating the basic principles guiding trade liberalization. The ALI appointed Henrik Horn, Petros C. Mavroidis, Kyle W. Bagwell, Gene M. Grossman, Robert W. Staiger, and Alan O. Sykes as reporters. Douglas A. Irwin has been invited to act as a coauthor in this first volume.

This book sets the stage for the subsequent volumes by exploring the circumstances that gave rise to the GATT in 1947. It examines the origin and evolution of specific provisions that comprise the GATT, as well as present government documents and negotiate drafts relating to the creation of the GATT. In the course of our research, we have accumulated many intellectual debts that we wish to acknowledge. We are grateful to Lance Liebman and Elena A. Cappella of the ALI for their support of this project. We are indebted to Todd Feldman at ALI for expert editorial assistance. Judith M. Cole and Sandrine Forgeron at ALI helped to organize a meeting at the Columbia Law School on November 8, 2007, in which we were able to receive valuable feedback on our work. We are greatly indebted to the conference participants for their helpful advice and comments: Steve Charnovitz, William Davey, Richard Gardner, Merit Janow, Anne Krueger, Åke Lindén, John Odell, and Joel Trachtman. We also received useful feedback on our work at a meeting sponsored by the John S. Dickey Center for International Understanding at Dartmouth College, and we thank colleagues – particularly Stephen Brooks, Jennifer Lind, and Benjamin Valentino – for useful feedback. We also benefited from the comments of participants at seminars in Washington, DC, sponsored by the American Enterprise Institute, the World Bank, and the International Trade Commission, particularly Claude Barfield,

Bernard Hoekman, Gary Horlick, John Jackson, Brink Lindsay, and Amy Porges. In addition, we wish to thank Susan Aaronson, Marc Bacchetta, Kyle Bagwell, Chad Bown, Geoffrey Carlson, "Coach" Vince Deluca, Wilfred Ethier, Bernard Gordon, Susan Howson, Harold James, Mark Koulen, Francine McKenzie, David Palmeter, Andrés Rodríguez-Clare, Simon Schropp, Robert Staiger, Richard Toye, Joel Trachtman, and Thomas Zeiler for helpful comments, encouragement, and assistance.

We are further indebted to John Dickson, Luigi Stendardo, and particularly Bruno Ventrone (all at WTO) for being continuously available and for helping us trace documents of utmost importance for this research project. Yahaira Alonzo, Luis Bello, Alexander Blechman, Kory Hirak, and Ashley "Pere-Pere" Pineda responded beyond the call of duty when preparing this book. We are further grateful to Susan Aaronson for providing us with many documents from the U.S. National Archives, which we have supplemented with our own research visits there. We also thank James Miller and Richard Toye for generously sharing with us their unpublished manuscripts on closely related topics. Finally, Irwin thanks the Rockefeller Center at Dartmouth College, and particularly its director, Andrew Samwick, for financial support for the archival research in this volume.

Foreword

The American Law Institute has sought since 2001 to assist the development of coherent and economically rational legal principles governing world trade. We have published three volumes analyzing recent decisions by the World Trade Organization. The chapters analyzing decisions, each the cooperative work of an economist and a lawyer, point the way to interpretations of the relevant treaty that would supply predictability and fairness valuable to nations and to economic actors.

Having focused on specific decisions by the WTO, we have now begun an effort to craft general principles governing this vital area at the intersection of law and economics. Engaged in our work are leading scholars of the field. As is always our practice, their drafts will receive constructive criticism from other engaged experts. Meanwhile, three distinguished professors have prepared this volume, a history of the General Agreement on Tariffs and Trade that supplies important background information for understanding where trade policy and trade law are today. Some aspects of the subject are dry, but this is also a riveting account of growing international interdependency and cooperation as World War II ended and of remarkable personalities, including the great John Maynard Keynes.

The large American Law Institute effort on trade law was conceived and is led by Professor Henrik Horn of the University of Stockholm and Professor Petros Mavroidis of Neuchatel University in Switzerland and Columbia University in New York. This book was authored by Professor Mavroidis, along with Professor Douglas Irwin of Dartmouth College in New Hampshire and Professor Alan Sykes of Stanford University in California. We are immensely grateful to them and to the many individuals who have suggested improvements when they read earlier drafts or attended conferences discussing earlier drafts. We also appreciate the generous financial support for our trade-law work from the Jan Wallander and Tom Hedelius Foundation in Stockholm and from the Milton and Miriam Handler Foundation in New York.

                                                Lance Liebman
                                                Director
                                                The American Law Institute

Introduction

At a conference in the *Palais des Nations*, in Geneva, Switzerland, representatives of 23 countries met from April to October 1947 and established two key pillars of the postwar world trading system. First, they created a legal framework for commercial policy by finalizing the text of the General Agreement on Tariffs and Trade (GATT). Second, the Geneva participants negotiated numerous bilateral agreements to reduce import tariffs, the benefits of which were extended to other GATT parties through the unconditional most-favored nation (MFN) clause. As a result, this landmark meeting produced a framework for postwar commercial relations in which governments agreed to rules about the use of certain trade barriers and to negotiate tariff reductions with one another. This system of multilateral cooperation has proven to be an enduring regime under which international trade has flourished for over half a century.

This book examines the origins of the GATT. There are many studies of the GATT from legal and economic perspectives, but relatively few that examine how the GATT emerged from the ashes of World War II. The goal of our study is to appreciate the original goals and intentions of its founders by reviewing the diplomatic history that gave rise to this remarkable agreement, and to understand why the GATT took the particular shape and form that it did, in terms of the various provisions included in or excluded from the text.

Chapter 1 focuses on the negotiations between the United States, the United Kingdom, and other countries during and immediately following World War II that led to the Geneva conference. The GATT grew out of discussions between government officials from the United States and the United Kingdom during the war. After seeing international trade stifled under the weight of protectionist measures during the 1920s and 1930s, officials from both countries had a compelling interest in pursuing policies that would reduce trade barriers and help expand world trade after the war. They sought to foster a more liberal trade system by developing a broad set of rules that would restrict the arbitrary use of trade restrictions, as well as initiate the process of negotiating reductions in existing trade barriers.

While the U.S. and UK governments agreed on the most important and basic principles to be included in a trade agreement, they differed on many substantive details that affected the shape of the GATT. Once these two countries agreed on a document that could serve as a basis for negotiation, other countries were invited to participate in shaping the provisions of the GATT and the charter for an International Trade Organization. Drawing on archival documents, the diaries and memoirs of participants, published and unpublished cable traffic and government memoranda, as well as many secondary sources, we aim to shed light on the political constraints on both sides of the Atlantic that affected the commercial-policy discussions.

Chapter 2 examines the evolution of the GATT as a legal text. The first draft of a proposed charter for an International Trade Organization (ITO) emerged from the State Department in August 1944. The first publicly released draft of the charter was published by the State Department in December 1945 on the basis of bilateral U.S.-UK discussions during the British loan negotiations. A revised draft emerged at the conclusion of multilateral consultations in London from September-December 1946. Officials in London appointed a drafting committee, which met at Lake Success, New York, in January-February 1947, to produce a formal draft of both a General Agreement on Tariffs and Trade and a charter for an International Trade Organization for consideration at the April 1947 Geneva meeting. This chapter traces how the provisions of the GATT evolved as a result of these meetings, and how the composition of the countries involved at each stage affected the specific details in the GATT text and shaped the form that it ultimately took.

In Chapter 3, we assess the GATT in light of recent economic and political theories that seek to understand the specific rationale for the existence of trade agreements. These theories include the idea that the GATT is motivated by terms of trade externalities across countries, by governments seeking external commitments to reduce the power of domestic interest groups, and by broader foreign policy and national security considerations. This chapter uses the history developed in the previous chapters to enhance our understanding of the motivations (sometimes different across countries) for why they chose to sign an international agreement on commercial policy.

In addition, we present an annex with key official documents whereby the reader can trace the evolution of government proposals and negotiating strategies that eventually produced the GATT in 1947. Annex A consists of documents that give us important insight into the American and British positions regarding a trade agreement. This includes such items as a short memorandum prepared in

Introduction

1942 by an economist working in the Economic Section of the War Cabinet, James Meade, which was perhaps the first official government document that explicitly envisioned a multilateral commercial agreement after the war, to various State Department cables that reveal the thinking of key officials as the negotiations evolved. Annex B includes the participants in the various committees and sub-committees that were established during the negotiation of the GATT.

The legal and diplomatic record of the 1940s is enormous and many interrelated issues were considered simultaneously by government officials. We strive to limit our focus to a narrow but important part of the bilateral U.S.-UK relationship, i.e., the commercial-policy discussions that led to the GATT. We do not address related issues, such as the 1944 Bretton Woods negotiations on the international monetary system, the British loan of 1945, or even the difficult 1947 Geneva negotiations over trade barriers and the major dispute over imperial preferences, except to provide background as they relate to the provisions of the GATT. Furthermore, given our exclusive focus on the GATT, we do not examine the ultimate failure of the ITO, a subject considered in greater detail by Diebold (1952), Aaronson (1996), Odell and Eichengreen (1996), and Zeiler (1999).

There is an abundance of excellent work on the GATT, yet many of the standard references take the GATT 1947 as their point of departure, giving only a cursory sketch of the events that gave rise to it. For example, the classic works of John Jackson (1969), Kenneth Dam (1970), and Robert Hudec (1975), have analyzed the GATT as an international legal text, and other important books, such as Gerard Curzon (1965) and Karin Koch (1969), have examined the early activities of the GATT as an international organization. Yet both types of work take the GATT as given and focus less on its origins or where the text originated.

Our work builds on the classic work of Richard Gardner, *Sterling-Dollar Diplomacy* (1956). Gardner was one of the first scholars to consider the Anglo-American economic negotiations during World War II, and his book has stood the test of time for clarity and insight. While he focuses on both the monetary and trade discussions, we focus exclusively, and in somewhat greater detail, on the trade negotiations and texts. Later works, particularly Thomas Zeiler's *Free Trade, Free World: The Advent of GATT* (1999), also examine in great detail the diplomatic maneuvering and national motivations in the negotiations that led to the GATT, as do Miller (2003) and Toye (2008). Susan Ariel Aaronson's *Trade and the American Dream: A Social History of Postwar Trade Policy* (1996) is also a notable, archival-based examination of U.S. trade-policy formation in the 1940s.[1] These works, however, tend to avoid discussion of the specific provisions

---

[1] There are also several country studies of trade policy, such as for Australia (Capling 2001) and Canada (Hart 1993, Rasmussen 2001), that examine how these countries responded to U.S.-UK proposals during the 1940s.

that eventually comprised the GATT text. While our book also does not aim to be a definitive history of the origins of the GATT, we hope it provides a deeper understanding of the basis for this important agreement.

We also hope that this book, which has been published shortly after the 60th anniversary of the 1947 Geneva conference that established the GATT, serves as a reminder of the remarkable and long-lasting achievements made just a little over half a century ago.

1 The Creation of the GATT

1.1 After the First World War

To understand the origins of the GATT, one must appreciate the traumatic events of the 1920s and 1930s. The period between World War I and World War II was a political and economic disaster, scarred by the Great Depression and the rise of fascism. A strong desire to avoid repeating this experience after World War II, along with the abandonment of isolationism by the United States in favor of a leadership role in world affairs, fostered support around the world for a new approach to international economic cooperation.

The outbreak of World War I in 1914 interrupted what had been a period of growing worldwide economic prosperity with moderate tariffs and expanding world trade supported by a well-functioning international monetary system (the gold standard). After the shock of World War I, the international trade and payments system recovered very slowly during the 1920s. Most countries only gradually phased out wartime controls on trade, while tariff levels remained higher than before the war. The United Kingdom did not return to the gold standard until 1925, and other countries waited even longer before restoring the convertibility of their currencies. Under the auspices of the League of Nations, the World Economic Conference of 1927 aimed to return the world economy to its previous state of vigor. But the Conference only started an international discussion of matters such as tariff levels, most-favored-nation clauses, customs valuation, and the like.

The gradual restoration of the world economy was interrupted by a worldwide recession starting in 1929. This economic downturn was met by greater protectionism, which in turn further reduced world trade. Although monetary and financial factors were primarily responsible for allowing the recession to turn into the Great Depression of the early 1930s, the spread of trade restrictions aggravated the problem. The commercial policies of the 1930s became characterized as "beggar-thy-neighbor" policies because many countries sought to insulate their own economy from the economic downturn by raising trade barriers. Blocking imports proved to be a futile method of increasing domestic employment because one country's imports were another country's exports. The combined effect of this inward turn of policy was a collapse of international trade and a deepening of the slump in the world economy.[1]

The United States bore some responsibility for this turn of events. What started out in 1929 as a legislative attempt to protect farmers from falling agricultural prices led to the enactment of higher import duties across the board in 1930. The Hawley-Smoot tariff of that year pushed already high protective tariffs much higher and triggered a similar response by other countries. According to the League of Nations (1933, 193),

> the Hawley-Smoot tariff in the United States was the signal for an outburst of tariff-making activity in other countries, partly at least by way of reprisals.

Canada, Spain, Italy, and Switzerland took direct retaliatory trade actions against the United States, while other countries also adopted higher tariffs in an attempt to insulate themselves from the spreading economic decline. The United Kingdom made a sharp break from its traditional free-trade policies by imposing emergency tariffs in 1931 and enacting a more general Import Duties bill in 1932. France and other countries that remained on the gold standard long after others had abandoned it for more reflationary policies imposed import quotas and exchange restrictions in an attempt to safeguard their balance of payments and stimulate domestic economic activity.

Many countries also turned to discriminatory trade arrangements in the early 1930s, both for economic and political reasons. At a conference in Ottawa in 1932, the United Kingdom and its dominions (principally Australia, Canada, New Zealand, and South Africa) agreed to give preferential tariff treatment for one another's goods. This scheme of imperial preferences involved both higher duties on non-British Empire goods and lower duties on Dominion goods and drew the ire of excluded countries for discriminating against their trade. Meanwhile, under the guidance of Reichsbank President Hjalmar Schacht, Nazi Germany concluded a series of bilateral clearing arrangements with central European countries that effectively created a new trade bloc, orienting the trade of these countries toward Germany at the expense of others. In Asia, Japan created the

---

[1] See the League of Nations (1942), Kindleberger (1986), Kindleberger (1989), and James (2001).

1.1 After the First World War

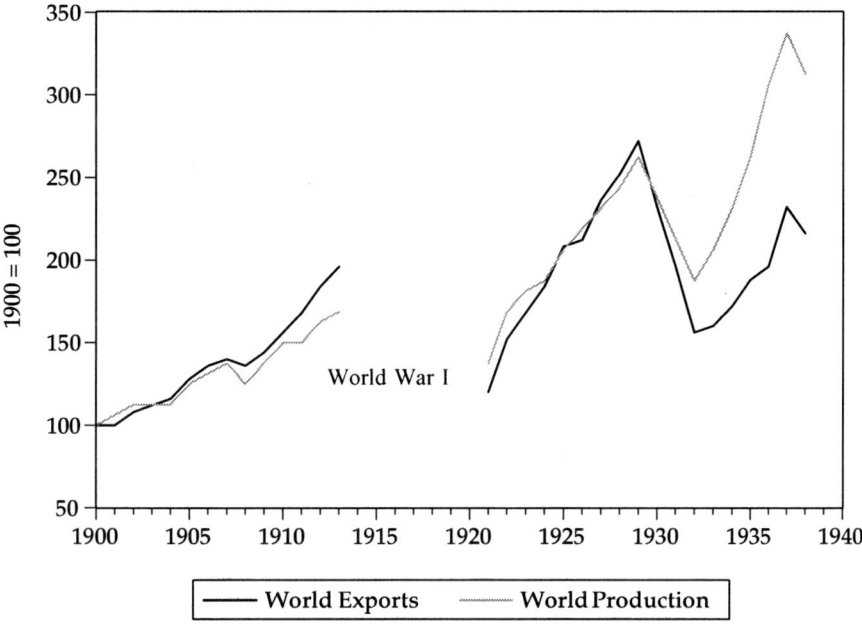

Figure 1.1. The Volume of World Trade and Production, 1900–1938. *Source:* Norbom (1962).

Greater East Asia Co-Prosperity sphere to extend its political and economic influence throughout the region and siphon off trade for its own benefit.

The outcome of these protectionist and discriminatory trade policies was not just a contraction of world trade, but a severe breakdown in the multilateral trade and payments system that the world economy had enjoyed prior to World War I and had started to revive in the late 1920s. Official conferences and multilateral meetings, notably the World Economic Conference in 1933, offered pronouncements to resist protectionism, but failed to stem the spread of inward-looking antitrade economic policies. The economic distress of the decade also had political consequences, undermining faith in democratic governments to manage their economies and hence abetting a turn to more authoritarian regimes in Germany and elsewhere.

Figure 1.1 shows the level of world exports and world production from 1900 to 1938. Although trade tended to grow faster than production prior to World War I and even in the 1920s, it collapsed to a much greater extent in the early 1930s. Even more important, having been saddled with a new and heavy layer of trade restrictions, world trade failed to rebound significantly after the recovery had begun. Even by 1938, world trade was still well below its 1929 peak. The growth of protectionist measures had stifled world trade and thereby, in the minds of many economic officials, hindered a full and complete recovery from the Depression.

However, having initiated the move toward greater protectionism in the 1930s, the United States also became one of the first countries to try to reverse these detrimental developments. For the first time in its history, the United States began to take a serious and active role in reducing trade barriers and expanding world trade in cooperation with other countries. After the Republican party that was responsible for the Hawley-Smoot tariff in 1930 was swept from office in the 1932 election, the Democratic administration of President Franklin D. Roosevelt formulated a new approach to trade policy. Recognizing that it could not undertake a unilateral reduction in American tariffs in the midst of the depression, the Roosevelt administration sought to negotiate bilateral trade agreements to reduce tariffs in concert with others. In 1934, the Democratic-majorities in Congress enacted the Reciprocal Trade Agreement Act (RTAA), which allowed the President to reduce American tariffs by up to 50 percent in the context of bilateral trade agreements that employed the unconditional most-favored-nation (MFN) clause. With this authority, originally granted for three years and subsequently renewed, the Roosevelt administration concluded more than 20 trade agreements during the 1930s.

Although these agreements had a limited effect in boosting world trade during the tumultuous 1930s, the RTAA marked a new beginning for U.S. trade policy, shifting it in a more liberal direction. The RTAA changed the course of American trade policy in several ways.[2] First, by enacting the RTAA, Congress effectively gave up the ability to legislate duties on specific goods when it delegated tariff negotiating power to the executive. Congressional votes on trade policy were now framed simply in terms of whether or not (and under what circumstances) the RTAA should be continued, so vote trading among particular import-competing interest groups was no longer possible. In addition, the national electoral base of the President is often thought to make the executive more likely to favor policies that could benefit the nation as a whole (such as open trade), whereas the narrower geographic representative structure of Congress would lead its members to have more parochial interests. For instance, the President may be more likely than Congress to take into account the broader foreign-policy ramifications of trade policy that affect the country as a whole.

Furthermore, the RTAA reduced the threshold of political support needed for members of Congress to approve executive tariff-reduction agreements. The renewal of the RTAA required a simple majority in Congress, whereas prior to the

---

[2] The academic literature on the RTAA is quite large. See Haggard (1988), Bailey, Goldstein, and Weingast (1997), Hiscox (1999), Irwin and Kroszner (1999), and Schnietz (2000).

1.1 After the First World War

RTAA any foreign-trade treaty negotiated by the President had to be approved by two-thirds of the Senate. Tariff-reducing agreements thus needed only the support of the median legislator, not that in the 67th percentile. This meant that protectionist forces would have to muster greater support to block tariff-reduction agreements under the RTAA, by refusing to renew the legislation, than under a treaty, when a minority could (and frequently did) veto it.

Finally, the RTAA helped to bolster the bargaining and lobbying position of exporters in the political process. Previously, import-competing domestic producers were the main trade-related lobby group on Capitol Hill since the benefits to these producers of high tariffs was relatively concentrated. Exporters were harmed indirectly by these tariffs, but the cost to exporters of any particular duty was relatively diffuse, and therefore exporters failed to organize an effective political opposition. The RTAA bundled foreign tariff reductions that were beneficial to exporters with lower tariff protection for import-competing producers. By directly linking lower foreign tariffs to lower domestic tariffs, the RTAA may have fostered the development of exporters as an organized interest group opposed to high tariffs and supporting international trade agreements.

The key figure behind this shift in U.S. trade policy was Cordell Hull, Roosevelt's Secretary of State. Hull was a southern Democrat, a politician from a region and party that had traditionally and strongly supported low tariff barriers to trade. As a member of Congress during World War I, Hull grew to appreciate the global ramifications of domestic tariff policy. In his memoirs, Hull (1948, 84, 81) recalled:

> When the war came in 1914, I was very soon impressed with two points.... I saw that you could not separate the idea of commerce from the idea of war and peace.... [and] that wars were often largely caused by economic rivalry conducted unfairly.... But toward 1916 I embraced the philosophy that I carried throughout my twelve years as Secretary of State.... From then on, to me, unhampered trade dovetailed with peace; high tariffs, trade barriers, and unfair economic competition, with war. Though realizing that many other factors were involved, I reasoned that, if we could get a freer flow of trade – freer in the sense of fewer discriminations and obstructions – so that one country would not be deadly jealous of another and the living standards of all countries might rise, thereby eliminating the economic dissatisfaction that breeds war, we might have a reasonable chance for lasting peace.

As a result, Hull was an early advocate of international cooperation on trade matters. In 1916, he called for the establishment of a permanent international congress that would consider

> all international trade methods, practices, and policies which in their effects are calculated to create destructive commercial controversies or bitter

economic wars, and to formulate agreements with respect thereto, designed to eliminate and avoid the injurious results and dangerous possibilities of economic warfare, and to promote fair and friendly trade relations among all the nations of the world (Hull 1948, 81–82).

The spread of illiberal trade policies and rise of international tensions in the 1920s and early 1930s confirmed to Hull the lessons he had learned during World War I. As he declared in 1937:

I have never faltered, and I will never falter, in my belief that enduring peace and the welfare of nations are indissolubly connected with friendliness, fairness, equality and the maximum practicable degree of freedom in international trade (Dam 1970, 12).

Having been chosen by Roosevelt to serve as Secretary of State, Hull was uniquely positioned to pursue his belief that freer trade might lead to economic and political conditions that would be more favorable to peace. Hull fought a long and hard bureaucratic battle to ensure that the official U.S. government position on international-trade policy was his State Department's vision of a world more open to trade and free from discriminatory commercial policies.[3] Hull helped design the RTAA and led the fight for its passage by Congress. The administration requested Congressional authority to reduce tariffs by no more than 50 percent on a selective, product-by-product basis to avoid injuring domestic industries. The goal was not "free trade" in the sense of zero tariffs, then an inconceivable objective, but simply to reduce "excessive" tariffs and allow some additional growth in foreign trade.

Hull was an especially sharp critic of imperial preferences because of their adverse effect on U.S. exports, particularly to the United Kingdom and Canada, two of America's most important markets. Testifying before Congress in 1940, Hull called imperial preferences "the greatest injury, in a commercial way, that has been inflicted on this country since I have been in public life" (Gardner 1956, 19). Hull particularly desired a trade agreement with the United Kingdom and Canada to reduce the discriminatory effect against U.S. exports. In 1938, the United States and the United Kingdom signed a reciprocal trade agreement, but the negotiation was difficult and the results were limited. Despite Hull's best efforts, the agreement failed to put a dent in Britain's system of tariff preferences.

---

[3] At least initially, the Roosevelt administration was deeply divided between internationalists in the State Department, foremost among them Secretary Hull, and economic nationalists elsewhere who supported the New Deal program of government price supports (in agriculture and through industrial codes) that might be undermined without controls on imports. For a study of Hull and the early trade-agreements program, see Butler (1998). Allen (1953) also examines Hull's trade beliefs.

1.1 After the First World War

Furthermore, the agreement went into effect in January 1939 but was rendered moot a few months later when Britain adopted extensive controls on imports with its entry into World War II in September.

During World War II, as we shall see, Hull inspired the State Department's efforts to develop more ambitious plans to reduce trade barriers after the war "based on a conviction that such liberal commercial policies and the development of the volume of commerce would constitute an essential foundation of any peace structure that civilized nations might erect following the war." While often criticized for being naive about the linkage of trade and peace, Hull firmly believed that

> a revival of world trade [is] an essential element in the maintenance of world peace. By this I do not mean, of course, that flourishing international commerce is of itself a guaranty of peaceful international relations. But I do mean that without prosperous trade among nations any foundation for enduring peace becomes precarious and is ultimately destroyed.[4]

Although Hull retired as Secretary of State in November 1944 and was not directly involved in the GATT negotiations, he gave the State Department a strong and lasting intellectual direction. As America's longest-serving secretary of state and imbued with a deep ideological attachment to the reduction of trade barriers, Hull shaped the State Department's approach to trade policy long after his departure. As Miller (2003, 12) put it:

> When Hull initiated postwar planning in 1939, he had already enjoyed six years in which to accrue trade policymaking power for the State Department. Over the course of his tenure, he carefully chose a group of men, based upon their views about trade, to formulate his favoured policies: if the officials arrived in the Department without decided views, then senior officials quickly inculcated them. Never before had trade policy originated in such a centralised, small, and carefully controlled location. More than any of their predecessors or successors, Hull's men shared several advantages: tremendous power relative to other branches of government, uniformity of opinion and purpose, and the Secretary's passionate commitment to their work and results.

While critics mocked his single-minded focus on trade policy, Hull ultimately persevered in his quest to develop a more liberal international trading system based on multilateral cooperation. Indeed, the reciprocal trade agreements program of the 1930s gave U.S. trade officials negotiating experience that allowed them to move with relative ease into discussions over postwar

---

[4] State Department *Bulletin* 8 (April 17, 1943), 329.

arrangements. By the end of the 1939, the United States had concluded trade agreements with 22 countries. While the impact of the tariff reductions in these agreements was modest, the provisions in the agreements formed the basis for a future multilateral accord. For example, in a template trade agreement from 1941, reproduced in Annex A-1, Article 1 is the unconditional most-favored nation clause. Other articles cover internal taxes, import quotas, exchange controls, monopolies and government purchases, customs administration, withdrawal or modification of concessions, safeguards, exceptions to MFN treatment, territorial application, and provisional application, among others. These provisions served as the basis for U.S. trade proposals during the war and many were ultimately included in the GATT. Hence, the GATT was not created from scratch, but represented a continuation and expansion of U.S. efforts during the 1930s.

In some sense, the goal of Cordell Hull's life was to further the objective of trade liberalization. For almost single-handedly repositioning U.S. trade policy in the 1930s and inspiring the efforts at postwar planning during the 1940s, Hull was the most important individual responsible for what ultimately became the GATT.

1.2 The Atlantic Charter and Article VII Negotiations

The outbreak of the European war in September 1939, and particularly the fall of France in June 1940, put the United States in the awkward position of formal neutrality and yet having a vital stake in the survival of the United Kingdom. With American public opinion opposed to any direct military involvement in the war, the Roosevelt administration sought to provide assistance to Britain through the Lend Lease program. Despite fears that this would embroil the country in the war, Congress passed the Lend Lease Act in March 1941. This enabled the federal government to transfer billions of dollars worth of equipment and supplies to the United Kingdom and later to other allies as well.

A key provision of Lend Lease was its deliberate disavowal of any requirement for a financial settlement for the goods provided. This provision aimed to avoid the difficult problems associated with debt repayments after World War I. Instead, as compensation for the U.S. assistance, Britain was required to provide a "direct or indirect benefit which the president deems satisfactory." This unspecified benefit became known as "the consideration" and was the price that Britain would have to pay for American aid.

The decision to settle Lend Lease debts without monetary or financial repayments had a profound impact on the shape of the postwar economic system. The United States decided to extract foreign-policy promises from the United

1.2 The Atlantic Charter and Article VII Negotiations

Kingdom and required its participation in a new world economic framework. This also meant that the State Department, rather than the Treasury Department, would be the lead U.S. government agency responsible for handling the consideration.[5] While the Treasury Department would have primary authority for handling postwar international monetary and finance issues, the State Department took the lead in most other postwar arrangements, such as creating the United Nations and negotiating postwar trade agreements.

This put Cordell Hull and the State Department in a much stronger position to eliminate imperial preferences than they had been in 1938 when they sought to do so in a reciprocal trade agreement. In 1941, Britain was in a much weaker position and desperately required American assistance. Hull therefore aimed to use "the consideration" to extract from the United Kingdom a pledge to abolish imperial preferences and to support a more liberal and nondiscriminatory international trade regime. Early State Department drafts of the lend-lease agreement called for the elimination of all imperial preferences.[6]

In June 1941, John Maynard Keynes, representing the UK Treasury, was dispatched to Washington to discuss the possible terms of a mutual aid agreement. At this point, Britain's goal was to postpone any specific commitments on postwar economic policy.[7] But U.S. officials were not to be dissuaded. On July 28, 1941, Assistant Secretary of State Dean Acheson presented Keynes with a draft aid agreement. Article VII of the draft read:

> The terms and conditions upon which the United Kingdom receives defense aid from the United States of America and the benefits to be received by the United States of America in return therefore, as finally determined, shall be such as to not burden commerce between the two countries but to promote mutually advantageous economic relations between them and the betterment of world-wide economic relations; they shall provide against discrimination in either the United States or the United Kingdom against

---

[5] In May 1941, President Roosevelt gave the State Department the principal responsibility for negotiating a Lend Lease agreement with the United Kingdom (FRUS 1941, III, 5). As Treasury Secretary Henry Morgenthau wrote, "As far as I am concerned, I am licked in the State Department.... Every time the President asks me to do something, Mr. Hull goes into a sulk and gets mad.... I am through being the President's whipping boy on the foreign affairs staff... Let the President of the United States tell Mr. Hull what kind of document he wants... " Quoted in Kimball (1971, 248).

[6] Reynolds (1982, 275ff) suggests that State Department officials Sumner Welles and Dean Acheson, rather than Franklin Roosevelt or Cordell Hull, argued for this tough position.

[7] "The Foreign Office advised stalling on any suggestion for commitment on post-war policy... This firm stonewalling reflected British optimism that either there would be no Consideration at all or that it might be largely and acceptably non-economic" (Pressnell 1986, 31).

the importation of any product originating in the other country; and they shall provide for the formulation of measures for the achievement of these ends (FRUS 1941, III, 15).

Keynes asked whether this raised the question of whether imperial preferences, exchange controls, and other trade measures would be restricted in the postwar period. Acheson replied that it did, but assured Keynes that

> the article was drawn so as not to impose unilateral obligations, but rather to require the two countries in the final settlement to review all such questions and to work out to the best of their ability provisions which would obviate discriminatory and nationalistic practices and would lead instead to cooperative action to prevent such practices (FRUS 1941, III, 11).

This produced a long outburst from Keynes, who was dismayed at what he perceived to be an attempt to force unilateral obligations on the United Kingdom by taking aim at imperial preferences and other trade controls that might be desirable in the postwar world.[8] Keynes privately dismissed this first draft of Article VII as the "lunatic proposals of Mr. Hull" (Harrod 1951, 512). In Keynes's view, the State Department had "taken the opportunity to introduce their pet idea in language which they meant to be technical; whereas the President himself had nothing so definite in view and meant only to require that we should agree to co-operate and to do so in a certain spirit and with a certain good purpose" (Pressnell 1986, 36).

Keynes made no promises and told Acheson that the British government was divided over postwar trade policy; some wanted a return to free trade, another group (including Keynes) believed in the use of import controls, and a third

---

[8] According to Acheson's minutes of the meeting: "Mr. Keynes then spoke for some time quite strongly about this provision. He said that he did not see how the British could make such a commitment in good faith; that it would require an imperial conference and that it saddled upon the future an ironclad formula from the Nineteenth Century. He said that it contemplated the impossible and hopeless task of returning to a gold standard where international trade was controlled by mechanical monetary devices and which had proved completely futile. He said that the only hope of the future was to maintain economies in balance without great excesses of either exports or imports, and that this could be only through exchange controls, which Article VII seemed to ban. He went on to say that the language used in Article VII had a long history; that it permitted all sorts of cunningly devised tariffs, which were in fact discriminatory and prohibited sound economic monetary controls. Finally, he said that at the end of the war we will probably have a great excess of exports, the British would require a considerable excess of imports, and that the formula provided in Article VII was wholly impossible. I replied to Mr. Keynes that I thought he was taking an extreme and unjustified position and that it must be clear to him that no one would be less likely to impose a rigid and unworkable formula upon future developments than the President." FRUS 1941, III, 12.

1.2 The Atlantic Charter and Article VII Negotiations 15

group wanted to maintain imperial preferences (FRUS 1941, III, 13). However, Keynes came around – "at the end of our talk he seemed more reconciled to the Article, but by no means wholly so," Acheson reported – and promised to take the draft to London for review.

The next day, after he had calmed down, Keynes wrote to Acheson:

> I should not like it to be thought because of my cavilling at the word "discrimination" that the excellence and magnanimity of the first part of that Article VII and of the document as a whole had gone overlooked.... My so strong reaction against the word "discrimination" is the result of my feeling so passionately that our hands must be free to make something new and better of the postwar world; not that I want to discriminate in the old bad sense of that word – on the contrary, quite the opposite.... But the word calls up, and must call up – for that is what it means strictly interpreted – all the old lumber, most-favored-nation clause and the rest which was a notorious failure and made such a hash of the old world. We know also that won't work. It is the clutch of the dead, or at least the moribund, hand. If it was accepted it would be cover behind which all the unconstructive and truly reactionary people of both our countries would shelter. We must be free to work out new and better arrangements which will win in substance and not in shadow what the President and you and others really want. As I know you won't dispute this, we shall be able to work something out. Meanwhile forgive my vehemence which has deep causes in my hopes for the future (FRUS 1941 III, 16–17).

Still, Keynes was shocked, in this instance and many others, at what he viewed as the State Department's outdated 19th-century laissez-faire ideology of simply reducing government trade intervention in the postwar era. For example, Keynes (1980, 239) dismissed one State Department memo on trade as

> a dogmatic statement of the virtues of laissez-faire in international trade along the lines familiar forty years ago, much of which is true, but without any attempt to state theoretically or to tackle practically the difficulties which both the theory and the history of the last twenty years has impressed on most modern minds.

Keynes strongly believed that government economic planning would be required to ensure full employment in the postwar period. Such planning, in his view, would necessarily include government controls on international trade.[9]

---

[9] An economic official at the U.S. Embassy in London, E. F. Penrose (1953, 18), recalled about this period: "At that time and later I did my best to impress on Mr. Keynes and other government economists that the desire for freer and for non-discriminatory trade in the State Department should not be written off as the product of a nineteenth century

The State Department and other U.S. agencies took a very different view. Not only did they want nondiscrimination as a key part of the world trading system, but they also wanted to ensure that most international trade would be left in the hands of private enterprise, not government planners.

The clash between Keynes and Acheson over imperial preferences would be repeated at nearly every Anglo-American meeting over the next six years. The next occasion for an exchange of views was in August 1941, when President Roosevelt and Prime Minister Winston Churchill met at Placentia Bay off the coast of Newfoundland. The two leaders sought to issue a joint declaration on the purposes of the war against fascism and the guiding principles to be followed after the war. Churchill presented a first draft of the Atlantic Charter that included the pledge that the two countries would

> strive to bring about a fair and equitable distribution of essential produce... between the nations of the world (Wilson 1991, 164).

Under Secretary of State Sumner Welles tried to introduce tougher language that called for the "elimination of any discrimination." Roosevelt softened this to say that mutual economic relations would be conducted "without discrimination," but even this proved to be unacceptable to Churchill. When presented with a draft stating that the countries

> will endeavor to further the enjoyment by all peoples of access, without discrimination and on equal terms, to the markets and to the raw materials of the world which are needed for their economic prosperity,

Churchill asked whether this would apply to the Ottawa Agreements. Wells said yes, but assured the Prime Minister that the phrase "will endeavor" meant that no commitments would be made. Churchill replied that any change in imperial preferences would require consultations with the Dominions and therefore discrimination could be eliminated only "with due respect for existing obligations" (Wilson 1991, 163–172). Over the strong objections of Welles, Roosevelt accepted this language.[10]

> laissez-faire attitude toward economic affairs, untouched by recent economic thought and experience.... In conversations in Washington both Acheson and Hawkins showed themselves progressive in outlook and under no illusion that freer trade alone was panacea for all economic ills. However, it soon appeared that the contrary view had been expressed to British officials in Washington by some U.S. officials outside the State Department." Markwell (2006) provides a good study of Keynes's views on international economic matters.

[10] As Welles later put it, "I said that in my own judgment further modification of that article would destroy completely any value in that portion of the proposed declaration. I said that it was not a question of phraseology, that it was a question of a vital principle which was

1.2 The Atlantic Charter and Article VII Negotiations

The final version of the Atlantic Charter read:

. . . .

Fourth, they will endeavor, with due respect for their existing obligations, to further the enjoyment by all States, great or small, victor or vanquished, of access, on equal terms, to the trade and to the raw materials of the world which are needed for their economic prosperity;

Fifth, they desire to bring about the fullest collaboration between all nations in the economic field with the object of securing, for all, improved labor standards, economic advancement and social security;

While the British were relieved at this outcome, Cordell Hull and other State Department officials, who were not present at the summit, were dismayed. Hull (1948, 975–976) later recalled that he was "keenly disappointed" with the fourth article because the "with due respect" qualification "deprived the article of virtually all significance since it meant that Britain would continue to retain her Empire tariff preferences against which I had been fighting for eight years." Indeed, State Department officials would not give up their attack on imperial preferences, which in their view "combined the twin evils of discrimination and politicization of foreign trade" (Woods 1990, 18).[11] Hull immediately sought clarification of the language with his British counterparts and pushed for stronger language in future meetings.

Meanwhile, American and British civil servants continued drafting the specific provisions and language of the Mutual Aid Agreement. The United

involved. I said that if the British and the United States Governments could not agree to do everything within their power to further, after the termination of the present war, a restoration of free and liberal trade policies, they might as well throw in the sponge and realize that one of the greatest factors in creating the present tragic situation in the world was going to be permitted to continue unchecked in the post-war world. . . . I said, however, that it seemed to be imperative that we try to agree now upon the policy of constructive sanity in world economics as a fundamental factor in the creation of a new and better world and that except through an agreement upon such a policy by our two governments there would be no hindrance whatever to a continuation later to the present German practices of utilizing their trade and financial policies in order to achieve political ends." FRUS 1941, I, 362.

[11] As the State Department saw it, "Britain under the Ottawa Agreements granted special low tariff duties and signed long-term bulk-purchasing agreements with empire trading partners in order to monopolize their raw materials and make sure that they took only British-manufactured products," writes Wood (1990, 18). "Imperial preferences could be used, then, not only to monopolize the trade of a particular nation or region; it also could be used to isolate and punish political and military rivals. In a political as well as an economic sense, the structure established by the Ottawa Agreements seemed the antithesis of multilateralism."

Kingdom did not respond to Acheson's draft of Article VII, which he had given to Keynes in July, until October 1941. The British reply contained a weak and ambiguous pledge to avoid discrimination with the qualification that any policy change would require the approval of the Dominions.[12] Acheson delivered an American redraft in December 1941, which added that the two countries would take action, "open to participation of all other countries of like mind," to expand world trade and seek "the elimination of all forms of discriminatory treatment in international commerce, and to the reduction of tariffs and other trade barriers" (FRUS 1941, III, 43–45). In explaining this language to the U.S. Ambassador in London, Cordell Hull insisted that unilateral obligations were not being imposed on the United Kingdom and that "with respect to the provision concerning discrimination, all that we ask is that the British sit down with us to work out the problems which lie ahead so that we may avoid substituting trade warfare in peacetime for the present wartime cooperation" (FRUS 1941, III, 49).

Despite these reassurances, British officials did not quite trust the State Department's continued attentive focus on imperial preferences and did little to resolve this impasse.[13] The British chose a strategy of delay not only because they had no desire to constrain future policy by any such commitments, but they also believed that Cordell Hull and the State Department were the only faction in the Roosevelt administration that really wanted the elimination of imperial preferences.[14] For example, in January 1942, six months after the Atlantic summit, Winston Churchill wrote to the UK Ambassador to the United States:

> All this fussing about what is to happen after the war is premature at the present time, when we are probably a long way from any satisfactory conclusion. It is only the State Department which is pressing. . . . I told the President

[12] The British draft retained the language of the American except: "they shall provide for joint and agreed action by the United States and United Kingdom, each working within the limits of their governing economic conditions, directed to securing as part of a general plan the progressive attainment of a balanced international economy, the avoidance of harmful discriminations, and generally the economic objectives set forth in the joint Declaration made by the President of the United States of America and the Prime Minister of the United Kingdom on August 12th [14th] 1941." FRUS (1941 III, 42).

[13] The U.S. Ambassador to the United Kingdom, John Winant, reported that "I could not get the Prime Minister himself to seriously consider the issue or the arguments." FRUS (1941, III, 50).

[14] As Winant cabled Washington, "The reason for failure to treat our position with sufficient seriousness is based on an assumption here that both the President and Mr. Morgenthau are themselves indifferent to that position and that it is rather a special position taken by Mr. Hull based on his general economic policy as expressed in the trade agreements which he has advocated so consistently for so many years. There is a further feeling that no great difficulty will be encountered in persuading the Congress to make the necessary appropriations under Lend-Lease now that we are in the war." FRUS (1942, I, 528).

1.2 The Atlantic Charter and Article VII Negotiations

that the Imperial Preference would raise great difficulties in England if raised as a separate issue now but that if raised at the end of the war as part of a large economic settlement, in which the United States would become a low tariff country, it would probably be easy to handle. He seemed to think this very sensible.... I should recommend you to stall any demand from the State Department with the usual diplomatic arts (Pressnell 1986, 50–51).

The precarious political position of the Churchill government was the key reason for its caution. Churchill himself had been a lifelong supporter of free trade and opponent of imperial preference. In 1903, Churchill left the Conservative party and joined the Liberals over Joseph Chamberlain's plan to introduce tariff preferences for the Empire, although he later rejoined the Conservatives. But as leader of a coalition wartime government, Churchill refused to take a strong stand on the issue. This is because the Conservative faction in the government, led by Leopold Amery, the Secretary of State for India, strongly supported close ties to the former colonies.[15] The Conservatives threatened to revolt, possibly bringing down the government, if a promise was made to dismantle imperial preferences. Amery was allied with Lord Beaverbrook, the newspaper baron and Minister of Supply, who clung to the ideas of imperial unity, freedom from foreign entanglements, and a distant relationship with the United States. By contrast, the Labour Party prided itself on antiimperialism, professed indifference to imperial preferences, and had a stronger free-trade than tradition the Conservatives.

Consequently, the British government was sharply divided over the Anglo-American mutual aid agreement. The Foreign Office supported accepting the American terms, while the Treasury – perhaps influenced by Keynes – opposed the agreement. The cabinet remained deadlocked, with a small but determined Conservative minority adamantly opposed.[16] As a result, Britain was unable to move.

[15] At the time of the Chamberlain debate, Amery attacked free trade in newspapers and wrote *The Fundamental Fallacies of Free Trade* (1906). According to Amery, the volume of British trade mattered less than remedying the country's deficiency in raw materials and foodstuffs by the export of its manufactures and services in partnership with the Empire's primary producers.

[16] In Winant's analysis: "The opposition is political. It is based on fear of a division in the Conservative Party. The idea that an agreement should be made with the United States in which the sovereignty of the unity of the Empire is questioned, even in the field of economics by the inclusion of the no discrimination clause in article 7, is opposed by Empire preference Tories who, in my opinion, are nothing more than imperialists. They represent a small but determined minority among the Conservative membership of the Parliament. [Anthony] Eden is the only man in the government who really fights to support our position and this in spite of the fact that Keynes and other economists have come to agree with our position." FRUS 1942, I, 528.

Yet the British belief that America's opposition to imperial preferences was simply a State Department obsession misread the stance of the U.S. government. The United States had a longstanding hostility to British imperialism and colonial trade networks. Furthermore, Hull reported directly to President Roosevelt; even if imperial preferences was an issue that only concerned Hull, if he could convince the president that it was an important issue, then the future of the Anglo-American relationship hinged on its resolution. To demonstrate that it was not just a State Department concern, Hull persuaded Roosevelt to cable Churchill and express his firm support for the draft. On February 11, 1942, Roosevelt telegraphed Churchill and urged him to conclude the mutual aid agreement soon.[17] But he added this reassurance:

> I want to make it perfectly clear to you that it is the furthest thing from my mind that we are attempting in any way to ask you to trade the principle of Imperial Preference as a consideration for Lend-Lease

because Britain was:

> no more under an obligation to get rid of Imperial Preference than the Americans were to get rid of their protective tariffs.[18]

Hull could not have been pleased with the President's language, but Roosevelt's assurance broke the deadlock in the British war cabinet. This persuaded Churchill, according to Cabinet minutes, that "Article 7 contained no commitment in advance to abolish Empire Preference, which should be excluded from our discussions," whereas Roosevelt clearly stated that everything should be put on the table and that nothing was excluded (Wilson 1991, 278, 369, n. 108). The

---

[17] While Roosevelt believed an agreement should be concluded quickly, he privately thought that the difficulties about discrimination were "unwarranted by the text" and even believed that "Further attempts to refine the language of Article VII would be wholly unprofitable and time-consuming" because of the "persistent misunderstanding of Article VII in London" (FRUS 1942, I 526).

[18] Roosevelt continued: "All I am urging is an understanding with you that we are going to have a bold, forthright, and comprehensive discussion looking forward to the construction of what you so aptly call 'a free, fertile economic policy for the post-war world.' It seems perfectly clear to me that nothing should now be excluded from those discussions. None of us knows how those discussions will turn out, although, as I told you when you were here last, I have great confidence that we can organize a different kind of world where men shall really be free economically as well as politically.... What seems to be bothering the Cabinet is the thought that we want a commitment in advance that Empire preference will be abolished. We are asking for no such commitment, and I can say that Article 7 does not contain any such commitment. I realize that that would be a commitment which your government could not give now if it wanted to; and I am very sure that I could not, on my part, make any commitment relative to a vital revision of our tariff policy." FRUS (1942, I, 535–536).

1.2 The Atlantic Charter and Article VII Negotiations

next day, Churchill informed the War Cabinet of Roosevelt's message when it met to discuss on Article VII and the mutual aid agreement. Roosevelt's assurance persuaded the War Cabinet that the Article VII language was acceptable and they endorsed the agreement.

This Cabinet decision paved the way for the Mutual Aid Agreement, which was signed in Washington on February 23, 1942. The key provision read:

> ARTICLE VII
>
> In the final determination of the benefits to be provided to the United States of America by the Government of the United Kingdom in return for aid furnished under the Act of Congress of March 11, 1941, the terms and conditions thereof shall be such as not to burden commerce between the two countries, but to promote mutually advantageous economic relations between them and the betterment of world-wide economic relations. To that end, they shall include provision for agreed action by the United States of America and the United Kingdom, open to participation by all other countries of like mind, directed to the expansion, by appropriate international and domestic measures, of production, employment, and the exchange and consumption of goods, which are the material foundations of the liberty and welfare of all peoples; to the elimination of all forms of discriminatory treatment in international commerce, and to the reduction of tariffs and other trade barriers; and in general, to the attainment of all the economic objectives set forth in the Joint Declaration made on Aug. 12, 1941, by the President of the United States of America and the Prime Minister of the United Kingdom.
>
> At an early convenient date, conversations shall be begun between the two governments with a view to determining, in the light of governing economic conditions, the best means of attaining the above-stated objectives by their own agreed action and of seeking the agreed action of other like-minded governments.[19]

Unfortunately, not only did this agreement fail to specify the precise terms of the consideration, but also both governments clung to different interpretations about what had been agreed to. Some in the State Department believed that Britain had definitively committed itself to eliminate imperial preferences. Yet UK officials believed that they had merely agreed to put preferences on the bargaining table as something to talk about at a future date. In its view, altering imperial preferences required consultation with the Dominions, which might perhaps agree to some preference reductions in exchange for American tariff

---

[19] Department of State *Bulletin*, February 28, 1942, pp. 190ff.

reductions. This divergence in interpretation persisted right down to the final hours of the Geneva GATT negotiations in October 1947.[20]

1.3 The Structure of Anglo-American Negotiations

The problems in securing an agreement over the language in Article VII foreshadowed the difficulties that the two countries would have in future negotiations over tariffs and trade preferences. Many of the difficulties concerned the substantive issues at stake. But there were important domestic political constraints that shaped the negotiating positions and attitudes of both sides as well. The structure of governmental decisionmaking, as well as domestic political views on the issue of trade, and even personality differences, had a critical impact on the negotiations and their outcome.

The U.S. and UK governments were not monolithic entities. Each was comprised of several departments and ministries, each of which had different institutional responsibilities and reflected different interests. Each bureaucratic agency had a different outlook on postwar economic problems and sought to have its views reflected in the shape of the postwar world trading system. Furthermore, within each agency a distinction can be made between the staff level and the political level of decision-making. The staff level (career civil servants or academics on leave from university) formulated policy options, drafted texts, conducted the actual negotiations, and attempted to resolve technical differences. Most of the bilateral contact was made at the staff level, and these specialists, often economists, on both sides were frequently willing to liberalize trade and set rules to a point far beyond where the political-level officials might be comfortable. Of course, ultimate decision-making powers rested with political-level officials, usually cabinet officers or appointed department heads who reported to the president or prime minister. These officials were constrained by a broader set of political forces, including interest-group pressure, electoral considerations, and legislative mandates, than were the civil-servant staff. They also had to deal with many foreign-policy issues in addition to trade and were usually not as committed as the staff to a particular outcome in the negotiations. On both sides of the Atlantic, at one time or another, the civil servants became very frustrated with decisions (or indecisions) of their political-level superiors.

In the United States, the Department of State was the lead agency in the trans-Atlantic commercial-policy negotiations.[21] Led by Secretary Cordell Hull,

---

[20] See Pressnell (1986, 57–59) on how Churchill's misinterpretation led the War Cabinet to approve the agreement.

[21] Of course, the Department of Treasury (and Assistant Secretary Harry Dexter White) led the American delegation at the Bretton Woods conference that created the International Monetary Fund.

1.3 The Structure of Anglo-American Negotiations

State Department officials strongly supported cooperative efforts to arrive at international agreements to reduce trade barriers and expand trade. Hull's State Department was also implacably hostile to discriminatory trade arrangements, foremost among them the British system of imperial preferences. While Hull provided the broad vision that became the State Department's mission, after his retirement in 1944 his goals were shared by and implemented at the political level by William Clayton. A southern businessman who established a successful cotton-brokerage firm, Clayton moved from the Commerce Department to the State Department in 1944, where he served first as Assistant Secretary and then Under Secretary of State for Economic Affairs. In some ways, Clayton was even more firmly committed than Hull to trade liberalization and the destruction of imperial preferences.

The State Department civil servants responsible for the actual trade negotiations were clustered in the Division of Commercial Policy and Trade Agreements.[22] This department had very close ties to Cordell Hull and Will Clayton due to their own deep interest in trade matters. The longtime head of this division was Harry Hawkins, an economist who earned universal respect in that position.[23] Hawkins had been an assistant professor of commerce at the University of Virginia before he joined the State Department in 1924. In 1944, Hawkins became Minister-Counselor for Economic Affairs at the U.S. Embassy in London.[24] In 1945, Clair Wilcox, a professor of economics at Swarthmore College,

---

[22] Notter (n.d.) provides a detailed history of this particular section of the State Department.

[23] Hull had enormous faith in Hawkins and relied on him for almost all commercial-policy-related issues. In his memoirs, Hull (1948, 366) praised Hawkins this way: "No one in the entire economic service of the Government, in my opinion, rendered more valuable service than he. Hawkins was a tower of strength to the department throughout the development of the trade agreements, and especially in our negotiation with other countries, which at times were exceedingly difficult." Notter's history of the Division of Commercial Policy attributes much of the Division's success to Hawkins's abilities. He notes that, under Hawkins's guidance, the Trade Agreements Committee never took a vote because he was so good at reaching a committee-wide consensus. In James Meade's view, Hawkins "has a most interesting and responsible job which he thoroughly enjoys and does extremely well.... In our commercial policy talks, he has been consistently acute and on the spot, but at the same time very sensitive to any difficulties or embarrassments which we may have been in; and instead of trying to score off any such embarrassments, he has always tried to help us out of our difficulties" (HM, 133). Riding in a car with John Fuqua, a State Department civil servant, Meade wrote: "We spoke about Hawkins who is his chief and whom he clearly worships (not unjustifiably I think)" (HM, 139). Another State Department civil servant, John Leddy, who drafted that GATT, said that Hawkins "was probably the most influential and important man second to Cordell Hull, in launching, operating, and administering the Reciprocal Trade Agreements program." http://www.trumanlibrary.org/oralhist/leddyj.htm#transcript (last visited Jan. 17, 2008). Unfortunately, Hawkins published very little, but did author a 1948 article on the ITO and a 1951 book on trade negotiations.

[24] In 1948, he moved to the Fletcher School of Diplomacy at Tufts University.

became director of the Office of Trade Agreements. In that position, Wilcox led the U.S. delegation (under Clayton) at the 1947 Geneva GATT negotiations and the 1947–1948 Havana ITO negotiations.

However, the political level of the State Department, as well as the president, had to be more attuned to the political constraints than the staff. In particular, they had to be very sensitive to the views of the Congress, which had constitutional authority over trade policy and delegated negotiating powers to the executive branch. Partisan factors also played a role in the relationship between the executive and legislative branches. The Democrats had long advocated lower tariffs, whereas the Republicans supported protectionist tariffs such as the Hawley-Smoot tariff of 1930, for which it was responsible. For most of this period discussed in this chapter, Presidents Franklin Roosevelt and Harry Truman enjoyed the support of a Democratic majority in both chambers of Congress, a majority that was broadly sympathetic to the administration's objectives. This enabled the critical 1945 renewal of the RTAA to move successfully through Congress, although with important constraints, as we will see. However, in November 1946, the Republicans captured the Congress and nearly derailed the 1947 Geneva conference on more than one occasion.

The State Department's enthusiasm for lower trade barriers was also somewhat restrained by other government bodies that participated in an interagency process to arrive at a unified government position. These agencies included the Departments of Agriculture, Labor, and Commerce, as well as the Treasury and the Tariff Commission. However, the State Department was clearly the lead agency, causing some resentment among the others, because the chain of command was clear: the Secretary of State reported directly to the President and could bypass other agencies if need be. As long as the Secretary had the support of the President, the State Department maintained a powerful hold on the administration's trade policy.

In the United Kingdom, policy formulation was quite different from that in the United States. Britain's cabinet government meant that policy was set by consensus at the cabinet level, rather than directly by the Prime Minister. (Parliament also played a secondary role, whereas Congress was always looming in the background in the United States.) Unlike Roosevelt, who did not rely on a cabinet consensus and whose party controlled Congress, Churchill had to compromise in order to ensure the survival of his wartime coalition government that was composed of both Conservatives and Labour ministers. These parties took differing positions on postwar trade policy. The Conservatives supported protectionist policies in the past and strongly defended imperial preferences with the Dominions. Conservative ministers, in particular Leopold Amery, the Secretary of State for India, Lord Beaverbrook, the Minister of Supply, and R. S. Hudson, the Minister for Agriculture, all opposed liberalizing trade or

1.3 The Structure of Anglo-American Negotiations

eliminating trade preferences. Meanwhile, the Labour party wanted to expand trade, but was also wedded to economic planning and socialism. They faced the daunting task of reconciling their desire for both a more socialist system and more liberal commercial policies to allow the expansion of world trade. Churchill actually received more support from Labour on the government's commercial-policy initiatives with the United States, but in order to maintain his coalition government he could not completely ignore the Conservative voices in his cabinet.

The Board of Trade was the lead government agency responsible for the commercial-policy negotiations. The Board formulated policy options and coordinated the approval process with other agencies before any proposal reached the Cabinet level. The Board was headed by Hugh Dalton (a Labour MP, a former student of Keynes, and previously a reader at the London School of Economics) from 1942 to 1945. From 1945 to 1947, the Board of Trade was headed by Sir Stafford Cripps (Labour MP), who played a pivotal role at the 1947 Geneva negotiations. The key civil servant at the Board of Trade was the Second Secretary, initially Sir Percivale Liesching (1942–1946) and later James R. C. Helmore (1946–1952).

The development of Britain's commercial policy was also influenced by the Economic Section of the War Cabinet Secretariat. The Economic Section, akin to the postwar Council of Economic Advisers in the United States, was staffed more by academics than career civil servants. From 1941 to 1945, the Section was headed by Lionel Robbins, a distinguished professor of economics from the London School of Economics. The wartime staff included economists James Meade and J. Marcus Fleming.[25] Previously, Meade had been a Fellow and Lecturer in economics at Hertford College, Oxford, and had worked at the Economic Intelligence Service at the League of Nations in Geneva. In 1940, Meade published a short book entitled *The Economic Basis of a Durable Peace* in which he examined the principles that might serve as the basis for a postwar international economic order. Echoing Cordell Hull, Meade (1940, 11) believed that an international economic body should be created as part of a postwar settlement because

> to a certain extent, the causes of international conflict are economic in character; and for this reason only an International Organization which is based upon a stable, just, and efficient economic foundation can hope to succeed in its primary political tasks.

---

[25] Fleming later served at the International Monetary Fund, where he helped develop the famous Mundell-Fleming model of open-economic macroeconomics (for which Mundell won the Nobel prize in 1999, Fleming having died in 1976).

International trade policy, he noted, would be one of the major concerns of such an organization. He joined the Economic Section in 1940 and was primarily responsible for developing the early commercial-policy proposals. After the war, Meade directed the Economic Section from 1946 to 1947 before taking a position at the London School of Economics, where he wrote his classic two-volume work *The Theory of International Economic Policy* for which he won the Nobel prize in economics in 1977.

The Economic Section provided advice and analysis to the Board of Trade in support of its commercial-policy initiatives, and Robbins and Meade were often included in the discussions with the United States. The interagency process was also more fluid in the British system. For example, unlike the United States, the Treasury played an important role in shaping Britain's position in the trade negotiations. Here, the formidable Cambridge economist John Maynard Keynes was a critical presence. Keynes was skeptical of the trade liberalism emanating from the Board of Trade and Economic Section, both because he doubted an acceptable multilateral agreement could be reached and because he did not want to limit domestic discretion to use trade controls (such as import quotas) as a means of ensuring full employment. Keynes was not a consistently strong supporter of the open, multilateral trading system, something that dismayed other economists, such as Meade, Robbins, and Fleming. Throughout the 1940s, the Treasury was constantly concerned about Britain's postwar balance-of-payments problems. In addition, the Dominions Office feared that any erosion in imperial preferences would offend the former colonies.

One of the remarkable aspects of the wartime Anglo-American trade discussions was that the staff level consisted of a small number of dedicated and internationally minded civil servants and economists who met each other frequently and grew to know each other well.[26] Harry Hawkins and his staff met frequently with Liesching, Robbins, and Meade. Relations were quite cordial and, at this level, they could convince one another of the merits of a particular

---

[26] See Ikenberry (1992). As E. F. Penrose (1953, 12–13), an economic official at the U.S. Embassy in London, put it: "In London, Ottawa, and Washington small groups of civil servants played a large part in the initiation as well as in the detailed preparation of plans for the postwar period. They were made up of an effective combination of permanent officials and of temporary officials who were drawn into government service for the war period, and some of whom were outstanding economists. The union of these two types of officials in wartime was fruitful in many ways: not only were the newcomers able to fill gaps which could not be filled from the ranks of permanent officials, but the experience and intellectual equipment of each type supplemented those of the other to the advantage of both of them. No such array of economic talent had ever before been mobilized in the service of government in the three capitals."

1.4 The 1942 Meade Draft for Commercial Union

position. For the most part, these economists did not always agree with decisions made at the political level, but they could do little to alter those decisions. One difference between the two countries at the staff level was that the Americans felt free to express their own views and speculate as to what might be possible, whereas the British felt constrained by their government's official instructions.[27]

However, bilateral relations at the political level tended to be more difficult mainly because these higher officials were responsible for handling disagreements that could not be resolved at the staff level. These disagreements brought into play more important national priorities and more sensitive domestic interests. Will Clayton and Stafford Cripps clashed frequently at the 1947 Geneva conference, for example, although those disputes were more about the degree of tariff reductions and elimination of imperial preferences than the provisions of the multilateral commercial convention.

We know a great deal about the Anglo-American trade discussions because many of the British participants, including Keynes, Meade, Robbins, Amery, and Dalton, kept diaries and other personal papers from the period. On the American side, unfortunately, there are no notable diaries; although Hull and Acheson have memoirs, there is not detailed discussion of commercial policy in them. However, there is an abundance of cable traffic and departmental memos in the National Archives and the *Foreign Relations of the United States* volumes that provide insight into the internal U.S. discussions.

The Anglo-American trade discussions took place during a unique period in history when a few individuals had enormous influence over the shape of postwar policy. These key officials, often internationally minded economists who had witnessed the interwar debacle, were set upon a special mission: to restore world trade to its previous flourishing condition.

1.4 The 1942 Meade Draft for Commercial Union

Having finalized Article VII of the Mutual Aid Agreement, government officials from the United States and the United Kingdom began to focus on the broad outlines of the postwar system of monetary and commercial relations. Soon after the Atlantic Charter was issued, British officials took the initiative and began drafting proposals on postwar economic policy before the Americans became committed to their own scheme. In June 1941, R. J. Shackle, a civil servant at

---

[27] As Meade noted, "Some Americans have no appreciation of the fact that when British civil servants have no instructions from senior officials or from ministers they necessarily become, in accordance with the traditions of their service, particularly constipated – unlike the Americans who in such circumstances feel freer than ever to express their most personal opinions without any sense of corporate responsibility" (HM, 121).

the Board of Trade, wrote a memorandum on postwar economic reconstruction that emphasized getting American support for a multilateral system of open trade, convertible currencies, and limited exchange-rate flexibility (Cairncross and Watts 1989, 96; CAB 123/53). Shackle stressed the importance of restoring convertible currencies as a means of financing trade, and his memorandum stimulated official thinking about the postwar economic system. James Meade at the Economic Section of the War Cabinet Secretariat promptly endorsed this proposal:

> The Board of Trade is right in emphasising the need for a regime of multilateral international trade after the war . . . as opposed to any system based upon bilateral barter, and preferential trade treatment between particular countries (Miller 2003, 132).

The importance of convertible currencies was widely recognized to be a prerequisite to a fully functioning multilateral trading system. This meant that the design of the postwar international monetary system was going to be a critical element of any agreement between the United States and the United Kingdom. As a result, John Maynard Keynes drafted a proposal for an International Clearing Union in late 1941, which was issued as a government paper in August 1943.

In July 1942, nearly a year after Shackle's memorandum, Meade wrote a short memorandum entitled "Proposal for an International Commercial Union," a precursor to what would eventually become the GATT (Annex A-2).[28] Meade argued that "if ever there was a community which had an interest in the general removal of restrictions to international commerce, it is the United Kingdom" and that it, "above all other countries," would gain from "a removal of those discriminations and rigid bilateral bargains which remove the opportunities for multilateral trading." But, he added, the country's strategy should be

> to implement these [Article VII] undertakings in a way which leaves room for state trading and which does not preclude us (a) from imposing restrictions or discriminations against us or (b) from restricting our payments to other countries if and when balance-of-payments difficulties make such action inevitable.

[28] "If any one event can be designated as marking the origin of the International Trade Charter and the International Trade Organization proposed at Havana in 1947, it took place in Whitehall in the latter part of 1942," wrote E. F. Penrose (1953, 89–90), an economic attache at the U.S. Embassy in London. "If any one person can be described as the originator of the movement for an International Trade Organization it is James Meade, who at the time was a member of the Economic Section of the War Cabinet secretariat."

1.4 The 1942 Meade Draft for Commercial Union

Meade highlighted several features of a possible multilateral trade convention. In his view, an International Commercial Union would have three essential characteristics: (i) open membership to all states willing to carry out the obligations of membership, (ii) no preferences or discrimination (with an exception for imperial preference) among the participants, and (iii) a commitment to

> remove altogether certain protective devices against the commerce of other members of the Union and to reduce to a defined maximum the degree of protection which they would afford to their own home producers against the produce of other members of the Union.

The exception regarding preferences would allow "discrimination of any degree desired against countries which were not members of the Commercial Union" and "would also permit discrimination of a defined and moderate degree in favour of a recognized political or geographic grouping of states, and would thus permit the continuation of a moderate degree of Imperial Preference."

Meade stated that the multilateral reductions in trade barriers would "not, however, imply laissez-faire, and are in no way incompatible with a system of state trading." Finally, a charter would create an International Commerce Commission "of a semi-arbitral semi-judicial nature" to which members could refer complaints "in order to obtain an opinion on whether the Charter of the Union was being broken by any particular action of a particular member of the Union." Meade viewed the dispute-settlement mechanism as "an essential part" of the Commercial Union, but noted that it was "premature at this stage to make detailed suggestions about the constitution of such a body."

Meade sent his draft to Hugh Gaitskell, the Principal Assistant Secretary at the Board of Trade, who reworked it and, in August 1942, passed it along to Hugh Dalton, the president of the Board of Trade. Impressed by the paper, Dalton got behind the proposal: "I agree generally with the policy proposed, though many points of detail are of first-class importance – and first-class controversial value," he wrote to Gaitskell (Pimlott 1985, 399).[29] Dalton requested that Meade

---

[29] As Dalton (1986, 476) noted in his diary entry for August 18, 1942: "Read, before going to bed, a paper by Meade and Gaitskell on Commercial Union. This is quite bright, though with some little defects, and ties up pretty well with the paper on the Clearing Union. I discuss this with Gaitskell next morning and agree that I will put it round to the officials, with a laudatory Minute, so that it shall emerge as a Board of Trade official paper. This will be better than a ministerial paper, since it is rather free trade and might, therefore, provoke outbursts from more than one quarter." Dalton was a Labour MP who, in his 1935 book *Practical Socialism for Britain*, advocated reducing import barriers with other countries either multilaterally or bilaterally. Such a proposal had an uneasy relationship with the economic planning that he and many in the Labour party later envisioned. See Toye (2000, 192, 195).

be seconded to the Board of Trade to help formulate the commercial-policy proposals in greater detail. In November 1942, Dalton circulated the paper to other ministries "having taken account, but not too much account of all the frightened and too prudent shrieks of my higher officials" (Dalton 1986, 506).

Dalton then formed an interdepartmental committee, headed by Arnold Overton Permanent, the Secretary of the Board of Trade, to formulate a consensus position on the country's commercial policy. In December 1942, the Overton Committee broadly endorsed the Meade proposal. Calling attention to the urgent need to expand world trade after the war, the committee proposed "a large-scale clearance of pre-war impediments to trade between nations" to enable British exports to grow sufficiently to pay for imports. Specifically, the Board of Trade called for a multilateral trade convention that would seek (i) deep multilateral tariff reductions, (ii) a three-year phase out of all quantitative restrictions (starting two years after the end of the war, after which they could be used only with the permission of an international commercial commission), and (iii) a cut in existing preferences and a ban on new ones. The Overton Committee even specified the degree of tariff-cutting: all countries, it was proposed, would agree to a 25 percent ceiling on MFN rates, 25 percent cut in all rates, subject to a right not to go below 10 percent, and a 50 percent reduction in preference margins, with a right not to reduce the margin below 5 percent (Cairncross and Watts 1989, 101). "By far the best course now is to seek big cuts in tariffs everywhere, and in other trade impediments, within a new international association, world-wide if we can make it so; if not, as wide as possible," the report stated.

> Politically it will be easiest to strike while the iron is hot and face transitional difficulties while the will for international cooperation is still strong. In many countries, especially enemy countries and those liberated after long occupation by the enemy, all will be fluid and all the vested interests at their weakest (Culbert 1987, 389).

A draft of the Overton report circulated within the British government in January 1943. It quickly became apparent that, while economists at the Board of Trade and Economic Section were pleased to support the plan for freer trade in the postwar world, not everyone in the British government agreed, not even other economists, particularly those in the UK Treasury. In a series of letters and memos in December 1942 and January 1943, John Maynard Keynes condemned the Overton report. In his view, the majority went much too far and exhibited a "strong free trade bias – too strong until we know more about the set-up of the postwar world" (Keynes 1980, 253). Keynes believed that postwar economic policy should put the highest priority on maintaining full employment.

1.4 The 1942 Meade Draft for Commercial Union

Achieving this objective, in his view, would likely require the use of trade controls and exchange restrictions. As Keynes (1980, 261) wrote to Overton:

> I do not like the appearance of special hostility to import regulation, since it seems to me to be, not merely temporarily, but permanently much the best technique open to us for the sort of things we are likely to want to do. I am not clear that it is yet fully appreciated how the growth of state trading and planning generally is likely to favour import regulation as the better technique compared with tariffs or subsidies.[30]

Keynes (1980, 251) also doubted that the United States was serious about liberalizing its import policy:

> We have to remember that the free trade element in the State Department, with whom we are in direct contact, represents almost nothing but themselves.[31]

Writing to Meade, Keynes (1980, 273) discounted the likelihood of a multilateral trade agreement because of the political difficulties it would cause in the United States. Keynes's harshly negative reaction to the trade-liberalization proposal led Meade and other economists to become wary of his illiberal and pessimistic tendencies on commercial-policy matters.

The Overton report also produced a sharp dissent from another Treasury economist, Sir Hubert Henderson (1955), who argued that the problem of postwar commercial policy should be approached in a spirit of cooperation but with this caution:

> Nonetheless, the fact that our means of paying for imports have been seriously reduced as a consequence of the war is necessarily a source of anxiety to us; and we are bound to have regard to that fact and to its implications

---

[30] At another point, Keynes (1980, 268) wrote that he was "arguing in favour of import regulation, not merely on balance of trade grounds, but also on the ground of maintaining stability of employment in new staple industries." Curiously, Keynes's own Clearing Union plan was designed to facilitate international payments in a multilateral system of credits without bilateral balancing and import quotas, and indeed specifically condemned quantitative restrictions (Pressnell 1986, 104).

[31] Although Keynes's view on this proved inaccurate, it was not completely without foundation. As Acheson (1969, 88) later recalled, "President Roosevelt's virtual exclusion of Secretary Hull from high-policy decisions during the war had more far-reaching effects than its contribution to the estrangement of the two men. It led directly to the theoretical and unreal nature of the State Department's – and hence the government's – thinking on postwar problems. Largely detached from the practicalities of current problems and power relationships, the Department under Mr. Hull became absorbed in platonic planning of a utopia, in a sort of mechanistic idealism."

in considering what commercial arrangements may be possible for us when the war is over (Henderson 1955, 209).

Henderson argued that the war had brought about "a drastic alteration" in the country's balance of exports and imports, wherein the loss of foreign markets produced a shortfall of exports in comparison to imports that could not be easily recovered. Hence, the "essential problem is to reconcile the aims of an expansion of international trade and equilibrium in the balance of payments." He therefore insisted that Britain's balance-of-payments situation after the war would not permit the abandonment of import restrictions: "so long as we have to correct an adverse balance of payments," Britain must "reserve the right to limit the volume of our imports by other means, such as some form of quantitative import control... we think it essential to make it clear that we see no likelihood... of being able to dispense with quantitative import control, as a means of correcting our adverse balance of payments for a considerable period after the war is over."[32] Because the options of countries facing a balance-of-payments deficit were narrowly circumscribed, countries with a balance-of-payments surplus (i.e., the United States) should be required to do the most to restore equilibrium by removing impediments to imports.

Henderson (1955, 215) also questioned the goal of nondiscrimination in trade:

> We cannot... accept the view that our preferential system is objectionable in principle, on the grounds that it entails discrimination.... In our view, the possibility ought not to be excluded that it may be desirable in postwar Europe to permit, and even to encourage, similar preferential systems between neighbouring groups of States, whose political solidarity it may be important to foster, but who may not desire to go so far as a complete Customs Union.

Keynes (1980, 253) praised Henderson's dissent as "a magnificent document, which, in my judgment, knocks the Overton Report sideways." Still, Keynes concluded that "the most advisable course very likely lies between the Overton Report and Henderson's critical rejoinder. But Henderson's impresses me as the more fundamental line of approach. His is a most powerful paper, and he makes the majority report look superficial."

[32] As Henderson (1955, 217) explained, "When a country is faced with the necessity of correcting an adverse balance of payments, quantitative regulation may be by far its most satisfactory means of conserving limited resources of foreign exchange for essential needs; and, as already indicated, we contemplate the probability that we shall have to use it ourselves for this purpose." Dalton (1986, 542) viewed Henderson's dissent, "as is usual with him, dangerously plausible and completely negative."

1.4 The 1942 Meade Draft for Commercial Union 33

In early January 1943, the Overton Committee debated the draft proposal, but Henderson found himself "quite isolated" at the meeting (Dalton 1986, 542). At the concluding gathering, a majority accepted the report with only Henderson dissenting (one of the two Treasury officials). Though he was not a member of the Overton Committee, eventually Keynes came around and approved the "general layout" of the plan after having raised objections to it.

A higher-level committee, led by Sir Alfred Hurst, then prepared the plan for consideration by the War Cabinet. The Hurst Committee produced a new draft in February 1943, which weakened the Overton proposal and attached "great importance to the retention, unimpaired, of the power to regulate imports" (Pressnell 1986, 105). This reflected the growing belief that the country's balance-of-payments situation after the war would be dire and would require it to discriminate between countries that would and would not accept UK exports on a favorable basis.

On April 8, 1943, the War Cabinet considered a memorandum prepared by the Board of Trade and the Dominion Secretary that outlined three possible approaches to postwar commercial policy based on the Hurst report.[33] View A involved a general multilateral reduction in trade barriers. View B was a less extensive plan that would give domestic authorities full discretion in the use of import restrictions for balance-of-payments purposes (i.e., a country would not have to request permission from an international body). View C anticipated modest international cooperation on trade barriers because it assumed that quantitative import restrictions would be used extensively as a part of national economic planning.

Amery (1988, 880-881) strongly endorsed View C and forcefully represented the skeptical faction in the government. With the Treasury worried about safeguarding the balance of payments, Amery (1988, 878) attacked a liberal, multilateral approach to trade on the grounds that other governments simply would not be interested in a proposal for more open trade after the war:

> no one would look at it and that it would not suit even our own interest.... Today our best chance lay in securing special terms for our exports by giving in return special facilities in our rich home market.

Amery (1988, 880–881) was not impressed by Churchill's conduct of the meeting, calling it:

> The most hopeless affair possible. Winston had read none of the papers and hadn't the slightest idea of the nature of the problems involved. Endless time was wasted in trying to make him even understand that some sort of

---

[33] PRO CAB 66/35 WP (43) 136.

restriction of imports was going to be necessary to protect our exchange after the war.... Winston had no notion of what were really the points at issue, and wanders about from one point to another revealing the most pitiful ignorance.... Winston has no doubt great qualities as a war leader, but when it comes to economics he is a quite out of date old man unaware of anything that has happened since 1880.[34]

But Amery reflected a minority position. Dalton (1986, 578) thought that Churchill knew from the start that View A should be adopted and "was most anxious that, whatever we said, we should 'use the right language.' We should make our approach in terms of the freest possible exchange of goods and services, freedom rather than restriction, abundance and not scarcity."

Eventually, "after much meandering and trite talk," Churchill asked for a vote on View A as amended to allow the use of quantitative import restrictions to safeguard the balance of payments as determined by national authorities and not an international body (Dalton 1986, 577). The cabinet voted 15 to 2 in favor of option A with the balance-of-payments reservation.

No decision was made on imperial preferences. Although Churchill was personally opposed to imperial preferences, he recognized that Conservative members of the cabinet (led by Amery) would revolt if they were dispensed with. However, Churchill insisted that it would be better to decide upon British policy first and then consult the Dominions, rather than try to formulate a wider imperial agreement on postwar trade policy.[35]

Having settled upon a general position on postwar commercial policy, the British government contacted the Dominions about the implications of a multilateral trade arrangement for their future relationship. The Dominions Secretary circulated a draft aide-memoire in April 1942 in preparation for a meeting of Commonwealth trade representatives.[36] Of all the Dominions, Canada was the most enthusiastic supporter of Britain's commercial-policy initiative. Canada was unique among the former colonies in having very close economic ties to the United States as well as to the United Kingdom. As such, Canada had a strong interest assuring its continued access to both markets by encouraging Anglo-American cooperation to develop a truly multilateral trade accord. From Canada's perspective, the worst possible outcome would be having to choose between the two markets, either continuing with imperial preferences but

---

[34] Churchill apologized for being rusty on matters of trade policy, but perked up when someone mentioned buffer stocks, which he heard to be "butterscotch."

[35] As Amery (1988, 880) noted, Churchill made clear "his dislike of having to consult the Dominions at all, 'these people' as he called them and he tried very hard to insist that we should consult the United States first."

[36] Reproduced in DCER 9, 638–639.

1.4 The 1942 Meade Draft for Commercial Union

with American protectionism intact, or concluding a bilateral agreement with the United States but facing restricted access to the British market. As the governmental advisory committee in Canada concluded in May 1943:

> the negotiation of a multilateral convention of commerce, providing for the tariff reductions and limitations and the removal of other barriers to the exchange of goods, is the soundest method of securing satisfactory conditions of trade between nations after the war. It is especially in Canada's interest, first, because our trade extends over many countries and it would be difficult, if not actually impracticable, to achieve any pattern of bilateral agreements which would serve our interest so effectively, and, second, because the United States will undoubtedly press for the removal of preferences" (DCER 9, 643).

If the United States and the United Kingdom could not agree, Canada would be put in the difficult position of trying to obtain better access to both markets.[37]

Trade representatives from the Dominions met in London for consultations in late June 1943.[38] Only the United Kingdom and Canada supported the multilateral approach, whereas Australia, South Africa, and New Zealand saw the merits in bilateral negotiations (McKenzie 2002, 99). The British quietly preferred the multilateral option because they feared that the Dominions, with an eye on the large American market, might be willing to trade away tariff preferences for access to the U.S. market in bilateral agreements.[39] Canada supported the multilateral approach to the reduction in trade barriers as a more efficient method of reducing trade barriers than the bilateral approach, but insisted that any reduction in imperial preferences should be contingent upon a significant,

---

[37] A memorandum from Norman Robertson, Canada's Undersecretary of State for External Affairs, to the Prime Minister noted that "it is strongly in Canada's interest to encourage and support" the U.S.-UK commercial-policy discussions because "Their approach, on the basis of a multilateral Convention of Commerce provide for tariff reductions and the removal of other barriers to the exchange of goods, is the only really sound and comprehensive method of securing satisfactory conditions of trade and perhaps, in the long run, of political security.... We would have very little, therefore, to gain by further negotiations on a bilateral basis. And must look to a multilateral convention, on the broad lines of the British proposal, if we are to secure ready access to the United State and to world markets. We should, therefore, I think, throw our whole weight behind the British proposal" DCER 9, 640.

[38] For a report, see DCER 9, 680–688. See also McKenzie (2002, 95ff).

[39] Sir Alexander Clutterbuck, the Dominion's Office representative on the Overton Committee, warned that the dominions might be willing to sacrifice imperial preferences for U.S. tariff reductions in bilateral agreements, so Britain had a stake in a multilateral agreement with everyone at the table; otherwise, "we are quite likely to see imperial preferences whittled away by the Dominions in return for little counterbalancing advantages for ourselves" (McKenzie 2002, 41).

across-the-board (nonselective) reduction in the high U.S. tariff. Australia also wanted priority put on measures to ensure full employment while also allowing protection of infant industries. New Zealand was generally supportive of the British proposal, South Africa made a "long and not always relevant statement" (according to the Canadian account) on the matter, while India did not want to rule out policy measures to promote industrialization.

Following these consultations, Canada discussed the London meeting with American officials. Norman Robertson, Canada's Undersecretary of State for External Affairs, repeatedly pushed the United States to think about bold and sweeping plans for postwar commercial policy. He insisted that the bilateral and selective approach of the RTAA was too cumbersome and should be abandoned for a multilateral approach. He also proposed that action be taken quickly because large tariff reductions could be implemented now while vested interests were disrupted, whereas it would be difficult to accomplish once the world's economies returned to normal conditions.[40]

State Department officials were encouraged by Canada's support, but were unable to move with the urgency that Robertson wanted. While the United Kingdom had moved ahead in 1942 by formulating its position around the Meade proposal, the United States had put commercial policy on the back burner. In 1941, the United States had cautiously put forward proposals for bilateral trade agreements with Australia, Canada, and the United Kingdom, but they were eventually dropped.[41] The year 1942 was lost as the United States entered the war following Japan's attack on Pearl Harbor. And in early 1943, rather than formulate an ambitious plan for postwar economic cooperation, the State Department focused on renewing the expiring trade-negotiating authority in the Reciprocal Trade Agreement Act. This effort was successful, given the large Democratic majorities in Congress and the sense that the renewal was

---

[40] As the U.S. Embassy in Canada reported: Robertson "is convinced that the best time to negotiate basic tariff reductions is during the depths of a depression when the inefficient industries have been driven to the wall and eliminated, or at a time, like the present, when because of the exigencies of war normal trade has been disrupted and directed into new channels which, under the control of governmental agencies, should be efficient channels.... With vested interests for the time being in the background he feels that this is the time to take basic action toward reducing tariffs. If we do not strike now, he is afraid we will drift back into the old pre-war methods under which, he feels, it will be impossible to effect adequate reduction of tariff barriers." FRUS 1943, I, 1104–05.

[41] See FRUS 1941, III, 112–128. According to this volume, "These trade agreement exploratory discussions were carried on for some time but did not lead to the opening of actual negotiations, apparently because of critical war conditions and the handling of wartime trade through Lend Lease operations."

superfluous in time of war. When Congress renewed the RTAA in June 1943, however, it did so for only two years with the understanding that it could not be used as the basis for designing a new postwar system of trade.

Still, the legislative renewal energized the State Department to pursue the issue of trade policy more aggressively. An interagency process was activated that considered a broad range of trade-related issues – not just tariffs and preferences but also quantitative restrictions, subsidies, cartels and restrictive business practices, and investment – that were of interest to the United States. In August 1943, Cordell Hull asked the U.S. ambassador in London about the latest British position and the status of the commercial-policy negotiations. Hull signaled his intention to resume discussions on these and other subjects covered by Article VII of the Mutual Aid Agreement (FRUS 1943, VI, 107–108). Having consulted with the Dominions, the UK government also cleared the way for a fall meeting with the United States on these matters. The Anglo-American discussions on postwar commercial policy were about to begin.

1.5 The Washington Seminar, September–October 1943

In September-October 1943, a delegation from the United Kingdom met in Washington with their American counterparts to discuss postwar economic issues. Led by Richard Law, a Minister of State in the Foreign Office, the UK delegation included officials from the Treasury (John Maynard Keynes), the Board of Trade (Percivale Liesching and James Meade, seconded from the Economic Section), the Economic Section (Lionel Robbins), and others from those offices and related government ministries. They met with a number of mid-ranking American officials, led by Harry Dexter White of the Treasury Department on financial policy and Harry Hawkins of the State Department on commercial policy. The purpose of the meeting was not to conduct formal negotiations involving official government commitments. Rather, these informal consultations allowed the two sides to exchange views and discover the areas of agreement and disagreement regarding postwar economic policy with the hope of formulating an agenda for higher-level Article VII negotiations.[42]

---

[42] As Pressnell (1986, 116) put it: "The informal, non-committal talks of September-October 1943 were the most important Anglo-American exchanges on economic issues not only during the war but also for many years before and since. They were indeed unique; they were conducted at a high intellectual level, ranging frankly over virtually the whole field of economic policy, and they have been appropriately described as having been 'in the spirit of a university seminar rather than of a formal international conference.'" Richard Gardner (1956, 104) used the term "university seminar" to describe the meeting.

Keynes, White, and the Treasury teams discussed postwar monetary and financial arrangements. Both sides recognized that any agreement on commercial policy was predicated on an agreement regarding postwar exchange rate and financial policy. Indeed, international trade could not flow smoothly without a well-functioning system of international payments and exchange rates in place. However, the discussions between White and Keynes did not go easily. Their strong personalities clashed frequently, and they tended to lace their comments with snide remarks and dismissive asides.[43]

By contrast, the commercial-policy discussions proceeded smoothly and cordially. Liesching, Meade, and Robbins discussed trade and commercial-policy issues with Harry Hawkins and other American officials. Both sides agreed on the fundamental idea that barriers to international trade should be reduced as much as politically possible. After the first few meetings, both Hawkins and Meade agreed that "phenomenal progress" had been made (HM 121). Meade was thrilled with this initial success, noting in his diary for September 21, 1943:

> Little did I think when, in May or so of last year, I first penned the words "Commercial Union" that I should now be present on the occasion when they were handed over by the British to the Americans, blessed by the War Cabinet, or that the Americans would receive them with such a welcome (HM, 111).

The main issues in the commercial-policy discussions were tariffs and preferences, quantitative restrictions, investment, employment, cartels, and state trading. Despite broad agreement on the basic principles, there were important differences of approach in each area. With respect to tariffs and preferences, the United States leaned toward bilateral negotiations to reduce tariffs on a product-by-product basis, as had been the practice under the RTAA. The United Kingdom strongly favored multilateral tariff reductions on an across-the-board basis in order to free up international trade to the fullest extent possible.[44] As

---

[43] As Meade recorded in his diary: "It augurs ill for the future unless these negotiations can somehow or another be got out of the hands of two such prima donnas as White and Keynes. There must be a growing accumulation of exasperation and bad temper as long as it goes on in this way" (HM 133). Meade went so far as to say that Keynes was "a menace in international negotiations" and that the monetary discussions were "seriously marred, I fear, by Keynes's ill-manners" (HM 135, 139).

[44] October 11, 1943, Meade recorded in his diary: "Went to a meeting of the Anglo-American Commercial Policy Group. What a battle! It appeared that some of them, particularly Ryder [Chairman of the U.S. Tariff Commission], really did believe that we might have an international convention outlawing quantitative restrictions and yet leave tariffs to be dealt with by bilateral agreements. We, i.e., Liesching, Robbins, and I battled with this and did our utmost to make it clear that there was no possibility of agreement whatsoever on those lines. . . . I hope that our firmness will at least have made it clear how much depends upon

1.5 The Washington Seminar, September–October 1943

the discussions progressed, the British representatives began to persuade their American counterparts about the merits of a broader multilateral approach, something that Canadian officials had also previously emphasized. U.S. officials did not rule out a multilateral approach to tariff reduction, and Hawkins himself seemed to favor it, but it ran counter to the traditional bilateral approach that had been pursued under the RTAA. Hawkins could not guarantee that the State Department would embrace it. Indeed, Meade was warned by a member of Hawkins's staff that

> Hawkins was a courageous and disinterested man who was running a terrific risk with his personal career in taking the grand line he was taking in favour of a multilateral approach to Commercial Policy, because the Secretary of State is an ultra-cautious man.

Meade drew the conclusion that "Hull is still extremely unconvinced of the multilateral approach, and that there may be real trouble when our joint report on Commercial Policy goes to higher authorities in the USA" (HM 139).

On the contentious issue of imperial preferences, the Americans demanded the elimination of all tariff preferences. The State Department maintained that cutting preference margins by 50 percent was insufficient because they were discriminations that had to be eliminated under Article VII of the Mutual Aid Agreement. They insisted that domestic politics in the United States required that preferences be addressed in a significant way. The British representatives resisted this effort, citing the close ties of kinship that bound Britain to the people of Canada, Australia, and New Zealand. The UK delegation stressed the domestic sensitivities regarding imperial preferences and argued that the extent to which preferences could be reduced was contingent upon the degree to which the United States would reduce its tariffs. But Meade admitted

> I feel some difficulty in helping to wage [the battle], as I feel that the American case is indeed very strong (HM 118).[45]

 their deciding to overcome the technical (and political) difficulties in the way of getting a radical reduction of tariffs" (HM, 135).

[45] The final text on preferences stated that the governments would "provide for agreed action looking not only toward the reduction of tariffs but also toward the elimination of all forms of discriminatory treatment in international commerce. No convention of the kind proposed would give final effect to these obligations unless it makes definite provision both for an adequate reduction of tariffs and for the ultimate substantial abolition of preferences. There remains for determination at the proper time the difficult question of what reduction of tariffs, at one step or by stages, would be adequate to make possible the substantial abolition of preferences. It has become clear in the course of the discussions that United States opinion would not consider it equitable or reasonable to contemplate drastic and

Still, both sides agreed on the centrality of the most-favored-nation clause. Regarding the MFN clause and the treatment of nonmembers, Meade reported:

> The Americans are in very much the same mind as ourselves on these issues; but they want it to be made compulsory for members of the Commercial Union not to extend the advantages of membership to non-members (HM 120).

Both sides agreed that quantitative restrictions should be eliminated in principle, but the United Kingdom insisted that they be permitted during a transition period and in case of balance-of-payments difficulties. On subsidies, the U.S. position was that export subsidies could not be abolished unless other countries restricted their use of domestic subsidies. The British took a more relaxed view of domestic subsidies but wanted to reign in export subsidies.

Cartels and restrictive business practices were also discussed and some differences arose. The United States took a firm line against cartels and restrictive business practices, essentially advocating the extension of its domestic antitrust laws, with their strong sanctions against any monopolistic behavior, to international trade.[46] The United Kingdom resisted the wholesale rejection of cartels and advocated a case-by-case policy with respect to monopolistic practices.

Despite these differences, both sides found remarkable agreement on the overarching principles of a multilateral agreement.[47] By October, Meade reported that:

> The Americans are drafting a report on Commercial policy, rather along the lines of our Commercial Union proposals, which is to be jointly agreed with us. Where there are unresolved differences, both views will be expressed. There could not be a more desirable outcome to our deliberations.... Ten years ago at Oxford I should never have dreamed that an economist could live

---

comprehensive reduction of tariffs (assuming this to be feasible) if it were not accompanied by the simultaneous substantial abolition of preferences" (DCER 9, 783–784).

[46] The U.S. position was presented by Corwin Edwards and Edward Mason, both notable industrial-organization economists at the time, the former from the University of Oregon who served in the Antitrust Division of the Department of Justice, and the latter a professor at Harvard University. See Edwards (1945) and Mason (1946).

[47] Meade summed up his reaction: "Sensible principles have been agreed for Commodity Policy. On Cartels we are taking back a good understanding of the American ideas, which will stimulate us to real work on this. On employment and investment very little has been done; but one can't ask for everything.... I think that we can be very pleased indeed with this final outcome, when one looks back on the expectations with which we started out. But there are plenty of snags ahead – and not only on tariffs and preferences" (HM 1990, 139, 141)

1.5 The Washington Seminar, September–October 1943

in such a heaven of practical application of *real* economic analysis!.... Our commercial policy report will be revolutionary if it finds acceptance and can be actually brought to birth (HM, 124, 130, 139).

On October 16, 1943, the two sides agreed to a joint statement (not publicly released) on the principles for a future commercial agreement (Annex A-3). The UK delegation left Washington in late October 1943 satisfied that the exchange had usefully clarified areas of agreement and disagreement, and that much had been accomplished on the possible shape of a postwar trading system. Of course, this small cadre of civil servants from the State Department, Board of Trade, and Economic Section were economists of a similar mind-set and all strongly supported the goal of reducing trade barriers.[48] Opposition to their plans lay elsewhere and would be revealed as the issues they discussed moved up to a higher political level. As a U.S. memorandum on the meeting noted:

> It is stressed that the United States Government had not formulated any position on the questions discussed, and the American officials participating in the conversations did so in their individual capacities. Thus the enclosed statement does not in any sense indicate the position of the United States Government, but is rather an annotated agenda of certain problems on which it appeared that official positions should be formulated for possible future discussions of a more formal character (FRUS 1943, I, 1115).

This caveat applied to the British side as well.

State Department officials quickly followed up on the joint discussions by forming a committee to set out concrete proposals for how to proceed. In December 1943, the committee issued an Interim Report that set out the two major postwar commercial-policy objectives of the United States:

> (1) the greatest possible expansion of international trade on a sound and non-discriminatory basis; and (2) the conduct of that trade so as to give widest possible scope to private competitive enterprise.

The Report argued that the United States was the only country that could take a leadership position in bringing this policy to fruition and that the war provided

---

[48] This explanation only goes so far because both Keynes and White were also economists, but dealing with more contentious macroeconomic issues. Still, the collegial commercial-policy discussions built a bond among these individuals that served both countries well in the future. As Penrose (1953, 16) wrote, the "informal and unobtrusive exchanges of personal views on postwar matters continued throughout the war, helping to clear the way for organized, official negotiations, removing misunderstandings, keeping a small and discreet group of officials in each capital in touch with the development of thought among their counterparts in the other and establishing a spirit of cooperation in a common Allied cause."

"a uniquely favorable time for thoroughgoing trade-barrier reform." And it is here that the British discussions left their mark: the British had convinced Hawkins and his staff that a multilateral approach would be superior to the RTAA's bilateral approach.

> It has seemed clear to the Committee, also, that not only should the various types of trade barriers be handled simultaneously, but that they should be dealt with simultaneously among a large number of countries, that is, on a multilateral basis. This approach is indicated primarily by the complexity of international trade relationships; i.e., by the fact that the volume of trade between any two nations is necessarily influenced by the trade barriers of other nations as well as their own (16).

The report continued:

> If workable multilateral tariff provisions acceptable to a large number of nations providing for a drastic reduction of tariffs without nullifying exceptions and reservations can be found, they would be superior to bilateral provisions alone. They would be superior because they would accomplish tariff reductions more quickly and because they would make it easier to accomplish the elimination of quotas and other nontariff trade restrictions (20–21).

However,

> In the event that the project for a general multilateral commercial policy convention should be abandoned, the Committee contemplates that the material prepared in connection therewith would serve as a basis for formulating more limited multilateral agreements (among a few large countries or restricted to one or two types of trade barriers) or a program of bilateral agreements (18).

Thus, the Report concluded:

> At a later stage, after further study and discussion, it is contemplated that specific recommendations, fully documented, will be prepared, including draft provisions for a proposed general multilateral convention on commercial policy.

In January-February 1944, the United States and Canada held discussions about a possible multilateral trade agreement. Canadian officials thought it "highly desirable to negotiate a multilateral commercial convention covering both import restrictions and tariffs" and recommended that it include all countries (developed and developing, private enterprise and state planned). They specifically proposed a uniform 50 percent reduction in import duties with a ceiling and floor on tariff levels. They also held that:

> import prohibitions and import restrictions such as quotas and licensing systems are among the devices most destructive of international trade, as, as part of a multilateral convention, should, except in certain special cases which would be held to a minimum and closely defined, be prohibited.

Finally, Canadian officials warned the United States that it would be unrealistic to expect the elimination of imperial preferences except by gradual erosion.[49]

With this advice, and on the basis of the Interim Report, the State Department spent much of 1944 coordinating a broad interagency process to arrive at specific proposals for international discussion.

1.6 Years of Deadlock and Delay, January 1944–September 1945

Although the Keynes-White Treasury discussions had been contentious, the American and British governments moved quickly to invite many countries to participate in the Bretton Woods monetary conference in New Hampshire in July 1944 (Pressnell 1986, Dormael 1978). This conference established an international monetary regime based on fixed but adjustable exchange rates, and two institutions: the International Monetary Fund for short-term balance-of-payments lending, and the International Bank for Reconstruction and Development (World Bank) for reconstruction and development assistance.

Yet, despite the broad Anglo-American agreement on trade and commercial-policy objectives, these negotiations languished for more than a year, mainly due to growing opposition within the British government. In reporting the results of the Washington discussions to his cabinet colleagues, Richard Law encountered fierce skepticism and hostility to the project from Conservatives in the cabinet (Amery, Hudson, and Lord Beaverbrook once again). This reluctance to reduce trade barriers stemmed from their support for imperial preferences in order to maintain close ties to current and former members of the British Empire. They also voiced strong support for the discretionary use of quantitative restrictions to limit imports and support the balance of payments. Hudson as Minister of Agriculture and Fisheries worried about exposing British farmers to foreign competition. Amery expressed skepticism that multilateral freer trade would

---

[49] See the report in DER 11, 1944–1945, 70–78.

resolve the problem of large prospective balance-of-payments deficits after the war:

> Is there the slightest possibility of our covering this [deficit] by increased exports, merely in consequence of some lowering of American and other tariffs, not to our exclusive advantage but to all the world under most favoured nation conditions? If Empire countries stand out, are we then, according to the Washington proposals, to be obliged to impose higher duties on them than on foreign countries which join the Commercial Union? Is Imperial Preference to be superseded by anti-Imperial discrimination? (Amery 1988, 926).

He pressed the point that "no general lowering of world tariffs... could compensate us for the loss of favoured markets in the Empire" (Amery 1988, 928).

Law attempted to counter all of these arguments. He reminded the cabinet that

> if we insist, for reasons of administrative convenience, upon retaining our right to impose quantitative restrictions upon agricultural products, other countries will have the same the same freedom to impose quantitative restrictions upon manufactured goods.

That, Law maintained, could have a devastating impact on Britain's export trade:

> surely it should not be beyond the wit of the Minister of Agriculture to fulfil his pledge to the agricultural industry without wrecking the whole economy of the country, and without mortgaging the incomes of the poor and future of the export trades (Miller 2003, 23).

But Law's arguments did little to quell the dissenters. As Pressnell (1986, 131, 134) writes about this period:

> On the trade proposals, Mr. Law's efforts did not satisfy the Cabinet doubters. Their flow of memoranda, verging on outright obstructionism, increased during the spring of 1944. The critics gained breathing space from Commonwealth considerations, which thrice during the early part of 1944 gave occasion or excuse for hesitation about commercial policy. Time was gained for determined opposition to harden towards the Washington proposals which, as had been feared, lost their impetus. In contrast to the protracted delays before the 1943 talks, it was now London that evaded, and the American administration which was anxious to resume, Article VII talks.... The main impression of British policy during these discussions was clear: cold feet were developing.

1.6 Years of Deadlock and Delay, January 1944–September 1945

Imperial preferences remained the central issue. Churchill himself believed that "world free trade would entirely justify the abandonment of the Ottawa Preferences," but he did not wish to impose his views for fear of losing the support of Conservatives in his fragile coalition government (Miller 2003, 231). Despite their differences, the War Cabinet agreed on one major point:

> We do not wish to abandon the Imperial preference unless or until we are in presence of a vast scheme of reducing trade barriers in which the United States is taking a leading part (Miller 2003, 229).

Still, the divisions within the British government brought the trans-Atlantic commercial-policy discussions to a halt. After the Washington meetings, Robbins (1971, 203–204) recalled, everything came to a stop on the British side:

> For more than twelve months there was silence on our side; we were forbidden to say anything to our American opposite numbers. Even after that, conversations were only resumed in London in the most informal way on the most strictly hypothetical basis.[50]

These ministerial equivocations dismayed the UK civil servants who had been involved in the commercial-policy negotiations.[51] Unfortunately, even Keynes remained an obstacle to those who sought a liberal multilateral trade agreement. As Cairncross and Watts (1989, 110) note:

> Keynes's correspondence during this time shows continuing efforts by the Economic Section to convince him – or keep him convinced – that the commercial policy proposals gave sufficient freedom to the UK to make justifiable use of quantitative import controls, and also that a change in

---

[50] In Robbins's words, "What had happened was that certain ministers had been alarmed at the progress of the initial talks in Washington; and under the leadership of Lord Beaverbrook, then as always the evil genius of British politics with his capricious enthusiasms and venomous hatreds – especially hatred of America and Americans – they had staged a revolt at the Cabinet level, a revolt which could invoke in its support many public attacks on the policy of multilateral expansionism, from both the extreme Right and the extreme Left, each propagating its own form of economic nationalism."

[51] On August 11, 1944, U.S. Ambassador Winant cabled Washington: "The following estimate of the present position here is based in part on further personal talks with leading officials concerned with commercial policy, who have expressed themselves frankly in strict confidence. The general position here since very early in the year has been that officials had given their advice, which was in favor of a prompt resumption of conversations on the basis of a progressive commercial policy. This advice was not acted on because of the ministerial position described in previous messages. The officials concerned were greatly irritated by ministerial attitudes and expressed themselves strongly in private to Ministers. One of them said he had been so annoyed that for some time he gave up working on the subject and turned full time to other work within his responsibilities." FRUS (1944, II, 67).

the exchange rate would be an effective way of improving the balance of payments in normal conditions and preferable to permanent quantitative import restrictions.

With the international monetary agreement moving toward fixed but adjustable exchange rates, Meade worked hard to develop an objective indicator of balance-of-payments difficulties – based on the level of foreign-exchange reserves – so that one could know if recourse to import quotas was justified. In addition, Meade sought to develop a method of ensuring the nondiscriminatory use of import quotas by auctioning off licenses. Yet Keynes and Treasury officials were dismissive of these efforts as they wished to preserve maximal domestic autonomy to impose quantitative measures when they deemed them necessary without any external constraints.[52]

Keynes was uncooperative in the efforts to rebuild a liberal trading system; Meade later agreed with the characterization of his attitude as "grumpy" (Worswick and Trevithick 1983, 130). Despite his misgivings, however, Keynes was not prepared to oppose the plans for a multilateral trade arrangement. In January 1944, Keynes (1980, 284) explained his position this way:

> In the case of the power to regulate imports, we are up against a very deep-seated difference of opinion. . . . James [Meade] seems to me to fail to give the only answer which carries any conviction to me, namely, that, if all the other countries in the world agree to fall in with the stipulations of his Commercial Union (which, in my judgment, is extremely unlikely), we shall gain more on the swings than we shall lose on the roundabouts. That we shall lose something on the roundabouts is, in my judgment, indisputable.

[52] Keynes and Meade had deep and fundamental disagreements about the efficacy of an exchange-rate depreciation in improving the trade balance and the balance of payments. In the event of a deterioration in the balance of payments, Keynes believed that imports had to be restricted to divert spending to domestic goods. Keynes feared that an exchange-rate depreciation would fail to expand exports and might deteriorate the terms of trade. Meade contended that exports would respond sufficiently to a fall in the exchange rate to remedy any shortfall in the balance of payments. Keynes (1980, 289) accused James Meade and Marcus Fleming of having "*laissez-faire* appendicitis," arguing: "I have no sympathy with the idea, which . . . I regard as vestigial, that, if imports have to be restricted, it is in some way sounder to raise their prices by depreciation of the exchanges than by any other technique." Fleming replied: "May I first make a few observations about 'laissez-faire', the price system etc. Perhaps I am just a relic of a by-gone age, but I certainly retain a strong attachment to the price system, not because I think it works perfectly, but because the alternative appalls me. In the past few years I have attended a good many meetings where people were engaged in allocating scarce resources between alternative uses; and no matter how high-minded and intelligent the allocators, I have always felt that the most imperfect of markets would have made a better and more sensitive job of it." See Keynes (1980, 291). Keynes was also very skeptical of Meade's plan to auction import quota rights as a way of ensuring their nondiscrimination application. See Meade's reply in Keynes (1980, 275-278).

1.6 Years of Deadlock and Delay, January 1944–September 1945

> Nevertheless, I am ready to be persuaded not to oppose the scheme, on the ground that our discretion is only restricted if others are also conforming to a strict code, and that the latter, if by a miracle it does come about, may be to our very considerable advantage.

Still, British indecision allowed the trade discussions to stall for many months. In February 1944, Dalton (1986, 705) complained that

> It is incredible how these rambling discussions succeed one another, every few months, with no new arguments and no one changing sides and never any really firm decisions.

A Commonwealth economic conference, held in London in February-March 1944, merely reinforced the resistance. Canada proposed a general 50 percent reduction in tariffs, with a lower limit of 10 percent, and an unbinding of all residual preferences. UK officials objected that this scheme would fail to narrow the gap between high- and low-tariff countries. They proposed a more modest tariff reduction, roughly 10 to 25 percent, with a tariff ceiling of 25 percent. Australia continued to emphasize full-employment policies, and along with New Zealand and South Africa expressed greater support for imperial preferences than they had in previous meetings (McKenzie 2002, 117ff, CDER 11, 65–66). Australia was particularly concerned that the United States would sink back into an economic depression after the war and bring other countries down with it unless some trade measures could be used to prop up domestic employment.

On April 14, 1944, Richard Law and Hugh Dalton made an attempt to secure Cabinet approval for the Commercial Union plans. After a contentious meeting, they backed off. Amery (1988, 978) reported that

> Dalton I think was frightened by the course of the discussion and instead of asking for immediate publication [of the Commercial Union] now suggested that his scheme would not be right until there has been further discussions with the American experts.

This outcome depressed the supporters of the commercial-policy initiative on both sides of the Atlantic. In April 1944, Dalton (1986, 738) recorded in his diary that "the State Department is very vexed at our delays" on commercial policy and

> it is generally realised at Washington, and that the Canadians understand in much more detail . . . that we are stuck, split, and in recession on Commercial Policy. The State Department is also pressing, in rather heated and indignant telegrams to the Foreign Office, and in high-level telegrams from President to PM, for an answer to their proposal to set up a Steering Committee on international economic problems.

Britain continued to stall by falling back upon the need to "consult with the Dominions."[53] In early May 1944, Britain's War Cabinet met with Dominion Prime Ministers and the outcome provided yet another opportunity for delay (McKenzie 2002, 122–126). Once again, Canada strongly supported efforts to secure a broad multilateral trade agreement on liberal terms. But the others dumped cold water on the proposal. The Prime Ministers of Australia and New Zealand spoke strongly in favor of continued high protection for industry, the importance of maintaining imperial preferences, and the necessity for quantitative restrictions on imports. The South African PM expressed doubt that the United States would ever reduce its tariff.[54]

With the exception of Canada, this lack of support at the highest political level in the British Commonwealth suggested that there was no consensus to move forward. Any momentum that had been achieved as a result of the Anglo-American discussions in September-October 1943 had been completely lost. Even though the United Kingdom needed to expand its exports drastically in the postwar period, Dalton (1986, 742) depressingly concluded that "there is just no hope of getting on, and that it would be a great tactical mistake even to suggest further discussions with the U.S. on this." With much regret, Dalton observed that moving forward on commercial policy

> was now quite impossible for political reasons in this country. There had been strong representations against it by the Conservative Party to the PM, who himself was in favour of it, so far as he had had time to study it, and there had even been a threat of resignation by at least one Conservative minister (Amery, though I did not name him). Liesching afterwards said to me that he quite realised the thing was now politically impossible here, and that he supposed what was most likely was a series of bilateral arrangements between the U.S. and the various Dominions, in which each of the latter would make concessions which would be helpful to them but not to us. None the less, by this most unsatisfactory means, the British Empire would be able to escape any American charge of bilking on Article VII. After an interval it may be possible, I think, to resuscitate our general plan. But not yet.

[53] On April 27, 1944, Dalton (1986, 739) noted in his diary: "War Cabinet on Commercial Policy. New subject! Finally agreed that I should prepare a fresh paper – this will be about No. 100! – to be put in for the Dominions P.M.s next week, making it as non-controversial as possible, and explaining that ministers here are not united and that an all-party government finds it much more difficult than a party government would, to reach agreement. Amery presses to be allowed to put in to the Dominion PMs an alterative programme, but the PM, very bored with him, shakes his head violently and says, 'No, no, no.' The PM is on my side – he says to me tonight, 'I agree very much with many of the things you say' – but is troubled by the split, and the active pro-Preference agitation, in the Tory Party."

[54] As for India and Southern Rhodesia, Dalton (1986, 742) noted, they "are rather obviously treated as being 'below the line.'"

1.6 Years of Deadlock and Delay, January 1944–September 1945

After the Prime Minister's conference, Dalton (1986, 745–746) met Canada's Norman Robertson "who is very sad at what he calls the 'confused and ignoble end of the Commercial Policy proposals.'" Indeed, Canadian officials watched with growing concern the crumbling of British support for multilateral trade initiatives. In March 1944, Robertson observed that

> The distance between the United States and the United Kingdom positions appear to have widened a good deal since they first met in Washington in October. In general, objectives seem to be shrinking and receding.

If the multilateral approach failed, Robertson suggested that Canada would have to cut its own bilateral deal with the United States:

> It seems to me that, as the multilateral programme becomes more modest and more remote, we shall have to look more seriously and more quickly at the specific problem of Canadian-American trade relations. I had envisioned a bilateral agreement with the United States, supplementing a general multilateral tariff reduction, but if effective multilateral action is to be indefinitely deferred and, when achieved, prove modest, then I think we may have to look at the question again from the continental perspective (DCER 11, 67).

Meanwhile, State Department officials grew increasingly frustrated with Britain's dithering, but proceeded with their own plans.[55] In the aftermath of the October 1943 meeting with UK officials and the December 1943 Interim Report, the United States began to formulate its own proposals on trade. In May 1944, the Executive Committee on Economic Foreign Policy (headed by Dean Acheson) appointed a Committee on Trade Barriers (chaired by

---

[55] In July 1944, Dalton (1986, 766) noted that "when months passed without replies to their suggestions and inquiries [on commercial policy], we gave the impression of having all gone to ground, and of being sulky, reserved and non-committal. This irritated the Americans a good deal." In September 1944, Cordell Hull wrote to Roosevelt noting that the British government faced strong and growing pressures to retreat from plans for a liberal postwar commercial policy. To put the postwar world "on as sound an economic foundation as possible must be accompanied by vigorous British efforts to join with us in pressing a world-wide program of multilateral reduction in barriers to international trade.... The British must be urged to implement these arrangements, and to join with us – through the Article VII conversations and otherwise – in thorough consideration of the remaining elements of our international economic program. It is of fundamental importance to the interests of the United States and to the establishment of the kind of economic conditions which we hope to see prevail in the post-war world that... we have assurances from the British that they will actively cooperate with us in achieving them. You are aware of the political situation in the British government which has impeded this, and I know you will agree that it is time that some forward steps be taken to resolve it" (FRUS 1944, III, 56).

William A. Fowler of the State Department) to draft a possible convention as the basis for further discussion. In mid-1944, the State Department circulated an options paper that weighed the pros and cons of five approaches to tariff reduction. Proposal A called for a horizontal tariff reduction plus safeguards to protect domestic industries harmed by imports. Proposal B called for selective tariff reductions on a bilateral basis, which could be accomplished under the existing RTAA legislation. Proposal C anticipated bilateral negotiations to reduce tariff and nontariff barriers. Proposal D suggested horizontal tariff reduction and supplemental bilateral trade agreements. Proposal E envisioned multilateral negotiations over nontariff barriers, cartels, commodities, and other areas, and then bilateral negotiations to reduce tariffs on a selective basis. Most State Department officials favored Proposal A, but recognized that proposal E might be more politically feasible (Aaronson 1996, 42–43). Assistant Secretary of State Will Clayton indicated that he preferred the multilateral to the multilateral-bilateral approach.[56]

In October 1944, the State Department-led interagency group completed a draft convention and presented it to Acheson's committee. The "Proposed Multilateral Convention on Commercial Policy" went far beyond the template reciprocal trade agreements of the 1930s (Annex A-4). The group suggested that the United States adopt the negotiating position of calling for a 50 percent horizontal tariff reduction, subject to a 10 percent floor, and a five-year window in which import quotas could be used in case of serious injury to any industry resulting from increased imports. All tariff preferences would be eliminated or reduced, and quantitative restrictions would be abolished, subject to permanent exceptions (when imposed under commodity agreements or in conjunction with measures to restrict domestic output) and temporary exceptions (liquidation of government surpluses) for no more than three years after the war. Other sections of the proposed convention dealt with exchange controls, state trading (guaranteeing equality of treatment), subsidies (both export and domestic prohibited, except transitional export subsidies and for products in chronic world surplus), and provisions on restrictive business practices, something President Roosevelt himself had instructed Hull to include.[57] Another provision gave developing countries more flexibility in adhering to the convention.

---

[56] Letter to William Fowler, 31 December 1944, National Archives II, LF 57-D, Box 60, 284.

[57] In September 1944, President Roosevelt wrote to Hull reminding him that the United States had "developed a tradition in opposition to private monopolies" and that "this policy goes hand in glove with the liberal principles of international trade." He urged Hull to keep an eye on ways to restrict cartels that interfered with the free flow of commerce between countries. Hull pledged to so do. FRUS (1944 II, 71–72, 87).

1.6 Years of Deadlock and Delay, January 1944–September 1945

In November 1944, Dean Acheson testified before Congress and gave one of the first public discussions of the administration's postwar commercial-policy plans. Acheson (1944, 660) warned:

> The pre-war network of trade barriers and trade discrimination, if allowed to come back into operation after this war, would greatly restrict the opportunities to revive and expand international trade.... Action by governments, working together to reduce these barriers and to eliminate these discriminations, is needed to pave the way for the increase in trade after the war which we must have if we are to attain our goal of full employment.

With the approaching transition from war to peace, he continued, the world was

> presented with a unique opportunity for constructive action in cooperation with other countries.... We therefore propose to seek an early understanding with the leading trading nations, indeed with as many nations as possible, for the effective and substantial reduction of all kinds of barriers to trade. The objectives of such an endeavor would be:
>
> To eliminate all forms of discriminatory treatment in international commerce;
>
> To make exchange restrictions on commercial transactions unnecessary, ...
>
> To achieve the progressive elimination of quotas, embargoes, and prohibitions against exports and imports;
>
> To reduce import tariffs;
>
> To lay down fair rules of trade, with reference to government monopolies and state trading, including trade between countries where private enterprise prevails and those where foreign trade is managed by the state;
>
> To create an international-trade organization to study international-trade problems and to recommend practical solutions.
>
> We propose, in other words, that this Government go on with the work which it has been doing during the last 10 years, even more vigorously, with more countries, and in a more fundamental and substantial way.

Finally, Acheson concluded,

> It is our purpose in the Department of State to press forward as firmly as we can in the general direction I have outlined, consulting fully with the

appropriate committees of the Congress. If exploratory discussions with representatives of other governments give encouragement to our efforts, a trade conference of the United and Associated Nations should be held at the earliest practicable date for the negotiation of an agreement for the reduction of all kinds of barriers to trade. This agreement would of course be submitted to the Congress for its consideration.

In December 1944, American and British officials met to discuss commercial policy for the first time since October 1943. Harry Hawkins briefed his British counterparts in London on the new U.S. proposals for a multilateral commercial agreement. According to Meade (1990, 14), the pertinent elements of the draft included

> a declaration about domestic employment policies; a cut in all tariffs by 50 per cent with a floor of 10 per cent; preference margins to be squeezed by applying these tariff cuts to the non-preferential rates and not to the preferential rates, with a maximum percentage limit to preference margins; quantitative restrictions to be permitted for five years from the signing of the Convention (provided the quota were not less than actual imports in a pre-war base period) and then to be continued only with the agreement of the proposed International Commercial Policy Organisation (IPCO) on a "tailing-off" basis and such quantitative restrictions could be imposed again later with the permission of the ICPO (which would be bound to allow them if they were necessary to ease a re-adjustment of industry due to some structural change) again on the basis that they would be "tailed-off" over a period of years.

Meade was enthusiastic about the American plan, believing that it "puts commercial policy on the map again.... It is difficult to see how we can lightly refuse an offer to halve the American tariff, when the Americans have gone out of their way to meet us (i) on employment policies, (ii) on not demanding the total elimination of imperial preferences, and (iii) on the quantitative regulation of trade" (HM 14, 18).

However, even as the commercial-policy civil servants welcomed the plan – Hawkins noted that their reaction was "wholly favorable" – other British officials reacted with skepticism and emphasized the outstanding problems.[58] Meade (1990, 18) noted:

> The talks with Hawkins have been continued. He has finished outlining the American proposals, which do not mention anything more very startling,

[58] See the U.S. account of the meeting in FRUS 1944, II, 99–101.

1.6 Years of Deadlock and Delay, January 1944–September 1945

but are bold and sensible. There was then a meeting of UK officials to decide how to proceed. Lionel [Robbins] tells me that this meeting was terrible. At it Liesching produced a paper by Shackle which was certainly lamentable – all full of the difficulties of a general multilateral agreement and emphasising every difficulty and disadvantage in the American proposals and overlooking all the many advantages of them. I really believe that the professional economists are the only people among officials (apart from Clutterbuck of the Dominions Office) who really wish to get an agreement. And yet an agreement is so patently in our interests and failure to agree with the Americans on it so patently dangerous.[59]

In fact, Britain responded to the American proposals by retreating from them. Ambassador John Winant cabled Washington with the disappointing British response, that there were "doubts as to the ability of the United Kingdom to fit itself into a multilateral system in the peculiar environment in which the country would find itself immediately after the war." They also wanted to create a special arrangement for agricultural trade outside any main agreement.[60] On state trading, "The United Kingdom officials emphasized strongly their desire to avoid having any words hostile to state trading either in the convention or in the records of negotiations."

These setbacks, in the form of new conditions and delays, delighted British opponents of a multilateral trade agreement. Amery (1988, 931) was heartened

---

[59] Hawkins sensed this negative British reaction. After a December 1944 dinner, Meade (1990, 20) wrote in his diary that Hawkins made "a very sad remark which wrung my withers. He argued how, if the USA and the UK really agreed together on the desirability of a liberal commercial policy, it would be irresistible throughout the world; and he said with a sigh that just as now the USA was turning rapidly towards the old English tradition of liberalising trade, just at that very moment the UK seemed to be moving as rapidly towards the evil old American tradition of high protectionism."

[60] See FRUS (1944, II, 99–104). "The United Kingdom have abandoned the idea of bringing agriculture wholly within the general provisions of the multilateral convention on commercial policy and instead have framed a plan for multilateral provisions for trade in food products which would be included in a multilateral convention on commercial policy. They support this stand on the ground that agricultural production is particularly subject to wide fluctuations and that ideas developed at Washington are not adequate for dealing with this problem.... Their conclusion is that such stability cannot be attained unless imports are regulated, that no single method is adequate for the purpose of such regulation, and that either tariffs or subsidies or quotas or a combination of two or all of them might have to be used in particular cases. They have therefore, as far as primary foodstuffs go, departed from the views expressed in Article VII talks in Washington favoring the use of subsidies instead of quotas and tariffs and do not wish to be restricted as to method of controlling imports, but will accept certain limitations on their use such as those outlined below" (FRUS 1944, II, 99–101).

that the increasing stress on full employment rather than trade liberalization appeared to slow the movement toward an agreement:

> Once things are seriously discussed from the angle of employment and wages I fancy that we shall hear little more of the American attempt to push us back.... into nineteenth century free trade and nondiscrimination. I believe we are slowly but steadily winning all along the line.

Keynes continued his skepticism about the commercial-policy discussions. In January 1945, Meade recorded a conversation with him in which Keynes reflected the prevailing attitude of indifference towards the American proposals. Meade (1990, 26) lamented that

> As often on this subject, Keynes was not at his best. He seemed to think that the thing to do was to go for a general "gentlemen's agreement" or statement of principles as to what countries would or would not generally do.... I maintained that many senior officials here were not simply trying to show Hawkins our very real difficulties; but they wished to put off the whole question, and this, I maintained, was riding for certain catastrophe as the USA certainly intended sooner or later to have some real liberalisation of commercial policy."

By early 1945, the European war was drawing to a close and the postwar era was no longer some distant period. Still, the plans for commercial policy had not yet reached an advanced stage. At this critical juncture, there were important personnel changes on both sides of the Atlantic. In the United States, after serving as Secretary of State for 11 years, Cordell Hull retired in November 1944. Although his successors (Edward Stettinius from November 1944 to June 1945 and James Byrnes from July 1945 to September 1946) did not share Hull's passionate beliefs about trade policy, Will Clayton, the new Assistant Secretary of State for Economic Affairs, embraced the cause of nondiscriminatory trade liberalization with even greater fervor than Hull. In December 1944, the incoming Clayton wrote to the retired Hull:

> The first letter I sign on State Department stationery is to you.... I want to assure you that your foreign policy is so thoroughly ingrained in my system that I shall always work and fight for it (Fossedal 1993, 136).[61]

Also in late 1944, Harry Hawkins left his position as director of the Division of Commercial Policy and Agreements and became the Minister-Counselor for

---

[61] As Clayton (1963, 501) said: "I have always believed that tariffs and other impediments to international trade were set up for the short-term, special benefit of politically powerful minority groups and were against the national and international interest."

1.6 Years of Deadlock and Delay, January 1944–September 1945

Economic Affairs with the U.S. Embassy in London where he continued to play a key role in the Anglo–American negotiations. In early 1945, Clair Wilcox, an economics professor at Swarthmore College, became the director of the State Department's newly named Office of International Trade Policy. Finally, President Roosevelt died in April 1945 and was succeeded by Vice President Harry Truman.

Britain also experienced important transitions. The wartime coalition government was dissolved after Germany's surrender and Winston Churchill's Conservative party lost the General Election of July 1945. Clement Attlee led a new Labour government that was committed to economic planning and full employment. Hugh Dalton left the Board of Trade and became Chancellor of the Exchequer. Sir Stafford Cripps, a staunch socialist Labour MP, became the new President of the Board of Trade. This left British policy in a very uncertain state. While the Labour party was not as wedded to imperial preferences as the Conservatives, and Dalton at the Board of Trade had supported multilateral freer trade, the Labour party was in a "theological maze" in trying to reconcile planning with a liberal trade system, according to a Treasury official.[62]

These transitions could have completely derailed the commercial-policy negotiations: President Truman could have held different views on commercial policy, the State Department without Hull could have abandoned its belief in the importance of liberal trade in the postwar era, and the Labor government could have halted the process by focusing exclusively on full employment and economic planning at home to the neglect of foreign-trade policy. Yet, despite these changes in personnel, American and British policy remained remarkably unaffected. In the United States, Truman and Clayton assured policy continuity. Truman had been a faithful adherent to the long-standing Democratic position on trade policy. In his first press conference as president, just days after taking office, Truman stated:

> I am for the reciprocal trade agreements program. Always have been for it. I think you will find in the record where I stood before, when it was up in the Senate before, and I haven't changed.[63]

In Britain as well, the Labour government opted for continuity, and was even more favorably disposed to open multilateral trade than Churchill's War Cabinet

---

[62] See Toye (2000) and Miller (2003, 204). Hugh Dalton summed up his view: "When people ask me whether I believe in free trade or protection, I reply, 'Neither, I believe in planning'" (Miller 2003, 254).

[63] This did not mean that he understood all the details of the negotiations or the issues at stake. After Clayton briefed the new president on the status of the postwar plans for commercial policy, Truman sighed, "I don't know anything about these things. I certainly don't know what I'm doing about them. I need help" (Fossedal 1993, 152).

had been.[64] In February 1944, a time when Conservatives such as Amery and Beaverbrook were causing problems and holding up decisions on commercial policy, Clement Attlee told Churchill and the War Cabinet that he favored the approach taken at the September-October 1943 Anglo-American meeting (Dalton 1986, 705). Once in power, however, Labour leaders found it difficult to relinquish imperial preferences under American pressure.

U.S. officials remained concerned about the languishing state of the trade negotiations. In February 1945, Secretary of State Edward Stettinius – who, coincidentally, had been a student of Harry Hawkins at the University of Virginia in the early 1920s – wrote to President Roosevelt that Churchill had the impression that the president was not interested in the Article VII discussions:

> This mistaken impression on the part of the Prime Minister has tended to encourage the British to take an unyielding attitude on the matter of their Empire preferences and trade barriers.

Roosevelt immediately wrote to Churchill, affirming the importance of the Article VII talks and urging that they be "re-invigorated" by his appointing a high-level delegation to meet with U.S. officials (FRUS 1945, Yalta, 962). Churchill rejected this suggestion and stalled again by citing the need to consult with other countries.[65]

In early 1945, the State Department's first trade-related priority was to renew the negotiating authority in the Reciprocal Trade Agreement Act, which was due to expire that summer. This renewal would be unlike previous ones because it would provide the statutory basis for the postwar tariff negotiations. The Roosevelt administration decided to ask for authority to reduce tariffs by up to 50 percent from their 1945 level, not their 1934 rates as in previous renewals, in executive agreements that did not require Congressional approval. This new tariff-cutting authority was sought because duties had been reduced significantly from their 1934 level under previous reciprocal trade agreements and the State Department wanted to be prepared for new and extensive tariff reductions in postwar negotiations.

The State Department also grappled with the key question of whether to ask for permission to reduce tariffs on an across-the-board basis or on a selective basis. The selective, product-by-product basis granted in previous RTAA renewals had been designed to avoid tariff reductions that would adversely affect

---

[64] See Toye (2000) on the Labour government's approach to foreign economic policy.
[65] According to Churchill, "The War Cabinet do not wish to commit themselves at this stage of the war to sending a high-powered delegation to Washington. This must involve bringing other countries into the discussions, notably France, at an early stage and of course the present mood of the Dominions must be ascertained before we go further on general policy." FRUS (1945, VI, 21).

1.6 Years of Deadlock and Delay, January 1944–September 1945

import-sensitive industries. In discussions with Britain and Canada, however, State Department officials had been persuaded of the merits of a broad, horizontal tariff reduction as a more expedient way of reducing import duties. This was written into the draft RTAA renewal legislation that the administration circulated for Congressional consideration.

In March 1945, senior State Department officials consulted with key leaders on Capitol Hill and reported that the initial reaction of the Speaker of the House Sam Rayburn and the chairman of the Ways and Means Committee was "very discouraging." While the Congressmen saw no problem with a three-year renewal of the negotiating authority under Section 1 of the proposed RTAA legislation, or even with the new 50 percent tariff reduction authority in Section 2, they regarded Section 3, permitting across-the-board tariff reductions as opposed to the selective approach, as very problematic. A State Department memo reported the reaction of Congressional leaders: "While they seemed to like the objective of the section, they were fearful that its inclusion would complicate and prolong Congressional consideration" of the new 50 percent authority and "make it very difficult, if not impossible, to get Section 2 unqualified by some form of Congressional approval. They did not close the door to Section 3 but Departmental officers who met with them came away with the feeling that the leaders felt very strongly that it should be dropped" (FRUS, 1945, VI, 27–28).

This left the State Department pondering whether to opt for the authority to reduce tariffs by up to 50 percent on a selective basis, or to reduce them by a smaller amount on a horizontal basis. Hawkins and other civil servants did not want to compromise and advocated pushing for the 50 percent authority on a horizontal basis. From London, Ambassador John Winant cabled Washington with his view that "the greatest importance should be given" to initiating multilateral negotiations along the lines of the general (not selective) authority, warning:

> I do not think renewal of the Reciprocal Trade Agreements Act, even with powers to make greater reductions in tariffs, would in itself make a great enough impression in UK to counteract the views either of the reactionaries who do not like article VII or the honest doubters who wish to support it but fear that we shall not do our part in implementing article VII. . . . sooner or later it will be necessary to obtain Congressional approval for a commercial policy measure that will go far enough to make a deep and convincing impression here and get the support of the British government (FRUS, 1945, VI, 29–30).

In the end, however, Dean Acheson and Will Clayton decided to ask for the authority to reduce tariffs by up to 50 percent on a selective basis.[66] On

---

[66] E. F. Penrose (1953, 106-107), an official with the U.S. Embassy in London, later recalled: "My impression is that most of the leading U.S. officials concerned with trade questions

March 26, 1945, the Roosevelt administration formally requested the enactment of legislation to this effect. In making the request, President Roosevelt stated that "trade is fundamental to the prosperity of nations" and:

> the reciprocal trade agreement program represented a sustained effort to reduce the barriers which the Nations of the world maintained against each other's trade. If the economic foundations of the peace are to be as secure as the political foundations, it is clear that this effort must be continued, vigorously and effectively. I shall continue therefore to explore the possibility also of reaching a common understanding with the friendly Nations of the world on some of the other international trade problems that confront us. . . . The purpose of the whole effort is to eliminate economic warfare, to make practical international cooperation effective on as many fronts as possible, and so to lay the economic basis for the secure and peaceful world we all desire.[67]

While Democrats were firmly in control of Congress, suggesting that the outcome of the 1945 renewal process should not have been in great doubt, the result clearly

> believed that a percentage reduction of all tariffs was a sounder and simpler method of reducing postwar tariffs than the method followed in the reciprocal trade agreements. There were indeed a number of difficulties of application, but they were not insuperable and it seems fair to say that if the decision could have been based on economic effects alone Washington and Whitehall would have been in substantial agreement on the subject. . . . The outcome of the discussion on this question was determined, not by economic reasoning, nor on grounds of equity but by what the Assistant Secretaries in the State Department believed it possible to pass through Congress. Here again the administration spokesmen had committed themselves, in the hearings on the renewal of the powers to negotiate reciprocal tariff reduction, to the principle of reciprocity and to the principle that each country should be left free to select the goods on which it was willing to reduce tariffs. They did not believe that Congress could be induced to go beyond the limits set by their Reciprocal Trade Agreements Act. In retrospect the validity of their judgment on this matter is doubtful, and in any case it seemed to some of us at the time that the attempt ought to have been made even if it failed." As State Department official John Leddy recalled: "And they – Acheson and Clayton – decided to go for 50 percent authority to cut tariffs, but on a selective basis, product by product. There were last minute appeals to the Department by the British and Canadians. Notably, one I recall, when Norman Robertson of Canada (Under Secretary of State in Canada at that time) came down here in a very strong appeal to Clayton that this was a disastrous decision. That if we went ahead on this basis that the chances of getting a really effective postwar agreement would be gone, go glimmering, and therefore, he appealed. He said, 'Almost anything would be better than what you seem to be thinking of doing.' And Clayton said, 'Well, I'm sorry but this is the way it is in this country. We just have no choice. We have no choice except to either throw up our hands at getting some kind of an improvement in the international situation or this, even though it may not meet your desires for a horizontal reduction,' And so the Canadians just sighed and went back home, and were really downhearted about this, but we put up the legislation and got it through." http://www.trumanlibrary.org/oralhist/leddyj.htm (last visited Jan. 17, 2008)

[67] "Recommendation for Renewal of the Trade Agreements Act," State Department *Bulletin*, April 1, 1945, 532–533.

1.6 Years of Deadlock and Delay, January 1944–September 1945

mattered more than in any previous renewal. Unlike the pro forma 1943 renewal, Congress was now very wary of granting the new authority. As State Department official John Leddy noted: "during the hearings on the Act we have played up selectivity probably more than during any previous renewal... to get the authority. There is likely to be considerable opposition to any plan involving horizontal reductions" (Aaronson 1996, 47).

Because of the strict majority-party rules in the House, which limited debate and the ability to offer amendments from the floor, the House's passage was expected to be relatively straightforward. Still, as in past renewals, Republicans repeatedly tried to restrict the president's powers and hoped to entice a few Democrats to support their more cautious approach. Republicans complained about the unchecked concentration of power in the executive branch over the life and death of American industries, as they put it. They supported a one-year extension without the authority to reduce tariffs by 50 percent from their 1945 level, a move that Democrats defeated. Then Rep. Harold Knutson (R-MN) proposed deleting all of section 2 of the proposed bill, the new 50 percent tariff-cutting authority, which was in his words "the crux of the whole fight" (Congressional Record, May 26, 1945, 5124). This move must have been anticipated because House Speaker Sam Rayburn then took to the floor to warn that "there is a big chance here to make a big mistake." He argued that the trade-agreements program should be strengthened to meet the demands of postwar cooperation and then read a letter from President Truman pledging that American industry and labor would not be sold out in the trade agreements.[68] The proposed amendment to eliminate section 2 was narrowly rejected by a vote of 174 yeas to 197 nays. A swing of just 12 members of the House could have reversed the outcome of this crucial vote and brought down the plans for extensive trade liberalization after the war.

Galvanized by the president's appeal, the Democratic leadership helped defeat the remaining amendments (12 in all) that would have given Congress veto power over any agreement, reduced or eliminated the new authority, or otherwise eviscerated the bill. Dean Acheson, who was the senior official responsible for ensuring its passage through Congress, was unimpressed by the Congressional debate which focused mainly on the impact on domestic

---

[68] The president wrote: "I assume there is no doubt that the act will be renewed. The real question is whether the renewal is to be in such a form as to make the act effective. For that purpose the enlargement of authority provided by section 2 of the pending bill is essential. I have had drawn to my attention statements to the effect that this increased authority might be used in such a way as to endanger or 'trade out' segments of American industry, American agriculture, or American labor. No such action was taken under President Roosevelt and Cordell Hull, and no such action will take place under my presidency." Congressional Record, May 26, 1945, 5148.

industries, not the foreign policy implications. As he noted at the time, it was

> a dreary and wholly unrealistic debate. Few of the claimed virtues of the bill were really true and none of the fancied dangers. The true facts lay in a different field from that where the shells from both sides were landing (Acheson 1969, 107).

Finally, in May 1945, the House voted 239–153 to renew the RTAA for three years. As usual, the final vote was largely along party lines: 95 percent of Democrats favored renewal while 81 percent of Republicans were opposed. Although the final margin was comfortable, Acheson (1969, 107) noted that "this does not tell the true story. It was very close on the critical amendments which would have killed the bill."

The renewal faced more dangers in the Senate. At the instigation of Sen. Robert Taft (R-OH), the Senate Foreign Relations Committee voted 10-9 to eliminate section 2 of the bill. The Senate rejected this recommendation by a vote of 33–47. Democrats defeated a bevy of other hostile amendments, including ones to require Senate ratification of any trade agreements, to prohibit any cuts in duties on agricultural commodities, to impose import quotas on textiles, and so forth. On June 20, 1945, the Senate voted 54 to 21 in favor of the RTAA's extension.

Buoyed by their success in Congress, the State Department sought to rejuvenate the languishing commercial-policy plans by resuming contact with their British counterparts.[69] However, British officials did not realize the choice the State Department had to make about the limitations in the legislative renewal. On June 27, 1945, in London, Harry Hawkins informed his British counterparts that, although Congress had approved legislative authority to undertake significant tariff reductions, it would only permit selective and not horizontal tariff cuts. Therefore, the United States proposed going ahead with a "multilateral-bilateral" approach wherein countries would negotiate on a bilateral, product-by-product basis with the principal supplier of the good in question, and the resulting tariff reductions would be generalized to other participating countries via the most-favored-nation clause (FRUS, 1945, VI, 57).

The British were sorely disappointed at this news. This was a huge blow to their ambitious hopes for a large multilateral tariff reduction on a uniform

---

[69] At this time, Meade (1990, 90–91) reported that the Americans "have now made it clear that they have a definite programme: first, they wish to agree with us behind the scenes a statement of principles on commercial policy; secondly, they intend then to publish it on their own initiative as their own document, after some discussion with Congress behind the scenes and possibly after some discussion with other countries; and finally, they intend to call a trade conference on the subject, this latter stage to be reached early in 1946."

1.6 Years of Deadlock and Delay, January 1944–September 1945

and nonselective basis. Wilfrid Eady of the UK Treasury told Hawkins that the abandonment of the multilateral approach with a general tariff cut "would be the end of all we hope to achieve... the end of everything worth having... the UK would go into [the negotiations] with no heart and no expectation of anything worthwhile coming out of it" (FRUS, 1945, VI, 58). Lionel Robbins made several objections to the U.S. approach: the length of time it would take to conduct bilateral negotiations, the negotiating complexity of undertaking multiple bilateral deals (a "nightmare conception"), and the lost psychological advantages of a simple uniform percentage reduction in all tariffs in which all countries sacrifice at once (FRUS 1945, VI, 57). Liesching also added that the Board of Trade only had enough qualified personnel to negotiate one commercial treaty at a time, reminding them that the 1938 US-UK trade agreement took 10 months to complete. He further argued that "the chances of dealing successfully with preferences would be much greater if a substantial uniform all round cut were made than if an attempt at gradually whittling down by a multitude of reciprocal pacts were made" (FRUS 1945, VI, 58). Robbins agreed that the United Kingdom would find it much easier to swallow a reduction in preferences in a multilateral context than it would under the bilateral method.[70]

The British officials also put forward a Draft Statement of Principles as a response to the American draft presented by Hawkins in December 1944.[71] The UK draft strongly favored a single international trade organization with subsections on commercial policy, commodity policy, and restrictive practices, and a separate section on employment, which had drawn the opposition of Meade and other economists.[72] But they now questioned whether an organization

---

[70] E. F. Penrose (1953, 109), who had been present at that meeting, later recalled: "I do not think that Whitehall ever again showed the zeal for tariff reduction which it had shown while hope remained for a comprehensive and fairly simple method of reducing tariffs at a single international gathering." However, the British government was also under pressure from the Agriculture Ministry to abandon the uniform method of tariff reduction, at least on agricultural products.

[71] These can be found as "Article VII: Specimen Draft of a Possible Statement of Principles," June 1945, PRO FO 371/45680. According to Meade (1990, 106), "Our statement of principles is, of course, put forward without commitment, merely as an illustration of the form which such a statement might take, etc. etc. Nevertheless it was only put forward after consultation with the Chancellor of the Exchequer and the President of the Board of Trade and in fact it marks a very definite step forward in the negotiations. The statement covers commercial policy, commodity policy and cartel policy in a quite unexceptional manner. It does, however, also have a section on Employment policy."

[72] The section on employment policy covered trade aspects of employment policy and contained a pledge to maintain full employment. In July 1945, Meade (1990, 106–107) wrote in his diary: "This seems to me to be all wrong, and Marcus Fleming and I have done our best to persuade Lionel Robbins that it is wrong. Of course, we want to get an international recognition of the fact that it is the international duty of countries to maintain their demand

could play an effective role under the bilateral arrangements envisioned by the Americans. Hawkins offered little prospect for a change in the U.S. position. He countered with the hope that a small nuclear group of important trading countries (the United States, the United Kingdom, and the Commonwealth, at a minimum) could get together and negotiate bilaterally but simultaneously and achieve something approaching a uniform tariff reduction.

In July 1945 in Washington and in Ottawa, Will Clayton and his deputies met with their Canadian counterparts to discuss the commercial-policy options.[73] The Canadians were also informed that the United States was constrained by the RTAA to undertake selective tariff reductions on a bilateral basis, rather than an across-the-board horizontal tariff reduction. Canadian officials were "deeply disappointed and dismayed" with this news. They said that this would require "a complete reappraisal of what could be expected to be accomplished in the trade-barrier field as well." They also warned U.S. officials that, while a horizontal approach might make a dent in imperial preferences, a selective approach would fail to do so (FRUS 1945, VI, 63, 67; DCER 11, 100). Canadian officials repeated the British view that the multilateral-bilateral approach would take years to complete because of the multiplicity of bilateral negotiations.

While Clayton indicated that the door was not completely closed to the idea of a horizontal tariff reduction, a joint U.S.-Canadian account of the meeting noted: "Both Mr. Acheson and Mr. Clayton were firmly convinced that, even apart from considerations growing out of the increased trade-agreements authority,

> for their goods. But it is quite wrong to connect this specially with the International Trade Organization, for two reasons. First, Employment Policy concerns monetary policy just as much as, if not more than, trade policy. It should, therefore, form the main task of the Economic and Social Council of the new world organization to co-ordinate action on employment policy. This task has already been recognised as belonging to the Economic and Social Council, and we should not therefore set up the International Trade Organisation as a rival in this field. Secondly, there is a very dangerous trend of thought in the USA, of which Will Clayton in the State Department may be taken as a symbol, that the way to cure unemployment is to have stable exchange rates and free trade rather than (what is much nearer the truth) that the only way to achieve the conditions in which one can establish freer trade and more stable exchange rates is for countries to adopt suitable domestic policies for maintaining employment. . . . My fear is that if employment policy is made a central feature of the trade convention we should get the cart before the horse once more and find the emphasis on the fact that we want free trade to give employment rather than that countries like the USA must take domestic measures to maintain employment if they want other countries to reduce trade barriers. My own view of the correct course is (i) that the trade convention should only have a passing reference to employment policy in its preamble and (ii) that the Trade Conference should pass a resolution saying that the successful operation of the trade convention depends upon domestic policies for full employment and asking the Economic and Social Council to get on with the subject."

[73] U.S. reports on the meetings can be found at FRUS (1945, VI, 61–74), while the Canadian report is DCER (XI, 99–106).

1.6 Years of Deadlock and Delay, January 1944–September 1945   63

legislative approval of the plan for horizontal tariff reduction could not be obtained and that it would be virtually useless to make the attempt" (FRUS 1945, VI, 68).

Canadian officials suggested that other countries should propose the horizontal approach as a way of forcing Congress to move in that direction, but the Americans rejected this, saying that Congress would be suspicious of such a proposal coming from other countries. Canada repeated its interest in a bilateral trade agreement with the United States should the multilateral initiative fail to materialize.

While disappointed with the multilateral-bilateral approach proposed by the United States, Canadian officials made a suggestion that soon took on immense importance. If the multilateral-bilateral approach had to be taken, the Canadians suggested, it would be undesirable to attempt to negotiate tariff reductions with many countries at the bargaining table:

> "judging from past experience, the presence at a general international conference of the less important, and for the most part protectionist-minded, countries, would inevitably result in a watering-down of the commitment which a smaller number of the major trading nations might find it possible to enter into" (FRUS 1945, VI, 71–72; CDER 11, 104).[74]

Therefore, Canadian officials suggested that a small "nuclear" group of eight to twelve nations start things off.[75]

This Canadian proposal is the first hint that something along the lines of a GATT might be a useful precursor to an ITO. And Canada's idea had an immediate impact on U.S. policy. As a result of these discussions, in late July 1945, the Executive Committee on Economic Foreign Policy recommended abandoning the multilateral-bilateral approach that had been proposed and instead adopting the "selective nuclear multilateral-bilateral" approach (FRUS

---

[74] For example, although U.S. and Canadian representatives agreed that employment measures were an important component of the trade package, "they also agreed that adoption of the extreme views put forth by the Australians, favoring a rigid international commitment to maintain employment and advocating an 'escape' clause from international commitments if employment were not maintained, would be impracticable and unwise" (FRUS 1945, VI, 64).

[75] They also worried about free riders under the selective approach. "Under the plan for horizontal tariff reduction it would have been possible to compel reluctant countries to participate in the plan by threatening to withhold the tariff benefits if they did not participate. This would have been politically feasible internationally because the requirements under the plan for a horizontal cut would be equitable, simple, and easy to understand. Any selective method of tariff reduction would be complicated and to some extent inequitable vis-a-vis outsiders and could not well be used as a weapon to force them in" (DCER 11, 100–101). Canada also proposed giving duty-free treatment for goods in which there was substantial bilateral trade.

1945 VI, 74–76). Under the selective nuclear multilateral approach, a group of about a dozen countries would negotiate bilateral agreements for selective tariff reductions and reach informal agreement on a code dealing with tariff preferences and nontariff barriers. This agreement would then be presented to a general international conference consisting of many other countries.[76] Thus, by July 1945, the United States had a rough conception of the process by which it could move from draft proposals to negotiated agreements, and also had in mind a two-track procedure that would lead to a GATT as distinct from the ITO.

In August 1945, Clayton met with British officials in London to discuss these plans. In the view of U.S. officials attending, "the general attitude of UK officials at this meeting was extremely pessimistic" as the British raised one objection after another (FRUS 1945, VI, 92).[77] They emphasized that the proposed separation of negotiations over tariffs and preferences was a nonstarter. British officials insisted that preferences should not be viewed as a distinct category of nontariff barriers, but must be discussed in the context of overall tariff reductions. They strongly criticized U.S. proposals on import quotas and export subsidies. They believed that granting permission to impose import quotas if limits were placed on domestic production, as the United States had in agriculture would open the door to all sorts of objectionable restrictions.[78] They also rejected allowing export subsidies on commodities in world surplus as blatantly inconsistent – Liesching called it "almost immoral" – with the overall proposal. On the other hand, the British also wanted fewer restrictions on the use of import quotas for balance-of-payments

[76] "Should the British refuse to accept the nuclear-multilateral procedure, this would provide an immediate and obvious occasion for reexamining the multilateral-horizontal approach with the Congress," the committee concluded (FRUS 1945, VI, 76). In August 1945, the State Department considered 11 countries as possible members of a nuclear group: the United Kingdom, Canada, Australia, New Zealand, South Africa, France, the Netherlands, Belgium, the Soviet Union, China, and Brazil. They excluded India because "the strongly protectionist sentiment in India makes it unlikely that India could be persuaded to join the nuclear group in expeditious tariff reduction" (FRUS 1945, VI, 88–89). In October, the United Kingdom requested that India be included.

[77] For the UK account of the meeting, see DBPO III, 6–10.

[78] "UK officials strongly criticized US proposals on quotas, maintaining that the provisions would permit quotas on the whole front. They did not agree that the provision that corresponding domestic restrictions must be imposed was a satisfactory check on the undue use of quotas. Shackle and Robbins maintained that it was most difficult to ascertain by how much domestic production was effectively restricted and whether such restriction was equivalent to the import restriction. Liesching, Robbins and Shackle objected to the proposals for subsidies on commodities in world surplus. Robbins said the main objection was to the idea that once it was agreed that a burdensome world surplus existed there should be a 'free-for-all' struggle with the use of export subsidies as a bludgeon to compel agreements that might not be satisfactory to all parties. Shackle said that distress at home should not be relieved by creating disturbances in other countries." FRUS 1945, VI, 92.

purposes.[79] Finally, they continued to pour cold water over the proposed bilateral negotiating approach: Keynes called it impracticable; Liesching said there were not enough qualified officials in Britain, let alone other countries, to negotiate with so many countries simultaneously; and Shackle thought that bilateral discussions would "drag on interminably" (FRUS 1945, VI, 91).[80]

Clayton said that the United States recognized the necessity for temporary controls on imports for a transition period of three to four years, but the British officials questioned whether that period would be sufficient (DBPO III, 60). Despite the advantages of the horizontal approach, Clayton believed that even a 20 percent horizontal cut would have been impossible to get through Congress. Still, the United States was determined to move forward. The two sides also differed over the number of countries that should participate, the United States favoring a small nucleus of about 10 countries, while the United Kingdom proposed no fewer than 17.[81]

1.7 The British Loan Negotiations, Washington, September–October 1945

In August 1945, shortly after Japan's surrender ended World War II, President Truman abruptly terminated Lend Lease aid to Britain and the allies. Clayton and others strenuously objected to this rash decision, but Truman (who later regretted the move) had been persuaded by aides who believed that he had no choice under the law's requirements. The decision stunned the British, who still lacked the ability to pay for vital imports of food, fuel, and raw materials. Keynes (1979, 410) warned the government that, without financial assistance,

---

[79] Commenting on the Anglo-American draft in July 1945, Keynes (1980, 325-326) said, however, "the discretion we retain for quantitative regulation is insufficient.... You must have some way of shutting off imports which you cannot afford. Of the various alternatives quantitative regulation is at the same time much the most effective and much the most in tune with the modern world. To try and create an international system which excludes quantitative regulation is out of date and, I should have thought, impracticable." He also described the American "multilateral-bilateral" method as "absolutely fatal from our point of view."

[80] However, they did concede that selective approach might make the infant-industry question and UK agricultural sensitivities easier to handle.

[81] According to the UK account of the meeting: "The Americans favoured as small a 'nucleus' as possible, so as to get quick results (indeed Mr. Clayton personally would have favoured the 'Big Five' Powers alone – including France and China). We on the other hand pointed out the risk of too narrow a limitation, which might lead to the formation of opposition blocs at the eventual Conference: we felt that there would have to be not less than 17 countries in the nucleus, while the Americans thought 15 should probably be the maximum" (DBPO III, 7, 9).

the country was facing a "financial Dunkirk." He was soon dispatched to the United States to seek transitional financing in order to cover Britain's postwar balance-of-payments shortfall.

Britain sought to secure a sizeable American loan on generous terms without any commitments on commercial policy.[82] In the expectation (or hope) that the negotiations would only concern financial matters, the British delegation consisted of Keynes and other Treasury officials alone. But in Washington, Clayton insisted that transitional finance would not be available for Britain without a satisfactory agreement on commercial policy. Although Keynes was confident that he could handle the trade negotiations by himself, U.S. officials rejected the idea of bilateral discussions without the participation of British commercial-policy experts. In fact, even British officials became alarmed at the thought of Keynes handling commercial-policy issues without supervision. Meade's (1990, 132) diary reaction for September 16, 1945 gives a flavor of the view in London:

> [Keynes] got himself sent to Washington without the commercial policy boys (Liesching, Lionel Robbins and Enfield) on the grounds that the mission was solely a financial one. He has now got set up in Washington an Anglo-American committee to discuss commercial policy, which he proposes to conduct himself, having at the last moment in England (while Liesching and Lionel Robbins were on leave) more or less sold to Ministers the crazy, lunatic, self-contradictory idea that we should join in with American in a general convention to reduce obstacles to trade all around but should maintain completely unfettered rights to programme (i.e. to restrict) our imports *ad infinitum* to any extent we desire! This week there has been a most resounding counter-attack on the part of Liesching and Lionel Robbins. Cripps at the Board of Trade has been magnificent, insisting on the need for a convention which prevents other countries from restricting their imports of our goods. (Query: How does this antiimport restriction view square with his apparent desire to "plan" everything quantitatively?) Dalton, to whom I sold the idea of the Commercial Union in the first place, who himself first launched the idea in Whitehall, who used to rant against us for not being willing to brush aside import restrictions quickly enough, and who used to pour scorn on Keynes's excursion into this field – now that he has moved from the Board of Trade to the Treasury seems to have swallowed this Keynes nonsense at least temporarily. But he was completely routed at the Ministerial meeting. Definite instructions have been cabled to Keynes instructing him not to touch commercial policy and to wait for a properly constituted team on the subject.

[82] The UK objectives for the mission are set out in DBPO (III, 74–77).

1.7 The British Loan Negotiations, Washington, September–October 1945

The British trade experts arrived in Washington in late September. With the financial future of the United Kingdom and the hopes for cooperation on postwar trade arrangements on the line, the stakes were very high; in Robbins's view, "there is nothing less at stake in this business than the future solidarity of the Western World" (HM 222).

Liesching and his colleagues began by proposing to narrow outstanding differences rather than to finalize the text of the proposed draft agreement. The Anglo-American negotiators first agreed that tariff negotiations among a select group of countries should be held in March 1946 and be followed by a general conference on trade and employment in June 1946. The officials then agreed to discuss five key issues: tariffs and preferences, subsidies, state trading, exchange controls, and cartels.[83]

Imperial preferences continued to be the most contentious issue and the United States handled it very clumsily. Clayton repeatedly tied American financial assistance to the elimination of imperial preferences, implicitly threatening that U.S. aid would not be forthcoming if Britain insisted on keeping preferences. Congress, he insisted, would not approve a loan unless Britain promised the complete abolition of discriminatory preferences. However, State Department civil servants took a softer line than Clayton, assuring their counterparts that there was no quid pro quo between preferences and financial assistance. Indeed, the U.S. Embassy in London warned the State Department that a heavy-handed American demand for an immediate and complete abolition of preferences as a condition for a loan would create a severe backlash in the United Kingdom. Whereas the United States thought the linkage was simply a form of conditionality, the United Kingdom viewed it as blackmail, as exploiting the country's weak economic position to America's advantage. However, Clayton and his staff were sending different signals to the British, and hence the U.S. message was somewhat contradictory: on the one hand, they wanted the two issues discussed in the same forum, but they did not insist that one depended upon the other.

Whatever the case, the British position was fixed: preferences should be subject to negotiation, but only in the context of American tariff reductions, and officials could not commit to their elimination without seeing the American tariff offers. British officials insisted that a unilateral abolition of preferences was neither equitable nor politically feasible. Liesching took the "uncompromising stand" that preferences should be discussed with all other tariffs, and not

---

[83] See the U.S. account in FRUS (1945, VI, 138) and on the British account in DBPO (III, 181–183). Keynes said that the U.S. draft commercial convention was "acceptable to us and indeed valuable," but there were four points of difficulty: preferences, state trading, import quotas, and the Bretton Woods provision about exchange controls.

considered as a separate category of non-tariff barriers.[84] Britain might be willing give up preferences in exchange for a major reduction in U.S. import duties, but noted that even a 50 percent reduction would still leave those tariffs at a much higher level than British tariffs. Liesching emphasized the domestic political sensitivities over eliminating preferences and again fell back upon the need to consult with the Dominions before committing to a major change in policy.

Even the British economists, who generally opposed preferences, were dismayed by the hard-line U.S. position. Robbins described the American stance as "crude and unimaginative" and Liesching thought it was "base" (HM 227). Like Churchill and Meade, Robbins was not a supporter of imperial preference and had opposed it at the time (in 1932), but confessed in his diary:

> I must say with complete sincerity that taking all the economic and political factors into account, I could not advise UK ministers to do anything but resist this kind of pressure (HM 228).[85]

He added that the Americans insisted that "an outright surrender of Imperial Preference is the price necessary to get the financial arrangements through Congress. As this is the one way in which we could *not* undertake to get rid of preferences, there is obvious trouble ahead" (HM 226).

Confronted with this resistance, U.S. negotiators ultimately backed down and accepted the British position that elimination of preferences was not a

---

[84] Hugh Dalton, now the Chancellor of the Exchequer, cabled Keynes and the British mission with this advice: "We have repeatedly expressed our willingness to consider preferences as part of a satisfactory tariff settlement, but not to treat them separately. Certainly there will be a very violent reaction here if preferences issue is formally linked, not with commercial talks, but with financial deal. Indeed, a financial settlement otherwise acceptable might be wrecked on this issue." DBPO III, 200.

[85] As Robbins (1971, 202-203) explained in his memoirs: "I do not think that any of us on the British side had any special penchant for discrimination per se. Some of us indeed, in earlier capacities, had played some part in elaborating the general arguments against it.... Nevertheless, there was an element of dogmatism in the American case which we all found it very difficult to swallow. Why should customs unions be permissible – as they were in the U.S. draft proposals – while anything short of complete union in the shape of mutual preferences be regarded as an ultimate iniquity? . . . Were the effects of Imperial Preference on the volume of world trade so manifestly more restrictive than those of the U.S. tariff as to deserve treatment as if in an entirely different category of offences? For all these reasons, even those who like myself had deplored the preferential innovations of the thirties, found no intellectual difficulty whatever in arguing, as our ministers had insisted, that preferences must be treated on all fours with other measures of trade regulations and that any progress towards their 'elimination' must be contingent on the nature of the bargain offered in the shape of reduction or elimination of other obstacles. And, in spite of much pressure from the other side, that remained our fundamental position to the very end. We were willing to enquire into possibilities. But we were not prepared to sign away anything until we saw what we were to get in return."

1.7 The British Loan Negotiations, Washington, September–October 1945   69

condition for American financial assistance. By November, the two sides agreed that "action for the elimination of preferences will be taken in conjunction with adequate measures for the substantial reduction in barriers to world trade on a broad scale" and that existing commitments would not stand in the way of actions to reduce preferences. Furthermore, no margins would be increased nor would new margins be introduced and the negotiated reductions in MFN tariffs would automatically reduce the margins of preferences (FRUS 1945, VI, 152).[86] In Meade's account (1990, 164–165):

> After sweating blood and tears with the Americans, Britain's position remained largely intact, although the introductory and concluding words... were drafted with the most skilful ambiguity so that the Americans, in explaining to their public, would be able to express greater hopes that in the negotiations on tariff and preferences to be undertaken next March preferences would be completely eliminated than we should be willing to admit. The Americans have in any case abandoned completely the idea that preferences should be eliminated in return for financial assistance;... but what they will not admit openly at any rate is that there is precious little prospect of us and the Dominions being offered a sufficient quid pro quo (particularly in view of the limitations under the US Trade Agreement Act for the extent to which they can reduce their duties) next March for us to feel able completely to eliminate preferences then."[87]

However, the United States insisted that further delay was no longer an option, that substantial progress had to be made toward an agreement on commercial policy by issuing a joint proposal at the conclusion of the negotiations. This proved easier than finalizing the details of the American loan because there was broad existing agreement on commercial policy and the United States accommodated the UK position on most outstanding issues. For example, there was no major difference in view with regard to state trading. On export taxes, the United Kingdom dissented from the American position that they should be

---

[86] The text of the agreement is in FRUS (1945, VI, 160–161). The final language in the *Proposals*: "In light of the principles set forth in Article VII of the mutual aid agreements, members [of the ITO] should enter into arrangements for the substantial reduction of tariffs and for the elimination of tariff preferences, action for the elimination of preferences being taken in conjunction with adequate measures for the substantial reduction of barriers to world trade, as part of the mutually advantageous arrangements contemplated in this document" (Annex A-5).

[87] After getting involved in drafting the language on preferences and Article VII, Meade (1990, 166) vented his frustration: "This is not economics. It is the psychology of symbols and is all very mystifying. How much easier affairs of state would be if rational men having agreed on a rational course of action were then permitted to give a rational account of it!"

abolished outright, preferring instead that export taxes be subject to negotiation just like import tariffs. As Robbins noted,

> To our great delight we were informed that they [the State Department] had completely accepted our views on state trading and export taxes. General subsidies and export subsidies are obviously going to be more difficult (HM 231).

On subsidies, the U.S. and UK positions were diametrically opposed: whereas the Americans planned to phase out domestic (agricultural) subsidies, it wanted to preserve export subsidies. Britain accused the United States of tailoring the text to its own domestic circumstances; instead, the United Kingdom wanted to keep domestic agricultural subsidies but abolish all export subsidies. Liesching announced his "uncompromising opposition" to the U.S. proposal to allow export subsidies on surplus commodities (FRUS 1945 VI, 140). In the final text, the two sides agreed that "members should undertake not to take any action which would result in the sale of a product in export markets at a price lower than the comparable price charged for the like product to buyers in the home market" within three years of an agreement, with a special provision for commodities in surplus.

On cartels, the United States continued to press for outright prohibitions on certain types of business practices in line with its domestic antitrust laws. Britain believed the proposed U.S. language was too strict. Although prepared to oppose cartels and restrictive practices in principle, British officials did not want to prohibit cartels whose effects were not considered harmful. They proposed a more flexible case-by-case approach rather than broad and sweeping prohibitions.[88] In this, as in most other areas, the United States essentially accepted the UK position.[89] After clashing on cartel policy, for example, Robbins was astounded to have the Americans return with a new draft that "more or less conceded our position.... [we could] scarcely believe our eyes" (HM 232).[90]

---

[88] Keynes still managed to annoy his hosts by sticking his nose into such issues as cartel policy. At one point Keynes interjected, "Isn't our scheme intended to get things done, whereas yours will merely provide a living for a large number of lawyers?," which produced an explosion from his American counterpart (Skidelsky 2000, 416). Dean Acheson (1969, 83) recalled that "Keynes did not like lawyers. He thought the United States 'a lawyer-ridden land' and believed that 'the Mayflower, when she sailed from Plymouth, must have been entirely filled with lawyers.'"

[89] These positions are reported in FRUS (1945, VI, 140ff).

[90] According to Robbins, one British negotiating strategy was simply to take advantage of the different positions of different U.S. agencies. For example, the negotiations on subsidies were "so far as we [i.e., the British] were concerned, very easy going; they quarreled so much among themselves (State Department versus Agriculture Department) that by invoking one or other of the antagonists, it was always possible to have a majority for our views. I

1.7 The British Loan Negotiations, Washington, September–October 1945

By the end of October 1945, the only remaining issue was the use of import quotas for balance-of-payments purposes during the transition period. Britain insisted upon the freedom to discriminate among different import suppliers in using quotas during the transition period, a disagreement that was resolved by requiring nondiscrimination after an unspecified transition period. In early November, Secretary of State James Byrnes reported to the U.S. Ambassador in London: "on all vital issues substantial agreement has been achieved or is in sight" and the draft proposal on commercial policy was soon transmitted to London (FRUS 1945, VI, 155–156). Britain consulted with the Dominions throughout the negotiations and received pledges of support from Canada and South Africa, but severe reservations from Australia and New Zealand.[91] On November 6, 1945, the British Cabinet approved the commercial-policy agreement after Hugh Dalton (Chancellor of the Exchequer) and Sir Stafford Cripps (President of the Board of Trade) strongly endorsed it (McKenzie 1998, 86).

The more difficult and protracted financial negotiations were completed a month later, in early December, when the details of a $3.75 billion U.S. loan were finalized. At the conclusion of the negotiations, President Truman and Prime Minister Attlee issued a joint statement congratulating themselves on having made progress "in establishing a world trading and monetary system from which the trade of all countries can benefit and within which the trade of all countries can be conducted on a multilateral, non-discriminatory basis."[92]

---

hate taking advantage of their lack of solidarity; for although, in part, it springs from bad organization and discipline, in part, it springs from greater candor and honesty than we regard as diplomatically appropriate. However, I go on doing it when necessary" (HM, 229).

[91] See McKenzie (1998, 138-155). According to a U.S. report, "The only serious British difficulty on commercial policy was with the Australians, where the Dominion's Secretary was said to be having "a hell of a time" with the Australian Minister for External Affairs "who is pouring in forcible protests against the commercial policy understandings" (FRUS 1945, VI, 153). Meade (1990, 171) noted that "Australia is making itself a frightful nuisance on the commercial policy draft by insisting on complete and absolute freedom from any shadow of a commitment on any part of it before the trade conference foreshadowed for March of next year." Robbins also noted: "Each delegation true to form – Canada first rate, South Africa debonair and friendly, New Zealand banal, Australia surly and unhelpful" (HM 233). Australia refused to recognize the priority of multilateral trade plans over full employment. In Canada's view, it was not objectionable and Canada did not oppose the substance. It actually "serves as a theoretical defense against a demand for the removal of trade barriers and the reduction of tariffs. It has a strong basis in the fact that, if full employment cannot be attained consistently with a high level of international trade, the political demands for protective measures are likely sooner or later to become irresistible. It is, however, in our view a dangerous doctrine if it is used to prevent or handicap an effort to secure full employment together with international specialization" (DER 11, pt. 2, 94).

[92] State Department *Bulletin* 13 (December 9, 1945), 906.

The Anglo-American commercial-policy discussions in October 1945 proved to be a critical breakthrough that ended two years of inaction.[93] Both sides agreed that the State Department should publish the proposed multilateral convention and invite 13 or 14 other countries to a March 1946 meeting that would negotiate tariff reductions. In December 1945, the State Department released its "Proposals for Expansion of World Trade and Employment" to the public, the first time that they were publicly disclosed (Annex A-5). The Proposals sought to address the four factors said to be responsible for the small volume of international trade: government trade restrictions, private trade restrictions (cartels and combinations), fear of disorder in primary commodity markets, and irregularity in domestic production and employment. Regarding the first factor, the Proposals stated that:

> Barriers of this sort are imposed because they serve or seem to serve some purpose other than the expansion of world trade. Within limits they cannot be forbidden. But when they grow too high, and especially when they discriminate between countries or interrupt previous business connections, they create bad feeling and destroy prosperity. The objective of international action should be to reduce them all and to state fair rules within which those that remain should be confined.

The *Proposals* called for an international conference on tariffs to be held "not later than the summer of 1946" and noted the following: "no government is ready to embrace 'free trade' in any absolute sense. Nevertheless, much can usefully be done by international agreement toward reduction of governmental barriers to trade."

1.8 Moving Toward the GATT

The United States now proceeded quickly on two tracks. First, with the publication of the Proposals in early December 1945, the State Department invited 15 countries to participate in a meeting of "nuclear" countries that would negotiate tariff reductions. By January 1946, 14 countries had accepted: Australia, Belgium, Brazil, Canada, China, Cuba, Czechoslovakia, France, India, Luxembourg, the Netherlands, New Zealand, South Africa, and the United Kingdom. The Union of Soviet Socialist Republics (USSR) was invited but apparently never responded.[94]

---

[93] One British official told the Americans that the delay over the previous year has served the negotiations well by allowing all parties in the United Kingdom to become comfortable with the issues (FRUS 1945, VI 153). Notes from the concluding meeting are in FRUS (1945 VI, 178-184).

[94] In Moscow, George Kennen of the U.S. State Department requested a meeting to discuss Soviet participation in the upcoming conference. Soviet officials never granted this request and never responded one way or another to the U.S. invitation, despite the fact that

1.8 Moving Toward the GATT

In August, at the request of the United Nations, Chile, Lebanon, and Norway received invitations as well.

Second, in February 1946, at the Economic and Social Council of the United Nations, the United States proposed convening a general UN conference on trade and employment. Although developing countries wanted prior assurances that their infant industries could still be protected, the United Nations agreed to move ahead and form a preparatory committee to prepare an agenda for such a conference. The goal of the UN conference was to prepare a charter for an International Trade Organization, not to undertake tariff negotiations. However, the preparatory committee would work in parallel with the smaller nuclear group that was planning on exchanging tariff reductions.

A February 1946 State Department memo indicated how the two tracks would be linked (Annex A-6):

> It is considered that the best means of preparing for the general world conference would be to develop in advance a body of definite and concrete international commitments on the various aspects of the Proposals which a broadly representative group of nations, including the major trading nations, would be prepared to support and adopt. Accordingly, it is believed

their delegates had participated in the UN Economic and Social Council discussion of the resolution-on-trade conference and voted for resolution. The State Department was skeptical that the Soviet Union, given the state monopoly control on foreign trade, could participate in a useful way in the tariff negotiations. Still, despite the lack of response from Soviet officials, the State Department decided to include the USSR on the list of countries with which it intended to negotiate, leaving the door open for their participation (FRUS 1946, I, 1354-1355). The U.S. Embassy in Moscow cabled back with this message: "We have noted with interest several recent reports from London of conversations with Soviet officials giving various explanations why Soviet Government does not participate in many international meetings, particularly ITO. Reasons given for nonparticipation range from lack of personnel to Soviet preoccupation with questions of security. While there may be some modicum of truth in these arguments, we believe that in regard to such institutions as the International [i.e., World] Bank, ITO and PICAO [i.e., Provisional International Civil Aviation Organization], the principal, if not the only, reason the Russians do not join is that they do not wish to. Kremlin insistence on keeping its independence of action in world affairs has even on occasion been frankly expressed by certain responsible Soviet officials, and, in any event, is self-evident in every aspect of Soviet policy in action." Furthermore, the cable added, for the Soviets "to join any organization which would require them to give statistics on national income, international trade, balance of payments and gold production, would imply a complete reversal of a basic and scrupulously maintained Soviet policy of state secrecy in such matters. On the other hand, whenever they stand to gain something concrete by participation in an international organ or run the risk of losing something important by failure so to do, they appear to find no difficulty in effecting such participation (UNRRA, telecommunications, whaling). It would appear unreal, therefore, in the absence of concrete evidence to the contrary, to base any policy on the belief that Russians actually desire to join such organs as ITO but are precluded because of personnel or other administrative considerations" (FRUS 1946, I, 1355–1356).

that the objective of the preliminary meeting should be to negotiate, and reach substantial agreement upon, a detailed international instrument incorporating such commitments (FRUS 1946, I, 1281).

Furthermore, these countries would exchange tariff reductions and therefore "the provisions of the Charter dealing with trade barriers would have a more definitive status (in respect of the countries participating in the preliminary meeting) than would the remainder of the Charter." The ITO charter itself would not deal with specific tariff reductions, so a protocol would have to be attached to the charter with the negotiated agreements to reduce or bind tariff rates. The resulting tariff schedules would be multilateral "both in scope and in legal application."[95]

But the State Department also envisioned that the protocol would enter into force before, and independent of, the ITO charter:

It is proposed, therefore, that the Protocol, consisting of the tariff schedules and of the non-tariff trade barrier provisions of the draft Charter which it may be agreed to incorporate in the Protocol by reference, should, at the close of the preliminary meeting, be signed and published by the countries participating in that meeting and should come into force, independently of the Charter, in accordance with provisions to be worked out. In order to make perfectly clear the relationship between the Protocol and the Charter, provision might be made whereby the Protocol could later be adapted to any changes in the provisions of the Charter relating to non-tariff trade barriers which might result from the action of the world conference (FRUS 1946, I, 1281).

Thus, by February 1946, the United States had a clear sense that a protocol (the GATT) would precede but ultimately become a part of the ITO.

However, the planned March 1946 meeting of nuclear countries never materialized. That date was simply too ambitious when invitations had only been issued just four months before. In April 1946, the State Department revised its

[95] "It has been the past international practice, with few exceptions, to confine negotiations on tariffs to agreements between two countries. In these bilateral agreements, such as those heretofore concluded by the United States under the reciprocal trade-agreements program, each of the two countries parties to the agreement granted reductions or bindings of its import tariffs on products of which the other was a principal or important supplier. While these concessions were, as a rule, generalized to third countries, either by virtue of most-favored-nation obligations or as a matter of policy, third countries had no contractual right to them independently of the existence of the bilateral agreement in which they were embodied. In other words, tariff reductions have been effected in the past either unilaterally or by means of a network of bilateral instruments, each separate from the other and dependent for its existence and continuation in force upon the policies and decisions of the particular pair of countries concerned" (FRUS 1946, I, 1282).

1.8 Moving Toward the GATT

schedule. Under the procedure established by the Reciprocal Trade Agreements Act, the federal government would have to release a list of items contemplated for duty reduction and allow time for public comment. The State Department anticipated giving public notice of the intent to negotiate in May 1946, holding public hearings in July, and then starting the tariff negotiations in September. President Truman received a memorandum in April 1946 asking for his permission to proceed on this schedule. The State Department warned that "experience has shown that once this list is published, minority interests will put strong pressure on the Administration for commitments that particular tariff rates will not be cut" and urged resistance to such pressures (FRUS 1946, I, 1307).

The timing of this request triggered alarm bells at the White House and State Department due to the upcoming November 1946 Congressional elections. When British officials requested permission in April to announce a specific date for the opening of the tariff negotiations, Secretary of State James Byrnes quickly replied that a date had not been set and hinted that it might be postponed (FRUS 1946, I, 1309). Just days later, Byrnes formally announced the decision – made jointly by him and the president – to delay the conference until early 1947. The rationale for the delay was that the Truman administration did not want to give the required 90-day public notice of the tariff items that would be subject to negotiation before Congress acted on the British loan sometime in mid-1946.[96] But then the public notice and public hearings would come uncomfortably close to the November elections. Therefore, to avoid stirring up political controversy over the trade proposals, Truman and Byrnes decided to issue the public notice immediately following the midterm elections, meaning that the negotiations could not begin until early 1947. Clayton sent an impassioned memo asking that Byrnes adhere to the original schedule because other countries were ready to act and further delay would risk the expiration of the 1945 RTAA renewal and possibly run into the 1948 election (FRUS, 1946, VI, 1311–1312). However, the decision had been made and this plea failed.

The State Department civil servants shared Clayton's fear of losing momentum, but also feared the politicization of the trade negotiations. In addition, they gained additional time to draft specific language for the charter and consult with other countries over its provisions. The United States circulated a draft charter in the summer of 1946 that was a slight revision of the December 1945 proposals. Hawkins visited France, the Netherlands, Belgium, Norway, and Czechoslovakia to test their interest in joining an International Trade Organization. He reported that Norway and Belgium expressed unqualified support, the Netherlands

---

[96] The United Kingdom also wanted to wait until the fate of financial agreement in Congress was determined before undertaking tariff negotiations (DBPO IV 293–294).

qualified only with respect to the interests of Dutch East Indies, while France expressed some doubt due to conflicting domestic political elements and Czechoslovakia much greater doubt due to its political relationship with the Soviet Union (FRUS 1946 I, 1347). All countries were concerned about transitional arrangements and objected to the cartels and intergovernmental commodity provisions, mainly because they did not share America's hostility toward cartels and commodity agreements.

From August to October 1946, other State Department officials went to Canada, Cuba, Brazil, Chile, New Zealand, Australia, South Africa, India, and China to brief them on the draft charter and get their reaction.[97] Canada was reported to be the most supportive of the whole effort, while the United Kingdom criticized the draft charter only as it differed from the December 1945 *Proposals*.[98] One State Department document summarized the reactions this way:

> A definite different opinion is to be found in the less-developed countries (Australia, New Zealand, India, China, Cuba, Brazil, and Chile) with regard to the reduction of trade barriers. These countries, deeply concerned with the problem of industrialization and full employment, want to use restrictive measures to protect their infant industries. In general, they remain unimpressed with our contention that subsidies offer the least objectionable method for this purpose. They point out that, while tariffs and subsidies both amount to charges on their economies, the very real difficulties in raising the revenue to pay subsidies make the latter impractical for them. The Cubans are reluctant to give up their preferential position in the US market, as are the New Zealanders in the UK. The British, however, are willing to negotiate on preferences if convinced of the sincerity of the US intention to lower substantially our tariff wall, as a defense against which the Empire preferential system was developed. A major point of difficulty will be faced in connection with our cartel provisions. The Dutch, the Czechs and the Belgians are not willing to concede that all cartels are bad. They would be willing to have the Charter state that certain practices may have undesirable effects, but they object to having the burden of proof put on those engaging in cartel arrangements, as our draft Charter now provides (FRUS 1946, I, 1349).

---

[97] Not surprisingly, Australian officials believed the draft failed to give sufficient emphasis on efforts to expand domestic demand (DAFP 10, 174–176).

[98] After reading the draft U.S. charter in September 1946, Meade (1990, 327) wrote: "A grand sign of the intention, at least of the [Truman] Administration, really to take this all seriously; and I personally confess that I am rather glad to hear that they propose next week to publish the whole draft charter, though the official view here is that this is dangerous since it will frighten off a number of countries. On the contrary, I believe now that anything which brings it all nearer to finality is to the good."

In light of these comments, the State Department revised the December 1945 *Proposals* and issued the U.S. *Suggested Charter* in September 1946.[99]

1.9 First Preparatory Meeting, London, October–November 1946

Although the tariff negotiations among the nuclear countries had been postponed until early 1947, plans for the ITO conference continued under the auspices of the United Nations. The first meeting of the UN Preparatory Committee for the International Conference on Trade and Employment convened at Church House in London during October-November 1946.[100] The U.S. delegation was headed by Clair Wilcox, the Director of the State Department's Office of International Trade Policy, with Harry Hawkins, the Minister-Counselor for Economic Affairs at the U.S. Embassy in London, as his principal deputy. The UK delegation was headed by H. A. Marquand, a member of Parliament, and included Helmore and Meade.

The London preparatory conference was the first formal meeting in which countries other than the United States and the United Kingdom were invited to participate. These countries included Australia, India, China, Ceylon, Lebanon, Brazil, and Chile, among others. As a result, the participation of others now began to shape the outcome of the multilateral convention. As will be discussed in Chapter 2, only Brazil and India submitted comprehensive reactions to the U.S. *Suggested Charter.* But many nations felt free to offer their criticism of the American proposals. For example, both Australia and Canada criticized the lack of disciplines in agriculture and sought greater constraints, but there was no consensus for stronger language.[101] (Chapter 2 explores the changes in the draft in detail.)

---

[99] "Suggested Charter for an International Trade Organization of the United Nations," State Department Publication No. 2598, September 1946.

[100] The documentation for the conference was published by the Economic and Social Council of the United Nations document series E/PC/T, which includes verbatim reports of plenary and committee meetings. The official report of the conference is in E/PC/T/33.

[101] Australia objected to the exclusion of agriculture from the general rules in the U.S. draft, that is, quantitative import restrictions and export subsidies were permitted in agricultural goods that would be detrimental to developing-country exporters. On Australia's view of the London meeting, see DAFP X, 400–407. "The Canadian delegation took the position that there should be no weakening of the Geneva draft which, in its opinion, had opened the door so widely that agriculture was almost written out of the Charter.... The exception which permitted the use of import restrictions on any agricultural or fisheries product, if associated with production control or a surplus disposal programme, was of great concern to the Canadian Delegation, for, if used, could nullify import concessions obtained from Members in the General Agreement on Tariffs and Trade" (Hart 1989, 38).

In a confidential summary of the meeting (Annex A-7), Wilcox wrote that:

The strongest support for the United States came from Belgium, France, Norway, and the Netherlands, with Canada and Cuba also agreeing with the U.S. approach. The strongest opposition came from Australia and India. These countries had two of the most effective delegations at the meeting. The Indians came with a chip on their shoulder. They regarded the Proposals as a document prepared by the U.S. and the U.K. to serve the interest of the highly industrialized countries by keeping the backward countries in a position of economic dependence.... The Australians were able, intelligent, and reasonable.... The differences between us were more a matter of emphasis than of substance and we succeeded in meeting their political necessities without surrendering anything that we regarded as a matter of fundamental principle" (FRUS 1946, I, 1362).

The main goal of the developing countries – particularly Australia, along with India, China, Brazil, and Chile – was to shift attention toward employment and economic development and to ensure that rules did not prevent them from using quantitative import quotas to promote those goals. As a result, new chapters of the draft ITO charter were included on both issues (FRUS 1946, I, 1361). Australia, in particular, stressed the importance of employment provisions and the necessity of countries to take affirmative action to undertake expansionary domestic policies to ensure full employment.[102] They believed that measures to ensure that the U.S. economy kept growing steadily would contribute much more to the expansion in world trade than simply reducing tariffs, many of which they wanted to retain in order to promote domestic industry. While Australia insisted on having a chapter on employment in the Charter, Wilcox (1949, 41–42) noted that no government "proposed any positive international measures directed toward that end.... The only affirmative provision with respect to the maintenance of employment adopted at London made it a matter of domestic policy; this was the proposal that had originally been made by the United States."[103]

[102] On Australia's position, see Crawford (1966) and Capling (2000).
[103] Hawkins (1948, 276) made this distinction between Australia's demand for full-employment provision and America's insistence upon disciplining the use of trade policy: "the difference between the problems presented is the difference between asking a man to obligate himself to remain prosperous and asking him to agree to a rule against deliberate attacks on the prosperity of his neighbors." With respect to the obligation to remain prosperous, it "could not, of course, be as absolute as in the case of the other matters which lie entirely within the volition and control of nations assuming the obligations of the charter." The United States resisted allowing exemptions from tariff discipline based on insufficiently full employment, but indirectly allowed them through the balance-of-payments exception. In other words, if the United States sank into depression, thereby affecting the exports of other countries, those countries might have recourse to trade remedies due to any export shortfall that materialized in the balance of payments.

1.9 First Preparatory Meeting, London, October–November 1946

Australia also joined with India in demanding a "developing country exception" that would permit the use of QRs to foster industrialization. To accommodate this, the U.S. delegation drafted a new chapter on economic development that permitted the ITO to allow the limited use of import quotas by developing countries. Wilcox noted that: "this was the only important concession made by the United States during the meeting and it was this that brought about the virtually unanimous acceptance of the charter as a whole" (FRUS 1946, I, 1361, Annex A-8).

At the same time, the United States sought to impose greater disciplines on the use of QR than in the *Proposals*. Indeed, Wilcox argued that:

> The major objective of the United States was the adoption of a rule that would outlaw the use of *import quotas* and other quantitative restrictions as a matter of principle, permitting them only with international approval in exceptional cases and requiring that they be administered, in such cases, without discrimination. In the absence of such a rule, it is virtually certain that all other nations will impose quotas on imports and that many nations will so administer these quotas as to discriminate against American goods (FRUS 1946, I, 1360).

The United States sought to end the transition period that allowed QRs for balance-of-payments purposes in December 1949, after which QRs would be permitted only in cases of severe balance-of-payments difficulties and only in conformity with the principle of nondiscrimination. Furthermore, after 1949, a country seeking to impose QRs for balance-of-payments reasons would be obliged to consult with the ITO. If the ITO members requested the removal of the QR and the country did not comply, the members could retaliate. Britain resisted this provision and held out for more discretionary use of QRs for balance-of-payments purposes. Although they were concerned that widespread use of QRs would have an adverse effect on their exports, British officials wanted a longer transition period and no ITO consultation.

As a result of the landmark London meeting, the participants agreed on most of the provisions of a draft charter for an International Trade Organization, although the draft was not yet binding on governments. The participants agreed to include a chapter on the need for countries to take measures to ensure a high level of employment and on the limited use of quantitative restrictions, exchange controls, and export subsidies, except under specific circumstances. In addition, chapters set out rules regarding state trading, economic development, restrictive business practices, intergovernmental commodity agreements, and the structure of the International Trade Organization.

Among the issues left unsettled at London were relations between member and nonmember countries, the conduct of state monopolies in foreign trade, and various technical articles on tariff valuation, freedom on transit, and the like. A staff memo to Clayton noted that:

> The new draft charter that has emerged is a truly international document to which all delegates at the conference have contributed. It embodies the essential principles of the American position as well as the contributions of other countries and is a better balanced and more complete document than the original American draft (FRUS 1946, I 1359).

More importantly, definite plans were made for a provisional agreement, the GATT, to take effect among the nuclear countries prior to the approval of the ITO charter.[104]

1.10 Toward Geneva, December 1946–April 1947

After the London meeting, a UN drafting committee met at Lake Success, New York, in January-February 1947 to improve the language of the articles where substantial agreement had been reached.[105] This meeting produced the first full draft of the GATT by drawing on the commercial-policy chapters of the draft ITO chapter. The GATT was considered necessary to protect the negotiated tariff concessions.[106] The New York meeting also decided that the GATT would not include articles involving domestic policy exclusively, which would be included in the ITO Charter, and that the GATT obligations would not take immediate effect but only after a transition period (E/PC/T/C.6/55 1947).[107] This, in turn,

---

[104] See in particular, E/PC/T/C.II/58, November 21, 1946.

[105] Lake Success, just outside of New York City on Long Island, was the temporary location of the headquarters of the United Nations.

[106] State Department official John Leddy assumed primary responsibility for drafting the GATT. As he later recalled, "Well, let's put it this way, I guess I was the guy who sort of pulled together and helped to guide through the interagency executive committee the old multilateral convention on commercial policy, that I spoke to you about, including various provisions on MFN, national treatment, marks of origin, customs formalities, customs valuation, quotas, the whole lot, ... We had in the U.S. Government worked on these provisions drawing them from the old bilateral trade agreements, as well as various multilateral instruments that had existed, like the Freedom of Transit Convention, the Convention on Abolition of Prohibitions and Restrictions, etc. In other words, we drew from both U.S. and international sources." http://www.trumanlibrary.org/oralhist/leddyj.htm (last visited Jan. 17, 2008)

[107] In his report on the Lake Success meeting, Leddy wrote: "The atmosphere at the New York meeting was generally good. The delegations of the United Kingdom, Canada, Australia and Cuba contributed substantially to the work of the meeting. Particular note should be taken of the attitude of the United Kingdom, which appeared to be much more cooperative than at the London meeting. . . . The Indian delegation did not, as at London, press for destructive amendments. . . . The delegations of Brazil and Chile were represented primarily by persons unfamiliar with the background or the subject matter and the attitude of the Brazilians was

1.10 Toward Geneva, December 1946–April 1947

cleared the way for the Second Preparatory meeting in Geneva set to open in April 1947.

Meanwhile, the United States consulted with the other "nuclear" countries about the procedures for negotiating the tariff reductions. Following the midterm elections in November 1946, President Truman approved the plans for the April 1947 conference in Geneva, signing off on the publication of the list of goods on which the United States was prepared to offer concessions.[108] But the outcome of the November 1946 election was stunning: a Republican sweep gave them control of Congress for the first time since 1932. Given the traditional Republican support for protection and past hostility toward the RTAA, this cast a threatening shadow over the impending negotiations. As more and more public concerns were aired about the impact of tariff reductions on import-sensitive industries, some conservative Republicans called for postponing the April meeting or even repealing the RTAA. In December 1946, Sen. Hugh Butler (R-NE) wrote a forceful letter to Will Clayton stating that the voters had repudiated the administration's tariff-reduction program and therefore the Geneva negotiations should "be temporarily suspended until the new Congress shall have an opportunity to write a new foreign trade policy." As Butler put it:

> The attempt to use the authority of the Trade Agreements Act, previously wrested from a Democratic Congress, to destroy our system of tariff protection, seems to me a direct affront to the popular will expressed last month.

Clayton rejected and countered every point in the Butler letter and refused to postpone the Geneva meeting.[109]

---

at times hostile. The Czechoslovak delegate, while personally friendly, made no constructive suggestions and was apparently under rigid instructions to avoid any amendments which would strengthen the provisions dealing with state trading. The delegations of China and New Zealand confined themselves to repeating, whenever appropriate, reservations made at London." Leddy to Wilcox, "U.S. Summary Report on the Interim Drafting Committee of the Preparatory Committee of the International Conference on Trade and Employment (Lake Success, New York)," p. 16. From National Archives II, Lot File 57D-284 – Box 8.

[108] As Wilcox (1949, 43) explained: "Public hearings on the tariff list were opened before the Interdepartmental Committee on Reciprocity Information in Washington on January 13, 1947. The statements presented in these hearings were then examined by the Interdepartmental Committee on Trade Agreements, together with studies made by the Tariff Commission and other relevant materials. On the basis of the recommendations made by this Committee, the President then set the limits within which the United States was permitted to negotiate."

[109] For example, he pointed out that "Far from intending 'to destroy our system of tariff protection,' our Government is entering into the projected trade negotiations for the purpose of insuring that tariffs, rather than discriminatory import quotas, exchange controls, and bilateral barter deals, shall be the accepted method by which nations regulate their foreign trade. If it were not for the initiative which our Government has taken in this matter,

In January 1947, Rep. Thomas Jenkins (R-Ohio) of the House Ways and Means Committee introduced a resolution to postpone the Geneva negotiations until the U.S. Tariff Commission had studied and reported on the impact of lower tariffs on domestic industries. Given the time it would take for this analysis to be completed, the Jenkins resolution would effectively derail the Geneva conference.

To avoid the impasse, two senior Republican leaders, Senators Arthur Vandenberg (R-MI) and Eugene Millikin (R-CO), chairmen of the Foreign Relations and Finance Committees, respectively, met with Under Secretaries of State Acheson and Clayton. Vandenberg supported multilateral negotiations to reduce tariff rates, but felt that the State Department put too much weight on foreign-policy considerations and discounted the potential harm to domestic producer interests as it sought tariff reductions. The Congressional leaders wanted to limit the executive's authority over tariffs without jeopardizing the entire trade-agreements program. These discussions resulted in an agreement that allowed the Geneva conference to go forward. In February 1947, Vandenberg and Millikin issued a statement that it would be "undesirable" to postpone the April conference in view of the extensive preparations for it, and that legislative changes to the RTAA would be "made more appropriately" in 1948, when it was up for renewal. However, they added, there was "considerable sentiment for procedural improvements leading to more certain assurance that our domestic economy will not be imperiled by tariff reductions and concessions." In particular, they requested several procedural changes to counter the fear that a "tariff adequate to safeguard our domestic economy may be subordinated to extraneous and overvalued diplomatic objectives" (Congressional Record, February 10, 1947, 912). In essence, Vandenberg and Millikin wanted escape-clause procedures that would make it easier for domestic industries to receive temporary protection.

A few days later, President Truman issued an executive order embracing most of the Vandenberg-Millikin recommendations. The executive order established a process for considering and acting upon complaints from domestic firms regarding the harmful impact of foreign competition as a result of a negotiated tariff reduction. The order mandated that, in all future trade agreements, the United States would retain the right to withdraw or modify concessions "if, as a result of unforeseen developments and of the concession granted by the United States on any article in the trade agreement, such article is being imported in such increased quantities and under such conditions as to cause, or threaten,

the world would be headed straight toward the deliberate strangulations of its commerce through the imposition of detailed administrative controls. I need hardly tell you that such a development would be seriously prejudicial to the essential interests of the United States." The exchange of letters was published in the Department of State *Bulletin*, January 26, 1947, 161–163.

1.10 Toward Geneva, December 1946–April 1947

serious injury to domestic producers of like or similar articles" (Congressional Record, February 26, 1947, 1411).[110]

In announcing the new procedures, Truman insisted that "the provisions of the order do not deviate from the traditional Cordell Hull principles," but "simply make assurance doubly sure that American interests will be properly safeguarded." This executive order did not incorporate all of the senators' suggestions, in particular one in which the Tariff Commission would recommend tariff limits below which a negotiated reduction should not go for fear of endangering a domestic industry. Still, Vandenberg and Millikin welcomed the president's action as "a substantial advance in the legitimate and essential domestic protections which should be part of an equally essential foreign trade program" (Congressional Record, February 26, 1947, 1413).

This compromise prevented a serious rift between the Republican Congress and the Democratic administration about the upcoming multilateral negotiations. While it did not necessarily win Republican support for trade liberalization, it at least secured their acquiescence to the Geneva Conference.

A month before the start of the Geneva conference, President Truman threw his support behind the meeting in a major speech at Baylor University in Waco, Texas. In a strong statement, Truman argued:

> If the nations can agree to observe a code of good conduct in international trade, they will cooperate more readily in other international affairs. Such agreement will prevent the bitterness that is engendered by an economic war. It will provide an atmosphere congenial to the preservation of peace. As a part of this program we have asked the other nations of the world to join with us in reducing barriers to trade. We have not asked them to remove all barriers. Nor have we ourselves offered to do so. But we have proposed

---

[110] In fact, the escape clause, permitting the withdrawal of tariff concessions when imports were causing serious injury to a domestic industry, was developed and inserted into the template reciprocal trade agreement in 1941 by the State Department. They did so in response to Congressional concerns, expressed during the 1940 renewal of the RTAA, about the impact of trade disruptions on American industries during and especially after World War II. State Department officials, who did not necessarily like the clause, acted to preempt Congressional action mandating such a provision. This clause allowed any domestic producer that felt harmed by foreign competition to petition the interdepartmental Committee on Trade Agreements for relief from imports. (At that time, the Committee was made up of representatives from the Departments of State, War, Navy, Treasury, Agriculture, Commerce, and the Tariff Commission.) The Tariff Commission would investigate the application and make a recommendation to the president "for his consideration in light of the public interest." If the Tariff Commission found grounds for restricting imports to prevent injury, the president then had the option of imposing restrictions on imports or rejecting the advice. The escape clause was first inserted in the 1942 U.S-Mexico trade agreement.

negotiations directed toward the reduction of tariffs, here and abroad, toward the elimination of other restrictive measures and the abandonment of discrimination. These negotiations are to be undertaken at the meeting which opens in Geneva next month. The success of this program is essential to the establishment of the International Trade Organization [and] to the strength of the whole United Nations structure of cooperation in economic and political affairs.... The negotiations at Geneva must not fail (State Department *Bulletin*, March 16, 1947, 483).

On April 3, 1947, Dean Acheson, Will Clayton, and Winthrop Brown (chairman of the interdepartmental Committee on Trade Agreements) met with President Truman to review the tariff concessions that the State Department was prepared to offer at Geneva and discuss the political sensitivities involved, particularly in the case of zinc, woolen textiles, cotton textiles, rubber, and tin. When told that he could expect strong political protests from some special interests, Truman replied, "I am ready for it." He then approved the recommendations (FRUS 1947, I, 914).

1.11 Second Preparatory Meeting, Geneva, Switzerland, April–October 1947

On April 10, 1947, the Second Preparatory meeting of the United Nations Conference on Trade and Employment opened at the *Palais des Nations* in Geneva, Switzerland. The purpose of the meeting was to prepare a draft version of the ITO charter for final discussion and ratification at the UN conference at Havana later that year. In addition, the meeting would allow the "nuclear" countries to negotiate tariff reductions and secure those reductions with an interim measure, a General Agreement on Tariffs and Trade.

The higher stakes of the meeting, as well as personnel changes on both sides of the Atlantic, meant that the negotiations lacked the cordiality of previous staff discussions. On the British side, Sir Stafford Cripps had replaced Hugh Dalton as head of the Board of Trade, and James Helmore had replaced Percivale Liesching as the Second Secretary. On the American side, Will Clayton continued in his role, assisted by Clair Wilcox.[111] As the highest-ranking officials, Clayton and Cripps met occasionally to discuss the most difficult and unresolved issues, while Wilcox, Helmore, and their staffs conducted most of the detailed negotiations. Despite the fact that the conference involved many countries, the final outcome

---

[111] Harry Hawkins and James Meade did not play as large a role as they had in the past. Furthermore, by this time, Lionel Robbins had returned to the London School of Economics, and John Maynard Keynes had died in April 1946.

1.11 Second Preparatory Meeting, Geneva, Switzerland, April–October 1947

still hinged largely on American and British decisions as their participation was crucial to the meeting's success.

The tariff negotiations started immediately, but detailed consideration of the multilateral convention did not begin until May 15, 1947. As Wilcox (1949, 44) later noted, "the text of the charter was reorganized, obscure passages were clarified, inconsistencies were removed, and the appearance of the document was generally improved." Because of the extensive negotiations in London, as Chapter 2 documents, the changes to the GATT text and ITO charter were relatively minor.[112] In July, Wilcox reported that the work on the employment, commercial policy, investment, and cartel sections of the charter were virtually complete.[113] From the American perspective, the charter received the most support from Belgium, the Netherlands, and Canada. The main area of dispute continued to be quantitative restrictions on imports, and Wilcox noted the "continuous assaults that are being made from all sides upon the controls developed at the London meeting dealing with the use and imposition of quantitative restrictions." In London, the United States reluctantly agreed to broaden the permission given to countries to introduce quantitative restrictions in the event of balance-of-payments difficulties. In Geneva, there was further pressure to widen the scope for using quantitative measures including general permission for developing countries to use them for the purpose of economic development. There was also pressure to eliminate the requirement that countries seeking to impose QRs had to justify their action and receive permission from the ITO before doing so. While the United States did not want to see a weakening in the discipline of QRs, countries such as New Zealand, Cuba, China, Chile, India, and Czechoslovakia wanted them for reasons dealing with state trading, economic development, and

---

[112] "Almost without exception," Wilcox (1949, 44–45) reported, "the changes that had been suggested in the United States were accepted and the draft was amended accordingly. Of particular importance was the inclusion of two new articles, one limiting the freedom of nations to discriminate against foreign motion-picture films and the other dealing with the treatment of foreign investment. The latter article, while unacceptable in substance, did serve to bring the subject of foreign investment within the scope of the Charter. On only one point did the United States suffer a reversal: at the instance of Canada, the Committee adopted an amendment forbidding the use of export subsidies without the prior approval of the trade organization. On this point the position of the United States was formally reserved."

[113] "Mr. Wilcox informed the Delegation that the United States negotiators have succeeded in having amendments to the Charter adopted to meet practically all of the suggestions made by the Senate Finance Committee, by the Foreign Trade Council, by the National Association of Manufacturers, by the International Commerce Commission and by the various interested parties who appeared at the public hearings on the Charter held in various cities throughout the United States. No changes, Mr. Wilcox said, have been made in the substance or patterns of the Charter. The changes that have been made related to matters of detail." FRUS 1947, I, 962.

balance of payments. The United States found that it had little choice but to accede to these demands.

Thus, by mid-August, the final text of the GATT and the draft ITO Charter had been finalized.[114] The purpose of the GATT was to prevent the tariff concessions from unraveling in the period before the ITO Charter took effect.[115] But at this point, there were few tariff reductions to be preserved because the tariff and preference negotiations were in a terrible state.[116]

Going into the conference, the United States faced the choice of revealing all of the authorized tariff reductions, showing the maximum degree to which the U.S. delegation could reduce its duties and thereby minimizing strategic bargaining, or holding some concessions back in the hopes of striking a better deal. As an act of good faith and to build good will, Clayton decided to put all of the American offers out from the start. Unfortunately, other countries professed not to be impressed, held back their offers, and the stalemate began. Canada's lead delegate, Dana Wilgress (1967, 153–154), later wrote:

> much frustration was experienced in getting the tariff negotiations started; each country had a good excuse for putting them off.... Some of the countries had come to the conference intending to obtain all they could in the way of concessions without giving too much in return. The United States... found it necessary to be very tough and this toughness brought forth recriminations, particularly from the Cubans.

In fact, the outcome of the negotiations was not guaranteed to be a success. The leading countries had some rough contingency plans for their trade strategy should the Geneva negotiations fail: Canada would seek a bilateral trade agreement with the United States, while the United Kingdom would retreat into the sterling bloc.[117]

---

[114] The official report of the conference was published in August 1947 as United Nations Publication E/PC/T/186. See Annex A-8 for the U.S. report on the Geneva negotiations.

[115] As Wilcox (1949, 47) put it, "All of these concessions were safeguarded by general provisions to prevent participating countries from canceling them out by resorting to other forms of restriction or discrimination. These provisions, paralleling the rules of the Charter, covered restrictive methods of customs administration, discriminatory internal taxes and regulations, quota systems and exchange controls, and the operation of state-trading enterprises. They insured the application of the principle of most-favored-nation treatment to a major part of the world's trade."

[116] See Zeiler (1999) and Toye (2008) for detailed discussions of the difficulties of the Geneva negotiations with respect to tariffs.

[117] On Canada's consideration of a trade agreement with the United States, see Hart (1989). In Britain, Toye (2003, 921) notes: "although the Attlee government, and Cripps in particular, continued to hope that the forthcoming conference would be a success – in spite of the fact that they did not anticipate the complete elimination of the preference system – they began

1.11 Second Preparatory Meeting, Geneva, Switzerland, April–October 1947

One important and politically sensitive commodity took on critical importance: raw wool. The American delegation was not authorized to reduce the tariff on wool at all. Even worse, as the Geneva conference began, the Republican Congress was in the process of enacting legislation that would further tighten restrictions on imported wool. This outraged the Australian delegation. Wool was the largest export of Australia and the main commodity on which they sought foreign tariff reductions. They threatened to leave the conference and take other members of the British Commonwealth with them if the United States failed to grant any concessions. This threat was credible: although a small country in world trade, Australia was a key player and, if it decided to pull out of the negotiations, Britain and the rest of the Commonwealth were likely to follow.

Clayton flew back to Washington to intervene at the highest political levels. Truman granted Clayton and his Secretary of Agriculture, Clinton Anderson, who supported the bill, 15 minutes each to make their case. Clayton urged the president to veto the bill, arguing that it would wreck the Geneva negotiations. Anderson argued that the president should sign the bill, maintaining that the Geneva meeting was a failure and the legislation would help rural farmers. Clayton managed to convince Truman to veto the bill on the grounds that it "contains features which would have an adverse effect on our international relations and which are not necessarily for the support of our domestic wool growers" (June 26, 1947).[118]

But Truman did more than this: he immediately gave Clayton the authority to reduce the wool tariff by 25 percent in the Geneva negotiations. The president's approval of a significant reduction in the wool tariff after Congress had just approved an increase was, in Clayton's (1963, 499) mind, "the greatest act of political courage that I have ever witnessed." Although the Australians grumbled about the small size of the tariff reduction, Truman and Clayton saved the conference with their quick and decisive action. Once the authorization to reduce the wool tariff was made official in August, the impasse over tariff reductions was broken and more offers were forthcoming.

With the wool problem resolved, the Geneva negotiations concentrated on the difficult and contentious issue of Britain's imperial preferences. On this issue, the conference had begun on an inauspicious note. At an opening press

---

to plan for other eventualities. In January 1947, the Cabinet agreed to the establishment of a group of outside economists, which would study the alternative policies which might be adopted in the event of a complete or partial breakdown of plans for an ITO. This was to be kept top secret. As it turned out, the group, which met from March to October, was unable to devise any satisfactory alternative to participation in a multilateral world trading system, and had little impact on policy."

[118] Hussain (1993) examines the wool issue in detail.

conference, when asked if a 50 percent U.S. tariff reduction would be sufficient to eliminate imperial preferences, Stafford Cripps tersely replied "no" (Toye 2008). He also gave a speech that harshly criticized the United States and disparaged the importance of tariff negotiations and the charter.

The negative British attitude cast a shadow over the conference. In June, the U.S. delegation in Geneva reported:

> In our opinion Helmore is not approaching negotiations here in spirits shown by Liesching and Robbins in Washington. We are convinced he desires face-saving charter draft and trade agreement but has no intention making serious modification in system of Empire preference. We believe he wishes to place responsibility on us for failure of conference to achieve purposes contemplated (FRUS 1947, I, 953).

This was not just the American perception; even the Canadians shared this view. As their delegation cabled back to Ottawa, "the UK delegation should have been led by someone from the Foreign Office capable of taking a long view rather than by technicians from the Board of Trade" (Hart 1993, 42).

In a key meeting on July 12, 1947, Clayton and Cripps clashed over preferences. Clayton insisted that the time had come for Britain to eliminate imperial preferences. Cripps completely rejected this demand. They squabbled over the degree to which the United States had reduced its tariff and thereby earned a reduction in preferences. Part of the difference between them was technical: Americans assessed the value of concessions by the percentage of items on which duties were reduced or bound, whereas the British used the prewar value of trade on which duties bound or reduced. But the British did not even pretend to make serious concessions. A U.S. cable described Cripps as "marked by complete indifference bordering on open hostility toward the objectives of the Geneva conference" (FRUS 1947, I, 965). At one point, Cripps

> made the amazing suggestion that a better balance might be achieved by the withdrawal or reduction of our offers. Helmore has sought an early termination of tariff negotiations and has indicated that we should be satisfied with modest results. In respect to preferences, the Commonwealth has placed us at a disadvantage in negotiations by taking the position that we must purchase every reduction or elimination of a preference twice – once from the country that receives it, and once from the country that grants it. On the basis of performance to date, it would appear that the United Kingdom will attempt to extract every concession that we will make toward easing their short-run situation without making any appreciable concessions with respect to long-run trade policy. The vested interests that have been built up under the preferential system are strong, and the United

1.11 Second Preparatory Meeting, Geneva, Switzerland, April–October 1947

> Kingdom has shown no willingness to take the political risks involved in reducing or removing the protection afforded them by the preferences which they enjoy. It appears that no concessions are made without the permission of the industry concerned. The real obstacle to effective action on preference exists, not in the Dominions, but in the United Kingdom (FRUS 1947, I, 975).

The Americans were flabbergasted that Cripps would suggest that the United States should withdraw some of its offers if it believed it had not received adequate concessions. Clayton was furious over Cripps's "callous disregard of their commitment on preferences" (FRUS 1947, I, 979). Canadian officials watched with grave concern the deterioration in the Anglo-American relationship at the conference:

> It is evident that temperamental differences between Clayton and Cripps have grown to the point at which they constitute a real obstacle to agreement (CDER 1947 13, 1192).

Cripps repaired some of the damage a few days later by publicly supporting the goals of the Geneva conference. But Wilcox was completely exasperated and warned that "there is a grave danger that the whole trade program will end in defeat."[119] In August, Wilcox reported that

> it now appears probable that we shall come out of the Geneva negotiations with a Charter that will be more acceptable in the United States than the earlier drafts. The prospective results of the tariff negotiations, however, are extremely discouraging.... It has been apparent, throughout the negotiations, that the United Kingdom has had no intention of making concessions that involve any real progress toward the elimination of preferences (FRUS 1947, I, 974).

Some context is needed to appreciate the intransigence on both sides. From Clayton's perspective, his personal credibility was at stake. In many statements before Congress, from the 1945 RTAA renewal to the British loan, he assured

---

[119] "American opinion regards the Hawley-Smoot tariff and the Ottawa system as related parts of inter-war trade restrictions. We are undertaking the liquidation of the Hawley-Smoot rates. We cannot support this action at home unless we obtain, in the process, the liquidation of the Ottawa system. We now have in our hands bargaining weapons that we may never possess again: (a) Our excellent offers on tariff reduction; (b) a cut on wool; (c) the possibility of easing the British financial crisis through relaxation on discrimination in the short run; and (d) the prospect of aid under the Marshall Plan. If we cannot now obtain the liquidation of the Ottawa system, we shall never do so. What we must have is a front-page headline that says "Empire Preference System Broken at Geneva." With this, the success of this whole series of negotiations is assured. Without it, there is grave danger that the whole trade program will end in defeat" (FRUS 1947, I, 976).

lawmakers that the British Empire would be cracked and the Geneva meeting would mark the end of Britain's discriminatory practices. Believing that Britain had agreed to eliminate imperial preferences as far back as the Atlantic Charter in 1941, he overestimated his ability to deliver on these promises. But Britain had always equivocated on this point. His State Department staff had a more realistic view of what could be achieved and tried to temper his view. They even had to persuade Clayton not to abandon the Geneva conference simply because Britain refused anything more than token compromises on preferences. As State Department official Winthrop Brown later recalled:

> Mr. Clayton wanted to get total elimination of all preferences. We civil servants knew it wouldn't be possible to do that. Mr. Clayton at one time really thought that Sir Stafford Cripps had agreed with that and there was a terrible misunderstanding. He was very hard to convince that we had to go ahead even without that total elimination having been agreed. So, we came to this impasse. At that point the boys came in with the total results of the tariff negotiations and each side found that so much had been accomplished that it could not be lost. This total accomplishment just had to be saved somehow.[120]

For his part, Cripps also took a very hard and uncompromising line in defense of imperial preferences.[121] His austere and stubborn personality may have played a role in exacerbating the tensions between the two sides, according to Toye (2008). But this intransigence was also related to the extreme economic difficulties that Britain faced after the war and the lingering resentments over the British loan negotiations in late 1945. The harsh winter of 1946–1947 required greater spending on imported fuels, depleting reserves that could have been spent on food and other consumer goods, and thereby necessitating additional austerity measures. Furthermore, under the terms of the loan agreement, the United Kingdom made the pound sterling convertible on June 15, 1947, shortly after the start of the Geneva conference. This early convertibility proved to be a disaster. The United Kingdom quickly lost a massive amount of dollar reserves due to pressure on foreign-exchange markets (Newton 1984).

---

[120] http://www.trumanlibrary.org/oralhist/brownwg.htm (last visited Jan. 17, 2008).

[121] As Toye (2003, 923) concludes: "there was some truth in Clayton's allegation that the British were not playing ball. They were not making all possible efforts to secure waivers from Commonwealth countries; rather the reverse. In July, Cripps warned the Cabinet that Canada's desire to be released from her own obligations to Britain represented a dangerous breaking of ranks: 'it sets a precedent to break away from agreements on preferences between Commonwealth countries, which... might lead to a gradual disintegration of the system.' These were not the words of a man negotiating in good faith for the abolition of preferences and frustrated only by the recalcitrance of other countries."

1.11 Second Preparatory Meeting, Geneva, Switzerland, April–October 1947

In a few short weeks, Britain spent a significant portion of its precious American loan defending the pound, and the government was forced to suspend sterling convertibility on August 20, 1947. The Attlee government also announced new austerity measures to stem the deteriorating balance-of-payments deficit.

Given the hard bargaining over the loan and the early convertibility requirement, the British were in no mood to make further concessions to American trade negotiators that might increase imports further.[122] With convertibility suspended, the United Kingdom informed the Geneva participants that it could not put the nondiscrimination clauses into force because of its severe balance-of-payments problems. The UK delegation further suggested that it could only apply the agreement "ad referendum" with no definite commitment to its coming into effect (FRUS 1947 I 967–973). "This would have been a body blow against the whole project of trade multilateralism," Toye (2003, 929) notes, "as it would have been very difficult to enact the Geneva tariff reductions without any general rules governing them." The United States insisted that the agreement should be signed and implemented as planned.

Britain's economic weakness was reflected not just in its concerns about the balance of payments, but its role in the world. The strong defense of imperial preferences could be read as reflecting fears about Britain's diminishing role as a world power. Britain clung to the Commonwealth as a way of boosting the perception that it remained a great power; indeed, in some ways, Britain needed the Commonwealth countries more than they needed Britain.[123] As the United Kingdom scaled back its global commitments, the United States increased its role further. When Britain withdrew its troops from Greece and Turkey in February 1947, President Truman responded by announcing the next month that the

---

[122] Britain was also dismayed by several U.S. policy actions that it believed detracted from stated goals of the GATT conference. First, the U.S. insistence on an escape clause was seen by Britain and others as potentially limiting the value of the negotiated tariff reductions. Second, the United States concluded a trade agreement with the Philippines in 1946 that gave the country an extended period of transition to tariff autonomy as the country achieved independence. The U.S.-Cuba preferential trade agreement also rankled the British who saw these as a marked contradiction in the U.S. stance against discriminatory trade arrangements. Clayton opposed these deals, the Philippines preferences would be phased out over 28 years, but Truman signed it (Zeiler 1990, 90).

[123] As Mackenzie (2002, 266) points out, "British officials continued to rely on the Commonwealth as a buttress to Britain's world position. Britain's enduring attachment to the Commonwealth option derived from the unshakeable conviction that international greatness was a birthright. Moreover, an historic identity as a global power could not be cast away lightly or suddenly." As Toye (2003, 917) also points out, "The Labour Party increasingly supported the preference system out of gratitude for the help afforded by the Dominions during the war."

United States would support Greece and Turkey with economic and military aid to prevent them from falling into the Soviet sphere (the Truman Doctrine).

Britain's economic and political weakness ensured that the United States would not push it too far in the trade negotiations. Indeed, the State Department had great concerns about the health of the entire European economy in 1947. In traveling throughout Western Europe in the spring of that year, Clayton became so concerned about the fragile state of the economic recovery that he wrote an impassioned memo warning of adverse political consequences if the situation did not improve. These dire warnings prompted Secretary of State George Marshall to propose a new program of aid for Europe – the Marshall Plan – at the Harvard commencement in June 1947. In Clayton's view, the Marshall Plan of foreign assistance made the Geneva trade negotiations "more important than ever because without sound permanent program of reciprocal multilateral trade, no temporary emergency program could possibly have any permanent worthwhile results" (FRUS 1947, I, 955).

American concerns about the political ramifications of economic weakness in Britain and in Europe played a key role in the end-game of the GATT negotiations. In late August, with the GATT text finalized but the tariff negotiations still at an impasse, Clayton cabled Under Secretary of State Robert A. Lovett in Washington and outlined four options:

(1) conclude an agreement without substantial elimination of preferences;
(2) conclude an agreement without substantial elimination of preferences by withdrawing some U.S. offers on tariff reductions, as twice suggested by Cripps;
(3) discontinue negotiations with the United Kingdom and conclude agreements with others on multilateral basis;
(4) adjourn the tariff negotiations indefinitely (FRUS 1947, I, 978).

Clayton was so dismayed with the British attitude that he endorsed the third option, although his staff disagreed with his negative assessment.

Lovett discussed the alternatives with President Truman. Truman rejected options (1) and (4) and favored (2) over (3), but did not want to raise the issue with Prime Minister Attlee. Lovett reported that the State Department officials agreed with the president that option (2) was the lesser of two evils. In explaining the decision, Lovett made it clear to Clayton that foreign-policy considerations were paramount. In particular, the President and State Department officials were concerned that a failure at the conference would further weaken Britain's economic and political position in the world and strengthen that of the Soviet Union.[124]

---

[124] Lovett noted that "we are attempting to give UK every assistance in getting over this difficult period and in avoiding irretrievable damage to their long-run position. Believe

1.11 Second Preparatory Meeting, Geneva, Switzerland, April–October 1947

This presidential decision, overriding Clayton's council to abandon hopes of an agreement with Britain because of its refusal to reduce its imperial preferences, ultimately ensured the success of the Geneva tariff negotiations. Many difficult maneuvers were still to be performed in the final agreement over preferences, but in late October 1947, the tariff negotiations were concluded. To Clayton's disappointment, Britain's imperial preferences remained largely intact.[125]

On October 29, 1947, President Truman hailed the completion of the General Agreement on Tariffs and Trade as

> a landmark in the history of international economic relations. Never before have so many nations combined in such a sustained effort to lower barriers to trade. Never before have nations agreed upon action, on tariffs and preferences, so extensive in its coverage and so far-reaching in its effects.... [and] it confirms the general acceptance of an expanding multilateral trading system as the goal of national policies.[126]

In Canada, Prime Minister Mackenzie King praised the outcome as

> the widest measure of agreement on trading practices and for tariff reductions that the nations of the world have ever witnessed... For Canada, the importance of the general agreement can scarcely be exaggerated. The freeing of world trade on a broad multilateral basis is of fundamental importance for our entire national welfare.[127]

---

[125] course of action leading to rupture trade negotiations inconsistent with policy we are following regarding financial agreement. (President referred to inconsistency our position if we should take alternative (3).) Important from point of view of successful relaxation convertibility and nondiscrimination provisions that some progress, even though slight, be made in commitment to reduce trade barriers. Believe alternative (3) likely to lead to strong resentment British public and considerable confusion and criticism in US. Would make more difficult consideration by Congress further assistance UK and Europe generally. As you know, UK Govt now under intense pressure from left wing members Labor party to curtail sharply UK foreign commitments, reduce arm forces and to withdraw British forces from Greece and Italy. We are concerned over likelihood that USSR will exploit fully any such differences between US and UK just as they are now trying to capitalize on British weakness by increasing pressure throughout Eastern Europe and Near East. Consequently best course seems to be to get best agreement possible in present highly unfavorable circumstances and reserve part of our negotiating position for use at more propitious time by trimming our offers correspondingly. From standpoint of public and congressional opinion here thin agreement of this kind we believe better than none, especially if made clear that present agreement only an initial stage in dealing with this problem" (FRUS 1947, I, 981).

[125] See Zeiler (1999) and Toye (2008) for details on the conclusion of the negotiations.

[126] On December 16, 1947, Truman issued proclamation 2761A "Carrying Out General Agreement on Tariffs and Trade Concluded at Geneva, October 30, 1947," making the agreement effective, provisionally, for the United States on January 1, 1948. 61 Stat. 1103; 3 CFR, 1943-1948 Comp., 139.

[127] Canada, House of Commons Debates, December 9, 1947, 99.

By contrast, British officials were more muted in their praise of the Geneva conference and more defensive about their participation. Speaking in Parliament, Harold Wilson, the President of the Board of Trade, noted that

> we have agreed to reductions in our own tariff or to reductions or eliminations of the preferences we enjoy in other Commonwealth countries only in return for concessions which we consider equivalent in terms of the trade thereby opened up to us.... I should like to repudiate here and now the suggestions made in certain quarters that we have at any time been putting pressure on other Commonwealth countries either to break up the preference system in general or to agree to any concession on preferences to which Commonwealth countries are contractually entitled....[128]

What had been achieved at Geneva? The finalization and implementation of the GATT text, the focus of Chapter 2, was a major accomplishment. The actual tariff and preference reductions, as well as the tariff bindings, were symbolically very important of the new direction in postwar commercial policy. In the first Geneva round, the 23 participating countries made no fewer than 123 agreements covering 45,000 tariff items related to about one-half of the value of world trade (GATT 1949, 11). But the reductions in duties were rather modest at the time, and many of those reductions had little effect on trade because quantitative restrictions and exchange controls remained in effect (Irwin 1995b, 139).

There are no precise estimates on the depth of the tariff cuts for most of the GATT participants. For the United States, according to official calculations, had the duties negotiated at Geneva been in effect in 1947, the average tariff on dutiable imports would have been 15.3 percent, instead of the actual 19.4 percent, a reduction of 4 percentage points, or 21 percent (U.S. Tariff Commission 1948, 19). About half of dutiable imports were subject to a tariff reduction, and the average reduction here was about 35 percent. The tariff reductions were not across the board or applied to import-sensitive sectors, such as agricultural goods or labor-intensive manufactures, but concentrated on industrial goods.

Because many import duties were specific duties, however, postwar inflation had a greater effect in reducing the ad valorem equivalent of duties than

---

[128] Hansard's *Parliamentary Debates*, 29 October 1947, 873. "We have further proceeded on the principle laid down at the London Session of the Preparatory Committee that the binding of a low tariff is equivalent to a reduction in a high tariff. Since, of course, our own tariff is made up predominantly of low rates, the agreement consequently includes a number of such bindings of low tariffs in exchange for reductions in some of the high rates in overseas tariffs."

negotiated tariff reductions.[129] In the case of the United States, the average tariff on dutiable imports turned out to be 13.9 percent in 1948, not 15.3 percent, and higher import prices accounted for the difference. Import prices rose 10.5 percent in 1948, which would have reduced the tariff by about 6.7 percent (Irwin 1998). Thus, in this one pivotal year (1947), fully one-third of the U.S. tariff reduction was due to higher import prices.

And despite all of the Anglo-American conflict over imperial preferences, postwar inflation also undermined much of their discriminatory effect. In the late 1930s, about half of British exports to and imports from the Commonwealth enjoyed preferences on the order of nearly 20 percent, on average. Therefore, the average preference on all trade was about 10–12 percent. By the early 1950s, the average margin of preference had shrunk to about five percent, about half way back to the pre-Ottawa levels, largely the result of higher import prices on specific duties (MacDougall and Hutt 1954).

1.12 Conclusion

The GATT took effect while the UN Conference on Trade and Employment was meeting in Havana, Cuba, from November 1947 to March 1948. Because this book focuses exclusively on the GATT, we will not examine the ITO Charter or its ultimate failure.[130] However, it is worth noting that, while the GATT was expected to be superseded by the ITO, there was also a foreboding sense that things may not work out as planned. As the chief U.S. negotiator, Clair Wilcox (1949, 47) later recalled:

> The [Havana] conference opened with a chorus of denunciation in which the representatives of thirty underdeveloped nations presented variations on a single theme: the Geneva draft was one-sided; it served the interests of the great industrial powers; it held out no hope for the development of backward states. Some eight hundred amendments were presented, among them as many as two hundred that would have destroyed the very foundations of the enterprise. Almost every specific commitment in the document was challenged.

As early as December 1947, Wilcox held the view that "it is unlikely that we will be able to get wide agreement on a Charter which is close enough to the

---

[129] Specific duties are a nominal amount charged per imported quantity, not an ad valorem (percentage) tax on the value of imported goods. The ad valorem equivalent of a specific duty is inversely related to the price of the imported good.

[130] On the ITO Charter, see Wilcox (1949) and Brown (1950). On the failure of the ITO, see Diebold (1952), Aaronson (1992), Zeiler (1999), and Odell and Eichengreen (1996).

Geneva draft to satisfy us" (FRUS 1948, I, 824). In February 1948, Wilcox reported that representatives from the major developed countries were

> buried in gloom. Wilgress [Canada] saw no hope at all. Coombs [Australia] was saying that we should adjourn the Conference and put the whole project on ice for a year or more (FRUS 1948, I, 872–873).

Even if the Havana negotiations had gone well, by 1948 the political environment in Washington had changed from what it had been just a few years earlier. More than two years had passed from Congress's extension of the RTAA in June 1945 to the completion of the GATT negotiations in October 1947. The era of grand economic institution building, as with the Bretton Woods conference in 1944, had passed, and the heady optimism of the early postwar period had given way to the Cold War. Policymakers in Washington had begun to focus on the Marshall Plan in 1948 and the creation of the North American Treaty Organization (NATO) in 1949. In January 1948, British officials reported that:

> Clayton admitted very frankly that he had found considerable difficulty in getting United States authorities at Washington to take any concerted interest in the Charter, their attention being almost entirely directed to Marshall Aid. This was one of the reasons why he was, he said, most apprehensive lest [the] Charter would be crowded out unless completed very shortly (Toye 2003, 294).

Clayton's sense turned out to be correct.

Congress insisted that the 1945 RTAA did not authorize the creation of any international trade-related institution or U.S. participation in any trade-related organization. Hence, the GATT was envisioned as an interim arrangement, not an organization, until the ITO charter could be formally approved by Congress. The GATT was not a treaty or an organization, but merely a trade agreement put into effect by executive order. As a result, participants were not "members" but "contracting parties" and State Department officials invented the Protocol of Provisional Application to bring it to effect. Parts I and III of the GATT were consistent with the negotiating authority granted in the 1945 RTAA, but Part II, which contained many of the trade rules, could only be brought into force only insofar as it was not inconsistent with existing legislation. Therefore, they were to be applied provisionally (Parts I and III applied definitively) until the Congress approved the Charter for the International Trade Organization. The original Article XXVIII of GATT bound tariff levels for only three years; only in 1958 did the bindings become indefinite.

This chapter has made clear that the GATT would not have come into existence without the leadership of the United States. However, there were

1.12 Conclusion

many junctures in which the United States and the United Kingdom could have abandoned the plans for a multilateral commercial agreement. In addition, other countries played an important role in shaping the GATT. Britain was responsible for pushing the United States into thinking in terms of a multilateral approach rather than a bilateral one. Canada was responsible for proposing that a small set of nuclear countries negotiate tariff reductions separately, rather than attempt to make reductions and finalize a charter at a large multilateral gathering. It is interesting to note that, despite its overwhelming economic strength in comparison to other countries, the United States could not dominate or dictate the outcome to other countries. Rather, the United States often accommodated the demands for exceptions or weaker language at various points in the negotiations to ensure the continued participation of other countries.

2 The Negotiation of the GATT

During the 1940s, as Chapter 1 described, the United States wanted to establish a new multilateral institutional architecture, a component of which would be devoted to the reconstruction of world trade. After the release of its proposed Charter in December 1945, the United States took concrete steps to bring this about: in February 1946, the U.S. delegate to the United Nations proposed that a resolution be adopted in order to convene a *United Nations Conference on Trade and Employment*, the purpose of which would be to draft the Charter for an *International Trade Organization* (ITO), also referred to as the Havana Charter. The General Agreement on Tariffs and Trade (GATT) would be an off-shoot of the broader and more ambitious ITO project.[1]

The GATT was drafted in a series of negotiations of the so-called *Preparatory Committee* for the ITO held between 1946 and 1948 in London, New York, Geneva, and finally in Havana. The *Preparatory Committee* was established pursuant to the 1946 UN resolution mentioned above. The *Havana Charter* was supposed to regulate government policy with respect to trade (e.g., trade in goods and commodity agreements), as well as establish rules regarding domestic employment, investment, economic development, and restrictive business practices (RBP).[2] The ITO was negotiated subsequent to the Bretton Woods negotiations, which

---

[1] The sequence of the words has not always been this one. In some negotiating documents, we find references to the General Agreement on Trade and Tariffs, see, for example, E/PC/T/C.6/21 of January 30, 1947 at p. 2.

[2] The ITO was definitely a far-reaching agreement. For example, Art. 7 discussed what today is referred to as *social dumping*. Charnovitz (1995) points out that social dumping in the ITO framework could provide the legal cause for an action on nullification and impairment (whereby, the affected trading partner will be requesting some form of compensation). In today's GATT, the only clause which might suggest that impermissibly low-cost products can be legitimately excluded from a given market is Art. XX(e) GATT, which allows WTO Members to block imports of products produced by prison labor.

2 The Negotiation of the GATT

led to the creation of the World Bank (WB), and the International Monetary Fund (IMF). A trade organization was contemplated by the participants in the Bretton Woods conference, but there is little evidence that the ITO was supposed to become an equal partner in the new international institutional architecture.[3] Nevertheless, it is certainly true that all three institutions shared one overarching goal: a genuine effort to help promote international economic cooperation in the post-World War II period. Through their design and aim, these three institutions distinguished themselves from the major institutional arrangement of that time, the United Nations (UN), which was intended to be the overarching international organization to help avoid another world war, without however addressing the underlying reasons for conflict. Their different function notwithstanding, the three institutions complemented the UN: promoting trade among nations, providing technical assistance to address development-related issues, and financing development policies were meant to be the international community's response to the ongoing quest of addressing the underlying causes of conflict.[4]

The GATT was first negotiated at the *London Conference* in 1946. However, the *London Conference* did not disentangle the GATT from the wider ITO negotiation. Indeed, the negotiation of the GATT, as we know it, was the work of *Committee II*, a committee established during the conference to deal with commercial policy. Other committees were established to deal with issues that were supposed to come under the ITO, such as employment, restrictive business practices (RBP), international commodity agreements, and organizational issues. The *London Conference* did not produce a final text, although negotiators managed to make considerable progress. They decided to continue their discussions and, based on agreed procedures, pursue multilateral tariff negotiations at a subsequent meeting. At that point, the GATT (or, more generally, a tariff agreement) would become necessary in order to safeguard the value of tariff concessions made during the negotiations.[5] The actual *ambit* of the GATT was not, nevertheless, definitively agreed at the *London Conference*.[6] Quoting from

---

[3] See the discussion in Jackson (1969) and Palmeter & Mavroidis (2004).
[4] Henry Cabot Lodge used to say that the United Nations system was designed to avoid hell, but it was no guarantee for heaven.
[5] The term *tariff concession*, which has customarily been used in the GATT-context and continues to be used in the WTO-era, does not make much economic sense: states make a concession to themselves as well since, at least those that cannot affect terms of trade, gain from trade liberalization. It does, nevertheless, make good legal sense, since it signals the transfer of sovereignty associated with the tariff promise: absent such transfer, trading nations would be free to increase or decrease tariff protection to their liking; through tariff concessions, they concede their sovereignty in this respect to the international plane.
[6] See on this score, Jackson (1969, pp. 42ff.).

the relevant documents, Jackson (1969, 43) suggests that it was agreed that the GATT would include "such other provisions as may be appropriate."

Other refers, of course, to provisions other than those dealing directly with tariff concessions. Which other provisions would be included? The negotiators held inconclusive negotiations on this issue already during the *London Conference*, and continued their discussion during the *New York Conference* (1947).

The *New York Conference* was held in Lake Success, New York, a village in northwest Long Island that served as the temporary headquarters of the United Nations from 1946 to 1951. Between January and February 1947, it became the place where a number of state representatives negotiated the GATT. A relatively homogeneous group (with few outliers) prepared the first draft of the GATT.[7] This time, nevertheless, it was not the *Preparatory Committee* that was holding the negotiations: during the *London Conference* already, negotiators had agreed to establish a *Drafting Committee* that was entrusted with the drafting of the first GATT text in Lake Success. The working assumption was that the GATT was not designed in any shape or form to be an institution; rather, it was simply a trade agreement that was to eventually come under the aegis of the ITO, once that institution was established and its Charter entered into force. Consequently, institutional provisions were not reflected in the GATT text. John Leddy, a civil servant at the U.S. State Department, trained in economics, was the main draftsman of the GATT.

The *Drafting Committee* decided to exclude *detailed* provisions dealing with pure domestic-policy issues, as well as provisions the existence of which depended on the coming into being of the ITO: the first *National Treatment* provision was negotiated during this Conference (Article 15, entitled *National Treatment on Internal Taxation and Regulation*). On the other hand, the negotiators did not address specific domestic instruments one by one, as had been the case during the *London Conference*, where they had embarked on a full-fledged discussion on *Employment* and had even drafted a provision dedicated to this issue.[8] This time, they opted for a nondiscrimination discipline to be imposed on an unidentified number of domestic instruments that affected the value of

---

[7] Recall the Chapter 1 discussion of the nuclear approach advocated by Canada. The participants were: Australia, Belgium, Brazil, Canada, Chile, China, Cuba, Czechoslovakia, France, India, Lebanon, Luxembourg, Netherlands, New Zealand, Norway, South Africa, Union of Soviet Socialist Republics (USSR), the United Kingdom, and the United States (see Drafting Committee of the Preparatory Committee of the UN Conference on Trade and Employment, Draft GATT, E/PC/T/C.6/85 of 15 February 1947). The USSR ultimately did not participate in the GATT/ITO endeavour.

[8] See E/PC/T/C.6/55.

2 The Negotiation of the GATT

tariff concessions. Finally, whereas no reservations would appear in the final text, reservations were allowed during the drafting stage.[9]

The negotiations produced the first full draft of the GATT text. Subsequently, the *New York Draft* underwent a series of changes during the *Geneva Conference* (1947). There, the state representatives *also* conducted, between April and October 1947, the first round of tariff negotiations at the European office of the United Nations in Geneva, Switzerland, under the institutional umbrella of the *Preparatory Committee* for the ITO.[10] The outcome of these negotiations together with the new GATT text constituted the *Geneva Final Act*. Under the terms of the *Protocol of Provisional Application* (PPA), signed to this effect, the governments that participated in the negotiations undertook to fully apply Part I of the GATT (dealing with tariff concessions, that is, the product of the tariff negotiations conducted in Geneva, as well as the most-favored-nation, or MFN clause), and Part III of the GATT (containing provisions dealing with administrative issues). These governments further undertook to apply Part II of the GATT (the heart of the GATT, covering national treatment, antidumping, subsidies, safeguards, balance of payments, prohibition of quantitative restrictions, general exceptions to the obligations assumed, and dispute settlement) "to the fullest extent not inconsistent with *existing* legislation."[11]

The GATT negotiations were successfully concluded on October 30, 1947, and the GATT, as described above, entered into force on January 1, 1948 by virtue of the PPA.[12] Its original 23 members were: Australia, Belgium, Brazil, Burma, Canada, Ceylon, Chile, Republic of China, Cuba, Czechoslovak Republic, France, India, Lebanon, Luxembourg, Netherlands, New Zealand, Norway, Pakistan, Southern Rhodesia, Syria, South Africa, the United Kingdom, and the United States. •

The application of Part II only to the extent consistent with existing *domestic* legislation is often referred to as "grandfather rights."[13] The states that had

---

[9] See § 2 of the Drafting Committee of the Preparatory Committee of the UN Conference on Trade and Employment, Draft GATT, E/PC/T/C.6/85 of February 15, 1947.

[10] See 55 UNTS 187 (1947). About 45,000 tariff concessions were negotiated, affecting roughly $10 billion worth of trade; see Drache (2003).

[11] See UNITS 308, 1(a) and (b) (1947).

[12] Jackson (1969, pp. 60ff.) has explained the reasons for sticking to the provisional application of the GATT. Essentially, it was felt that through provisional application one would avoid discriminating across countries that had adopted the GATT only provisionally, and countries that had done definitively so.

[13] A good example is the U.S. countervailing-duty law, which did not require a determination of material injury as required by Article VI in Part II of GATT, until the United States agreed to include such a requirement for signatories to the so-called 1979 Tokyo Round Subsidies Code or for other countries that entered into comparable bilateral agreements with the United States.

signed the GATT *and* had existing legislation inconsistent with provisions of the GATT, at the time it entered into force, were allowed to continue applying these GATT-inconsistent measures. The inconsistency of domestic legislation of some member states with provisions of the GATT did not create many problems since the grandfathering provision was meant to be temporary as set out in Art. XXIX.2 GATT:

> Part II of this Agreement shall be suspended on the day on which the Havana Charter comes into force.

More generally, Art. XXIX GATT governed the legal relationship between the GATT and the ITO in the following terms:

> *Article XXIX*
>
> *The Relation of this Agreement to the Havana Charter*
>
> 1. The contracting parties undertake to observe to the fullest extent of their executive authority the general principles of Chapters I to VI inclusive and of Chapter IX of the Havana Charter pending their acceptance of it in accordance with their constitutional procedures.
> 2. Part II of this Agreement shall be suspended on the day on which the Havana Charter enters into force.
> 3. If by September 30, 1949, the Havana Charter has not entered into force, the contracting parties shall meet before December 31, 1949, to agree whether this Agreement shall be amended, supplemented or maintained.
> 4. If at any time the Havana Charter should cease to be in force, the CONTRACTING PARTIES shall meet as soon as practicable thereafter to agree whether this Agreement shall be supplemented, amended or maintained. Pending such agreement, Part II of this Agreement shall again enter into force; *Provided* that the provisions of Part II other than Article XXIII shall be replaced, *mutatis mutandis*, in the form in which they then appeared in the Havana Charter; and *Provided* further that no contracting party shall be bound by any provisions which did not bind it at the time when the Havana Charter ceased to be in force.
> 5. If any contracting party has not accepted the Havana Charter by the date upon which it enters into force, the CONTRACTING PARTIES shall confer to agree whether, and if so in what way, this Agreement in so far as it affects relations between such contracting party and other contracting parties, shall be supplemented or amended. Pending such agreement the provisions of Part II of this Agreement shall, notwithstanding the provisions of paragraph 2 of this Article, continue to apply as between such contracting party and other contracting parties.

2 The Negotiation of the GATT

6. Contracting parties which are Members of the International Trade Organization shall not invoke the provisions of this Agreement so as to prevent the operation of any provision of the Havana Charter. The application of the principle underlying this paragraph to any contracting party which is not a Member of the International Trade Organization shall be the subject of an agreement pursuant to paragraph 5 of this Article.

Thus, negotiators did not sever the link that tied the GATT to the ITO: they intended to see the GATT eventually come under the institutional umbrella of the ITO. In this vein, they focused on finalizing the remaining provisions of the ITO Charter during the *Havana Conference*, which took place after the entry into force of the GATT. Still, some GATT provisions underwent changes during the *Havana Conference*. The (eventual) nonadvent of the ITO meant that the GATT was the only tangible multilateral trade contract across nations.

The *Review Session* of 1955 further refined some provisions of the GATT, while *Part IV* on *Trade and Development* was added to the original text in 1965. To date, no subsequent amendments to the GATT have been recorded.[14]

It follows from these brief introductory remarks, that the GATT was largely completed in the 1940s. It has successfully withstood the test of time for over 60 years and continues to provide the bedrock of the world trading system today.

In this Chapter, we discuss in detail the various drafts of the GATT. We follow a chronological order starting, in Section 2.1, from the first session of the *Preparatory Committee* which gave rise to the *London Draft* (E/PC/T/33). In Section 2.2 we move to discuss the *Drafting Committee's New York Draft* (E/PC/T/34) as well as the various revised drafts that were prepared in that session (E/PC/T/135, 189, 196, and 214/Add. 1/Rev. 1).[15] In Section 2.3, we will discuss the *Geneva Conference* that gave birth to the GATT Final Act (October 30, 1947, published in 55 UNTS 152). In Section 2.4, we deal with the changes that the *Geneva Draft* underwent during the *Havana Conference*; Section 2.5 focuses on the *Review Session* of the GATT (1955), whereas Section 2.6 is dedicated to the introduction of Part IV to the GATT, that is, the last of the changes that the GATT text has undergone. In Section 2.7 we discuss how the content of the various GATT provisions evolved from the *London Conference* to their modern appearance, whereas Section 2.8 is an attempt to establish the property rights of the GATT.

---

[14] The GATT 1994 added some legal instruments to the GATT, without modifying any of its provisions.
[15] Drafts of the GATT also appear in other documents such as E/PC/T/180, 186.

2.1 London Calling: the London Draft

2.1.1 The Mandate

The *Preparatory Committee* did not dedicate its first session exclusively to the preparation of the GATT; it had a wider mandate: to prepare draft articles for "a Charter of, or Articles of Agreement for an International Trade Organization."[16] The *Preparatory Committee* did not start negotiating from a clean slate because the U.S. proposal to establish an ITO (the *Suggested Charter*) served as the basis for the negotiations. In anticipation of the *London Conference*, the U.S. government prepared a *Suggested Charter* for the ITO in September 1946, a revision of the December 1945 proposals.[17] This was in name a U.S. initiative, but very much the product of extensive consultations between the U.S. and UK governments. The *Suggested Charter* was divided into seven Chapters: I, Purposes; II, Membership; III, Employment provisions; IV, General Commercial Policy; V, Restrictive business practices; VI, Intergovernmental commodity arrangements; VII, Organization. In this Chapter, we are mainly concerned with Chapter IV because these provisions provided the basis for the GATT provisions, the focus of this volume. The *London Draft* was effectively the response of the participating nations to Chapter IV of the *Suggested Charter*.

The U.S. proposal was not the only document considered by the negotiators assembled in London. They also had a draft Charter proposed by Brazil, a detailed commentary on the U.S. proposal by the Indian government, and a memorandum on employment policy submitted by the UK delegation.[18] The Brazilian document was, in fact, a joint effort between the American and the Brazilian delegations and largely reproduced the ideas already included in the U.S. *Suggested Charter*.[19] India's reaction could be qualified as semi-official, since India was not an independent state when the *London Conference* was launched. Thus, we read on page 1 of the document:[20]

> The views expressed in these notes are the personal views of the experts concerned but they have found considerable support in India and are likely to play an important role in the formulation of the Government of India's policy.

Still, this document reflects much of the negotiating positions that India later, after gaining its independence, presented in subsequent negotiations. India

---

[16] See E/PC/T/33 at p. 4.
[17] See "Suggested Charter for an International Trade Organization of the United Nations," State Department Publication No. 2598, September 1946.
[18] See UN Information Centre, Geneva, Press release No. 36 of April 8, 1947.
[19] See E/PC/T/W.16 of October 18, 1946. [20] See E/PC/T/W.14 of October 21, 1946.

2.1 London Calling: the London Draft

understood the U.S. proposal to be a common endeavour of the U.S. and UK governments, and viewed the proposal as protecting the interests of developed countries only. For example, in India's view, developing countries with limited financial resources would not be in a position to protect infant industries, which developed countries could easily protect through domestic subsidies. India questioned whether the new institution would still allow it to pursue a policy of industrialization (that it favors), and whether the non-discrimination obligation embedded therein will help it make the income necessary to finance its policy choices. In short, India held the view that the U.S. *Suggested Charter* did not sufficiently address the asymmetries across the participants, and, consequently, did not take into account the development needs of the weaker players. The Indian experts went on to provide, in a 75-page-long document, detailed comments on each and every provision included in the U.S. *Suggested Charter*.

The *London Draft* (E/PC/T/33) provided the input to the discussions of the *Drafting Committee*, which produced the first GATT text in the subsequent *New York Conference*. However, the participants decided during the *London Conference* to give effect to *certain* provisions of the proposed (by the U.S. *Suggested Charter*) ITO Charter by means of a General Agreement on Tariffs and Trade. At the very least, it was contemplated that the advent of the GATT would precede that of the ITO. The rationale advanced was as follows: one of the objectives of the proposed ITO Charter was the substantial reduction of tariffs and (eventual) elimination of tariff preferences. To this effect, a detailed schedule for organizing tariff negotiations was elaborated.[21] It was felt that:

> once agreed upon, the tariff schedules resulting from the negotiations among members of the Preparatory committee cannot easily be held in abeyance pending action by the general international conference on trade and employment and the adoption of the Charter by national legislatures.[22]

Consequently, the GATT was conceived as the institutional vehicle to bring *immediately* into life the agreed tariff schedules: to this effect, the various commercial-policy provisions would be combined with the agreed schedules of concessions, and together form the GATT. Some necessary institutional arrangements, such as the establishment of the *Interim Tariff Committee*,[23] were made in order for the GATT to be temporarily operational, until the entry into force of the ITO; the *Interim Tariff Committee* would eventually cease to exist since, with the advent of the ITO, such disputes would come under the aegis of

---

[21] See *Preparatory Committee*, Report of Committee II, E/PC/T/30 of November 24, 1946, Annexure, pp. 8ff.
[22] Id. at p. 12.
[23] This Committee was in charge of resolving disputes relating to tariff negotiations.

the "normal" ITO adjudication procedures. This was the necessary "regulatory" minimum to ensure that the tariff schedules could become *provisionally* operational, until they would later come under the aegis of the ITO.

In this Chapter we focus on the provisions of the *London Draft* (and the subsequent drafts) that provided the basis for GATT provisions. Of course, it should not be forgotten that beyond trade liberalization and the establishment of a permanent institutional machinery for consultation and collaboration in trade and trade-related matters, the ITO was designed to accomplish other tasks as well: promote the maintenance of employment in member countries; promote their economic development; and provide an orderly procedure under agreed rules for the negotiation of intergovernmental commodity arrangements. Such objectives either disappeared completely from the final GATT preamble, or were retained without specific provisions to make them operational. It is questionable whether they retain any value in helping us understand the GATT provisions.

Finally, it should be noted that the *Preparatory Committee* was acting as a group of experts without committing the represented governments.[24] Formal commitment would come much later, at the end of the second session during the Geneva meeting.

2.1.2 Institutional Issues

At its first session on February 18, 1946, the UN Economic and Social Council (ECOSOC) established the *Preparatory Committee*.[25] Its members were: Australia, Belgium, Luxembourg, Brazil, Canada, Chile, China, Cuba, Czechoslovakia, France, India, Lebanon, the Netherlands, New Zealand, Norway, South Africa,[26] the Union of Soviet Socialist Republics (USSR), the United States, and the United Kingdom. The USSR indicated that it was unable to participate as, by its own admission, it had not found the time to devote to this project.[27] At its second session (May 31, 1946), the ECOSOC announced that the necessary arrangements were in place for the Preparatory Committee to convene its first meeting in London on October 15, 1946.[28] The London negotiations went until November 20, 1946,[29] and were also attended by countries that were members

---

[24] See Foreword, Preliminary Draft Charter for the International Trade Organizations of the United Nations, Department of State, December 1946, Publication 2728, Commercial Policy Series 98.
[25] See E/PC/T/117 Rev. 1 of July 9, 1947 at p. 1.
[26] Union of South Africa was the official name of the country. We use the term South Africa throughout this book.
[27] Id. at p. 2.   [28] See E/PC/T/33 on p. 3.
[29] See E/PC/T/117 Rev. 1 of July 9, 1947 at p. 1.

2.1 London Calling: the London Draft

of the UN, but not of the *Preparatory Committee*,[30] by UN specialized agencies,[31] by other international organizations,[32] and by nongovernmental organizations (NGOs).[33] The *Preparatory Committee* held two meetings (sessions):

(a) from October 15, 1946 to November 20, 1946, as indicated above, in London (first session);
(b) from April 10, 1947 to October 30, 1947, in Geneva (second session).

In between, from January 20, 1947 to February 25, 1947, the *Drafting Committee*, an organ appointed by the *Preparatory Committee*, met in New York and prepared the first comprehensive draft of the GATT.

The *Preparatory Committee* established the following working committees:

(a) Committee I: *Employment and Economic Activity;*
(b) Committee II: *General Commercial Policy;*
(c) Committee III: *Restrictive Business Practices;*
(d) Committee IV: *Intergovernmental Commodity Arrangements;*
(e) Committee V: *Administration and Organization.*

Committee II is our main interest because it is under its aegis that the first draft GATT articles were prepared. Committee II established a series of Sub-committees which were requested to report their findings to the main Committee (II): chief among them, the *Technical Sub-committee*, which dealt with a number of provisions appearing in the GATT, ranging from customs valuation to national treatment. Participation to the *Technical Sub-committee* was open to delegates for all the countries represented on the *Preparatory Committee*. Delegates of six different nationalities acted as rapporteurs, Leddy (US), being one of them. The other Sub-committees were drafting committees: issues were first negotiated in detail within Committee II, and were then referred to them so that they were put in a form that would be acceptable to the *Preparatory Committee*.

[30] Colombia, Denmark, Mexico, Peru, Poland, and Syria sent observers to both the first and the second session of the *Preparatory Committee*; Colombia, and Mexico, to the *Drafting Committee* (which became operational during the *New York Conference*, see infra); Afghanistan, Argentina, Ecuador, Egypt, Greece, Iran, Saudi Arabia, Sweden, Syria, Turkey, Uruguay, Venezuela, and Yugoslavia sent representatives to the second session of the *Preparatory Committee*. Note that the Syrian delegates were representing the Syro-Lebanese customs union, see E/PC/T/117 Rev. 1 of July 9, 1947 at p. 2.

[31] The International Labour Office (ILO), and the Food and Agriculture Organization (FAO), see E/PC/T/117 Rev. 1 of July 9, 1947 at p. 2.

[32] The International Bank for Reconstruction and Development (World Bank, WB), and the International Monetary Fund (IMF), see E/PC/T/117 Rev. 1 of July 9, 1947 at p. 2.

[33] The American Federation of Labor (AFL), the International Chamber of Commerce (ICC), the International Co-operative Alliance (ICA), the World Federation of Trade Unions, and the International Federation of Agricultural Producers, see E/PC/T/117 Rev. 1 of July 9, 1947 at p. 2.

With respect to participation in the various committees, it is worth noting that not only during the London Conference, but throughout the negotiation of the GATT:

(a) delegates from the United Kingdom and the United States participated in all sub-committees;
(b) delegates from the United Kingdom and the United States were jointly present in all but one of the groups established;
(c) delegates from the United Kingdom and the United States were often appointed rapporteurs.

Although points (a), (b), and (c) are imperfect measures of influence in the drafting process, the presence of UK and U.S. delegates in every sub-committee enhanced their chances to have a substantial impact on the negotiations.

2.1.3 The Output

The *London Draft* discussed the following issues that later became provisions in the final GATT agreement: MFN; tariff reduction; internal taxes; transit; antidumping and countervailing duties; customs formalities; marks of origin; publication and administration of trade regulations; quantitative restrictions; balance of payments; exchange restrictions; subsidies; state trading; safeguards; general exceptions to assumed obligations; consultations; and preferential arrangements. It further contained provisions on boycotts, information, statistics, and trade terminology, which were not included in the final GATT text.[34] Negotiators managed to agree on 74 out of 89 articles included in the *Suggested Charter*.[35] However, the agreement did not *ipso facto* end the negotiation because the participants did not have legal authority to commit their governments yet. Still, agreement was not inconsequential either: as we will see, in the vast majority of cases, minor changes only to the agreed text were made in subsequent negotiations. The absence of agreement, on the other hand, did not mean that negotiators would start from scratch in the following phases of the negotiation. Bracketed texts were put before them first in New York and then in Geneva, and it is on this basis that they proceeded.

---

[34] We provide at the end of this Chapter, a discussion on the details of the negotiation of each and every GATT provision during the London Conference, as well as the modifications they underwent in subsequent negotiations.

[35] See Foreword, Preliminary Draft Charter for the International Trade Organizations of the United Nations, Department of State, December 1946, Publication 2728, Commercial Policy Series 98. Recall, nevertheless, that the *Preparatory Committee* did not have the powers to *formally* engage the international responsibility of the participating delegations. The Brazilian delegate to the *Drafting Committee* (Parangua), nevertheless, claimed that only 66 articles were agreed, see E/PC/T.6/4 of January 21, 1947.

2.1.4 An Assessment

As noted, the *London Draft* is, for all practical purposes, a renegotiation of the *Suggested Charter*. Reading the two documents side by side, several key differences can be found:

(a) *Preferences*: whereas the *Suggested Charter* included a carve-out for long-standing preferences only (such as the US-Cuba trade arrangement, and imperial preferences), following requests by other participants, the scope of the carve-out was broadened so as to include many preferences in existence before 1946. The U.S. delegate (Hawkins) tried in vain to restrict the carve-out to long-standing preferences only.[36] The position advocated by the Chilean delegate (Videla) to expand the carve-out to other contractual arrangements that could not qualify as long-standing was echoed by a number of delegations, and such arguments managed, ultimately, to carry the day;[37]

(b) *Tariffs*: the *Suggested Charter* dealt with tariffs only, whereas it was agreed in the *London Draft* that all other duties and charges imposed at the border (but not the internal taxes, for which a separate provision was made available) should be disciplined as well. It was further agreed that no negotiations on the state trading margin be held, since it was felt that the provisions on state trading enterprises (STE) of the *London Draft* dealt adequately with all issues relating to STE;

(c) *Safeguard*: it was made clear that, in exceptional circumstances, emergency action could take place even in the absence of prior consultations with affected parties (the opposite was the case in the *Suggested Charter*);

(d) *Customs union*: the *London Draft* allowed for exceptions from MFN not only for existing customs unions (as was the case under the *Suggested Charter*), but also for arrangements that would eventually lead to the formation of customs union.

(e) *Government procurement*: there is no obligation to observe MFN in the *London Draft* (the opposite was the case under the *Suggested Charter*). Moreover, a distinction was now being made between purchases with the intent to resell (which would be covered by the STE disciplines), and purposes

---

[36] In his words, "... I begin to get a little nervous every time a suggestion is made for additions, because if we added all preferences that might be thought of you might get a very long list and perpetuate a good many preferences....," see E/PC/T/C.II/PV.8 at p. 15. His position was echoed by the Canadian delegate (McKinnon), see id. at p. 29.

[37] Id. see pp. 12ff. for the Chilean position, and pp. 19ff., and 33ff. for the eventual compromise. Lebanon, speaking for the *Arab League*, requested the possibility to allow for regional preferences, that is, preferences that would allow Arab countries to coordinate their economic policies, see Brown (1950) at p. 72.

for governmental use (which would be part of the government-procurement carve-out).

The basic approach of the *Suggested Charter* survived the *London Conference*: the GATT would emerge as an international contract among nations who agreed to use tariff protection only (and domestic subsidies, assuming availability of funds) for domestic producers, keeping in mind that the level of tariffs would be reduced through ongoing multilateral negotiations; who would, eventually, abolish all preferential treatment; who would unilaterally continue to pursue their domestic (nonnegotiable) policies and thus subject trade liberalization to their own social preferences (assuming, nevertheless, that the latter would be exercised in a nondiscriminatory manner). It bears repetition that the ideas incorporated in the *Suggested Charter*:

> although formulated by a technical staff within the Government of the USA, they represent, in the words of the British Prime Minister, not only the constructive thought of the US Government, but the culmination of a long process of study and exchange of ideas between our own experts and those of the USA.[38]

One cannot overlook the identity of players who directly, or indirectly (but quite decisively) influenced the shaping of the GATT. It is probably true that public service is particularly appealing to the elite in times when history is being made. And 1945-1946 was indeed such a time: the construction of the post-world-war era is a defining moment in world history. The UK delegation counted James Meade (Nobel Prize for Economics, 1977) and Lionel Robbins (Professor of Economics, LSE) in its ranks, whereas the hand of John Maynard Keynes is visible any time short-term, macro-economic solutions (such as the balance-of-payments exception) were advanced and found their way into the GATT. Harry Hawkins (later, of Tufts University) of the U.S. delegation was yet another important figure in the negotiations. And it seems that participation of such remarkable individuals was not confined to the *London Conference* only: the French philosopher Alexandre Kojève was a member of the French delegation participating in the *Drafting Committee* that continued the work in New York and Geneva. The final product is in part due to these remarkable people.

Furthermore, it is remarkable, especially for modern lawyers, to see the manner in which national delegates viewed the negotiating process as an integral

---

[38] See E/PC/T/W.14 at p. 4. So the G4 as we now know it (Brazil, India, European Union, United States) has had a quasi-identical composition already in the '40s, the only difference being that the United Kingdom was occupying the place of the European Union. At that time, of course, neither Brazil nor India were important players, as they are today.

2.2 Atlantic Crossing: the New York Conference (1947)

part and parcel of their wider international commitments. Besides the treatment of preferences, a number of international agreements that were relating to issues also covered by the ITO Charter negotiation were explicitly mentioned during the negotiations and provided substantive input; the willingness to ensure uniformity across the GATT and other, prior international arrangements is evident throughout the negotiating process.[39] A look into the negotiating documents leaves us with the impression that delegates stressed the importance of prior commitments, and aimed at ensuring compatibility of the ITO Charter with such prior commitments. This attitude is so different from today's negotiating techniques which, essentially, view the negotiation of an international contract as some sort of a self-contained enterprise.[40]

The *London Conference* ended with a decision to appoint a *Drafting Committee* that was entrusted with formalizing the text of the agreement reached in London. The *Drafting Committee*,[41] originally convened in New York, in Lake Success in January–February 1947, and then completed its work in Geneva later in the same year. It comprised 53 national delegates, as well as eight observers (one from Mexico, one from Colombia, one from the ILO, one from the WB, one from the IMF, and three from the FAO).[42] The size of the *Drafting Committee* was kept intentionally limited in order to speed up the process.[43] In New York, the first textual separation of the GATT from the ITO was made.

2.2 Atlantic Crossing: the New York Conference (1947)

2.2.1 The Mandate

The agreed function of the *Drafting Committee* was to prepare a draft report no later than February 28, 1947:

(a) editing for clarity and consistency these portions of the text on which the *Preparatory Committee* has come to substantial identity of views;
(b) preparing alternative drafts of those portions on which remains a division of general views; and

---

[39] On this score, see the discussion of the detailed provisions in Section 2.8 of this Chapter.
[40] There is a lot of discussion today on the fragmentation of international law, but so far we have yet to see something adding to the disciplines embedded in the *Vienna Convention on the Law of Treaties* (VCLT). Although the VCLT had not entered into force when the GATT was being negotiated, the attitude of the negotiators is evidence that, in this respect, it indeed codifies customary international law: negotiators took previous obligations seriously.
[41] See E/PC/T/C.6/2 of January 20, 1947 at p. 1.
[42] See E/PC/T/C.6/77 of February 13, 1977, and the revised list in E/PC/T/C.6/Rev. 1 of February 24, 1977, where one more delegate was added.
[43] See E/PC/T/C.6/2 at p. 1.

(c) preparing suggested drafts covering such uncompleted portions as are referred to by the *Preparatory Committee*.[44]

2.2.2 Institutional Issues

The final *New York* draft is divided in two parts: the first part is a redraft of the ITO Charter; the second part is the first draft of the GATT. Since the two documents shared some provisions, a committee (the *Sub-committee on Tariff Negotiations*) was designated to decide which articles of the ITO Charter would be included in the GATT. The GATT has, of course, a narrower scope than the ITO. Moreover, the common provisions do not necessarily have identical content: an appropriate illustration is offered by the disciplines imposed on subsidization; as we will see in Section 2.7 infra, the disciplines on subsidies included in the ITO Charter differ drastically from those included in the GATT.

It was decided early on to adopt flexible working procedures. The *Drafting Committee*[45] would meet in plenary sessions. Whenever a specific complicated point arose, an ad hoc group of a maximum of four delegates would be established to deal with it; it was also anticipated that the establishment of two to three sub-committees, comprising at most four delegates each, was necessary in order to deal with some self-contained issues.[46] Although the sub-committees were of restricted membership, all delegates to the *Drafting Committee* were accorded the right to participate in the proceedings of the sub-committees at any time, and frequently availed themselves of this facility.[47]

It was further decided that a small group would eventually be established to do the edit and put in proper legal language the outcome of the negotiations.[48] The group would be called *Legal Drafting Sub-committee*. This group would essentially do legal editing and, whenever substantive issues arose, they would be referred back to one of the ad hoc drafting committees that were established to this effect.

The various drafts would go through two readings before the relevant sub-committee and then would be referred to the *Legal Drafting Committee*. From there, they would be included in the final report that was submitted for approval.[49] The *New York Draft*[50] is the final output of the *New York Conference*.

---

[44] See E/PC/T/C.6/2 of January 20, 1947 at p. 1.
[45] See E/PC/T/C.6/4 at p. 1.
[46] In Annex B, we provide a detailed account of the composition and the mandate of each of these sub-committees.
[47] See E/PC/T/C.6/102 at p. 4.   [48] See E/PC/T/C.6/2 at pp. 2–3.
[49] See E/PC/T/C.6/W.44 of February 3, 1947.
[50] See E/PC/T/34 of March 5, 1947.

2.2 Atlantic Crossing: the New York Conference (1947)

2.2.3 The Output

The *New York Draft* carried the ball forward. The final outcome could be described as follows:

(a) a bifurcation was operated, whereby the GATT text was separated from the larger ITO Draft. This is the confirmation that the GATT would precede the entry into force of the ITO;
(b) The overlapping provisions however, do not necessarily have identical content. The subsidies provision, discussed in more detail in Section 2.7 infra, is an appropriate illustration to this effect: the prohibition on export subsidies figures in the ITO provision on subsidies, but not in the corresponding GATT provision. A probable explanation is, as alluded to supra, that the GATT text was narrowed down to what was strictly required to ensure that tariff concessions would not be circumvented. The introduction of nonviolation complaints (NVCs) was probably considered an adequate safeguard to this effect, and there was no need to introduce an absolute prohibition as well;
(c) some progress was made with both agreed (during the *London Conference*), and nonagreed provisions: the former were further streamlined (Section 2.7), whereas the disagreements on some of the latter were smoothened out.

2.2.4 An Assessment

The *New York* GATT Draft contains, all in all, 27 articles.[51] There are minor differences between this and the *London Draft, as far as their GATT component is concerned*. Some provisions appearing in the *London Draft* (boycotts; information about statistics) were left out from the *New York* GATT *Draft*.[52] In terms of the New York GATT Draft and New York ITO Charter, most of the overlapping provisions appear in identical terms in the two texts. Some provisions (tariff valuation, customs formalities, publication and administration of laws, STE) exhibit some superficial differences in drafting, or, as in the case of tariff valuation, differences relating more to the context within which they will operate: Negotiators had early on expressed their willingness to standardize tariff valuation; this task, nonetheless, it was judged, could not be handled in an appropriate manner by the GATT, a temporary arrangement anyway. As a result, the tariff-valuation

---

[51] Shortly before the end of the *New York Conference*, the U.S. delegation prepared a comprehensive draft of the GATT, which summed up the discussions (see E/PC/T/C.6/W.58 of February 7, 1947). It contained 23 provisions and made room for minimal institutional arrangements that were deemed necessary for the provisional operation of the GATT. The Secretariat circulated its comments to the U.S. draft in a separate document (see E/PC/T/C.6/65/Rev. 2 of February 12, 1947).

[52] But they continued to appear in the New York ITO Draft Charter.

provision appearing in the *New York* Draft ITO Charter contains one additional paragraph calling for efforts to standardize this process since, it was felt, that only under the aegis of a true institution, such as the ITO, would a similar task come to fruition. The only substantive difference between the two texts concerns the treatment of export subsidies. We have already alluded to the reason why this is the case supra, when we discussed the rationale for omitting a discipline on export subsidies from the *New York* GATT Draft.

Finally, there are some terminological differences that are the direct consequence of the common perception of the GATT as a multilateral, contractual arrangement, as opposed to the ITO, which was viewed as an authentic international organization. In this vein, the ITO *Members* are GATT *contracting parties*.

At the end of the *New York Conference*, it was clear that negotiators would reconvene in Geneva to finalize their agreement on the GATT text, as well as hold the first round of multilateral trade negotiations. A UK proposal suggested that the GATT should enter into force for an initial period of three years.[53] No definitive decision was made on this point. The *Drafting Committee* decided to provide a list of all texts where agreement had been reached, keep in brackets the texts where future negotiation was required, provide alternative texts with commentary, if necessary, and also include a list of all reservations that were maintained at the end of the New York Conference.[54]

2.3 GATT Finalized: the Geneva Conference (1947)

2.3.1 The Mandate

> I am heartened to learn of successful conclusion of tariff negotiations begun under auspices Preparatory Committee in April. Successful conclusion of these negotiations is encouraging evidence of intention of United Nations to take common action to press on with the economic organisation of peace with a view to attaining the higher standards of living and economic progress envisaged in Article 55A of the UN Charter. Stop. Your agreement in Geneva is also a happy augury for successful outcome to the UN Conference on trade and employment which is to open in Havana next month.

This is how the President of the *Preparatory Committee*, Mr. Suetens[55] opened his remarks on October 30, 1947, the date when the *Geneva Final Act* was

---

[53] See E/PC/T/C.6/W.40 of February 1, 1947 at p. 1.
[54] See E/PC/T/C.6/82 of February 14, 1947.
[55] On Suetens's election as Chairman, see E/PC/T/PV.2/1 at p. 10.

2.3 GATT Finalized: the Geneva Conference (1947)

open for signature by the delegations.[56] In 370 days, the *Preparatory Committee* managed to produce not only a text on a very complicated issue which, with minor changes that we will be discussing infra, has withstood the test of time for more than 60 years now, but also conduct the first round of multilateral tariff negotiations.[57] The negotiators held 453 meetings in Geneva, 58 in Lake Success, and 150 in London, for a total of 626 meetings in order to finalize their agreement on the GATT.[58,59]

The mandate of the Geneva negotiators was two-fold:

(a) to finalize the agreement on the GATT;
(b) to hold the first round of multilateral negotiations to reduce tariff rates, the results of which would become an integral part of the GATT.

2.3.2 Institutional Issues

Since the mandate covered both the wrap up of the GATT and the first multilateral round of tariff negotiations, institutional arrangements were made in order to ensure that the two negotiations will proceed smoothly. Five of the most experienced negotiators (from China, Cuba, Czechoslovakia, India, and Norway) would be acting as vice-chairmen in order to assist with the negotiation.[60] Two Commissions were established (*Commission* A and *Commission* B) and distributed the negotiated subject matter. *Commission* A dealt with commercial policies and restrictive business practices, whereas *Commission* B would focus on international commodity agreements, subsidies, and the institutional aspects of the ITO.[61] These Commissions were further in charge of appointing

---

[56] See Press Release No. 479 of October 30, 1947.
[57] The poor hotel accommodations in Geneva might have contributed toward speeding up the process. In his welcoming speech, Mr. Moderow, the chief of the European Office of the UN, apologized for the hotel conditions due to the fact that the city had to simultaneously offer accommodation to various international conferences that were being held in Geneva at that time, see E/PC/T/PV.2/1 at pp. 6–7. On the other hand, one should not underestimate that amendments of the GATT are difficult, by virtue of the consensus rule applicable to such decisions.
[58] See E/PC/T/PV.2/5.
[59] As was the case with the *London* and *New York Conferences*, Chinese, English, French, and Spanish were kept as the official languages of the *Preparatory Committee*, while English and French were the chosen working languages for the meetings in Geneva, see E/PC/T/39 and 40.
[60] See E/PC/T/DEL/20 at p. 2.
[61] See E/PC/T/72 of May 19, 1947. The Chairman of Commission A was Suetens (Belgium), and the vice-chairmen were Colban (Norway) and de Vilhena Ferreira Braga (Brazil); Wilgress (Canada) acted as Chair for Commission B, whereas Royer (France) acted as vice-chair, see E/PC/T/180.

Committees, Sub-committees, Working Parties, and ad hoc groups that dealt with specific issues (see Section 2.7). The study of the different proposals was streamlined by the *Working Party on Tariff Negotiations*, which operated under the Chairmanship of Wilgress (Canada), produced the first GATT draft that resembles quite closely the current text.[62]

2.3.3 The Output

The changes to the *New York GATT Draft* are neither many nor substantial. In Geneva, negotiators contributed, with few exceptions, clarifications and, of course, provided the necessary legitimacy to a text agreed by representatives who lacked the official negotiating authority to commit their governments to a particular text. The most notable exceptions are discussed in Section 2.7 infra.

The *Geneva Conference*, as mentioned before, also provided the forum for the first multilateral trade negotiations. The plan for the negotiations on tariff concessions had already been agreed to during the *London Conference*.[63] In brief:

(a) negotiations should be based on reciprocity, which meant that countries should not be expected to grant concessions unilaterally;
(b) prior international commitments, *with respect to tariff treatment*, should not stand in the way of the negotiations;
(c) stand-still provisions should be agreed regarding residual preferences (they could not be increased after that date), new tariffs, and other restrictive measures;
(d) negotiations should take place between a small subset of the members of the *Preparatory Committee* (two to four), the concessions agreed, nevertheless, should be extended to all members;
(e) negotiations should take place in accordance with the *principal supplier rule*: countries should be expected to grant concessions on products of which the other members of the *Preparatory Committee* were likely to be the principal supplier;[64]

---

[62] A comparative table also exists in E/PC/T/180 of August 19, 1947.
[63] See E/PC/T/33, Annexure 10.
[64] The rationale for the *principal supplier rule* and its link to *reciprocity* are adequately explained in an official press release: "Since the supreme rule of the most-favored-nation treatment governs the relationship between the negotiating parties it must be expected that importing country A will be interested in granting to exporting country B concessions on products of which B is the main supplier, because in this way country A will secure the highest concessions from B on other goods which A exports to country B," see UN Information Centre, Geneva, Press release No. 36 of April 8, 1947 at p. 6.

2.3 GATT Finalized: the Geneva Conference (1947)

(f) additionally, concessions should also be granted on products for which no single principal supplier existed among the members of the *Preparatory Committee*, but a principal part of which was supplied by various members of the *Preparatory Committee*;
(g) negotiations would roll over four stages, which largely reflect a (bilateral) request and offer, and a multilateral review of concessions made;
(h) 16 schedules would be completed that would incorporate the MFN and the preferential rates of duty.[65]

At the time, the *Harmonized System* (HS), which provides a common description of all traded goods, did not exist. Negotiators used its predecessor, the *Geneva Nomenclature* (GN), which came into force on July 1, 1937.[66] It was also clear that, following a U.S. proposal to this effect,[67] all preferences were negotiable. A *Tariff Steering Committee* was established to guide the work on tariff negotiations.[68]

The trading nations committed a number of negotiating teams that focused on exchange of tariff concessions: Australia came with three teams, Benelux with six, Brazil with four, Canada with one, Chile with one, China with two, Czechoslovakia with one, France with two or three, India with four, Lebanon-Syria with one, New Zealand with one, Norway with two, South Africa with two, the United Kingdom with three, and the United States with eleven.[69] There was consistent monitoring of negotiations,[70] and fortnightly reports were issued to this effect.[71]

---

[65] The 16 schedules would belong to Australia (Schedule I), Belgo-Luxembourg-Netherlands customs union (II), Brazil (III), Canada (IV), Chile (V), China (VI), Cuba (VII), Czechoslovakia (VIII), France (IX), India (X), New Zealand (XI), Norway (XII), Syro-Lebanese customs union (XIII), USSR (XIV), the United Kingdom (XV), and the United States (XVI). By the time the Geneva Conference convened, it was highly unlikely, if not out of the question altogether, that the USSR would participate. For preferential rates, the option was given to either include them in the schedule, or in a separate schedule, see Annexure 10, op. cit.

[66] The GN was subsequently replaced by the *Brussels Convention on Nomenclature for the Classification of goods in Customs Tariffs* (BTN) in 1959. The BTN was replaced in 1974 by the *Customs Cooperation Council Nomenclature* (CCCN) in 1974, which was replaced by the HS in 1988. The HS has been amended three times since 1988, (in 1992, 1996, and 2002), largely to account for changes in classification.

[67] See E/PC/T/W/146 of May 30, 1947 at p. 3.

[68] E/PC/T/C.6/88/Rev. 1 of February 17, 1947 at p. 5. See also E/PC/T/C.6/88, which provides additional information as to the planning of the Geneva-held negotiations.

[69] See E/PC/T/58 of April 29, 1947.

[70] See, for example, E/PC/T/73 of May 19, 1947, E/PC/T/70 of May 27, 1947.

[71] See, for example, E/PC/T/152 of August 5, 1947.

The Secretariat[72] had also an important role to play. It was agreed that it should:

(a) help the *Tariff Steering Committee*, whenever requested to do so;
(b) provide expert assistance to national delegations;
(c) act as liaison across negotiating groups; and
(d) provide statistical assistance, when necessary.[73]

The tariff negotiations did not take place in a self-contained manner. Frequent meetings with various nongovernmental organizations (NGOs) were held, whereby the Chairs of the various groups would inform the wider public on the progress of the negotiations.[74] According to the GATT (1949, p. 11), in the first Geneva negotiation the 23 participating countries made no fewer than 123 bilateral agreements covering 45,000 tariff items related to about one half of the value of world trade. However, in terms of its effect on tariff levels, the outcome of the Geneva negotiations has been difficult to assess. The best information concerns the United States. The U.S. Tariff Commission (1948, p. 18) calculated that had the tariff cuts from the first GATT round in Geneva (finalized in October 1947, implemented in January 1948) been applied to actual imports in 1947, the average tariff would have declined 21.1 percent, from 19.4 percent to 15.3 percent. Thus, the United States reduced its tariff by about 20 percent in the Geneva conference. The actual U.S. tariff fell by a somewhat greater margin because of the impact of import price inflation in reducing the *ad valorem* equivalent of specific duties.[75]

There is not much information regarding how much other countries reduced their tariffs at the *Geneva Conference*.[76] It is generally acknowledged that the

[72] Since the beginning of the negotiations (*London Conference*), a small Secretariat (something akin to today's WTO Secretariat, that is, international officials, who, however, lacked this status at the time) had been established that would help negotiators with their numerous tasks. As of the *Geneva Conference*, the role of the Secretariat became more important. It was agreed that Eric Wyndham-White would serve as Executive Secretary heading the established Secretariat, see E/PC/T/PV.2/1 at p. 15.

[73] E/PC/T/C.6/88/Rev. 1 of February 17, 1947 at p. 7.

[74] See E/PC/T/87 of June 4, 1947 on meeting with ICC, and E/PC/T/88 of June 4, 1947 on meeting with the World Federation of Trade Unions, E/PC/T/99 of June 17, 1947 on meeting with representatives of IFAP (International Federation of Agricultural Producers).

[75] See Irwin (1998a). The average U.S. tariff in 1948 turned out to be 13.9 percent and higher import prices fully account for the difference. Import prices rose 10.5 percent between 1947 and 1948, which (Irwin calculates) would have reduced the tariff by 6.7 percent. Applying both the 21.1 percent reduction due to the GATT negotiations and the 6.7 percent reduction due to higher import prices to the 19.4 percent tariff in 1947 yields 14.0 percent, just 0.1 percentage points from the actual 13.9 percent. In this one pivotal year, therefore, fully a third of the U.S. tariff reduction was due to higher import prices.

[76] See Irwin (1995) for an assessment regarding Western Europe.

2.3 GATT Finalized: the Geneva Conference (1947)

United States made the deepest tariff cuts, but there is not much data on the extent to which other countries cut their tariff rates. In any event, it was widely believed at the time that import tariffs were not then the binding constraint on international trade; rather, exchange restrictions and some import quotas reduced trade to a much greater extent. Indeed, the Geneva tariff cuts may have been larger than otherwise politically possible because they were viewed as ineffective in view of the other nontariff barriers. As Curzon (1965, p. 70) explains:

> countries believing that quantitative restrictions would be a permanent feature of the post-war world gave sham but very substantial reductions on their tariff rates in exchange for real reductions from the only country not to apply quotas on manufactured goods, i.e., the United States.

Even the Economist magazine (April 23, 1949, 757) argued that:

> As quotas and discriminatory use of import licensing fade, ultimately vanish, the concessions exchanged at Geneva.... will acquire real substance.[77]

2.3.4 An Assessment

The *Geneva Draft* contains few substantive changes from the *New York Draft* (Section 2.7). The innovation was the successful completion of the first round of multilateral trade negotiations. The successful completion of both negotiations (GATT text, tariff reductions) enabled the entry into force of the GATT provisionally through the Protocol of Provisional Application (PPA) on January 1, 1948. The GATT text agreed in Geneva underwent some changes during the Review Session of 1955, and in 1965 when Part IV was added. We discuss these two events in the following Sections. After 1965, it underwent no change.[78]

The GATT could have entered into force definitively, had the number of countries provided for in its relevant provision agreed to do so: according to Art. XXVI GATT, this would happen when countries representing 85 percent of all trade would accept to do so. It never happened though, probably because, as Jackson (1969) explains, it was thought that discrepancies between those who had accepted it provisionally and those who would do so on a definitive basis should be avoided.

---

[77] On this issue, see also pp. 26–30 of World Trade Report, the WTO: Geneva, 2007.
[78] The GATT text did not change. Nevertheless, it was agreed during the *Uruguay Round* that the GATT 1994, that is today's GATT, comprises not only the text of the GATT as it was modified in 1965, but also a series of decisions that the GATT CONTRACTING PARTIES, the highest organ of the GATT, adopted during the GATT years.

The parts of world trade of the signatories at the time when the GATT entered into force were as follows:

Australia	3.2%
Belgium-Netherlands-Luxembourg	11.0%
Brazil	2.8%
Burma	0.7%
Canada	7.2%
Ceylon	0.6%
Chile	0.6%
China	2.7%
Cuba	0.9%
Czechoslovakia	1.4%
France	9.5%
India (Pakistan)	3.3%
New Zealand	1.2%
Norway	1.5%
Southern Rhodesia	0.3%
Syro-Lebanese customs union	0.1%
South Africa	1.7%
United Kingdom	25.9%
United States	25.4%

Source: Annex G of E/PC/T/135

2.4 The Havana Conference (1947–1948)

2.4.1 The Mandate

With the GATT in place as of January 1, 1948, negotiators moved to Havana in order to complete the negotiation of the ITO. Nevertheless, some changes to the agreed GATT provisions were still agreed. The *Havana Conference* signals the first meeting of the GATT CONTRACTING PARTIES, the highest organ of the GATT, which had entered into force on January 1, 1948.

2.4.2 Institutional Issues

The GATT Contracting Parties' meetings ran from January 31 to March 17, 1948.[79] Various committees were established during the *Havana Conference*

---

[79] See UN Conference on Trade and Employment, reports of Committees and principal sub-committees, Interim Commission for the International Trade Organization, Geneva, September 1948, hereinafter CRH (Committee Reports Havana) at p. 40.

2.4 The Havana Conference (1947–1948)

in order to honor the mandate. For the purposes of this work, it is the *Third Committee* that is of interest: it focused on commercial policy, that is, essentially, the overlap between the GATT and the ITO Charter. This Committee established a series of sub-committees and working groups that provided the institutional cover for the negotiations (see Section 2.7).

2.4.3 The Output

A series of Protocols include the changes agreed during the *Havana Conference*.[80] Note that the changes were formal amendments, since by the time the *Havana Conference* was under way, the GATT had already entered into force. They have been included in Volume I of the *Basic Instruments and Selected Documents* (BISD) series: this was until the end of the *Uruguay round*, the official GATT publication which included all acts of the CONTRACTING PARTIES.[81] Some of the changes were quite dramatic, such as the acknowledgement that FTA as well, and not CU only as had been the case, can legitimately constitute a deviation from Art. I.[82]

---

[80] See The GATT Analytical Index, 3rd revision, The GATT: Geneva, 1970 at p. 1ff.
[81] There is now a corresponding WTO publication.
[82] In the official account on the Havana Conference, Wilgress, the head of the Canadian delegation, provides us with a very interesting personal evaluation of the situation as it unfolded and the attitude of the various trading partners: In his view, the Latin countries were able to act as a "solid block" and dominated the first part of the negotiations. They had embraced the socialist ideas, and felt that the developed nations should be helping them with concrete measures. They were quite unhappy with the fact that the U.S. government had decided to help European countries only (Marshall Plan). While all of them were looking to secure measures that would allow them to protect their domestic industry, Argentina had, in his view, the more nationalistic attitude, Brazil was quite cooperative, whereas Mexico favored the use of tariffs to this effect over QR. Among developing countries, India had, in his view, a very able negotiating team. Among developed nations, Wilgress notes the handicap that the U.S. delegates suffered, as a result of their staunch resistance to proposals to prohibit the use of QR on farm products, and their equally firm commitment to exempt export farm subsidies from the outright ban on export subsidies. The UK delegates were keen to allow for discriminatory QR in case recourse to BoP had been made. The Benelux countries had adopted a pro-free-trade stance from early on, while Switzerland wanted to widen the permissible recourse to QR. French delegates alerted their partners to their negotiating position: because of the rise of the socialist and communist parties, the only chance they had to secure approval of the final text was by presenting the (amended) GATT along with an ITO Charter signed by a large number of trading nations. Australia held a similar position (no GATT without an ITO). As a result, Wilgress describes the situation early on during the negotiation as hopeless. In his view, absent comprehensive last-minute horse-trading, no agreement would have been possible. Three were the keys for successful resolution: (i) allowing for extension of justified deviations from the prohibition to have recourse to QR (so as to include economic development, and protection of industries established during the war, the so-called "war babies"); (ii) a split among Latin countries (some preferred protection of farm products, some of

2.4.4 An Assessment

There are few, but notable changes, as explained in detail in Section 2.7. Chief among them, figures the agreement that FTA should also come under the purview of preferential (regional) agreements, alongside CU. On the other hand, following a Cuban proposal to this effect, participants agreed to include a sentence in the provision regulating antidumping, whereby dumping would be condemned, although not outlawed. Dumping would of course, be condemned, only if it was injurious. The legal significance of the condemnation of dumping should not be underestimated: numerous WTO panels, and the WTO Appellate Body as well, have insisted on this aspect of Art. VI GATT, in order to adopt a less demanding standard of review when dealing with antidumping cases, than is the case when it deals with safeguards; in its view, such a standard is warranted in light of the fact that antidumping is an instrument aimed at taming *unfair*, as opposed to *fair*, trade practices.[83]

2.5 The Review Session of 1954–1955

2.5.1 The Mandate

During their ninth session, the CONTRACTING PARTIES of the GATT undertook a comprehensive review of the GATT. It was felt that the time was ripe to review the various GATT provisions that had already been in place for over six years. It was quite clear, by that time, that the ITO would not be entering into force. The Truman administration had already decided to withdraw the ITO Charter from congressional consideration in 1950, and the entry into force of the ITO without the participation of the United States was inconceivable.

2.5.2 Institutional Issues

A *Steering Group* was established that was in charge of the organization of the negotiating process. Wilgress (Canada) acted as Chair, whereas Garcia Oldini (Chile), and Seidenfaden (Denmark), acted as vice-chairs.[84] The *Steering Group* proposed that negotiations would take place in three stages: for the first two,

---

the nonfarm industry); (iii) a last-minute U.S. proposal to allow for discriminatory QR when recourse to BoP had been made by developing countries, see Report of the Canadian Delegation to the United Nations Conference on Trade and Development at Havana, No. 165, 1948.

[83] For a survey of the literature on this score, see Mavroidis (2007).
[84] See SR.9/1 of October 29, 1954.

2.5 The Review Session of 1954–1955

plenary sessions were envisaged, and for stage three, a series of Working Parties would be established:[85]

(a) Working Party I on Quantitative Restrictions;
(b) Working Party II on Tariffs, Schedules, and Customs Administration;
(c) Working Party III, on Other Barriers to Trade;
(d) Working Party IV, on Organizational and Functional Questions.[86]

Each of the Working Parties could establish *ad hoc* working groups to discuss specific issues.[87] A series of sub-groups mandated to review the work of Working Parties were established.[88] Finally, a *Legal and Drafting Committee* was established with a double mandate:

(a) to give expert advice on legal issues; and
(b) to remove drafting imperfections.[89]

2.5.3 The Output

Three instruments that amended the GATT were agreed to. However, only one of the three instruments, the Protocol amending the Preamble, and Parts II and III of the GATT, entered into force.[90] Parts II and III, nevertheless, constitute the bulk of the GATT obligations: only MFN and scheduling of concessions are missing out. The Draft Protocol amending Parts II and III of the GATT, which reflects all the changes, was agreed to in early March.[91]

2.5.4 An Assessment

The *Review Session* was quite comprehensive and produced a series of amendments in the GATT that should not be overlooked: clarifications in the discipline with respect to QRs; the manner in which developing countries could use QRs; the process for renegotiating consolidated tariffs, etc.[92]

---

[85] See W.9/2 of November 3, 1954.
[86] See W.9/10 of November 10, 1954.
[87] Such as, for example, the *Technical Group on Customs Administration* that Mr. Ashford (United Kingdom) chaired, see SR.9/26 of December 24, 1954 at p. 13.
[88] See W.9/64 of December 2, 1954.
[89] Perez Cisneros was appointed Chair, and the members were: Abramson (United Kingdom); von Bargen (Germany); Haguiwara (Japan); Hollis (United States); Monaco (Italy); de Saint-Légier (France); and Stuyck (Belgium), see SR.9/28 of January 10, 1955, its terms of reference are reproduced in detail in the same document. Germany eventually replaced von Bargen by Partsch, see SR.9/20 of January 21, 1955 at p. 1, and France replaced de Saint-Légier by Dubais, see SR.9/32 of February 2, 1955.
[90] See The GATT Analytical Index, 3rd revision, The GATT: Geneva, 1970 at p. 1ff.
[91] See W.9/242 of March 4, 1955, and W.9/246 of March 6, 1955, which contain all the changes.
[92] For a detailed discussion, see Section 2.7 infra.

2.6 Development Enters the GATT: Negotiating Part IV (1965)

2.6.1 The Mandate

We have seen above that many developing countries were feeling that the original GATT rules were not dealing adequately with the particular situation of developing countries. They increasingly questioned the appropriateness of the MFN-rule as a one-size-fits-all rule for developed and developing economies alike. Although, in the various renegotiations of the original GATT contract, developing countries managed to introduce many rules that were better suited to their own preferences and preoccupations, developing countries still felt that a more drastic redraft of the GATT was warranted. The GATT CONTRACTING PARTIES requested that a special group, headed by the distinguished trade economist Gottfried Haberler of Harvard University, examine the issue. The famous *Haberler report* concluded that claims by the less-developed trading partners, to the effect that, the existing rules on trade liberalization would not necessarily work to their advantage, were not entirely unjustified.[93] This report examined both the short- and long-term trends in commodity prices and the factors influencing them. The report concluded that existing protectionist policies in the agricultural sector by developed (industrialized) nations, as well as tariff-escalation practices by many developed nations, operated adversely to the growth of developing countries. The *Haberler report* made a series of recommendations to address the issue: reduction of the existing protectionism was one of the measures suggested. Importantly, it sensitized the trading partners to the fact that not all participants gain from the existing regime; something needed to be done to address the concerns of those who were being left behind.

In 1961, the CONTRACTING PARTIES adopted a *Declaration on the Promotion of trade of less-developed countries.* In this Declaration, the CONTRACTING PARTIES introduce many of the elements/conclusions of the *Haberler report.* There was, thus, an increasing recognition that liberalization of trade in farm products was very much a concern for developing countries, as the first comprehensive studies on the welfare implications of such a démarche started to appear. At the same time, arguments to the effect that there was an asymmetry in trade liberalization were gaining pace all the time: in areas of interest to developed nations (manufactured products), liberalization (in the form of tariff reductions) was progressing fast; in areas of interest to developing nations (farm products), this had hardly been the case.

---

[93] GATT (1958), *Trends in International Trade*, Geneva.

2.6 Development Enters the GATT: Negotiating Part IV (1965)

During the *Kennedy round* of international trade negotiations (1963–1967), the *Committee on Legal and Institutional Framework* worked on a chapter on *Trade and Development*. In May 1963, the GATT Ministers recognized the need for an adequate legal and institutional framework necessary to enable the contracting parties to discharge their responsibilities in connection with the work of expanding trade to developing countries. They decided to establish a special group that would dedicate its work to the study of this issue: this was the Committee III.[94] Committee III (1958) was established in order:

> To consider and report to the CONTRACTING PARTIES regarding other measures for the expansion of trade, with particular reference to the importance of the maintenance and expansion of export earnings of the less developed countries to the development and diversification of their economies.[95]

The mandate of Committee III (1958) was wide enough to provide negotiators with the necessary flexibility to design the mechanisms for improving the condition of developing countries within the multilateral trading system. Time, nevertheless, was an important factor, and as Lacarte (Uruguay) astutely observed, it is because of time that the discussion was limited to nonreciprocal tariff preferences, and was not extended to other issues: Uruguay and Brazil, for example, had a comprehensive proposal on the table regarding the necessary, in their views, reforms to the dispute-settlement system; absent such reforms, the system would not operate in the interests of developing countries. This and similar proposals were ultimately not discussed.[96]

The negotiations concerned the acknowledgment that unilateral tariff (i.e., nonreciprocal) preferences should become part of the GATT edifice, and the modalities (legal technicalities) under which this should be the case. The *Working Party on Preferences*, established to this effect, held comprehensive discussions on the ambit of preferences, their form, the list of beneficiaries, the duration of preferences, and the necessary (in light of the MFN) institutional amendments to the GATT that would allow preferences to take place.[97]

---

[94] To avoid confusing it with Committee III that dealt with RBP, we will be referring to it as Committee III (1958) in the rest of the document.

[95] See 7S/BISD at p. 29. BISD stands for *Basic Instruments and Selected Documents*. Unlike previous occasions, there was widespread participation in Committee III (1958): Argentina, Australia, Brazil, Canada, Ceylon, Chile, Cuba, Czechoslovakia, Dominican Republic, France, Germany, Ghana, Greece, India, Indonesia, Israel, Japan, Netherlands, Nigeria, Pakistan, Peru, Rhodesia, Sweden, Tanganyika, Turkey, United Arab Republic, United Kingdom, United States, Uruguay, Yugoslavia, see L/2079 of November 6, 1963.

[96] See SR.21/11 at p. 169.   [97] See L/2073 of October 24, 1963.

2.6.2 Institutional Issues

Committee III (1958) was the forum where proposals regarding measures destined to satisfy the requests of developing countries would be discussed. This is the forum where what became Part IV of the modern GATT was successfully negotiated. The other institutions, relevant for the coming into being of Part IV, were the already mentioned *Committee on Legal and Institutional Framework* (which had proposed a Charter on Trade and Development),[98] and the *Working Party on Preferences*, which had been created to discuss preferences by industrialized to developing countries, as well as between developing countries.

2.6.3 The Output

Part IV was finalized in a Special Session of the CONTRACTING PARTIES, held from November 17, 1964 to February 8, 1965, and was added by virtue of an amending protocol to the GATT where it now appears as Part IV. Part IV came into effect on June 27, 1966.

Developing countries were all in favor of introducing tariff preferences. Developed countries, with some notable exceptions, were not opposed to the idea either. The first draft of what became Part IV was submitted, as Evans (United States) recalled, by the U.S. delegation; many delegations reacted, and the final product is to a considerable extent a compromise among the various national positions.[99] Six governments submitted early on specific proposals to this effect: Australia, Brazil, Chile, India, United Arab Republic (UAR), and the United States.[100] Ceylon, Japan, Nigeria, and Uganda submitted their proposals at a later stage.

The mainstream position held by developing countries was a reflection of the idea then prevailing in the writings of *some* economists (Hans Singer, Raoul Prebisch) that the terms of trade between primary and manufactured goods tend to deteriorate over time: countries that export commodities (that is, mainly developing countries) would be able to import less and less for a given level of exports.[101] Prebisch went on to argue that, for this reason, developing countries should strive to diversify their economies and lessen dependence on primary commodity exports by developing their manufacturing industry. This led to the drive for import-substitution industrialization. For industrialization to be achieved, though, developing countries would need extra income. This would

---

[98] See 2SS/SR.2.
[99] See 2SS/SR at pp. 4ff.
[100] See SR.21/11 at pp. 166ff.
[101] This is often referred to as the Prebisch-Singer hypothesis.

2.6 Development Enters the GATT: Negotiating Part IV (1965) 127

come from additional exports that would be guaranteed through unilateral (tariff) preferences in favor of developing countries. Shah, the delegate from India, for example, citing the terms of trade pessimism during the negotiations, stated that exports of developing countries had not progressed as fast as those by developed countries, and that (the eventual) Part IV should be conceived to deal with this issue.[102]

The challenge for negotiators was not so much to agree on the principle, but rather to agree on the modalities to accommodate the principle, in light of the inconsistency of what they were after with MFN.[103] *Committee III* (1958) had proposed the insertion of additional paragraphs and/or amendments to existing provisions. India, at first, supported by the United Arab Republic, supported the inclusion of the new provision immediately following Art. I (MFN):

> Notwithstanding anything contained in this Agreement, and without prejudice to the rights of contracting parties in Article I, paragraphs 2, 3, and 4, contracting parties may accord, with respect to all matters in this Agreement, preferential treatment to products originating in less-developed countries, with a view to promoting the economic development and international trade of less-developed contracting parties. Such preferential treatment granted to any contracting party shall be applied automatically and unconditionally to like products originating in all other less-developed contracting parties.[104]

Chile, as well, was in favor of a clause to this effect.[105] Note that preferential treatment granted by developed nations to products originating in developing nations, would *not*, in accordance with this proposal, be limited to tariff preferences only. Subsequently, Lall (India) proposed that the draft Charter should become Arts. XXXVI etc. of the GATT. By giving it a separate entity, negotiators would implicitly at least, acknowledge its special status.[106]

Interestingly, the negotiations on Part IV opened up the door to other *quid pro quos* as well: Suzuki (Japan), for example, stated that its country would not be willing to become a donor country, absent the removal of the nonapplication clause that some (potential) beneficiaries kept still in place against Japan.[107]

Australia's proposal was framed so as to provide developing countries with added flexibility with respect to import commitments, judged necessary in order to promote a particular industry.[108] Australia was unequivocally in favor of

---

[102] See 2SS/SR.5 at pp. 3ff.
[103] See L/2196 and Corr. 1.
[104] Id. at pp. 7–8.
[105] Id.
[106] See 2SS/SR.2 at p. 5.
[107] See 2SS/SR.2 at p. 7.
[108] See L/2195 of March 20, 1964 at pp. 13ff.

including an *enabling clause* in Part II that would explicitly allow for deviations from MFN in favor of products originating in developing countries.[109]

Brazil did not limit its proposals to tariff preferences only. With respect to the latter, it pronounced in favor of including a declaration to the effect that no distinction across developing countries should take place by the donors.[110] It insisted on centrally planned economies opening up more to products originating in developing countries.[111] It was, nonetheless, particularly sensitized by the evolution of dispute settlement: it held the view that asymmetry of bargaining power largely explained why developing countries have had recourse to it and developing nations had not done so, and proposed concrete measures aiming at redressing this issue: the effects of measures on developing countries should be taken into account in calculating compensation; financial compensation should be introduced when developing countries are hurt (this was a joint proposal with Uruguay); and permanent panelists should be introduced as well.[112] Brazil went so far as to suggest that collective action might be necessary to address the imbalance between big and small markets, and it should be allowed when developed countries, through their policies, were hurting the interests of developing countries.[113] Since, however, negotiations were limited to tariff preferences, all these proposals were not seriously debated.

The UAR delegation wanted the GATT to be empowered to lend money to developing countries without, however, transforming the GATT into a lending institution.[114] An expert group with the participation of delegates from the United Arab Republic, Argentina, Ghana, India, the United Kingdom, the United States, the European Economic Community (EEC), and Japan was established to study this issue.[115] The discussions led nowhere.

The U.S. delegation took the view that developing countries would profit more from MFN tariff cuts and elimination of NTBs, rather than from extension of tariff preferences.[116] The U.S. delegation, on the other hand, was in favor of non-reciprocity, cutting down or imposing no duties at all on products of interest to developing countries, and was prepared to sympathetically examine other measures that might help developing countries.[117]

Nigeria was opposed to a one-size-fits-all approach, and opted for preferences tailor- made to the development needs of the beneficiaries.[118]

---

[109] See L/2196/Rev. 1 at p. 7.
[110] Id.
[111] See L/2195 at p. 19.
[112] See L/2195 at pp. 20ff.
[113] See L/2195/Rev. 1 of April 13, 1964.
[114] See L/2080 of November 7, 1963 at pp. 9ff. Argentina supported this proposal.
[115] Id. at pp. 11ff. Sweden was keen in helping developing countries with export-promotion activities, id. at pp. 13ff.
[116] See L/2196/Rev. 1 of April 2, 1964.
[117] See L/2136 of February 13, 1964.
[118] Id. at p. 8.

2.6 Development Enters the GATT: Negotiating Part IV (1965)

Australia, Brazil, Chile, India, and the United Arab Republic all tabled proposals in favor of allowing for preferences among developing nations.[119]

Then came the thorny issue, who should qualify as a developing country? A number of delegations were in favor of introducing pure quantitative criteria, *per caput* income being the one most countries would agree upon (Japan, UAR, and Uganda, which, however, wanted to distinguish between developing and least-developed countries).[120] As is by now known, such criteria were not finally introduced in the GATT. As to what the identity of the donors should be, Japan wanted all industrialized countries to grant preferences; the UK delegation did not object to this approach, it would rather see all developed countries act parallel though.[121] There was no disagreement that preferences should be non-reciprocal.[122] As to the product coverage, various proposals were submitted: some delegations wanted to see all products covered (Nigeria and Uganda), whereas others wanted to see that products be specified (Ceylon); Brazil wanted non-primary products only to be covered; Chile preferred a vague reference to products of special interest to developing countries; Japan preferred a cross-reference to the products included in the lists established by *Committee III* (1958); finally, the United Arab Republic would rather see semi-manufactured and manufactured products covered.[123]

As to the nature of preferences, we observe the following: Brazil would not agree that preferences are limited to tariff preferences only; India would like to introduce special arrangements that would be different from tariff preferences (that is, *tariff* preferences should not exhaust the realm of preferences granted to developing countries); Uganda, on the other hand, favored tariff preferences only.[124] Note that some delegations, such as the United Arab Republic and Uganda, wanted to introduce a specified margin of preference (50 percent), whereas others (United Kingdom) were categorically opposed to such an endeavor.[125]

On the duration of preferences: some suggested that preferences should be withdrawn when domestic industries became competitive (Italy, Nigeria); others wanted an agreed phaseout (Japan); and yet others linked them to MFN: when MFN duties would be driven down to zero percent, so would the margin of preference (Uganda).[126]

Many developing countries felt that, whatever the outcome of the negotiations, this was just the beginning: Letts (Peru) speaking for Argentina, Brazil, Chile, Dominican Republic, Peru, and Uruguay stressed this point, hoping that

---

[119] Id. at pp. 10ff.
[121] Id.
[123] Id. at pp. 13ff.
[125] Id. at p. 15.
[120] Id. at p. 12.
[122] Id.
[124] Id. at p. 14.
[126] Id. at pp. 15–16.

the whole idea of assisting developing countries would be an ongoing theme in the multilateral trading system.[127]

The agreed Part IV contained three new legal provisions:

(a) Principles and objectives (Art. XXXVI GATT);
(b) Commitments (Art. XXXVII GATT); and
(c) Joint action (Art. XXXVIII GATT).

None of the three provisions was conceived to be a binding legal obligation. A look at the wording of each provision makes it clear, that they are "best endeavors" clauses, whereby GATT contracting parties recognize the validity of the claim that something must be done to help developing countries, and a subset of the whole group, the developed nations, promise to undertake in the future concrete action to this effect. A number of developing countries had negatively reacted toward the proposal to include best-endeavors clauses in Part IV, and chief among them was Cuba, through their delegate Camejo Argudin.[128] Their voices were heard some years later, when concrete action came through the establishment of the generalized preference schemes (GSP).

Art. XXXVI GATT is a formal recognition that market access for products of export interest to developing countries[129] has to be improved. Art. XXXVI GATT does not prescribe the measures that should be adopted to this effect. It does, however, lay down one important principle: nonreciprocity. Recall that the introduction of this principle was a joint request by developing countries. To avoid any misunderstandings as to what this principle should capture, § 8 of the provision pertinently reads:

> The developed contracting parties do not expect reciprocity for commitments made by them in trade negotiations to reduce or remove tariffs and other barriers to the trade of less-developed contracting parties.

The *Interpretative Note ad* Art. XXXVI GATT sheds some additional light on this issue:

---

[127] See 2SS/SR.5 at pp. 2ff. Except for some specific interventions, this proved to be rather wishful thinking. The Doha round is the first comprehensive negotiation since the '60s axed on development issues. The views of economists about what trade and other economic policies are conducive to economic development have changed significantly since the 1960s. See Krueger (1997).

[128] See 2SS/SR.2 at p. 6.

[129] The degree of homogeneity across developing countries, as understood in those years, was relatively higher in the early 1960s. It was thus easier for them to reach consensus among them, and formulate common demands that corresponded more or less to similar needs.

2.6 Development Enters the GATT: Negotiating Part IV (1965)

It is understood that the phrase "do not expect reciprocity" means, in accordance with the objectives set forth in this Article, that the less-developed contracting parties should not be expected, in the course of trade negotiations, to make contributions which are inconsistent with their individual development, financial and trade needs, taking into consideration past trade developments.

Later, during the final stages of the *Kennedy round*, this provision was further interpreted as follows:

There will, therefore, be no balancing of concessions granted on products of interest to developing countries by developed participants on the one hand and the contribution which developing participants would make to the objective of trade liberalization on the other and which it is agreed should be considered in the light of the development, financial and trade needs of developing countries themselves. It is, therefore, recognized that the developing countries themselves must decide what contributions they can make.[130]

In a nutshell, Art. XXXVI GATT should be understood as embodying the principle that, from now, it should be expected that concessions by developing countries will first and foremost be compatible with their development process.[131] One would expect that, at least in the areas where they cannot influence terms of trade, it would not make much economic sense for developing countries to impose trade restrictions, absent some public-order justification.

Art. XXXVII GATT was some sort of a general clause recommending various actions that developed states should undertake in order to help promote issues of interest to developing countries: chief among them, the incitation to reduce the gap between (high) barriers on processed goods, and (low) barriers on primary products. This is the often-quoted "tariff escalation" argument. The validity of this argument can be put into question though: the problem seems to be the high tariff on processed goods, rather than the gap in protection between primary and processed goods. Hence, this item should not be placed in the agenda in terms of a relative difference (gap in protection between primary and processed goods), but, instead, in absolute terms (high protection on processed goods).[132]

---

[130] See GATT, COM.TD/W/37, p. 9.

[131] Rodrik (1999) notes that the negotiations in the 1950s and the 1960s coincide with the excessive faith that many developing countries placed in import-substitution strategies. There was a widespread belief that government intervention could achieve a lot in terms of promoting development policies.

[132] A series of discussions with Henrik Horn on this issue are acknowledged.

The remaining part of Art. XXXVII GATT deals with issues that were further detailed in subsequent agreements: for example, developed countries, when imposing countervailing or antidumping duties, or introducing safeguard measures, were to "have special regard to the trade interests" of developing countries and "explore all possibilities of constructive remedies before applying such measures." In the *Uruguay Round* AD agreement, this provision has become a binding legal obligation. In the context of antidumping, for example, it has been interpreted as an obligation to examine the feasibility of introducing price undertakings on dumped imports originating in developing countries, before antidumping duties are eventually imposed.

Art. XXXVIII GATT was meant to provide the institutional vehicle that would make the best-endeavors clauses reflected in the two aforementioned provisions happen: institutional arrangements for furthering the objectives of Part IV should be made, collaboration to this effect with the United Nations and its organs and agencies was envisaged, and some monitoring of the rate of growth of the trade of developing countries should be introduced.

Besides the introduction of these provisions, the GATT CONTRACTING PARTIES agreed on the establishment of the *Committee on Trade and Development* (CTD), which was established in 1964.[133] Its mandate was to review the application of the provisions of Part IV. Also in 1964, the *International Trade Centre* (ITC) was established, with the aim of promoting trade of developing countries. The ITC became later a joint agency of UNCTAD and GATT.

2.6.4 An Assessment

It is impossible to compare this with any previous negotiation: the subject matter of the negotiation of Part IV is unique. We will, thus, limit ourselves to an assessment of the usefulness of the provisions contracted into the body of the GATT. The feeling among developing countries has been that Part IV has fallen short of substantively contributing to the development policies pursued. First, it is simply not the case that trade liberalization is a substitute for development policies *in toto*. Depending on the importance of international trade on the GDP, it can be an important or a relatively unimportant aspect of a wider development strategy. On the other hand, even within these narrow(er) parameters, Part IV could not have had much of an impact in light of the fact that it was, for all practical purposes, a set of best-endeavor clauses, a list of "I wish to do" items, deprived of binding language in any direction.

Still, Part IV exercised some influence to subsequent developments: the *Enabling Clause* essentially reproduces the nonreciprocity idea, first embedded

---

[133] See 2SS/SR.5 at pp. 20ff. The terms of reference are set out in 2SS/SR.6.

2.7 The Evolution of the GATT Provisions
133

in Art. XXXVI.8 GATT. It is the Enabling Clause that led to the adoption of the various national GSP-schemes, an instrument that is being viewed with increasing skepticism.[134] In a way, Part IV could be seen as the instrument that first operated as the institutional awareness that something needed to be done to address the concerns expressed by developing countries, and then paved the way to concrete reforms of the world trading system.

The AB, in its report on *EC – Tariff Preferences*, noted that the *Enabling Clause* has become an integral part of the GATT, by virtue of Art. 1(b)(iv) of GATT 1994, since, as noted above, the *Enabling Clause* was adopted as a decision of the CONTRACTING PARTIES. In the same report, the notes that since the *Enabling Clause* enables WTO Members to grant tariff preferences to a subset of the WTO Membership (namely the developing countries), it constitutes a *legal exception* to Art. I GATT (§ 99).

2.7 The Evolution of the GATT Provisions[135]

2.7.1 MFN

London Conference

The MFN obligation was reflected in Art. 14 of the *London Draft*. The negotiation of MFN was intimately linked to the issue of imperial preferences. As Brown (1950, pp. 70ff.) points out, the MFN was the principle and the imperial preferences the exception: the latter could not be increased beyond the level existing on July 1, 1939, or July 1, 1946, whichever was lower. The drafters of the MFN clause were inspired by the formulation of the MFN clause as developed by the *League of Nations*. In turn, the League of Nations based its formulation of the MFN clause on the numerous bilateral trade treaties during the 1920s and before World War I.[136] Many of those treaties were signed by the United States.[137] The

---

[134] For a survey of the literature, see Grossman & Sykes (2005).

[135] Many of the provisions that found their way in the final GATT text appeared in bilateral agreements that the U.S. government had signed with various other states. Jackson's (1967) thorough analysis is the leading paper in this respect. Two agreements (U.S. – Mexico, 1942; U.S. – Uruguay, 1942) are the prime sources of inspiration. The two agreements were almost identical and contained provisions on all GATT provisions with the exception for films, antidumping, marks of origin, export subsidies, and assistance on economic development. Similar provisions had been also reflected in agreements that the U.S. government had signed with Canada (1938), Costa Rica (1936), El Salvador (1937), and Peru (1942).

[136] See E/PC/T/C/33 at p. 9.

[137] In the 1942 reciprocal trade agreement with Mexico, Article I read: "With respect to customs duties and charges of any kind imposed on or in connection with the importation or exportation, and with respect to the method of levying such duties and charges... any advantage, favor, privilege or immunity which has been or may hereafter be granted by

negotiation of the MFN was one of the sticking points between the UK and the U.S. delegations. The idea was that all preferences should be subsequently negotiated and eventually eliminated.[138] Because it was recognized that some preferences would be provisionally maintained, the negotiation shifted towards what else should be carved out. During the *London Conference*, it was agreed that in addition to imperial preferences, other long-standing preferences, such as those between Cuba and the United States, would be permitted temporarily.[139] The actual MFN text is quite broad ("*any* advantage, favour, privilege or immunity") so, unless a (trade-related) measure is not explicitly exempted from the coverage of this provision, it is inevitably subjected to it. It was quite clear, nevertheless, that some practices, such as *Government Procurement*, and *Buy National* policies, would not be covered by the MFN.[140] The text under discussion in London was viewed as being far from a completed work: it was thought that some key terms, such as *like products*, should not be defined any further; this should be left for a later stage and should be the job of the ITO.[141]

New York Conference

This is Art. II of the *New York* GATT Draft, and Art. 14 of the *New York* Draft ITO Charter. Only cosmetic changes were made, a normal development in light of the fact that with respect to this provision, an in-principle agreement was already obtained during the *London Conference*. We find it noteworthy to mention a proposal by the delegate of Lebanon who argued in favor of introducing tariff preferences for trade between developing countries, although it was not accepted.[142]

---

the United States of America or the United Mexican States to any article in or destined for any third country shall be accorded immediately and unconditionally to the like article originating in or destined for the United Mexican States or the United States of America, respectively." 57 Stat. 835.

[138] See E/PC/T/C/33 at p. 9.   [139] See E/PC/T/C/30 at p. 3.

[140] See E/PC/T/C/33 at p. 1. This discussion is featured under the heading MFN in the *London Draft*, although it is explicitly acknowledged that it relates to national treatment. It is probably the case that its placement was justified by its strong link, in practice, with *Government Procurement*. However, during the negotiations, this issue was discussed under the heading *National Treatment*, as we will see infra. As to *Buy National* policies, we should already signal that, while the U.S. delegation was firmly against such practices, such was not the will of the other trading nations.

[141] Id. at p. 1.

[142] In the words of the Lebanese delegate: "Members recognize that the development of industry in small nations is hampered by the lack of a sufficiently large market for manufactured goods. Consequently, the Organization shall give the most favourable consideration to any proposal for preferential tariff arrangements presented to it by small Member nations belonging to one economic region, aiming at the development of that region, with a view to releasing from their obligations under Chapter V." This proposal did not concern

2.7 The Evolution of the GATT Provisions

Geneva Conference

The U.S. delegates proposed to regroup Arts. 14, 15, and 24 of the *New York ITO Draft Charter* (MFN, tariffs, and national treatment); the proposal was not, however, that a single article should emerge, but rather, that the link between them would be more explicit. The rationale was that the three provisions were very closely interlinked: all tariff concessions would have to be applied on an MFN basis, and trading partners should not be undoing their tariff promises through domestic instruments. The necessary consequence was that it would, thus, become even clearer that national treatment served as an anti-circumvention provision.[143] The current GATT text reproduces this approach (Art. I: MFN; II: tariff concessions; III: national treatment).

Havana Conference

There was no change in the text, except for the addition of § 3, which concerns the special position of certain countries of the Near East (*Ottoman Empire*).[144] Some annexes, nevertheless, were added, so that some preferences could qualify for exemption. The annexes concerned Portuguese territories, and the special regime between Italy, San Marino, and the Vatican.[145]

Review Session

No change is reported.

2.7.2 Tariff Reduction

London Conference

The title of Art. 24 of the *London Draft* is *Reduction of Tariffs and Elimination of Preferences*, and it perfectly captures the quintessence of the negotiations on this score. The trade off (between the UK and the U.S. delegations) was between the ambit of (essentially, U.S.) MFN tariff reductions and the corresponding ambit of cuts in (essentially, UK) preferences. No sector-specific negotiations took place during the *London Conference*; such negotiations were held for the first time in 1947 in Geneva. Instead, the negotiators of the *London Draft* put together the institutional framework for international negotiations aiming at tariff reductions.

> North-South preferences, as we know them from modern GSP schemes, but rather, South-South preferences aiming at developing industries within regional blocks, see E/PC/T/C.6/W/25 at p. 14.

[143] See E/PC/T/W/179 of / June 1947.
[144] See The GATT Analytical Index, 3rd revision, The GATT: Geneva, 1970 at p. 3ff.
[145] See CRH at pp. 47–49.

Art. 24 contains two important elements:

(a) it imposes an obligation on all states to negotiate tariff reductions, if requested to do so;
(b) if this obligation has not been observed, injured states might be authorized (by the ITO) to withhold the extension of MFN rights on tariff reductions negotiated with third partners (*non adimpleti contractus*).

This is a remarkable provision, which was omitted from subsequent drafts, in that it conditions the enjoyment by a given state of increased market-access opportunities on the obligation to negotiate its own tariff reductions.[146] There is a caveat though: countries with low tariffs could justifiably refuse to negotiate because their pre-negotiation level was not a serious obstacle to international trade. What constituted a low tariff was nowhere defined.[147] This provision was later dropped. Both tariff-and preferences-reductions (eliminations) were considered to be concessions. The negotiators did not spend any time discussing the thorny issue of a common tariff nomenclature, since no negotiations took place during the *London Conference*. There is evidence, nevertheless, that the negotiators did have in mind the potential problems created by the absence of such a common framework:[148] the League of Nations had started some work that was to be completed later by the *Brussels Nomenclature*, prepared by the *Customs Cooperation Council* (CCC).[149]

New York Conference

This is Art. VIII of the *New York* GATT Draft. Negotiators essentially reproduced their agreement during the *London Conference*.[150] Still, some very noteworthy proposals were submitted: the UK delegation, for instance, proposed the addition of a paragraph that would call for negotiations any time an ITO Member

---

[146] In doc. E/PC/T/30 at p. 4, it is explained that it is only *unjustifiable* refusal to negotiate that will be punished.
[147] See E/PC/T/30 at p. 10.
[148] See E/PC/T/C.II/64 of November 22, 1946 at p. 6.
[149] When mentioning the problems created by the tendency of states to unilaterally subdivide concessions agreed in order to avoid the catch of MFN, Jackson (1969, p. 211ff.) pays tribute to the legislative genius of the framers of the 1904 Swiss-German Treaty reducing tariffs on "... large dapple mountain cattle reared at a spot of at least 300 meters above sea level and having at least one month grazing each year at a spot at least 800 meters above sea level."
[150] See E/PC/T/C.6/9 of January 23, 1947, /13 of January 24, 1947, and E/PC/T/C.6/W.4 of February 3, 1947. We note that, although *export taxes* did figure high on the U.S. wish list (Proposals, p. 3), they were considered to be a nontariff barrier and were not originally discussed under this provision, which concerned import tariffs only.

2.7 The Evolution of the GATT Provisions

changes its method of tariff valuation or its tariff classification so as to increase the duty payable.[151] This proposal did not make it to the final text.[152]

Geneva Conference

No change is reported with respect to the manner in which consolidation of tariffs would operate. The re-negotiation of consolidated duties became a separate provision (Art. XXVIII GATT). During this conference, as already reported above, the first round of multilateral negotiations took place.

Havana Conference

No change is reported. We note, however, an Argentine proposal to replace the term *substantial* reduction of tariffs by the term *progressive* reduction of tariffs, so as to ensure that countries could comply with their duties, as long as they agreed to *some* reduction. This proposal was rejected. The reaction to the Argentine proposal is evidence of the reigning spirit among national delegations to move forward quickly.[153]

Review Session

The re-negotiation of Art. XXVIII GATT (renegotiation of duties) revealed the many important differences within the group. The divergence of opinion led to imperfect drafting of these provisions.[154] The most important questions regarding the operation of this provision were debated during this negotiation: Should re-negotiation take place at any time, or within fixed periods only? Negotiators privileged the latter option. Should arbitration take place in case negotiations have failed to result in a mutually acceptable compensation? Negotiators did not manage to include a provision to this effect, and this is still very much a tantalizing issue in practice.[155] Should unilateral withdrawal of concessions occur even when no compensation has been agreed?[156] The negotiators opted for an affirmative response in order to increase the embedded flexibility in this provision. The outcome of the negotiations suggests that consensus could only

---

[151] See E/PC/T/C.6/W.15 of January 23, 1947.
[152] The WTO *Argentina – Footwear* dispute dealt with similar facts: Argentina changed its method of valuation (*ad valorem* – specific), and the Appellate Body eventually held that it was entitled to do so if the payable duty did not increase as a result. The report is problematic in that it is unclear how (at which point in time) equivalence between the two valuation methods is established.
[153] See CRH at p. 55.
[154] The current drafting has led to important disagreements across GATT/WTO Members in practice, as evidenced in the survey of practice by Hoda (2001).
[155] See W.9/19 of November 17, 1954.
[156] See SR.9/16 of November 22, 1954, and SR.9/17 of November 23, 1954.

emerge around extra flexibility for the renegotiation of concessions, and not on extra rigidity as some had wanted.[157] One should also note that Brazil submitted a proposal to the effect that transposing duties from specific to *ad valorem* could not be done unilaterally; in its view, in such cases the procedure laid down in Art. XXVIII GATT should be followed.[158] This proposal was not followed, and, as already stated supra, transpositions can now be performed unilaterally, provided that the bound level has not been superseded.[159]

2.7.3 Internal Taxes (Domestic Regulation)

London Conference

This is Art. 15 of the *London Draft*. The negotiations on internal taxes (and, more generally, domestic regulation) were inconclusive. The *London Draft* makes it clear that the final decision was to consider this item further at a later stage.[160] Nevertheless, some progress was made that proved to be crucial for the eventual agreement. First of all, there was general dissatisfaction with the term *like products* that had been retained in order to delineate the coverage of this provision. The dissatisfaction was twofold:

(a) on the one hand, it was felt that the term was obscure, and that it would be necessary for the ITO to try to clarify at a subsequent stage;[161]
(b) on the other, it was felt that, since the *Suggested Charter* contained references to *like products* only,[162] with no reference at all to competitive products, what is now known as directly competitive or substitutable products (DCS), something should be done to address cases where a domestic tax on imported coffee was higher than that imposed on domestic chicory.[163] In the words of the Dutch delegate, Mr. Van den Berg, the additional paragraph that was being negotiated during the *London Conference*, and that dealt with competitive products aimed "to guard against the more concealed types of discriminatory taxation."[164]

---

[157] See L/329 of February 24, 1955 at pp. 11ff.   [158] See W.9/118 of December 17, 1954.
[159] See AB, *Argentina – Footwear*. This ruling, nonetheless, has not contributed much to legal security since questions can legitimately be asked concerning the timing of the conversion, etc. One can only deplore that the Brazilian proposal was not ultimately followed.
[160] See E/PC/T/33 at p. 28.
[161] See E/PC/T/C.II/54 at p. 36. Recall our discussion of the same term supra, under heading 2.3.2.1, where we reflected the dissatisfaction of negotiators with the term *like products*, which also appears in the MFN discipline.
[162] See the *Suggested Charter*, op. cit., at p. 4.
[163] See E/PC/T/C.II/W.2 of October 29, 1946 at pp. 5ff.
[164] Id. The level of sophistication of the arguments made is remarkable. See, for example, an exchange between the Australian (Mr. Morton) and the U.S. (Mr. Johnson) delegates

2.7 The Evolution of the GATT Provisions

As the title of our heading shows, the negotiations initially focused on internal taxes, which were distinguished from customs tariffs in that they were decided unilaterally by every state and were applied to both domestic and foreign products. Eventually, the negotiators moved on to other areas of internal regulation of non-fiscal nature. The inconclusive negotiations on this latter issue notwithstanding, it is noteworthy that its ambit was heavily discussed. Still, the negotiations reflected a tendency to exclude specific transactions rather than provide a benchmark for inclusion. To this effect, we note that it was the UK delegation that initially proposed (what later became Art. IV GATT) the exclusion of films from the coverage of Art. 15 of the *London Draft*. In the words of the UK delegate (Mr. Rhydderch):

> he would prefer a note to the Article to say it did not apply to films. There were cultural, as well as commercial, considerations to be taken into account in the case of films.[165]

This is probably one of the first expressions in favor of a *cultural exception* in the postwar world trading system. Although the objective of a national-treatment-type provision was clear in the negotiators' minds,[166] no provision equivalent to the current Art. III.1 GATT was included in the *London Draft*. Recall that this provision sanctions any domestic regulation (of fiscal or nonfiscal character) that operates so as to afford protection. It was left for later to explicitly state that such should be the objective of this provision.

New York Conference

This is Art. II of the *New York* GATT Draft, and Art. 15 of the *New York* Draft ITO Charter.[167] Two days into the negotiations, the U.S. delegation submitted its first proposal concerning a re-draft of Art. 15 of the *London Draft*.[168] Negotiations

---

on the legality of some Australian mixing requirements and preferential tariff rates, see E/PC/T/C.II/W.2 at p. 7.

[165] See E/PC/T/C.II/E.14 of November 4, 1946 at p. 5. Incidentally, the UK position was supported by Czechoslovakia, France (later, an ardent supporter of the "cultural exception"), New Zealand, and Portugal).

[166] See, for example, the French proposal where, in application of the French doctrine of *abus de droit*, France requested the insertion of a paragraph to the effect that "The members undertake not to institute or maintain internal taxes on the products of other member-countries the object of which might be a disguised form of protection for national production." This is one of the first statements to the effect that the national-treatment obligation would operate as an anticircumvention provision: ITO Members should not circumvent through internal taxes their obligations with respect to tariff treatment of foreign products. Producer welfare would thus be legally protected through tariffs only.

[167] Recall the bifurcated approach adopted during the *New York Conference* that, essentially, resulted in the preparation of a GATT, as well as a preparation of an ITO Charter.

[168] See E/PC/T/C.6/6 of January 22, 1947.

were smooth.[169] It became gradually clear that the GATT would not contain any *detailed* obligations concerning domestic policy, other than the obligation not to discriminate.[170] There are various reasons that mandated this approach:

(a) more detailed provisions regarding (some) domestic instruments would be included in the ITO Charter, the advent of which would supersede the GATT. The GATT was conceived as some sort of regulatory minimum necessary to ensure that tariff concessions would not be circumvented. To this effect, an obligation not to discriminate was considered as adequate insurance policy against the danger of circumvention;
(b) at least in the United States, non-tariff barriers (NTBs) did not matter much since few were in place;[171]
(c) many NTBs were simply not known to negotiators since they were "hidden" behind high tariffs. It was, thus, quite rational to first address tariff barriers before moving to discuss, in a more elaborate manner, NTBs.[172]

The corresponding provision in the *London Draft* underwent some changes without altering its rationale or basic design (and expanded from two to five paragraphs).[173] Importantly, a chapeau was agreed denoting the objective function of this provision: halt to protectionism through domestic instruments (anti-circumvention). With respect to internal measures of non-fiscal nature, South Africa proposed the insertion of the terms "laws, regulations and requirements" that denote the coverage of this provision, and that now constitute the core of the discipline embedded in Art. III.4 GATT.[174] The terms *identical or similar products* were changed to *like products*.[175] India wanted a carve-out for taxation "strictly for the purposes of raising revenue," but this proposal was not accepted.[176] Czechoslovakia and Norway also backed the New Zealand and the United Kingdom's proposal to exempt cinematograph films from the obligation to accord national treatment.[177] The re-draft was not unanimously accepted. It was decided, however, to leave it to Cuba, Norway, and India to consider whether

---

[169] It is New Zealand only that objected to the redraft insisting for some sort of arrangement that would take care of its *film hire tax*, see E/PC/T/C.6/8 of January 23, 1947. The *film hire tax*, however, was a delayed customs duty levied at the point where the real value of the film had become apparent. The New Zealand delegate eventually conceded that this imposition could form the subject matter of tariff negotiations under Art. 24 of the *London Draft*. New Zealand was not, at the time, producing films, other than educational and newsreels, see E/PC/T/C.6/55/Rev. 1 at pp. 7–8.
[170] See E/PC/T/C.6/67 at p. 1.   [171] See Proposals, pp. 2ff.
[172] See, on this score, the excellent analysis of Baldwin (1970).
[173] See E/PC/T/C.6/55 at pp. 2ff.   [174] See E/PC/T/C.6/55 at p. 3.
[175] Id.   [176] See E/PC/T/C.6/W.19 of January 24, 1947.
[177] See E/PC/T/C.6/55 at p. 7.

2.7 The Evolution of the GATT Provisions

they would maintain their objections. Cuba wanted an exemption for protection of infant-industry purposes; India's desired carve-out regarded, as mentioned above, the possibility to tax discriminate in order to raise government revenue; Norway requested a carve-out in order to be in position to tax discriminate, if necessary, to maintain uniform prices for a given product in its domestic market.[178]

Geneva Conference

During the negotiations, it was made clear that there was no room for preferential internal taxes, such as those previously practiced in some parts of the world (New Zealand, United States).[179] Key terms such as *like products* continued to provoke a lot of discussion: Brazil mentioned the existence of a Committee (*Comisão de Similares*) that they had established to deal with determinations of like products precisely because the term was hard to define. It was felt that some similar action should be undertaken at the multilateral level as well, but it was left for the ITO:

> ... later on to establish a jurisprudence on the meaning of this term.[180]

Following a U.S. proposal to this effect, the obligation of national treatment was extended to cover not only *like*, but also *directly competitive or substitutable* (DCS) products,[181] the intent being to ensure that, in the absence of domestic production of like products, taxes could not be used to favor domestic DCS products.[182] China wanted to limit the national treatment-obligation to taxes (fiscal measures) only, but this attempt was thwarted by others.[183] The UK delegation continued to think of films not only as economic, but as cultural goods as well. The continued support of Chile, Czechoslovakia, New Zealand, and now India,[184] Norway, and South Africa, left only the U.S. delegation opposing the UK view. The United States saw no reason to treat films differently from other goods; in the view of its delegates, the preference of the audience should determine the trade in films.[185] It was clear, nonetheless, that the U.S. delegation was fighting a losing battle on this issue. Eventually, a separate provision applicable only to films and justifying an exception to national treatment would be agreed to in

---

[178] See E/PC/T/C.6/55/Rev. 1 at pp. 3ff.
[179] See E/PS/T/W/179 at p. 3.
[180] See E/PC/T/A/PV/40(1) at p. 14.
[181] See E/PC/T/W7150 at p. 5.
[182] See E/PC/T/174 at p. 6. This is more or less what subsequent case law has repeatedly confirmed.
[183] See E/PC/T/W/181 at p. 3. In China's view, hence, there should be no national-treatment obligation with respect to regulatory (nonfiscal) domestic instruments.
[184] Before the expansion of Bollywood.
[185] See E/PC/T/W/181 pp. 7–8.

subsequent negotiations (the current Art. IV GATT). The continued negotiations on *mixing requirements* might seem a bit unwarranted from today's perspective. The proliferation of such schemes during the time the GATT was being negotiated very much explains why this instrument ultimately earned specific mention in a provision that only mentioned a few domestic instruments (the others being subsidies and government procurement). The U.S. delegation tabled a proposal to make it clear that the rationale for prohibiting the use of mixing requirements was to ensure that no protection would be afforded to domestic production through this instrument.[186]

Havana Conference

Negotiators aimed to make it even clearer than before, that the rationale behind this provision was that domestic taxes and laws should not operate so as to afford protection to domestic production (and thus, circumvent, tariff concessions agreed to). The negotiators nonetheless seemed quite conscious that the term *protection* is not that easy to assess. As a result, the negotiating history of this provision, during the *Havana Conference*, reveals some interesting discussions where negotiators advance specific examples to demonstrate their understanding of the term. Although the legal relevance of such examples specifically mentioned in the negotiating documents is limited, some of them bear mention: for example, the final text, which provided for the outright elimination of taxes protecting DCS products in cases in which there was no substantial production of the domestic like product;[187] it was stated, nevertheless, that, an internal law that might help a domestic product (say, butter), but which hits equally imported and domestic oleomargarine (a DCS product), does not violate the national-treatment provision, if domestic production of oleomargarine is substantial.[188] To what extent such constructions are still good law is at least debatable, since it seems that modern constructions of Art. III GATT would outlaw such practices as well.

Review Session

No change is reported.

---

[186] See E/PC/T/W/181 at pp. 10ff.   [187] See CRH at p. 61.
[188] See CRH at pp. 61–67. On pp. 62–63 in response to a question by Chile, Lebanon, and Syria, the Sub-committee responded that impositions (a) whose characterization under domestic laws is not the final word, (b) are collected at the time of and as a condition to entry of goods, and (c) that apply exclusively to imported goods are import duties and not internal taxes. P. 64 The term *internal* was used to make it clear that this provision was not covering international shipping.

2.7 The Evolution of the GATT Provisions

2.7.4 Transit

London Conference

The disciplines on transit were supposed to be reflected in Art. 16 of the *London Draft*. The negotiations on this issue were inconclusive, and it was decided that the issue be re-negotiated at a later stage.[189] Still, some progress was made. For one thing, negotiators agreed that air traffic should be exempted from the eventual disciplines because it was being dealt with by the *Provisional International Civil Air Organization*. On the other hand, it was generally felt that transit was adequately covered by the *Barcelona Convention* of April 20, 1921, and that the latter's disciplines should be kept in mind when drafting the GATT disciplines on transit.[190]

New York Conference

This is Art. III of the *New York* GATT Draft, and Art. 16 of the *New York* Draft ITO Charter. There was no departure from the *London Draft*, and it was agreed that the Secretariat would draft a text[191] that would reflect the discussions held (where the U.S. delegation had a leading role).[192] The proposed text corresponds more or less to current Art. V GATT, and largely reproduces the U.S. proposal to this effect.[193]

Geneva Conference

No change is reported.

Havana Conference

No change is reported.

Review Session

No change is reported.

---

[189] See E/PC/T/33 at p. 28.
[190] See E/PC/T/C.II/54/Rev. 1 of November 28, 1946 at pp. 7ff.
[191] See E/PC/T/C.6/7 of January 22, 1947. The Secretariat, that is, the sum of international officials that had been helping out the negotiators since the *London Conference*, is quite active during the *New York Conference* and produced texts on various provisions of the *London Draft*, see, for example, E/PC/T/C.6/W.17 of January 23, 1947, which reflects the Secretariat draft on balance of payments, exchange arrangements, etc., and E/PC/T/C.6/65 of February 10, 1947, which reflects comments by the Secretariat on various provisions.
[192] See E/PC/T/C.6/16 of January 27, 1947.   [193] See E/PC/T/C.6/55 at pp. 8ff.

2.7.5 Antidumping and Countervailing Duties

London Conference

This was Art. 17 of the *London Draft*. Negotiators made substantial progress on this issue but failed to agree on a proposal. As a result, it was decided that Art. 17 of the *London Draft* dealing with antidumping (AD) and countervailing (CVD) duties would be renegotiated at a subsequent stage.[194] Negotiators devoted their time to discussing *responses* to dumping, rather than regulating dumping itself. Dumping does not figure under the list of restrictive business practices that ITO Members should try to eliminate.[195] Recall that the *London Draft* regulates both subsidies and CVDs. At the *London Conference*, there was no statement that dumping constitutes an unfair practice and should, therefore, be condemned. In fact, neither the *London Draft*, nor the U.S. *Suggested Charter* contained a reference to this effect.[196] Instead, dumping came to be recognized as an unfair practice at a later stage. The general goal of the London negotiators was to introduce language that would reduce, if not eliminate altogether, the potential for abuses when imposing AD/CVD duties. While recognizing that there were four types of dumping (price, service, exchange, and social), the U.S. delegate (Johnson) acknowledged that the U.S.-backed provision on antidumping was concerned with price dumping only.[197] The Australian delegate (Morton) expressed his antithesis to the proposal that AD duties could be lawfully imposed "such as to prevent the establishment of a domestic industry." In his view, this provision would provide countries with the incentive to resort to AD measures "when actually there was little likelihood that a domestic industry would be established."[198] In similar vein, the Dutch delegate (Van den Berg) emphasized the intentional use of the term *serious injury*: in his view, serious is a higher evidentiary standard than "normal" injury: in turn, this should mean that AD duties could only be imposed in case serious injury resulted from dumping.[199] More dramatically, the French delegate (Roux) disagreed with the U.S. delegate,

---

[194] See E/PC//T/33 at p. 28.

[195] See E/PC/T/33 at p. 34 (Art. 39.3 of the *London Draft*). The argument is often voiced that the GATT, being a government-to-government contract, cannot regulate dumping, a purely private activity. The ITO did impose on its Members the obligation to eliminate certain RBP (Art. 39.3 of the *London Draft*). It stopped short, nevertheless, from adding dumping to the list of RBP that should be eliminated.

[196] See Preliminary Draft Charter for the International Trade Organizations of the United Nations, Department of State, December 1946, Publication 2728, Commercial Policy Series 98 at p. 8 (Art. 17).

[197] See E/PC/T/C.II/48 of November 11, 1946 at pp. 1ff.

[198] Id. at p. 5. [199] Id. at p. 10.

2.7 The Evolution of the GATT Provisions

and requested that a paragraph be added that would make it clear that the country imposing AD/CVD duties should carry the burden of proof and justify its measures.[200]

New York Conference

This is Art. IV of the *New York* GATT Draft, and Art. 17 of the *New York* Draft ITO Charter. Negotiators repeated more or less the proposals made during the *London Conference*.[201] Some interesting proposals were advanced, such as Canada's proposal that language be added to the nonagreed text of the *London Draft* that would make it clear that only injury to the "domestic industry supplying a reasonable percentage of the normal domestic consumption of the commodity in question" would count as injury in the sense of this provision. Ultimately, this was rejected.[202] The focus of negotiators continued to be on disciplining antidumping, and consequently dumping was still not condemned.[203]

Geneva Conference

There was no change from the text agreed in New York. Being dissatisfied with the current provision, which simply regulated the conditions under which AD duties could be legally imposed, Cuba insisted on the inclusion of a paragraph condemning dumping. The Cuban request was not adopted.[204]

Havana Conference

Cuba finally got its wish to insert a paragraph condemning injurious dumping. This paragraph now figures prominently in the current Art. VI GATT. It has not been carried over in the WTO Agreement on Antidumping, but continues to be legally relevant, since the WTO Appellate Body has consistently held that the two documents (Art. VI GATT, WTO Agreement on Antidumping) must be read together.[205]

---

[200] Id. at p. 16.

[201] There was, nevertheless, a proposal to limit AD only in cases where the dumping margin exceeded a five percent threshold. This was an Australian proposal, which ultimately, at the request of the U.S. delegation and others supporting it, was not retained, see E/PC/T/C.6/18 at p. 3.

[202] This proposal was not met with enthusiasm, and in today's world the only safeguard against microdefinitions of the domestic industry is the term *like product*; case law has traditionally interpreted this term narrowly and it, thus, suggests that the danger that Canada anticipated when making its proposal is very much present, see E/PC/T/C.6/W.20 of January 27, 1947, at p. 2.

[203] See E/PC/T/C.6/55 at pp. 16ff.   [204] See E/PC/T/103 at pp. 7ff.

[205] See, on this score, Mavroidis (2007) pp. 338ff.

Review Session

The discussions on antidumping did not lead to any meaningful change. New Zealand suggested that a discipline on dumping be inserted, which was rejected by the other trading partners.[206]

2.7.6 Tariff Valuation

London Conference

Unsurprisingly, it is the most sophisticated customs administrations that took the lead on this score, and the final text corresponds to a U.S. proposal with input from the UK delegation.[207] It was made clear early on that the purpose of this provision should be to ensure that there is no under-invoicing, and that customs authorities will follow agreed procedures that will enable them to apply the proper customs duty on the transaction at hand. The negotiations produced a draft that reflects the spirit of the current GATT provision, but not necessarily the actual wording. This happened through subsequent streamlining of the language used.

New York Conference

This is Art. V of the *New York* GATT Draft, and Art. 18 of the *New York Draft ITO Charter*. The discussions do not reveal any substantial change from the line followed during the *London Conference*.[208] Some streamlining did occur: the U.S. delegation proposed that the *actual value* of a merchandise import becomes the benchmark for tariff-valuation purposes (what is now § 2(a) of Art VII GATT).[209] For the rest, the final text resembles the current text,[210] following a comprehensive last-minute U.S. proposal to this effect with input from the UK delegation.[211]

Geneva Conference

No substantive change is reported.

Havana Conference

There was no substantive change compared to the *Geneva Draft*.[212]

---

[206] See Jackson (1969) pp. 408ff.
[207] See E/PC/T/C.II/50 of November 15, 1946.
[208] See E/PC/T/C.6/W.20 at p. 3.
[209] See E/PC/T/C.6/22 of January 30, 1947 at p. 2.
[210] See E/PC/T/C.6/55 at pp. 22ff.
[211] See E/PC/T/C.6/W.76 of February 13, 1947.
[212] See CRH at p. 75.

2.7 The Evolution of the GATT Provisions

Review Session

Nothing much changed. It is still noteworthy that negotiators invited the head of CCC to give an opinion on this matter, and explain the rationale behind the cases where actual value should and should not be followed.[213]

2.7.7 Customs Formalities

London Conference

This was Art. 13 first, and 19, later, of the *London Draft*. Under this heading, negotiators discussed items that correspond to today's ODC (other duties and charges) and *fees and formalities* coming under the ambit of today's Art. VIII GATT. Both ODC and fees and formalities were distinguished from ordinary customs duties (OCD), which were the subject matter of Art. 24 of the *London Draft*, as we saw above.

The negotiators agreed that such duties and charges should not be used as indirect protection for domestic products.[214] Thus, this provision was intended to operate as an anti-circumvention provision, ensuring that Art. 24 *London Draft* would not be undermined through the imposition of other (than ordinary customs duties) duties and charges. The negotiators further believed that some harmonization (standardization) of national practices was probably necessary in order to reduce this risk.[215] This provision echoes the *Geneva Convention* of November 3, 1923. In fact, France originally, and with the support of Belgium, Luxembourg, Czechoslovakia, Netherlands, and the United Kingdom later, held the view that this provision would be useless if all members (of the ITO) adhered to the *Geneva Convention* of November 3, 1923.[216] The *World Economic Conference* of 1927 had made similar recommendations, and a number of countries following France wanted to ensure consistency across its recommendations and the eventual ITO provision.[217] Nevertheless, the negotiators could not agree on the modalities. The extent of the obligation imposed on signatories was an area of concern: on the one hand the Dutch and Belgian (Luxembourg) delegates wanted to impose a strict deadline by which all members would have to implement the obligation; on the other, the delegates of Australia and New Zealand were in favor of a more pragmatic solution, whereby members would have to review

---

[213] See W.9/54 of December 1, 1954. Similar attitude in other areas. WP III, for example, invited the FAO delegate to explain its institution's programme on disposal of surpluses, see W.9/71 of December 6, 1954.

[214] See E/PC/T/C.II/50 of November 15, 1946 at p. 1; E/PC/T/C.II/4 at p. 20; E/PC/T/C.II/64 at p. 5.

[215] See E/PC/T/C.II/54 at pp. 16ff.   [216] See E/PC/T/C.II/54 at p. 21.

[217] See E/PC/T/C.II/12 at p. 4.

their customs procedure only upon request.[218] Another area of disagreement was the availability of penalties depending on the gravity of the act (negligence, accidental error).[219] At the end, although negotiators managed to agree on an indicative list of charges coming under the purview of this provision,[220] they felt that their disagreements were serious enough to justify that their draft be considered further at a later stage.[221]

New York Conference

This is Art. VI of the *New York* GATT Draft, and Art. 19 of the *New York* Draft ITO Charter. Negotiators did not substantially depart from their positions already expressed during the *London Conference*.[222] The new U.S. proposal was met with objections by many delegations, especially regarding the obligation to review operation of laws. The U.S. delegation had submitted a similar proposal during the *London Conference* that had not been unanimously accepted. During the *New York Conference*, the same dividing lines were reproduced, with those objecting essentially requesting some dilution of the obligation to review operation of domestic laws relating to customs formalities.[223]

Geneva Conference

No substantive change is reported.

Havana Conference

The first paragraph was re-drafted because the *Geneva Draft* was unclear as to the scope of this provision. Negotiators made it clear that they wished to include all payments of any character required by a member in connection with importation or exportation.[224]

Review Session

The UK proposal on Art. VIII GATT was largely followed by the negotiators, and the opening paragraph (which denotes the spirit of this provision) follows almost verbatim the UK proposal to this effect.[225]

---

[218] See E/PC/T/C.II/50 at p. 1.
[219] See E/PC/T/C.II/54 at p. 22.
[220] See E/PC/T/C.II/54 at p. 23. The list comprises items such as consular fees, licensing, exchange regulations, statistical evidence, inspection, quarantine sanitation, and fumigation (plant, animal, and human).
[221] See E/PC/T/33 at p. 28.
[222] See E/PC/T/C.6/W.20 at p. 3.
[223] See E/PC/T/C.6/55 at pp. 28ff.
[224] See CRH at p. 76.
[225] See W.9/69 of December 3, 1954.

2.7.8 Marks of Origin

London Conference

This is yet another provision on which no agreement could be reached (Art. 20 of the *London Draft*).[226] Negotiators aimed to strike a balance between consumer protection and burdens on commercial transactions. It was felt that the former should be protected without unduly burdening the latter. So they were, in essence, searching for a necessity type of discipline.[227] Marks of origin had been previously regulated in various international agreements, such as the *Madrid Convention* of April 14, 1891, the *Washington Arrangement* of June 2, 1911, the *Hague Arrangement* of November 6, 1925, as well as the *Union Agreement of Paris/Brussels* of December 14, 1900. Once again, negotiators requested that the ITO provisions be compatible with the provisions of the afore-mentioned agreements.[228] France, which played a prominent role in the discussion of this provision, wanted to bring under the heading *Marks of origin* a discussion on marks of *geographical or regional origin* as well.[229] The majority of delegates, however, thought that this should not be an issue of concern for the ITO Charter, and that such issues were more appropriately dealt with in bilateral consultations, or, at most, that a multilateral conference should be organized to specifically discuss this matter.[230] The current Article 23 of the TRIPs agreement addresses this issue.

New York Conference

This is Art. 20 of the *New York* Draft ITO Charter, and it was not included in the *New York* GATT Draft. The various countries essentially reproduced their negotiating positions already expressed during the *London Conference*;[231] France insisted on the protection for geographical or regional origin (wines, etc.), referring to the obligations already imposed on signatories of the *Madrid Convention* of 1891 on the protection of such names who would become ITO Members.[232] On the other hand, a joint U.S./UK proposal, aiming at eliminating

---

[226] See E/PC/T/33 at p. 28.
[227] See E/PC/T/C.II/W.30, E/PC/T/C.II/48 at pp. 21 ff., and E/PC/T/C.II/54 at pp. 23ff.
[228] See, for example, the proposals of the French delegation at E/PC/T/C.II/12 of October 26, 1946 at p. 5.
[229] See E/PC/T/C.II/12 at p. 6.   [230] See E/PC/T/C.II/50 at pp. 13ff.
[231] See E/PC/T/C.6/W.20 at p. 4. Much is the U.S. proposal, see E/PC/T/C.6/22 at pp. 6ff.
[232] See E/PC/T/C.6/30 of January 31, 1947 at p. 4. France, in this document, proposed a national-treatment type of obligation, like those recorded in the *Madrid Convention*, whereby Spain and Portugal would be precluded from selling "Bordeaux" wines, whereas France would be precluded from offering for sale "Madeira" wines.

compulsory marks of origin, was tabled.[233] It was eventually decided to defer this issue to the ITO.[234]

Geneva Conference
The *Geneva Draft* essentially reproduced the partial agreement reached in New York.

Havana Conference
No substantive change compared to the *Geneva Draft* is recorded.[235]

Review Session
No change is reported.

2.7.9 Publication and Administration of Trade Regulations

London Conference
This was Art. 21 of the *London Draft*. Absence of agreement led the negotiators to a decision to re-negotiate this item at a later stage.[236]

New York Conference
This is Art. VII of the *New York* GATT Draft, and Art. 21 of the *New York* Draft ITO Charter. The U.S. delegation took the initiative on this issue as well, tabling a comprehensive proposal.[237] The various negotiating documents reveal the tendency of negotiators to stick to their original positions.[238] There was a proposal to absorb certain existing international agencies such as the *Brussels Tariff Bureau*; this proposal did not materialize in anything concrete, but is yet another demonstration of the tendency of negotiators to view the creation of the GATT as part and parcel of their wider international commitments.[239] The agreement was partial, and the final product closely resembles the current Art. X GATT.

Geneva Conference
No change is recorded.

---

[233] See E/PC/T/C.6/55 at pp. 33ff.
[234] See E/PC/T/C.6/55 at p. 37. This decision probably explains the *provisional* (as we will see) exclusion of this provision from the GATT Draft.
[235] See CRH at pp. 78–79.   [236] See E/PC/T/33 at p. 28.
[237] See E/PC/T/C.6/W.18 of January 24, 1947.
[238] See E/PC/T/C.6/W.20 at pp. 4–5; see also E/PC/T/C.6/55 at pp. 38ff.
[239] See E/PC/T/C.6/55 at p. 39.

2.7 The Evolution of the GATT Provisions

Havana Conference
Following a proposal by Uruguay, it was decided that suitable facilities should be provided for traders to consult with governmental authorities. Following a U.S. proposal to this effect, the term *published* was changed to *made public*.[240]

Review Session
No change is reported.

2.7.10 Quantitative Restrictions

London Conference
Art. 25 of the *London Draft* states that all imports and export quotas (that is, excluding domestic quotas) are, in principle, prohibited; the words *in principle* are critical. A number of transactions mentioned in the same provision are excluded from the coverage of the prohibition: measures dealing with postwar shortages; shortages/surpluses of foodstuffs and other farm goods; international commodity agreements, etc. Moreover, under the influence of the UK delegation, additional exceptions to the prohibition were agreed to, for reasons having to do with the safeguarding of balance of payments or the exchange rate (and became eventually, separate provisions of the *London Draft*). As a result, the prohibition agreed to was really only *in principle*. Assuming a quantitative restriction had been lawfully imposed, it should be administered in a nondiscriminatory manner (Art. 27 of the *London Draft*), unless for reasons stated in Art. 28 of the *London Draft*. These two provisions eventually became Arts. XIII and XIV, respectively, of the current GATT text.

New York Conference
Various provisions concern this item: Art. IX of the *New York* GATT Draft (Art. 25 of the *New York* Draft ITO Charter) makes it clear that import and export quotas are illegal; the non-discriminatory administration of exceptionally permitted quotas, what eventually became a separate provision in the final GATT text (Art. XIII), is regulated in Art. XI of the *New York* Draft (Art. 27 of the *New York* Draft ITO Charter); finally, the exceptions to nondiscriminatory administration of quotas are dealt with in Art. XII of the *New York* Draft (Art. 28 of the *New York* Draft ITO Charter). Negotiations during the *New York Conference* did not produce any major change as to the basic obligation already agreed during the *London Conference*.[241] Disagreements concerned the extent of the carve-out

---

[240] See CRH at p. 79.
[241] See E/PC/T/C.6/14 of January 24, 1947, and E/PC/T/C.6/W.4 at pp. 3ff.

from the basic obligation to abolish quotas: whereas Norway insisted that only farm products should be covered, Chile continued to press in the opposing direction requesting that the carve-out should not be limited to farm and fisheries products only.[242] Neither were there major changes with respect to the obligation to administer (legal) quotas in a non-discriminatory manner.[243] The discussion of this particular provision offers a very appropriate example of the negotiating techniques followed during the *New York Conference*: negotiators established a small *ad hoc* group (made up of delegates from Cuba, France, the United Kingdom, and the United States), which prepared a partial re-draft of this provision that now constitutes the cornerstone of the current obligation included in Art. XIII GATT.[244] There were no major changes with respect to the list of exceptions from the obligation to administer legal quotas in a non-discriminatory manner either.[245] It is noteworthy that India proposed an amendment that eventually became Section C of the current Art. XVIII GATT: in its view, Members should be free to choose any measure they thought was necessary for their development and, to that effect, they should not be constrained by the prohibition of import and export quantitative restrictions. This is probably the first official pronouncement of the *infant-industry* exception to the (agreed) obligation not to impose import and export quotas.[246]

Geneva Conference

The negotiations yielded no changes in the text as agreed in New York. There is no change in the text concerning the administration of QRs either.[247] Looking into the various negotiating documents, it is obvious that *domestic quotas* were not meant to be covered by the discipline on QRs: the requirement that existing internal quantitative regulations not expressly approved by the ITO should be

---

[242] See E/PC/T/C.6/W/43 at p. 13. In the same document, we witness yet another very sensible proposal (this time by Belgium-Luxembourg), which, unfortunately, did not make it to the final text: "Restrictions imposed under this exception should be strictly limited to the period during which the aforementioned circumstances occur, and should not be imposed on seasonal commodities at a time when like domestic products are not available." Had it been adopted, a serious proxy to detect protectionist behavior would have been added to the legislative arsenal.

[243] See E/PC/T/C.6/W.31 of January 28, 1947, E/PC/T/C.6/26 of January 30, 1947, and E/PC/T/C.6/61 of February 10, 1947.

[244] See E/PC/T/C.6/W.55 of February 6, 1947, and E/PC/T/C.6/W.81 at pp. 5ff.

[245] See E/PC/T/C.6/W.69 of February 10, 1947, and E/PC/T/C.6/W.81 at pp. 8ff.

[246] See E/PC/T/C.6/17 at p. 2. For the rest, nothing much changed during the negotiations, except for the occasional expression of a topical (sectoral) interest, such as Canada's preoccupation with electricity, and its unwillingness to treat it as a "good" and thus subject it to the disciplines on import and export quotas, see E/PC/T/C.6/17 at p. 3.

[247] See E/PC/T/141 of August 1, 1947.

2.7 The Evolution of the GATT Provisions

terminated was removed from the text.[248] Australia proposed the carve-out (from abolition of QRs) for temporary restrictions applied to prevent critical shortages of foodstuffs.[249] This proposal eventually became the current Art. XI.2(a) GATT. Cuba expressed its support for inclusion of a carve-out in favor of promoting the domestic infant industry, a proposal originally tabled by India.[250]

Havana Conference

The provision remained as it had been agreed during the *Geneva Conference*.[251]

Review Session

The current Art. XII.4 GATT was the outcome of these negotiations. The current Art. XVIII GATT was redrafted, during the same conference, with major input by various developing countries.[252] The negotiators used the UK and U.S. proposals as basis for discussion.[253] India carried the flag for developing countries by insisting that a distinction should be even more clearly drawn between ordinary QRs on the one hand, and QRs aimed for economic development on the other (leading to the current Art. XVIIIc GATT).[254] India tabled a series of proposals on this score,[255] and, ultimately, its proposals were to some extent echoed in the current drafting of Art. XVIII.c GATT.[256] Pakistan should be credited with the formulation of two of the current GATT provisions: first, Art. XVIII.5 GATT, which requires that consultations be held every time a country's exports of primary commodities have seriously declined; and, second, with what is now Art. XX(h) of the GATT, that is restrictive measures are justifiable because they purport to observe intergovernmental commodity agreements.[257]

2.7.11 Balance of Payments

London Conference

This is Art. 26 of the *London Draft*. In today's world, the balance-of-payments exception is practically a nonissue: countries experiencing such problems will rather devaluate than impose a quantitative restriction. In the 1940s, however, the world was one of exchange rates with *fixed parities*, and the devaluation option was subject to important restrictions. Following UK proposals to this

---

[248] See E/PC/T/174 at p. 8.
[249] See E/PC/T/W/223 at p. 3.
[250] See E/PC/T/A/PV/40(1) at p. 18.
[251] See CRH at pp. 86–87.
[252] See L/332 of February 25, 1955.
[253] See W.9/106 of December 15, 1954.
[254] See SR.9/15 of November 22, 1954 at pp. 6ff.
[255] See W.9/212 of February 21, 1955.
[256] See SR.9/40 of March 9, 1955.
[257] See L/327 of February 22, 1955 at p. 34.

effect, Art. 26 of the *London Draft* provided for the possibility to lawfully impose import restrictions in order to safeguard the balance of payments.[258]

New York Conference

This is Art. X of the *New York* GATT Draft, and Art. 26 of the *New York* Draft ITO Charter. Once again it was the U.S. delegation that took the lead and proposed the first draft which, for all practical purposes, reproduced the agreement already reached during the *London Conference*.[259] Negotiations were smooth and an agreement on this issue was reached.[260]

Geneva Conference

The UK delegation had to vigorously defend the need to keep the BoP provision in place against a late proposal by Belgium to delete it altogether.[261]

Havana Conference

Except for a change in the title, no change was made.[262]

Review Session

This was one of the provisions that was heavily re-negotiated. With respect to BoP, it became immediately obvious that the positions represented were diametrically opposed: some wanted more stringent rules (mainly developed nations), whereas others (mainly developing countries) favored additional flexibility.[263] The U.S. proposal aimed to bridge the gap by insisting on the necessity to acquire prior approval for any restriction based on BoP grounds, whenever the petitioner was a developed nation; conversely, it was prepared to accept flexibility when developing countries were acting as petitioners.[264] The U.S. insistence on some sort of multilateral prior clearing for BoP measures was ultimately defeated.[265] Yet the U.S. position found some, probably unexpected, allies: South Africa opposed the extension of unauthorized BoP restrictions, because it had

---

[258] Note that France wanted to insert a provision that would make it explicit that the burden of proof is on the country imposing restrictions that would be required to demonstrate its balance-of-payments problems, see E/PC/T/C.II/12 at p. 3. Modern case law has anyway moved into this direction, see *India – Quantitative Restrictions*.

[259] See E/PC/T/C.6/W.11 of January 22, 1947.

[260] See E/PC/T/C.6/15 of January 27, 1947, E/PC/T/C.6/W.43 at pp. 6ff., and E/PC/T/C.6/W.81 of February 19, 1947 at pp. 1ff.

[261] See E/PC/T/A/PV/41 at p. 15.   [262] See CRH at p. 95.

[263] See W.9/18 of November 17, 1954.

[264] See SR.9/14 of November 17, 1954 at pp. 4ff.

[265] See W.9/73 of December 6, 1954, and also L/332, and L/332 Rev. 1.

2.7 The Evolution of the GATT Provisions

important trade links with countries that, in its view, would be availing themselves of this possibility too frequently; thus, South Africa was particularly against the envisaged possibility to extend the coverage of § 17, which would allow members to introduce measures inconsistent with the General Agreement.[266] The UK delegation tabled a proposal that would make prior authorization a necessity only when a restriction would exceed one year.[267] This was an honorable effort to bridge the gap between those who insisted on some prior authorization, and those who did not see any merit in such a proposal. It became obvious to developed nations that consensus could emerge in favor of expanding and widening consultations, but not in favor of expanding the prior-authorization rule.[268] There was not much sympathy for proposals aiming to introduce fixed time limits within which BoP measures should operate.[269] Thus, the more lenient (toward petitioners) expression (consultations) won the argument at the end of the day.[270]

2.7.12 Exchange Restrictions

London Conference

Art. 29 of the *London Draft* provided that quantitative restrictions can also be imposed for reasons having to do with the exchange rate of national currencies. For matters relating to balance of payments or exchange arrangements, a procedure of cooperation between the ITO and the IMF was established under the same provision. To avoid complications, ITO Members that were not IMF members were requested to join the latter, or make exchange arrangements with it in case they decided to leave it.

New York Conference

This is Art. XIII of the *New York* GATT Draft, and Art. 29 of the *New York* Draft ITO Charter. It is a quasi verbatim reproduction of the text agreed during the *London Conference*.[271]

Geneva Conference

The discussions centered around the degree of deference to the IMF: on the one hand, the U.S. delegation pushed for the IMF to have the final word on

---

[266] See W.9/175 of February 4, 1955, and W.9/184 of February 8, 1955.
[267] See W.9/22 of November 19, 1954. [268] See W.9/208 of February 18, 1955.
[269] See W.9/174 of February 3, 1955. [270] See W.9/74 of December 6, 1954.
[271] See E/PC/T/C.6/24 of January 30, 1947, E/PC/T/C.6/W.69 at pp. 3ff., and E/PC/T/C.6/W.81 at pp. 10ff.

exchange restrictions, and thus relieve the GATT of the necessity to build up a separate staff of technical experts duplicating the work of Fund experts;[272] on the other, New Zealand did not wish this to be the case.[273] The reason why the U.S. delegation insisted on this point had to do with the fact that its opinion carried more weight in the IMF because of the *weighted voting*, that is the decision-making procedure that the IMF followed: whereas in the GATT, every contracting party would have one vote; countries had a number of votes that more or less corresponded to their economic power in the IMF. Representatives of the IMF who participated in the conference were implicated in the drafting of this provision. The UK compromise allowed the ITO to define what financial matter is (the domain of this provision), but to accept the IMF evaluation on issues such as what is decline in monetary reserves, and what constitutes a low level of monetary reserves.[274]

Havana Conference

No change is reported, although it is interesting to note a French/U.S. compromise, according to which the former would support the U.S. point of view (finality of Fund determination in this matter), and the latter would support France on a host of other issues.[275] The final compromise, as now reflected in the GATT, calls for substantial deference to the IMF for matters coming under its purview. It is for a WTO panel to establish at last resort, however, whether a violation of Art. XV GATT exists.

Review Session

No change is reported.

2.7.13 Subsidies

London Conference

Art. 30 of the *London Draft* reflects the first multilateral regulation of subsidies. A bifurcated approach was privileged, whereby:[276]

(a) export subsidies are, in principle, prohibited. There are some exceptions provided for in this provision, such as price-stabilization schemes;[277]

---

[272] See E/PC/T/W/233 at p. 34.
[273] See E/PC/T/A/PV/41 at p. 65.
[274] See E/PC/T/A/PV/41 at pp. 66ff.
[275] National Archives, NARS 927302, January 8, 1948.
[276] This provision largely reproduces Art. 25 of the U.S. *Suggested Charter*.
[277] This provision was diluted in subsequent GATT drafts, as we will see infra. It should be noted, nevertheless, that the obligation to abolish export subsidies would not kick in immediately but within three years from the entry into force of the ITO.

2.7 The Evolution of the GATT Provisions

(b) all *other* subsidies (that is, domestic subsidies) must be notified and, assuming they cause serious prejudice to the interests of another country, the subsidizing state would be requested to enter into consultations with such affected country (-ies). This provision explicitly deals with tax exemptions: with remarkable clarity (which, alas, we have been missing in subsequent drafts), it provides that tax exemptions on goods not consumed in the domestic market should not be construed as contravening the letter and the spirit of Art. 30 of the *London Draft*.

The bifurcation was deemed necessary "in view of the fact that export subsidies are recognized as being more likely to distort trade than so-called 'domestic' subsidies."[278] This provision should be read in conjunction with Art. 17 of the *London Draft*, which regulates unilateral responses to subsidization.

New York Conference

This is Art. XIV of the *New York* GATT Draft, and Art. 30 of the *New York* Draft ITO Charter. The U.S. delegation provided, in this instance yet again, the first text that reproduced, with some cosmetic changes, the text already agreed during the *London Conference*.[279] This text found widespread support[280] and retained the distinction between domestic and export subsidies (the former tolerated, the latter prohibited), as agreed in the *London Conference*.[281] Then, during the discussion within the *Sub-committee on Tariff Negotiations*, a document was circulated that did not include any disciplines on export subsidies; it merely reproduced the discipline on domestic subsidies, as agreed during the *London Conference*. Note that, with respect to export subsidies, there was no agreed obligation to abolish them right away; rather, the agreed obligation was to abolish them within three years from the advent of the ITO. A majority of countries felt that the discipline on export subsidies should be part of the ITO Charter, but

---

[278] See E/PC/T/33 at p. 16. The bifurcation was a Canadian proposal. The U.S. delegation did not want to go any further than a discipline that would request trading nations to ensure that they do not result with an unreasonable share of world trade, irrespective of whether they use domestic and export subsidies. To some extent, the disciplining of subsidies provoked the U.S. decision to seek a waiver for its farm subsidies, see Brown (1950, pp. 118ff.).

[279] See E/PC/T/C.6/W.21 of January 27, 1947. New Zealand continued to insist that price-stabilization schemes that sometimes resulted in export prices higher, and sometimes lower, than domestic prices should not be considered subsidies in the sense of the Agreement. Its proposal was ultimately not retained, see E/PC/T/C.6/W.23 of January 27, 1947.

[280] See E/PC/T/C.6/W/21 and 23, and E/PC/T/C.6/23. Recall that the United States was not a wholehearted partisan of the bifurcated approach. In Brown's (1950, p. 119) account, they accepted the idea until the multilateral effort was given "fair trial."

[281] See E/PC/T/C.6/W.69 at pp. 5ff., and E/PC/T/C.6/W.81 at pp. 11ff.

not the GATT. Consequently, the provision on export subsidies was included in Art. 30 of the *New York* Draft ITO Charter, but not in Art. XIV of the *New York* Draft GATT. Only the delegates from Brazil and New Zealand reserved their position on this score.[282]

Geneva Conference

The *Geneva Draft* kept the bifurcation between the GATT Draft, which contained no mention of a discipline on export subsidies, and the ITO Draft, which explicitly prohibited the use of export subsidies.[283] No other change is reported.

Havana Conference

No change of substance is recorded.[284]

Review Session

The preparatory work shows that discussions centered around the link between concessions and their erosion through subsidies.[285] The divide between the positions advocated by developed and developing nations was not as apparent in this group as it was in other groups: delegates of developed nations favored a strengthening of the disciplines on subsidies,[286] with some of them going as far as proposing an outright ban on export subsidies. While delegates of developing countries did not object to this idea, they backed India's proposal for a series of exceptions for developing countries.[287] Denmark expressed support for a ban on export subsidies, whereas the UK and U.S. delegates argued in favor of an *in principle* only ban, with some exceptions explicitly provided for.[288] The U.S. delegate should be credited with the discipline that subsidies should not lead to the subsidizing state acquiring more than an *equitable share of world trade*, which was very much the original U.S. position on this issue.[289] Faced with stringent rules, the United States requested, and in 1955 received, a waiver for their *Agricultural Adjustment Act* during the same session.[290] The most extreme position against subsidies was advocated by Australia, which went so far as to request a ban not only on export but on domestic subsidies as well.[291] Documents L/334 and L/334

---

[282] See E/PC/T/C.6/85 of February 15, 1947.
[283] See E/PC/T/124 pp. 4ff.   [284] See CRH pp. 106ff.
[285] See W.9/220 of February 22, 1955.   [286] See W.9/20 of November 18, 1954.
[287] See SR.9/23 and SR.9/24 of December 22, 1954.
[288] See W.9/102 of December 15, 1954, W.9/103 of December 15, 1954, and W.9/104 of December 16, 1954.
[289] See SR.9/17 at p. 11. See also Brown (1950, op. cit.).
[290] In fact, for Section 22 of this Act, see SR.9/33 of February 7, 1955.
[291] See W.9/67 of December 6, 1954.

2.7 The Evolution of the GATT Provisions 159

Add. 1 (Section B) reflect the final compromise on subsidies, according to which the additional disciplines would be imposed on export subsidies only and would not amount to a total ban.

2.7.14 State Trading

London Conference

This is yet another evidence of the remarkable influence that the UK delegation has had on the *London Draft*: three provisions were dedicated to disciplining state trading. Two of them were of peripheral interest: Art. 32, which dealt with state monopolies of individual products; and the bracketed (that is, not fully agreed) Art. 33, which dealt with the extraordinary case of *complete* state monopolies of import trade. It is Art. 31 of the *London Draft*, however, which reflects the original understanding upon which the current disciplines on state trading enterprises (STE) have been built. This provision accomplishes three different objectives:

(a) it makes it clear that state trading should be distinguished from government procurement, in that the latter concerns purchases for governmental use and not for resale, as the former does. With respect to government procurement, ITO Members would simply have to grant fair and equitable treatment to products of other countries, with no further obligation;[292]
(b) it defines STE by using a simple control criterion: any enterprise effectively controlled by the state should be considered STE;[293]
(c) it makes it clear that STE have to respect the MFN discipline when purchasing goods. To this effect, they should act in accordance with commercial considerations, such as price, quality, etc.[294]

New York Conference

This is Art. XV of the *New York* GATT Draft, and Art. 31 of the *New York* ITO Draft Charter. The U.S. delegation produced the first draft which did not

---

[292] This is, of course, a rather weak obligation, since it falls short of MFN, and, hence, discriminatory treatment could thus not be excluded.
[293] The contract thus would be *completed* through subsequent case law. The judge retains substantial discretion to define what effectively amounts to control.
[294] The term "commercial considerations" is of course, open-ended. Negotiating history suggests that it was meant to operate as the opposite of purely *political* considerations. At any rate, the indicative list added to Art. 31 helps the judge avoid type – II errors: he/she must review whether price, quality, etc. had been examined by the STE when making a purchase.

deviate from the *London Draft*.²⁹⁵ There were, nonetheless, some interesting discussions concerning key terms of this provision, which appeared to be quite open-ended. For example, the U.S. delegation attempted to remove doubts as to the consistency of some practices with the obligation imposed on STE to base their actions on commercial considerations:

> The charging by a state enterprise of different prices for its sales of a product in different markets, domestic or foreign, is not precluded by the provisions of this Article, provided that such different prices are charged for commercial reasons.²⁹⁶

This proposal eventually found its way in the *Interpretative Note ad Art. XVII GATT*, as we know it today. Arts. 32 and 33 dealt with specific cases of STE (state monopolies of individual products, and expansion of trade by state monopolies, respectively).

Geneva Conference

Czechoslovakia, on the brink of a communist takeover, showed increasing interest in the negotiation of STE. In its view, the GATT should allow countries of

> whatever political, economical or social structure to collaborate peacefully in the attainment of the purposes of the Charter.²⁹⁷

It was thus requesting a modification to ensure the necessary flexibility so that participation in the GATT would not be reserved to market economies only. France opposed this provision; it was quite hostile to the idea of including flexibility and, essentially, wanted to ensure that STE behave like private enterprises.²⁹⁸ The discussions produced, as the U.S. delegate put it, cleaner drafts of the spirit of the *London Draft*.²⁹⁹ Still, the negotiating documents shed light on the intent behind some key terms appearing in the provision. Chile, for example, speaking for many delegations, stated that the term *commercial considerations*, the key obligation imposed on STE, should be understood to mean that STE could not base their decisions on political considerations.³⁰⁰ Finally, Art 33 of the *New York GATT Draft* on the expansion of trade by state monopolies was deleted.³⁰¹

---

[295] See E/PC/T/C.6/W.22 of January 27, 1947, E/PC/T/C.6/W.69 at pp. 7ff. and E/PC/T/C.6/W.81 at pp. 14ff.
[296] See E/PC/T/C.6/27 of January 30, 1947 at p. 5.
[297] See E/PC/T/W/198 of June 16, 1947. [298] See E/PC/T/W/239 of July 10, 1947 at p. 2.
[299] Id. at p. 5. [300] Id. at p. 6.
[301] See E/PC/T/160 of August 9, 1947.

2.7 The Evolution of the GATT Provisions

Havana Conference
No change of substance is recorded.[302]

Review Session
The discussions on state trading did not lead to any meaningful change.

2.7.15 Safeguards

London Conference
The negotiators laid down the essential conditions for safeguard (emergency) action under Art. 34 of the *London Draft*: assuming a contingency has occurred (injury resulting from unforeseen developments), a country would be in position to withdraw benefits it accorded to its trading partners (by raising its tariffs, or, by imposing a quota). A country wishing to avail itself of this possibility was required to enter into consultations with all other members having a substantial interest in the withdrawn benefit. Only in exceptional circumstances would this obligation be waived. Even in such cases, nevertheless, negotiations would resume as soon as practicable after the imposition of the safeguard. Absence of agreement, between the country imposing safeguards and those having a substantial interest, would allow the latter to withdraw benefits as well. Thus, a country imposing safeguards would not face countermeasures, only in cases where the safeguards imposed were the outcome of a negotiated solution.[303] One can trace the safeguard clause to a number of bilateral treaties that especially the United States had signed much before the negotiation of the GATT/ITO.[304]

New York Conference
This is Art. XVIII of the *New York* GATT Draft, and Art. 34 of the *New York* Draft ITO Charter. The text is a re-production of the corresponding provision in the *London Draft*.[305]

---

[302] See CRH at pp. 113ff.
[303] As noted in Chapter 1, the U.S. State Department developed the escape clause in 1941 after Congress expressed concerns about the impact of war and postwar disruptions on U.S. industries. It was a component of the December 1941 template reciprocal trade agreement reproduced in Annex A-1. In addition, as the chapter notes, Congress required a safeguard measure in all executive trade agreements as a result of a deal with the Truman administration in February 1947.
[304] See also Art. 5 of the Preliminary Draft International Agreement for the Abolition of Import and Export Prohibitions and Restrictions, League of Nations, Economic and Financial, 1928.II.7.
[305] See E/PC/T/C.6/28 of January 31, 1947, and Rev. 1 of February 8, 1947; see also, E/PC/T/C.6/W.66 of February 11, 1947 at pp. 1ff., and E/PC/T/C.6/W.87 at pp. 1ff. Canada and Chile,

Geneva Conference

The discussion focused on whether consultation (with affected parties) should always precede the imposition of safeguards or not. Canada, Chile, Cuba, and France were in favor of prior consultations; Australia, Brazil, India, South Africa, and the United States were against it.[306] Canada broke the deadlock by proposing a compromise: if safeguard action would take place without consultation, then counteraction should be permitted. The U.S. delegation proposed that no prior consultation should be required, because delays due to consultations might be damaging to the country wishing to avail itself of the possibility to impose safeguards. Its proposal eventually found its way to the current Art. XIX GATT.[307]

Havana Conference

No substantive change is recorded, except that it was made clearer that there is no limitation on the types of measures (safeguards) that trading nations could take. The negotiating documents further reveal a consensus that there should be a relation of cause and effect between increased imports and obligations assumed (i.e., imports have risen because tariffs had been reduced, or because QR cannot be lawfully imposed).[308]

Review Session

No change is reported.

2.7.16 General Exceptions

London Conference

Delegates could not agree on a text on this matter and, hence, what was supposed to be Art. 37 of the *London Draft* remained, originally, an open issue.[309] The discussions are quite revealing of what negotiators had in mind when tackling this issue. *First*, it is clear that negotiators unanimously held that Art. 37 should be dedicated to *permanent*, rather than *emergency* action.[310] *Second*, the

---

nevertheless, continued to be opposed to the idea of allowing safeguard action without prior consultations, even though, according to the agreed text, such action would be limited to exceptional circumstances only, see E/PC/T/C.6/Rev. 1 at p. 3.

[306] See E/PC/T/W/224 of June 24, 1947 at pp. 1–7.
[307] See E/PC/T/146 of July 31, 1947.   [308] See CRH at p. 83.
[309] This provision was modeled after the corresponding provision in the 1927 International Convention for the Abolition of Import and Export Prohibitions and Restrictions (World Economic Conference of 1927), the first attempt to multilateralize international trade. The refusal of Poland to ratify it signaled its definitive demise.
[310] See E/PC/T/C.II/50 at p. 4. Those interested in tracing the roots of this provision, could further check Art. 4 of the Preliminary Draft for the International Agreement for the Abolition

2.7 The Evolution of the GATT Provisions

function of the list included in Art. 37 seems to be at odds with its subsequent re-incarnations, and, ultimately, its modern construction in WTO case law. The UK delegation originally proposed what became the current chapeau of Art. XX GATT (the corresponding to Art. 37 provision). They seemed to have in mind a provision that would operate as an exception to import and export restrictions only, and not to internal measures:

> The undertakings in Chapter IV of this Charter *relating to import and export restrictions* shall not be construed to prevent the adoption or enforcement by any member of measures for the following purposes, provided that they are not applied in such a manner as to constitute a means of arbitrary discrimination between countries where the same conditions prevail, or a disguised restriction of international trade.[311] (emphasis added).

Third, the ambit of some of the exceptions negotiated under Art. 37 seems to be at variance with their modern-day construction: the points made by the Indian delegate (Ganguli), with respect to the carve-out for exhaustible natural resources, suggest that negotiators had in mind protection for non-living organisms only.[312] Subsequent discussions[313] confirm this impression, at least as far as some delegations were concerned. As Charnovitz (1991) notes, in a parallel negotiation concerning an international commodity agreement (fisheries and wildlife), the same term had been used to cover living organisms as well. A remark by the temporary chairman of the working group discussing the international commodity agreement (Eric Wyndham-White), to the effect that the term *exhaustible natural resources* appearing in Art. XX(g) GATT covered fisheries as well (that is, living organisms) lends to confusion as to the exact coverage of this term.[314] The better arguments, however, rest with the understanding of the term as covering nonliving organisms only.[315] For a start, the discussion about fisheries was within a different context, that of an international commodity agreement, which would come under the ITO and not the GATT itself. Moreover, subsequent discussions during the *Havana Conference* confirm that negotiators treated fisheries and wildlife as a special case.[316]

---

of Import and Export Prohibitions and Restrictions, (1927 World Economic Conference), League of Nations, Economic and Financial, 1928.II.7, and the ensuing discussion.

[311] See E/PC/T/C.II/50 at pp. 7ff., and E/PC/T/C.II/54 at pp. 32ff.
[312] See E/PC/T/C.II/50 at pp.5ff.
[313] See E/PC/T/C.II/50 at pp. 34ff. Only a few of them, however, (those mentioned in 2.3.2) concerned the GATT.
[314] See E/ PC/T/B/SR/27 at p. 14 and the discussion in Charnovitz (1991).
[315] A conclusion that Charnovitz (1991) does not exclude.
[316] See E/CONF.2/C.5/9 at p. 21, and E/CONF.2/C.5/SR.7 at p. 2, and the corresponding discussion in Charnovitz (1991). In light of this record, it should come as no surprise that the Appellate Body avoided references to the *travaux préparatoires* of the term *exhaustible natural resources*, in its judgment on *US – Shrimp*.

New York Conference

This is Art. XX of the *New York* GATT Draft, and Art. 37 of the *New York* Draft ITO Charter. With respect to the grounds justifying deviation from general obligations assumed under GATT included in this provision, there is little, if any, change compared to the *London Draft*. The innovation is the inclusion of a chapeau which corresponds, more or less, to the current chapeau of Art. XX GATT.[317] As already briefly alluded to supra, the provision regarding environmental protection included in the 1927 International Convention for the Abolition of Import and Export Prohibitions and Restrictions (World Economic Conference of 1927) substantially influenced the negotiations of the *General Exceptions* clause. One of the key differences however, between the two documents is that, in the GATT text, the chapeau includes both an MFN clause and an NT clause, and not just an NT clause, as was the case before.[318] The negotiating documents further reveal that the drafting of Art. XX(b) GATT (protection of human, animal, and plant life) should be attributed to a joint proposal by Chile, Czechoslovakia, France, New Zealand, and the United States.[319]

Geneva Conference

The *New York Draft* was not substantially altered. Benelux (Belgium, the Netherlands, and Luxembourg) and French delegates should be credited with the expression "nothing in this agreement will be construed," which was included in the chapeau of this provision and generalized the application of the list of exceptions included herein.[320]

Havana Conference

A provision was included allowing for measures that were deemed necessary to protect *public safety*, this term being considered to include *public order*.[321]

Review Session

Art. XX(j) GATT, dealing with justifiable restrictions on products in short supply, was agreed during the *Review Session*.[322]

---

[317] See E/PC/T/C.6/41 at p. 3, and E/PC/T/C.6/55 at pp. 48ff. Canada, on the very last day of negotiations, stated a reservation requesting the addition of a paragraph that would make it possible for an ITO Member to prohibit a commodity the domestic production of which was also prohibited, see E/PC/T/C.6/W.85 of February 20, 1947. This addition was probably unnecessary anyway, but was meant to provide some ex ante clarity.

[318] See Charnovitz (1991).   [319] See E/PC/T/C.6/55/Rev. 1 at p. 47.

[320] See E/PC/T/103 at p. 43. In fact, the delegates of Benelux and France were reinserting the language that was used in the corresponding provision of the International Agreement for the Abolition of Import and Export Prohibitions and Restrictions, op. cit.

[321] See CRH at p. 84.   [322] See L/334 of March 1, 1955 at p. 10.

2.7 The Evolution of the GATT Provisions

2.7.17 Consultations – Dispute Settlement

London Conference

Art. 35 of the *London Draft* discussed consultations in general, that is, regarding *any* issue that might form the subject matter of a dispute, whereas Art. 24 discussed disputes arising from tariff negotiations and dealt within a specific procedure that we discuss infra. The negotiations on consultations were intrinsically of institutional nature and, thus, very much dependent on the overall success of the wider ITO negotiations. With this caveat in mind, we note that, besides bilateral consultations on a disputed issue across interested parties and, eventually, discussions among all those participating in the ITO, an institutional link with the International Court of Justice (ICJ) was envisaged as well. Requests for advisory opinion, even direct appeals to the ICJ, were contemplated.[323] Three forms of complaints [violation complaint; nonviolation complaint (NVC); situation complaint], were already discussed and, in principle, agreed to during the *London Conference*.[324] Disputes arising from tariff negotiations would be submitted to an *Interim Tariff Committee* comprising delegates from all countries that would have agreed to abide by the *General Agreement on Tariffs and Trade* by a specified date (Art. 67 of the *London Draft*).

New York Conference

This is Art. XIX of the *New York* GATT Draft, and Art. 35 of the *New York* Draft ITO Charter. The text is a reproduction of the spirit of the corresponding provision in the *London Draft*.[325] Some streamlining did occur though: we find, for example, a draft by the UK delegation concerning nonviolation complaints (NVCs) that resembles very closely to the current provisions of the GATT and the WTO Dispute Settlement Understanding (DSU).[326]

Geneva Conference

No substantive change is reported.

Havana Conference

No substantive change is reported.

---

[323] See E/PC/T/C.V/33 of November 20, 1946 at p. 7. On this issue, see the excellent account of Rubin (1949), who explains the various mutations of dispute settlement since the London Conference, as well as the national positions on this score.

[324] NVC is an instrument that the United States had already used in its pre-GATT bilateral agreements, see for example, Art. XI of its 1935 Reciprocal Trade Agreement with Sweden pp. 3755ff.

[325] See E/PC/T/C.6/28/Rev. 1 at pp. 2ff., and E/PC/T/C.6/W.87 at pp. 2ff.

[326] See E/PC/T/C.6/W.63 of February 10, 1947.

Review Session

With respect to dispute settlement, negotiations centered on two issues: the form of reparation, and the composition and overall nature of dispute-adjudicating bodies. In the eyes of at least some delegations, dispute settlement should eventually lead to a re-balancing of concessions. In other terms, in their view, the GATT was introducing *liability rules*,[327] whereby a party breaching the contract would have the option to comply or pay instead of complying, and not *property rules*, whereby the breaching state had no option but to comply with its obligations: Denmark, Norway, and Sweden proposed that a new paragraph be introduced that would clarify that the purpose of dispute settlement is the maintenance of the level of reciprocal concessions, and that recourse to retaliation would be authorized only when "all other possibilities had been explored." This proposal was defeated. The rationale for defeating it gave extra arguments to those espousing the view that rebalancing in case of breach was an option:

> The Working Party considered that the requirement in paragraph 2 of the Article that the circumstances must be "serious enough" limits the possibility of authorizing a contracting party or parties to take appropriate retaliatory action to cases where endeavours to solve the problem through the withdrawal of the measures causing the damage, the substitution of other concessions, or some other appropriate action have not proved to be possible, and here there is considered to be substantial justification for retaliatory action, as in cases in which such authorization appears to be the only means either of preventing serious economic consequences to the country for which a benefit has been nullified or impaired, or the only means of restoring the original situation.[328]

Regarding the organization of dispute settlement, we find, probably counterintuitively so, that it was the Danes who first proposed that *panels* of experts (individuals proposed by contracting parties) should be adjudicating *all* disputes submitted for adjudication: they originally wanted to entrust panels of experts with the adjudication of BoP-related disputes only, and, eventually, expanded their proposal to cover all disputes.[329]

---

[327] Negotiators did not use terms such as *liability rules* and *property rules*. The thrust of the discussions held, nonetheless, points to this direction.

[328] See W.9/164 of January 31, 1954. As many have argued, however, it is difficult to reconcile this response with the current drafting of Art. 22.1 DSU.

[329] See W.9/171 of February 3, 1955. Panels were, of course, being used before 1955 as well. What the Danish delegate proposed was that this practice be extended, as a matter of principle, across all cases submitted for adjudication.

2.7 The Evolution of the GATT Provisions

2.7.18 Preferential Arrangements

London Conference

Art. 38 of the *London Draft* deals with one form of preferential arrangements: *customs unions* (CU). Free-trade areas (FTA) did not enter the GATT disciplines until the *Havana Conference*). This provision does not prevent the formation of a customs union (or, a customs territory, defined as an area with separate tariffs and other regulations of commerce than the country under the sovereignty of which it operates), provided that two conditions have been met: there is substantial trade liberalization across CU members, and the common tariffs applied to the rest of the world are not higher than the *average level of duties* applicable to the constituent parts of the CU, before the latter had been formed. These two conditions were further refined (and, in part, modified) in subsequent drafts of the GATT.[330]

New York Conference

This is Art. XXI of the *New York* GATT Draft, and Art. 38 of the *New York* Draft ITO Charter. This provision continues to deal with frontier traffic and customs unions only.[331] No major change from the *London Draft* is, thus, observed.

Geneva Conference

No substantive change is reported.

Havana Conference

The exemption for preferential arrangements encompasses as of this moment, not only CU, but also FTA. Until the recent, very persuasive research by Chase (2006), the view has been held by many that the inclusion of a provision on FTA was there to accommodate the European integration process. For a number of reasons, this view should be rejected: we already alluded to the fact that, in Acheson's record, Jean Monnet revealed his plans on European integration later

---

[330] It is highly unlikely that the provision on customs unions was designed with the European integration process in mind. The first Schuman plan was unveiled on May 6, 1950 (that is, four years after the *London Conference*), and, in Acheson's (1969, pp. 382ff.) account, "Schuman urged the utmost secrecy upon us." Moreover, the Schuman plan concerned two products only, coal and steel, and thus could hardly satisfy the requirements of this provision. As a result, the *European Coal and Steel Community* (ECSC) eventually requested and was granted a waiver, and its consistency with the provision relating to preferential arrangements was not an issue, see SR.9/4 of November 4, 1954. It is more likely that this provision reflects the need to accommodate the Belgo-Luxembourg-Netherlands customs union, a "genuine" customs union in place at the time, or even the Syro-Lebanese customs union.

[331] See E/PC/T/C.6/W.66 at pp. 3ff. and E/PC/T/C.6/W.87 of February 24, 1947 at pp. 3ff.

than the *Havana Conference* took place. Chase (2006) drawing from a series of archival records, demonstrates that it was the U.S. negotiators that designed this provision in order to accommodate a trade agreement that they had secretly reached with Canada. The U.S. – Canada FTA, alas, was never ratified.[332] The term *average level of duties* was replaced by the term *general incidence of duties*: as a result, no mathematical average was required by members of a preferential arrangement that aimed to satisfy the external requirement imposed through the GATT discipline. The inserted flexibility was deemed necessary in order to facilitate the establishment of such arrangements.[333]

Review Session
No substantive change is reported.

2.7.19 Institutional Provisions

London Conference
No discussion on institutional provisions took place, since it was (at least originally) clear that the GATT would be part of the ITO, the agreement that would contain all necessary institutional provisions. With the exception of the *Interim Tariff Committee*, the function of which we discussed supra, no particular arrangements were negotiated during this conference.

New York Conference
It was by now clearer that the GATT would enter center stage before the ITO. Consequently, negotiators felt that it was required to introduce in the GATT text some institutional provisions that would help administer the tariff bargain and the various other commitments. To this effect, Art. XXII of the New York GATT Draft renamed the *Interim Tariff Committee* (agreed in the *London Conference*) to *Interim Trade Committee*, which becomes the organ entrusted with the day-to-day operation of the multilateral trading system, including the settlement of disputes (Art. XXIV.2). The *New York Draft* further contains a host of other provisions necessary for the GATT to fulfill its intended functions: a provision

---

[332] Chase (2006) is also a great account of the evolution of the current Art. XXIV GATT from the *London Conference* onward until its modern design.

[333] See CRH at pp. 50–52. Another, less dramatic, amendment of the provision would have provided GATT contracting parties with the possibility to enter into CU with noncontracting parties. In Brown's (1950 at p. 242) account, this was necessary in light of the decision of France (a contracting party) to enter into a CU with Italy (not a contracting party). The current Art. XXIV.5 GATT, nonetheless, does not allow for this possibility, since it envisages preferential arrangements across WTO Members only.

2.7 The Evolution of the GATT Provisions

regarding revision, amendment, and termination of the agreement (Art. XXIII, a UK proposal);[334] a provision on entry into force of and withdrawal from the GATT (Art. XXV); and, finally, a provision regarding accession to the GATT (Art. XXVI). Two provisions (Arts. XVI and XVII, 4 and 13 of the *New York* Draft ITO Charter, respectively) deal with maintenance of domestic employment, and a conciliation provision in case pursuance of the establishment of a domestic industry might encroach on the tariff commitments entered by the country at hand. The former was completely eliminated from subsequent drafts (except for a brief mention of hortatory nature in the GATT Preamble); the latter was reduced in scope and, eventually, became an integral part of the current Art. XVIII(c) GATT.

Geneva Conference
The institutional arrangements agreed already in New York were confirmed.[335]

Havana Conference
No substantive change is reported.

Review Session
No substantive change is reported.

2.7.20 Boycotts

London Conference
This provision was not included in the final GATT text. In essence, this provision requested from ITO Members not to actively participate in campaigns aiming to discourage consumption of imported goods (Art. 23 of the *London Draft*). Negotiations on this item were quite substantive during the *London Conference*, but failure to agree meant that it would be further discussed at a later stage.[336] Still, negotiators drew a clear line between participating in (inciting) boycotts and *Buy National* policies: whereas there was agreement to ban the former, there was, by now, widespread momentum in favor of allowing the latter.

New York Conference
This is Art. 23 of the *New York* Draft ITO Charter.[337] Note that this provision was omitted from the GATT text prepared during the *New York Conference*. The

---

[334] See E/PC/T/C.6/87 of February 17, 1947 at pp. 1ff.
[335] See E/PC/T/136 at p. 5.   [336] See E/PC/T/33 at p. 28.
[337] In part, the letter of current Art. XI GATT, and in part case law have filled the gap left by the omission of this provision from the final GATT.

negotiations essentially reproduced the spirit of discussions already held during the *London Conference*: the distinction between boycotts and *Buy National* policies was retained, and the latter were exempted from the obligation not to participate in boycotts.[338] Still, the U.S. delegation, while not entering a formal reservation on this provision, stated a preference for the original stipulation (as included in the *Suggested Charter*), whereas China, India, and Lebanon entered formal reservations.[339]

Geneva Conference
This provision was omitted from the GATT text.

Havana Conference
The U.S. delegate suggested that the initial rationale for boycotts was to preclude *Buy National* policies, but, since no agreement on this score could be achieved, the provision should be scrapped altogether, and so it happened.[340]

Review Session
No discussions on this provision are reported.

2.7.21 Information, Statistics, and Trade Terminology

London Conference
Similarly, disagreements among negotiators led to the decision to renegotiate what was supposed to emerge as Art. 22 of the *London Draft*.[341] Several delegations pointed to the fact that similar ground was covered by the *Brussels Convention* of December 29, 1913 (establishment of international commercial statistics), and the *Geneva Convention* of December 14, 1928 (economic statistics) and that, as a result, negotiation should aim at achieving a result that would be consistent with the provisions included in the two agreements.[342]

New York Conference
This is Art. 22 of the *New York* Draft ITO Charter, and was excluded from the *New York* GATT Draft.[343] The discussions during the *London Conference*

---

[338] Following the exclusion of this provision from the GATT, and assuming a *Buy National* policy can be attributed to a government, it will, in all likelihood, be judged illegal in today's world. The WTO, though, has yet to face such an issue head on.
[339] See E/PC/T/C.6/W/20 at p. 5, E/PC/T/C.6/41 of February 4, 1947 at p. 2, and E/PC/T/C.6/55 at pp. 46ff.
[340] See CRH at p. 81.   [341] Id.
[342] See E/PC/T/C.II/54 at pp. 30ff.
[343] This time, that is, contrary to what is the case with marks of origin, the exclusion of this discipline was definitive. In part, this role has been assumed by the WTO Secretariat.

2.8 Property Rights on the GATT

showed that the *Suggested Charter* contained disciplines that were viewed as too demanding by many delegations. As a result, the negotiators aimed to tone down the existing disciplines, and to request the ITO Members to communicate information about their external trade in goods, revenue from import/export duties, etc., "to the extent reasonable," or "so far as possible," etc.[344]

Geneva Conference
This provision was not included in the GATT text.

Havana Conference
No change was made to this provision, which was discussed, however, as part of the ITO Draft Charter and not of the GATT text anymore.[345]

Review Session
No discussion is reported under this item.

2.8 Property Rights on the GATT

By accepting the GATT, trading nations signed up to a trade-liberalization model, whereby they accepted that they could, in principle, protect their domestic producer through tariffs only: QR are illegal, and domestic instruments should not operate so as to afford protection. Trading nations further accepted that tariffs would be negotiated down in successive rounds of trade liberalization and that, in principle again, all tariff advantages would be extended to all their trading partners that have signed up to the GATT. Nevertheless, the ambit of non-discrimination was tempered essentially, by accepting that imperial (and other, following the insistence of Chile to this effect) preferences would remain in place, at least during a transitional phase. This bargain is very much the outcome of the negotiation between the two transatlantic partners, the United Kingdom and the United States. As Chapter 1 suggested, the implicit *quid pro quo* between them was the reduction of imperial preferences for an extension of MFN. The U.S. government entered the negotiations with considerable contractual experience, since it had negotiated similar trade deals before. The experience of the UK government in international trade issues was quite substantial as well; from a negotiating perspective, however, the United Kingdom was an ailing empire, while the United States emerged from the Second World War as the undisputed hegemonic power.

It was, thus, quite natural that the two transatlantic partners dominated the negotiations on the GATT/ITO, as they had also dominated the negotiations

[344] See EP/C/T/C.6/55 at pp. 43ff.   [345] See CRH at p. 80.

during the Bretton Woods conference a few years before. As we saw, from early on, UK and U.S. delegates participated in all committees, groups, etc. established. As we unveil the negotiating history of the GATT, it becomes apparent that this observation holds true throughout all stages of the negotiations.[346] Although, as briefly alluded to supra, participation in negotiations is no perfect proxy to measure the influence that participating delegations have had on the final text, few would argue with the point that participation is a necessary (albeit, not sufficient) condition for influencing the eventual outcome. It bears repetition that UK and U.S. delegates are the *only* national delegates that participated in all committees, groups, etc. Their point of view on each and every provision that made it to the final GATT text has been consistently discussed (and often, as we saw, retained). With one exception, they were simultaneously present in all committees during the *London Conference*, where the "heart and soul" of the GATT was constructed.

The basic bargain of the GATT was the tariff bargain, whereby trading nations promised each other reductions of their pre-GATT levels that they would consolidate and apply on an MFN basis. The GATT, however, could not have contained just a provision on tariff consolidation and the MFN. For one thing, negotiating history reveals that negotiators were quite aware of the equivalence propositions: an import tariff can be decomposed to a domestic tax on consumption and a domestic-production subsidy that will produce comparable effects to that of the import tariff. This is why negotiators felt that a provision disciplining domestic instruments was a necessary addition that would operate as an anticircumvention provision that would insure trading nations who had to "pay" through their own tariff concessions, for the tariff concessions obtained by their trading partners against the risk of seeing the value of concessions obtained, diluted through recourse to domestic instruments. A similar function explains of provisions such as the disciplining of state trading, and the introduction of NVC in the GATT text.

The GATT text, nevertheless, contains many provisions additional to those necessary to ensure that the tariff bargain would not be undermined: antidumping, balance of payments, safeguards, institutional provisions, etc. In our view, at least the following important explanatory variables have determined what else should have been added in the GATT (that is, what else *next* to the basic bargain):

(a) the influence that the failure to conclude the ITO has had on the negotiation of the GATT;

---

[346] In Annex B, infra, we provide information on the composition of all committees, etc. established until and including the Review Session of 1955.

2.8 Property Rights on the GATT

(b) that the leading nation at the time (United States) was unwilling to undo some key trade-related legislation of its own;
(c) the different perceptions of the UK and the U.S. delegations on the role of the state in the handling of international trade relations;
(d) the emergence of some developing countries who became serious negotiating partners over the years.

The first point explains the inclusion of institutional provisions in the GATT. Although the GATT was not conceived to be an international organization, negotiators felt that some institutional provisions had to be agreed so that it could function as such until the entry into force of the ITO.[347] It also explains the *ambit* of some GATT provisions. Recall our discussion on the disciplining of subsidies: the ban on export subsidies was included in the ITO Charter, where disciplines on RBP were also included, but not in the GATT, which contained no such disciplines. Point (b) explains the inclusion of provisions such as antidumping. In its original conception, antidumping was not supposed to function as a flexibility clause.[348] An omission to antidumping, nevertheless, would probably make it even more difficult for the U.S. delegation to get the necessary political support for the GATT/ITO project. As a result, the doubts about its intellectual underpinnings notwithstanding, antidumping found its way into the GATT.[349] Point (c) has been documented in many other accounts, and more recently in Miller (2000). Briefly stated, it is upon the insistence of the UK delegation that the provisions relating to BoP, state trading, and the re-negotiation of tariff concessions entered the GATT. This does not mean, however, that the U.S. delegation did not see any role for state intervention; after all, the GATT was largely negotiated by a Democratic administration. The safeguards clause, for example, was modeled after similar clauses that had been included in previous contractual arrangements that the U.S. government had adhered to, such as the trade deal with Mexico. Recall that some European countries (Benelux) were staunchly against flexibility-type provisions. Point (d) explains the inclusion of provisions such as protection of infant industry, and, importantly, eventually, the inclusion of Part IV: it is developing countries that insisted and, ultimately, obtained the inclusion of these provisions. The term *developing countries* (or *less-developed countries* in the lingo of the '40s) should

---

[347] See the excellent analysis of Jackson (1969) on this score.
[348] Although in modern literature, there are increasing arguments to this effect. See, for example, Finger and Nogués (2006).
[349] Originally, antidumping was supposed to be the instrument to combat international predation. However, the emergence of the effects doctrine seriously undermined this function, see Hoekman and Mavroidis (1996).

not necessarily be equated to modern-day developing countries. It is true that India and Brazil, that even nowadays qualify as developing countries, have been prominent in the formulation of developing countries' positions since 1946, as we saw in the first part of the Chapter where we examined the Brazilian and Indian reaction to the *Suggested Charter*. Australia, on the other hand, was quite vocal on infant-industry protection, and largely contributed to the final text as embedded in Art. XVIII(c) GATT, where India, as we saw, played a leading role.[350] It was considered to be a developing country during the time of the negotiation.

The GATT, however, was very much the property of industrial countries and, as Hudec (1975, p. 57) put it:

> they did not have to accommodate the rest of the world.[351]

The *nuclear approach* suggested by Canada, even though weakened through compromises, had a lot to do with it. Two more factors have been identified in literature: Johnson (1968) explains that the principal-supplier rule, followed in the original negotiation, effectively barred developing countries from effective participation, since no developing country was a principal supplier in any commodity. MFN somewhat diminished the effects of non-participation in the tariff negotiation, but is not a perfect substitute. In his words (p. 368):

> ... the real trouble with the GATT is not the institution of bargaining for tariff reductions, but the techniques for bargaining...

The negotiating rules changed only in the fourth round (Geneva), as reported in Kock (1969). Moreover, Wilkinson & Scott (2007, 10ff.) point out that many developing countries were more active during the ITO negotiations, since they thought that the GATT would effectively come under the aegis of the ITO. The failure of the ITO means, ipso facto, that their negotiating efforts were in vain.

The transatlantic partners should be also credited with the provisions regarding customs valuation, fees, and formalities. This is the natural consequence of the fact that they possessed the more sophisticated customs administration. In this respect, the influence of other contracting parties such as France and the Benelux countries should not be underestimated. European countries had entered into international arrangements (mentioned above) dealing with similar

---

[350] Concurring Wilkinson and Scott (2007).
[351] On the role of developing countries during the GATT negotiation, see the excellent analysis in Hudec (1987).

2.8 Property Rights on the GATT

issues, and they were bringing into the negotiations the experience they had gained from such participation. More generally, the study of the negotiating history reveals a respect for prior commitments, which negotiators tried to incorporate into the GATT to the extent possible. The only area where they decidedly wanted to break with the past was prior *tariff* commitments. This, of course, is quite natural in light of their resolve to establish a multilateral trade order.

3 The Rationales for the GATT

The two previous chapters examined the origins and evolution of the GATT as a text. In this brief chapter, we turn to the broad question of how the historical evidence relates to existing academic theories of why countries seek to negotiate and join multilateral trade agreements. The classical theory of international trade and commercial policy examines the benefits of trade and the impact of trade-policy measures, but not, until recently, the value of international trade agreements.[1] This has prompted economists and political scientists to search for the deeper economic and political rationales for trade agreements such as the GATT. These theories seek to answer questions such as: Why do we have the GATT? What is the underlying objective of the agreement, and what purpose does it serve?

The preamble (*chapeau*) of the GATT sets out the major purposes of the agreement, at least in the eyes of the founders:

> Recognizing that their relations in the field of trade and economic endeavour should be conducted with a view to raising standards of living, ensuring full employment and a large and steadily growing volume of real income and effective demand, developing the full use of the resources of the world and expanding the production and exchange of goods,
>
> Being desirous of contributing to these objectives by entering into reciprocal and mutually advantageous arrangements directed to the substantial reduction of tariffs and other barriers to trade and to the elimination of discriminatory treatment in international commerce, ...

---

[1] Indeed, the 19th century British classical economists were skeptical of trade agreements between countries, believing instead that each country should reduce trade barriers unilaterally (O'Brien 1976).

3.1 Economic Theory and Trade Agreements

In light of Chapter 1, there is little reason not to take this language at face value, but economists and political scientists have sought to understand the deeper roots of trade agreements such as the GATT. This chapter briefly summarizes the various theories about the rationale for trade agreements and then evaluates them in light of the historical evidence that we have presented.

3.1 Economic Theory and Trade Agreements

The economic approach to trade agreements begins with an assumption that governments are motivated to pursue policies that increase national income, although they sometimes are forced to depart from that objective for political reasons (such as to maintain political support, raise campaign contributions, or redistribute income to favored groups, etc.). Therefore, economists have focused on trade agreements as a way to reap the real income gains as a result of lower trade barriers.

In this approach, Jones (1969) has pointed out that the gains from trade can be decomposed into changes in the terms of trade and in the volume of trade. That is, the more favorable the terms of trade (the price of a country's exports relative to its imports) and the larger the volume of trade (for a given tariff), the larger the gains in real income will be.[2] Therefore, a country might find it advantageous to pursue a trade agreement if it is likely to improve the terms of trade or expand the volume of trade.

In theory, a small country – i.e., one that cannot influence its terms of trade – can maximize its real national income by adopting free trade unilaterally. However, on economic grounds it might still want to sign trade agreements in order to expand the volume of its trade to an extent greater than would be possibly by unilateral liberalization. In addition, a small country would probably see its terms of trade improve if a larger country were to grant it better access to its markets (especially since, if they do not seek such agreements they risk being left completely out of lucrative export markets, or treated in a discriminatory manner). Yet small countries that cannot affect the prices of their exports and imports are unlikely to have much bargaining power vis-à-vis their larger trading partners and hence are more likely to be ignored by them.

The issue is more complex for a "large" country that can affect the prices of its exports and imports. Standard theory suggests that large countries should avoid free trade, in the sense of forgoing taxes on trade, but should want to impose

---

[2] In notation, $\Delta y = -M \Delta p^* + (p - p^*) \Delta M$, where Δy is the change in real income, M is the volume of imports, Δp^* is the change in the relative price of imports (the inverse terms of trade), $p - p^*$ is domestic valuation of the imported commodities (p) relative to the world price (p^*), and ΔM is the change in import volume.

an "optimal" tariff in which the loss from a reduced volume of trade would be more than offset by an improvement in the terms of trade. A terms-of-trade gain arises for the large country because foreign exporters will reduce their prices and absorb a portion of the tariff and thereby lower the price of a country's imports, or because foreign consumers will absorb a portion of the tax and accept higher prices for the country's exports. It follows that a large country should be reluctant to reduce its tariff unilaterally for fear that it might deteriorate its terms of trade and possibly make it worse off.

In this setting, international trade agreements may be driven by a desire to internalize a terms-of-trade externality between countries. Harry Johnson (1953–1954) noted that if two large countries were to choose their optimal tariffs independently, that is, taking the policy of the other country as given, the resulting non-cooperative Nash equilibrium would be inefficient. In essence, when each country imposes trade barriers in an attempt to manipulate the terms of trade to its own advantage, these actions tend to cancel each other out. The result of the higher trade barriers will be a much lower volume of trade with potentially little net change in the terms of trade, giving rise to the possibility that both countries would be worse off than if they had refrained from such policies.

In this situation, the terms-of-trade externality arises from the *unilateral* nature of the tariff setting. Acting independently, countries may not be able to avoid the inefficient equilibrium because, if one of them were to reduce its tariffs alone, the other country would still have a unilateral incentive to maintain its duties on the tariff-reducing country. This logic was used by economists such as Mayer (1981) to demonstrate that countries can overcome this inefficient equilibrium by cooperating in binding agreements to reduce trade barriers. A similar approach to trade agreements was developed by Bagwell and Staiger in a series of papers during the 1990s, which are synthesized in Bagwell and Staiger (2002). Bagwell and Staiger use this approach to analyze a host of GATT institutions ranging from non-discrimination and MFN to safeguards, and offer an explanation of these GATT institutions through the lens of the terms of trade. They show that two features of the GATT, non-discrimination and reciprocity, are simple rules that allow governments to reach efficient trade agreements.[3]

---

[3] We should also note that there is a small but growing body of research on imperfect competition in trade and the motivations for trade agreements. While these models are of theoretical interest, it is less clear whether such issues played much of a role at the time of the original GATT, when raw materials and primary products formed a larger proportion of world trade than today and much of the focus was on commodity agreements. Nonetheless, we cannot rule out the possibility that issues relating to market access for goods characterized by product variety and economies of scale had some bearing on the negotiations.

3.1 Economic Theory and Trade Agreements

One difficulty with the theory originally developed by Johnson and elaborated by Mayer was the assumption that the objective function of the government was to maximize national welfare. This assumption was at odds with much observed behavior in the trade arena, leading other economists to search for theories that rested on more realistic assumptions about government objective functions. Grossman and Helpman (1994) developed a model of trade-policy formation at the national level in a small country, in which political officials determine trade policy on the basis of an objective function that blends conventional national welfare with their own self interest in securing campaign contributions. The Grossman and Helpman model assumes that some industries are well organized to participate in the political process and some are not (a very realistic assumption). The resulting political equilibrium then involves a mix of policies favoring organized interests that can deviate from the policies that would achieve national welfare maximization.

Grossman and Helpman (1995) then extended the analysis to consider two large countries whose actions influenced their terms of trade. When acting unilaterally, each government is responsive only to its domestic interest groups, and thus the Nash equilibrium entails inefficiencies due to the international terms of trade externality. A trade agreement then has the potential to improve the welfare of both countries (as measured by their political objective functions) by addressing this externality problem. Because governments are not national-welfare maximizers, however, the terms of a cooperative agreement may deviate significantly from the policies that conventional joint-welfare maximization would require. Bagwell and Staiger (2002) also consider a wide variety of potential government objectives in their analysis of terms-of-trade motivated trade agreements.

Despite the impressive pedigree of the terms-of-trade theory, a number of economic commentators have expressed skepticism about it. For example, Krugman (1997) has remarked that "the optimal tariff argument plays almost no role in real-world trade disputes." A frequent criticism of the terms-of-trade rationale is that the GATT does not constrain the use of export taxes, which are a potentially important instrument for manipulating the terms of trade because certain countries have market power over their exported goods.[4] Ethier (2004) takes issue with the terms-of-trade theory on precisely these grounds.[5] He observes that the GATT does not include any prohibition of, or general constraints

---

[4] For example, it is often the case that a country has the market power to influence the terms of trade via its exports, e.g., the Organization of Petroleum Exporting Countries (OPEC) and oil, Chile and copper, Morocco and phosphates, and Russia and South Africa and gold and diamonds.

[5] For additional criticisms, see Regan (2006).

on, export taxes. To be sure, export taxes can be the subject of negotiation and binding in GATT negotiating rounds. Yet, as a matter of fact, very few export taxes are bound into national schedules of concessions. Thus, if governments were really tempted to use trade-policy instruments to improve their terms of trade in the absence of cooperation, one must wonder why they do not use (unbound) export duties to influence terms of trade in the GATT environment today.[6]

These points are not beyond rebuttal. The GATT may do little to constrain export taxes in practice simply because governments rarely use them due to political constraints. An export tax may improve the terms of trade for a large country, other things being equal, but it will also generally reduce the profitability of the export industry that is taxed (and the government appropriates the surplus through tax revenue). For this reason, export industries may organize to resist export taxes, and governments may avoid using them. Import tariffs may be a much more likely device for manipulating the terms of trade, by contrast, because the domestic interests harmed by them are often poorly organized consumers and not well organized producers, as in the case of export taxes. The fact that GATT seems much more focused on import tariffs than on export taxes, therefore, is perhaps not so puzzling after all.

This economic approach has been influential among economists in providing plausible rationale for trade agreements such as the GATT. Is it consistent with the historical evidence? One approach is to simply examine data on the two sources of the gains from trade. Figures 3.1 and 3.2 present the terms of trade and the volume of trade for the United States, the United Kingdom, and Canada for the years around the formation of the GATT. The period prior to GATT was not a period of deteriorating terms of trade for the major players. In fact, the terms of trade of the United States improved dramatically between 1926 and 1935, and then leveled off. The UK's terms of trade similarly increased during this period, while Canada's fluctuated around a stable mean.

By contrast, the volume of trade for these countries fell significantly during the interwar period, by a much greater margin than domestic production or output. The volume of exports slumped dramatically in the early 1930s as the world economy entered the Great Depression. But what is remarkable is that, for

[6] One might add that a similar critique of the terms-of-trade theory arises if we replace export taxes by domestic instruments: an import tariff can be decomposed into a domestic tax on consumers and a subsidy on producers. This critique is less powerful, however, in that the GATT early on devised a doctrine to prohibit the use of new subsidies to frustrate the market-access expectations resulting from a bound tariff. Also, note that in the European Community context, a scheme whereby the proceedings from domestic taxation are used to finance domestic producers is outright illegal. There is standing case law to this effect, see, for example, *Capolongo*, 77/72, ECJ Reports (1973) 611; *Cucchi*, 77/76 ECJ Reports (1977) 987; *CELBI v. Fazenda publica*, C-266/91, ECJ Reports (1993) I-4333; *Fazenda publica v. UCIAL*, C-347/95, ECJ Reports (1997) I-4911.

3.1 Economic Theory and Trade Agreements

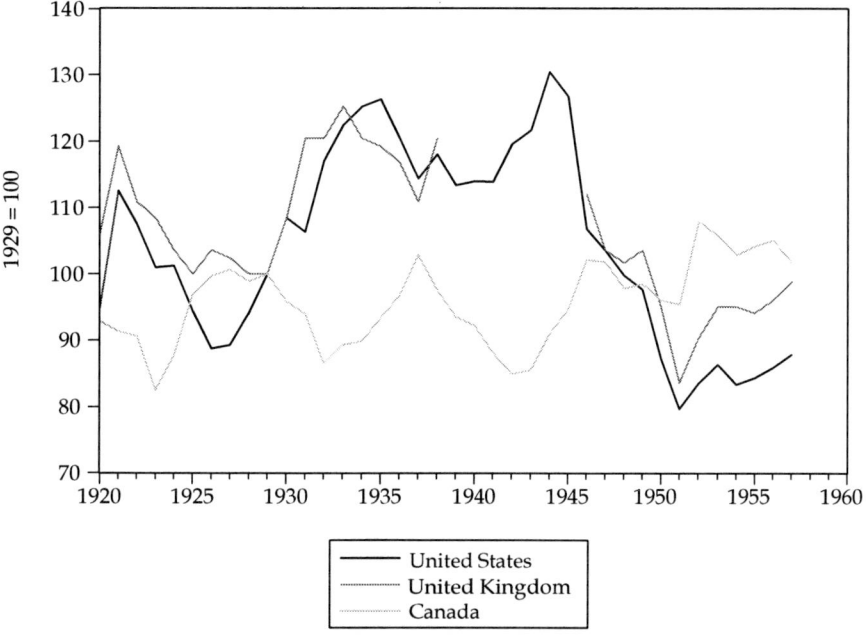

Figure 3.1. Terms of Trade of the GATT Founders, 1920–1957. *Source:* For United Kindom: Mitchell (1988, 577). For United States: U.S. Bureau of the Census (1975, series U 226, U238). For Canada: Leacy (1983), series G388.

both the United States and the United Kingdom, the volume of exports in 1938 had not yet reached its 1929 interwar peak, despite the fact that domestic output in both countries by then had exceeded its 1929 peak. In other words, while domestic output recovered from the depression, the trade of these countries lagged significantly behind the overall recovery. The failure of trade to recover from the shock of the depression may be due to the accumulation of trade barriers in the early 1930s that put a significant burden on the expansion of trade.

These data suggest that the United States and the United Kingdom may have been motivated to initiate a multilateral trade agreement because of the declining volume of world trade, not a shift in the terms of trade against them. But in fact, these data may not be inconsistent with the terms-of-trade theory of trade agreements. It would be a mistake to suppose that nations sought to enter the GATT to "improve" their terms of trade. Indeed, as a logical matter, it would be impossible for all nations to improve their terms of trade relative to each other – an improvement in the terms of trade for one nation is inevitably a worsening for another. After all, as argued before, terms of trade concerns can provide the impetus for trade liberalization.

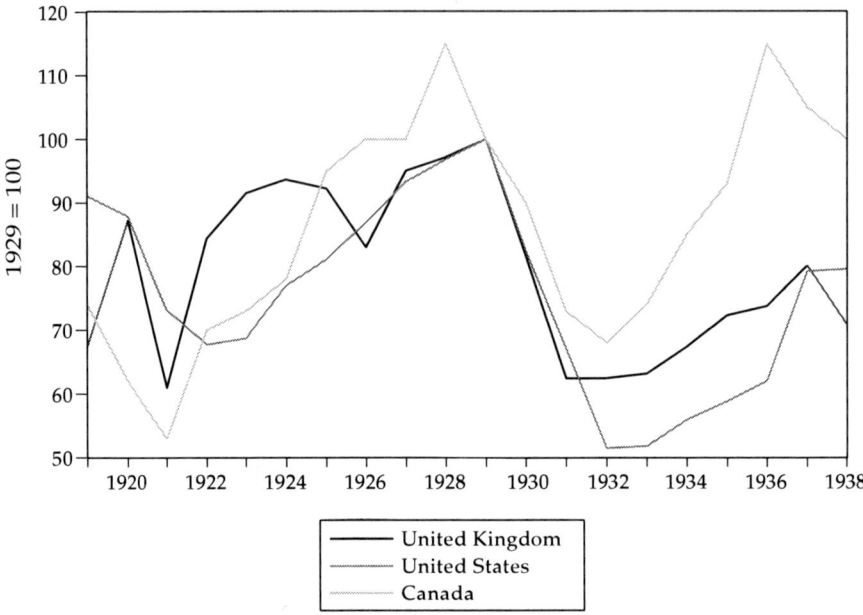

Figure 3.2: Export Volume of the GATT Founders, 1919–1938. *Source:* For United Kingdom: Mitchell (1988, 527). For United States: U.S. Bureau of the Census (1975, series U 226, U 238). For Canada: Leacy (1983), series G 386–388.

That theory holds that unilateral tariff policies in equilibrium lead to a set of tariffs around the world that may or may not improve the terms of trade for any given country, but that surely choke off the volume of trade. Cooperation to reduce those barriers may yield little or no net improvement in terms of trade for the cooperating nations, but will enhance their mutual prosperity by expanding the volume of trade.

Furthermore, the aggregate measures of the terms of trade may miss significant changes in bilateral terms of trade. As Mundell (1964) explained in a three-country model, tariff preferences exchanged between two countries are likely to improve their terms of trade vis-à-vis the rest of the world while deteriorating the terms of trade of the excluded country.[7] This may explain the American obsession with eliminating Britain's imperial preferences. Discrimination against U.S. exports in the United Kingdom and Canada, two of the country's most important trading partners, may have adversely affected America's terms of

---

[7] Chang and Winters (2002) find empirical support for this result in the context of the Mercosur agreement in South America.

3.1 Economic Theory and Trade Agreements

trade (and volume of trade) with respect to those countries. For example, in 1937, the average preference on UK goods receiving preferences in the Commonwealth was about 20 percent (MacDougall and Hutt 1954). In 1946, Canada's average tariff on total imports was 6.6 percent as applied to the United Kingdom and 12.9 percent as applied to the United States.[8] This margin of preference deterred U.S. exports and, as we have seen, the elimination of discrimination in imperial preferences was one of the principal objectives of the United States in creating the GATT. While we cannot provide definitive evidence that America's terms of trade deteriorated as a result of imperial preferences, such an outcome is highly plausible.[9]

Another way of assessing the rationale for the GATT is by examining the statements made by national representatives at the opening of the Geneva conference. While taking such statements at face value may divert attention from hidden motives or agenda, not to examine such statements would be to discard potentially interesting evidence about the reasons for having a GATT, particularly if the statements go beyond mere standard invocations of the common good.

The statements by developing-country representatives provide limited support for the terms-of-trade hypothesis. That is, these representatives seemed to want to increase the prices of their commodity exports, either by improving their access to other markets or by establishing a commodity agreement in the ITO that would stabilize those prices. De Vilehna Ferreira Braza (Brazil) did not hide that his country was particularly pre-occupied with the international trade for commodities, and thus, was very much geared towards achieving a solution to the persistent problems that commodity trade was facing.[10] Sitzcovich (Chile) expressed a position very similar to that advocated by Brazil: his country was largely dependent on exports of raw materials. Reducing, if not eliminating altogether, fluctuations in world prices for raw materials was very much what he was after. The signing of inter-commodity agreements was thus a priority for his government, and a measure indeed appropriate to help developing countries increase their production and export earnings.[11] Clark (Cuba) was in the same vein with Chile, and Brazil. Commodity trading preoccupied him, and more importantly the stabilization (and perhaps improvement) of prices for sugar and tobacco.[12]

---

[8] See Leacy (1983), series G 486–487.
[9] Eichengreen and Irwin (1995) report evidence from an empirical gravity-equation model that imperial preferences may have diverted trade away from nonparticipants.
[10] See E/PC/T/PV.2/4 at pp. 20ff.   [11] See E/PC/T/PV.2/4 pp. 3ff.
[12] See E/PC/T/PV.2/4 pp. 17ff.

3.2 Commitments and Trade Agreements

Another explanation for trade agreements is that they serve as a commitment device that allows governments to ignore pressure from domestic interests (import-competing producers) to impose trade barriers. Two different but related commitment theories can be distinguished: economic commitment and political commitment. In both cases, trade agreements serve as a "hands-tying" mechanism that improves the bargaining position of each signatory government in relation to various domestic pressure groups. According to this approach, governments want to pursue a trade policy that will maximize national welfare, but special interests (such as domestic producers that compete against imports) make it politically impossible for domestic authorities to implement such a policy. So the government signs a trade agreement with other countries that takes trade policy out of the hands of domestic politicians and also raises the costs of returning to a discretionary policy of high tariffs.[13]

The economic-commitment approach considers the case where governments sign binding agreements that reduce tariff levels. The economic-commitment theory differs fundamentally from the terms-of-trade theory in that there is no international externality associated with trade-policy choices. This approach has been championed by Tumlir (1985) and, more recently, by Maggi and Rodríguez-Clare (1998, 2007). Maggi and Rodríguez-Clare (1998) focus on a small country (thereby ruling out terms-of-trade effects) in which factors of production are sector specific in the short run but mobile in the long run. Even if the government reaps some political benefits (from the specific factors) by imposing trade restrictions in the short run, it may nevertheless wish to commit to a free-trade agreement to avoid the economic distortion to resource allocation. In their framework, the speed of adjustment of factors over time between sectors, as well as the preferences of the government for campaign contributions over economic efficiency, determine the political outcome: the faster the adjustment and the more efficiency is valued, the more likely a government will prefer the improved allocation of resources as a result of trade agreements to the forgone

---

[13] The essence of the problem is one of time consistency – the government wishes to pursue a certain policy at time A, but knows that political developments at time B may pressure it to adopt a policy that undermines those objectives. For example, suppose that a government wishes to encourage the development of an industry that uses steel as its primary input. To do so, it would like to commit to maintain a low tariff on steel. But it knows that at some future time, an economic shock to the domestic steel industry might put great pressure on it to raise steel tariffs. Because the domestic steel-consuming industry is aware of this problem, it will not invest in its own expansion as the government desires. To avoid this problem, the government enters a trade agreement binding steel tariffs at a lower level. See Staiger and Tabellini (1987).

3.2 Commitments and Trade Agreements

rents from the political process by maintaining trade restrictions. Maggi and Rodríguez-Clare (2007) extend the analysis by blending standard terms-of-trade externalities with a desire by governments to commit themselves through trade agreements.

A number of authors have taken issue with important features of the commitment theory. Srinivasan (2005), for example, asks why is there need for an *international* commitment, if the source of the problem is domestic? One could respond that the commitment theory does not pretend that it offers the first best response to a domestic distortion: it simply offers *one* plausible response.

How useful is the economic theory of commitment? The validity of this approach largely depends on the credibility of the commitment, but one can question how strong GATT commitments are in practice. First, the GATT contains a number of provisions that allow deviation from commitments in the face of domestic pressures to do so (safeguards, antidumping, etc.). Second, the GATT explicitly provides for re-negotiation of tariff commitments, which members can undertake in response to domestic pressures to deviate from them. Finally, flat-out violations of the GATT contract are possible, since GATT remedies are, as a matter of practice, prospective only. (Indeed, we observe persistent violations of the GATT contract over the years. For some countries at least, those who can "afford" countermeasures, commitments theory does not seem to be a persuasive explanation as far as their participation to the multilateral trading system is concerned.)

In light of all of the above, it is questionable whether GATT really serves to tie the hands of signatory governments very effectively. The commitment theory cannot be dismissed simply on this basis, however, because the GATT could raise the costs of adopting certain antitrade policies enough to reduce their likelihood. This may have some value to signatory governments in their bargaining game with domestic interest groups. For example, Staiger and Tabellini (1999) present evidence that GATT rules do in fact allow governments to commit to lower tariffs. Commitment theory might also be useful in explaining specific behavior: for example, a government might be willing to take a dispute and lose before the GATT, only to turn then to its domestic constituency and explain that its hands are indeed tied, or, that, at the very least, it would be now quite costly to disregard the GATT ruling. This is what Robert Hudec called "use GATT as an excuse." One might have difficulty in *proving* that this is indeed what happened in particular cases, although one might legitimately speculate along these lines.[14]

---

[14] We can probably explain, along these lines, Mexico's nonappeal against the Panel report on *Mexico – Telecoms*, where Mexico lost on rather shaky legal grounds. The WTO report provided Mexico with a golden opportunity to "tame" its telecoms monopolist, *Telmex*,

On the other hand, the gradual completion of the multilateral trade contract – from GATT in 1947, to GATS, TRIPs, DSU, and all other trade agreements nowadays – has arguably added to the persuasiveness of this theory: the more complete the contract (in the sense of more and more meaningful international disciplines), the higher the value of this explanation for signing trade agreements. Our study, alas, concerns the GATT as originally negotiated, and not today's GATT. The commitment theory, finally, also suffers from a lack of research explaining the various GATT instruments *in light of* commitment theory.

With reference to the domestic commitment theory, no country's representative explicitly stated that it wanted to adopt an international trade agreement so that it could ignore domestic protectionist interests. That would have offended those interests and have been too impolitic. To the contrary, several representatives stated that they wanted *more* flexibility and fewer constraints in the agreement in order to pursue various domestic objectives, such as using trade-policy measures for economic development. In his speech to the *Preparatory Committee* during the opening of the *Geneva Conference*, Coombs (Australia) stressed that high levels of employment and demand would do much to promote a high volume of world trade. His country sought rules that would be flexible to accommodate countries at different stages of development and with different political philosophies. He was preaching in favor of understanding the *various* purposes that tariffs pursue as a precondition for a successful meeting.[15]

Chundrigar (India) argued for introducing more flexibility in the ITO Charter to allow developing countries the ability to adjust based on their different economic circumstances. The ITO charter should not be conceived to be just a policeman, in his view, but rather a contributor to development. Nonetheless, he rejected blind protectionism, arguing that flexibility should be used in order to promote development, and not to protect domestic producers' welfare.[16] Moubarak (Lebanon) agreed with India's insistence on flexibility. In his view, a transition was necessary for his country's customs union with Syria in order to adjust to the rules in the GATT/ITO.[17] Holloway (South Africa) stressed his country's interest in trade expansion but without neglecting the need for some governments (like his) occasionally to protect their domestic market.[18]

However, as reported in Chapter 1, there is some evidence – particularly among Canadian officials – that they saw the GATT as an opportunity to head off domestic protectionist interests after the war. Canadian officials repeatedly emphasized the importance of early action before vested interests had a chance

without having to take the political blame for its actions that could be attributed to an exogenous force, the WTO Panel.

[15] See E/PC/T/PV2/1 at pp. 3ff.
[16] See E/PC/T/PV.2/4 at pp. 7ff.
[17] See E/PC/T/PV.2/4 at pp. 14ff.
[18] Id. pp. 9ff.

3.2 Commitments and Trade Agreements

to kill the chances for a multilateral accord. A memo reporting on Canadian-American commercial-policy discussions in January-February 1944 noted:

> such an attempt should be made at the earliest possible moment while conditions of relative commodity scarcity still obtain and foreign competition is of relatively little concern to domestic producers and before demobilization of war industry has set in and vested interests in war-time restrictions on imports become too highly developed (CDER 11, 70).

And as the U.S. Embassy in Canada reported, a senior trade official (Norman Robertson)

> is convinced that the best time to negotiate basic tariff reductions is during the depths of a depression when the inefficient industries have been driven to the wall and eliminated, or at a time, like the present, when because of the exigencies of war normal trade has been disrupted and directed into new channels which, under the control of governmental agencies, should be efficient channels.... With vested interests for the time being in the background he feels that this is the time to take basic action toward reducing tariffs. If we do not strike now, he is afraid we will drift back into the old pre-war methods under which, he feels, it will be impossible to effect adequate reduction of tariff barriers (FRUS 1943, I, 1104–1105).

From this report, some Canadian officials viewed the GATT as serving the purpose of domestic commitment.

Still, the GATT does not appear to have been a strong economic contract for lowering trade barriers, not only because countries were reluctant to reduce their tariffs and preferences in Geneva but also because the GATT text includes a multitude of escape clauses that all parties desired.

A second approach to commitment is political. Even if the GATT contract only weakly constrains the use of tariffs and trade instruments, a trade agreement by itself may affect domestic politics in a way that it allows the government use it as a commitment. Of course, the degree to which a country can make a political commitment via a trade agreement depends upon its political system. In this regard, the changing domestic politics of trade as a result of the Reciprocal Trade Agreements Act of 1934 in the United States has been a major focus of research. According to many political scientists, such as O'Halloran (1994), Bailey, Goldstein, and Weingast (1997), Schneitz (2000), and others, the RTAA fundamentally changed the domestic political economy of U.S. trade policy by shifting tariff determination away from the special-interest dominated, logrolling-prone legislature to the national-interest-minded executive. Rather than undertake an easily reversible unilateral tariff reduction by Congressional legislation, the Roosevelt administration opted to reduce U.S. tariffs in the context of foreign-trade agreements. This method bundled domestic tariff reductions with foreign tariff reductions on U.S. exports, and therefore strengthened the interests of exporters in promoting this policy (Gilligan 1997). The RTAA supported a political commitment to more liberal trade policies by making it more difficult for the legislature (Congress) to reverse them. For example, the president always had authority to sign trade agreements that would take effect with the approval of two-thirds of the Senate. But this meant that a minority, only one-third, of the Senate could block a trade-liberalizing agreement. By requiring a simple majority for its approval, the RTAA raised the bar for the number of legislators to impede trade-liberalizing agreements from one-third to one-half.

Yet just as with the economic commitments in the GATT, the political commitment in the RTAA system is also imperfect. A unified Republican government could easily have repealed the RTAA and withdrawn from the trade agreements. Indeed, as Irwin and Kroszner (1999) and Hiscox (1999) point out, it was not until there was bipartisan support for the RTAA approach that it became politically secure. This did not occur immediately; as late as 1940, Republicans voted consistently against the RTAA. Bipartisan support was fragile even in 1945. Yet ultimately a consensus did emerge, perhaps promoted by the RTAA itself, which activated exporting groups to become more politically active and thereby counterbalanced import-competing interests.

Thus, the delegation of power from Congress to the executive branch and the use of trade agreements appear to have played important roles in securing domestic political support for lower trade barriers, at least in the United States. Further research is needed to determine whether trade agreements proved to be a useful way of securing a domestic political commitment for lower trade barriers in other countries.[19]

3.3 Foreign Policy Motivations for Trade Agreements

Robert Baldwin (1986, 91) has noted that "economists tend to judge the rules of organizations such as the GATT on the basis of whether they promote economic efficiency, growth, and stability." Yet, in his view, "maximizing the collective economic welfare of individuals making up either a country or the world is, however, not the main policy objective of the GATT." Rather, "the broad objective is to help to maintain international political stability by establishing

---

[19] See, for example, Verdier (1994).

3.3 Foreign Policy Motivations for Trade Agreements

rules of 'good behavior' as well as mechanisms for settling disputes." Baldwin believes that "the objectives of those establishing the organization were mainly political" and that "even if the above reasoning by trade economists is valid in most cases, it seems to be more the result of a happy coincidence of economic and political objectives rather than of foresight and deliberate choice by the founders of the GATT."

In assessing these political motivations, one starting point for thinking about international trade policy in the field of political science has been hegemonic-stability theory. Often associated with the work of Charles Kindleberger (1973, 1981), this influential theory seeks to explain the structure of the international trade regime. Broadly speaking, Kindleberger suggested that only a single, strong and dominant actor in international politics can provide and maintain a stable international economic order. The leadership of a hegemonic power can produce a collectively desirable outcome for all states by providing certain international public goods, such as a monetary system (gold standard or dollar standard) and an open trade regime. Providing these public goods fosters order and stability in the world, and thereby serves the national and foreign-policy interests of the hegemon.

The burden of the hegemon is that it must underwrite the costs of providing these public goods and seek the support of other countries for the maintenance of the regime. But the hegemon is willing to bear these costs and undertake this effort because the alternative is conflict and chaos (from which the hegemon will suffer). In the absence of a hegemonic leader, coordination problems and the prisoners' dilemma will prevent countries from cooperating to establish an open, liberal international economic system. Thus, in periods where there is no such dominant state to provide such public goods, the international system is characterized by disorder and is thus an undesirable outcome from the standpoint of all states.

The theory of hegemonic stability has generated an enormous debate among political scientists.[20] The initial appeal of hegemonic-stability theory was that it seemed to explain three phases in the world economy: the late-19th-century period of open trade and financial relations (overseen by the United Kingdom, which supported the gold standard and open trade policies), the chaos of the interwar period (when trade and financial relations broke down because there was no dominant actor to provide stability to the system), and the post World War II period (when the United States provided the leadership in the system). Upon closer inspection, political scientists have dissected the theory and found it

---

[20] For a short survey of the literature, see Lake (1993).

wanting on historical grounds (it does not fit the 19th-century British experience very well) and theoretical grounds (it lacks sharp predictions about the behavior of the hegemon), but it may still explain the creation of new international regimes.[21]

One basic question is whether an open international trade regime is a public good or not. A public good is defined as non-rival (consumption or use by one state does not impinge or diminish its benefits for another), and non-excludable (other states cannot be prevented from enjoying its benefits). Trade may be non-rival, in the sense that it is mutually beneficial to both parties, but the benefits of an open trading system such as the GATT may be excludable if non-GATT signatories are not granted MFN status. Therefore, the trading system may not have the collective-action problems associated with the provision of public goods and may not require a leader to create it.[22]

Another ambiguous element of the theory is whether a hegemon will pursue benevolent policies aimed at improving world welfare or coercive policies aimed at improving its own welfare, possibly at the expense of others. In Kindleberger's view, the dominant power will provide public goods and is, therefore, benevolent because it bears the costs of maintaining an open system while others who benefit do not pay those costs. Alternatively, Krasner (1976) and others have suggested that hegemonic states will use their power to structure the trading system to their own advantage and then impose the system on others.

Regardless of whether it was providing a "public good," the United States certainly provided international economic leadership during the 1940s, but whether it was able to act as a powerful hegemon is highly questionable (Ikenberry 1989). In the case of the GATT, the evidence in Chapter 1 clearly points to the United States modifying and tempering its proposals for the postwar trading system based on the demands of other states that it wished to include in postwar arrangements. In particular, despite its unique and preponderant power, the United States accommodated many British demands, notably its desire to retain imperial preferences. In addition, many developing countries, led by Australia, Brazil, and others, insisted upon and were granted many exceptions from the disciplines in the GATT. This behavior is hard to reconcile with the Krasner (1976) view that the powerful hegemon constructs the international economic order with only its interests in mind. As Stein (1984, 358) argues, a hegemon simply cannot create an international trading system based on low tariffs because that requires bargaining between sovereign states.

[21] For example, in the 19th century, the United Kingdom was the world's hegemonic power, but it did nothing to create an open trading system. See McKeown (1983) and Stein (1984).
[22] See Conybeare (1984) for an analysis; he argues that international trade is more akin to a prisoners' dilemma than a public good.

3.3 Foreign Policy Motivations for Trade Agreements

One reason for the accommodating stance of a hegemon toward others is that it has noneconomic objectives in mind. As Stein (1984, 359) points out:

> The hegemon's willingness to accept asymmetric trade agreements is not a function of economic interests alone. Both trade agreements and trade disputes have inherently international political underpinnings; their foundations are not solely economic: Great Britain and the United States had important political objectives for which they were prepared to make economic concessions.

The most important political motivation for the GATT, for which the United States was prepared to make economic concessions, was world peace, in particular, the idea that flourishing trade reduces conflict among nations. The liberal argument that trade promotes peace goes back at least to the 18th century and is associated with Baron de Montesquieu and Immanuel Kant. The idea was later expounded by 19th-century liberal thinkers, such as Richard Cobden and John Stuart Mill.[23]

As Chapter 1 noted, Cordell Hull enthusiastically embraced this view. As Hull wrote in 1934: "The truth is universally recognized that trade between nations is the greatest peace-maker and civilizer within human experience." The Roosevelt administration's program

> to secure trade agreements with the principal nations is the first step in a broad movement to increase international trade. Upon this program, rests largely my hope of insured peace and the fullest measure of prosperity (Schatz 1970, 86–87).

Indeed, Schatz (1970) points out that Hull envisioned the reciprocal-trade-agreements program in the 1930s as the first step in a worldwide campaign to restore political stability.

Was Hull correct in his view that international trade promotes peace and cooperation among nations? At the time, Hull was certainly perceived as being

---

[23] Mill (1909 [1848], 582) expressed the idea this way: "It is commerce which is rapidly rendering war obsolete, by strengthening and multiplying the personal interests which act in natural opposition to it. And it may be said without exaggeration that the great extent and rapid increase of international trade, in being the principal guarantee of the peace of the world, is the great permanent security for the uninterrupted progress of the ideas, the institutions, and the character of the human race)." Norman Angell's *The Great Illusion* (1909) was an influential statement of this view, but its publication just prior to the outbreak of World War I served to discredit the trade-peace doctrine. However, Angell did not argue that war was impossible, rather that it was futile. His view that war is economically irrational was subsequently distorted to become a claim that wars would not occur because of economic integration.

correct in the eyes of many. In 1945, he was awarded the Nobel Peace Prize for his efforts to promote international political and economic cooperation.[24] In the opening public statements at the Geneva conference, there is much support for the view that economic cooperation would promote political cooperation. In particular, countries that had been directly involved in World War II, and that had suffered great material damage and casualties, saw the GATT as a part of a new era of international cooperation that would reduce the risks of war in the future. In the view of Baron van der Straten-Waillet (Belgium), the economic union between his country, the Netherlands, and Luxembourg offered an appropriate example of how economic nationalism can be defeated; it should be extrapolated to the world sphere. While acknowledging the leading role that the U.S. government was playing, he argued in favor of emulating at the world level his own country's experience.[25] Wilgress (Canada) offered a similar view to that of the Benelux countries: he preached in favor of relaxing (to the extent necessary) one's national sovereignty in order to promote the common good.[26] Philip (France) stressed the positive role that bilateral trade agreements could play, and argued in favor of ensuring that they coexist with ITO, since they share the same objective: to open up markets.[27] Huysmans (Netherlands) urged the ITO to open up to enemies as well, since, in his view, the contribution to world peace would be increased as more and more joined the ranks of the ITO.[28]

Sir Stafford Cripps (UK) started by stressing that "we all failed to appreciate sufficiently the direct relation between international economic policies and the danger of war." In his view, the GATT and ITO project demonstrated the will for international cooperation and the abandonment of dangerous unilateral policies.[29] Finally, Wilcox (United States) emphasized the links between the GATT/ITO with the other Bretton Woods institutions, and the wider peace process. Echoing the spirit of Hull, he explained his government's view that the establishment of the world trading system was a major contribution to the new

---

[24] As the Chairman of the Nobel Committee noted in his presentation, "Cordell Hull has devoted his entire life to the stabilization of international relations. Best known to the public are his untiring efforts in the field of commercial policy, efforts inspired by his desire to counteract autarchic tendencies both in the U.S.A. and abroad.... This is the driving spirit behind his fight against isolationism at home, his efforts to create a peace bloc of states on the American continents, and his work for the United Nations Organization." http://nobelprize.org/nobel_prizes/peace/laureates/1945/press.html (last visited Jan. 17, 2008).

[25] See E/PC/T/PV.2/1 at pp. 25ff. [26] See E/PC/T/PV.2/2 at pp. 2ff.
[27] See E/PC/T/PV.2/2 at pp. 13ff. [28] See E/PC/T/PV.2/3 at pp. 22ff.
[29] See E/PC/TPV.2/3 at pp. 3ff.

3.3 Foreign Policy Motivations for Trade Agreements

world order that nations would be jointly building in order to break with the past.[30]

Is it true that trade fosters peace?[31] There are several channels by which increased international trade or economic interdependence may reduce the chances of war and increase the likelihood of cooperation. The higher incomes that are associated with greater trade increase the opportunity cost of military conflict. Glick and Taylor (2005) document the large and persistent effects of war on trade and find that the economic costs of disrupted trade may be as large as the conventionally measured "direct" costs of war. Trade also provides an alternative mechanism for extracting resources from other countries; goods can be acquired by mutually beneficial exchange rather than by military conquest. Thus, the fear of the potential economic consequences from the disruption of trade, and the reduced benefits of obtaining resources via military means, may deter some states from initiating a conflict.

Another channel by which trade can reduce the likelihood of war is by increasing communication across states. Recent theories of strategic bargaining suggest that war results from asymmetric information about states' interests and capabilities rather than calculations about the costliness of war itself. Economic interdependence provides more information across states, thereby promoting transparency and facilitating costly signaling, and thereby reducing asymmetries of information.

However, conflict theorists have also suggested that trade can increase conflict. As Morrow (1999, 487) notes:

> current theory on the initiation and escalation of disputes casts doubt on the idea that trade prevents international conflict. If higher interdependence reduces a nation's resolve for war with its trading partners, the effect of interdependence on conflict is indeterminate. It could make the initiation and escalation of dispute more or less likely. Trade makes war less attractive to both parties, but the target's lower willingness to fight makes coercion of the target easier and more attractive to the initiator.

---

[30] See E/PC/T/PV.2/4 at pp. 26ff.

[31] Some political scientists, particularly those from the "realist" school that focuses on international conflict as a function of raw power politics, are skeptical about any relationship between trade and peace. For example Gilpin (1987, 58) argues that there is no relationship between the two: "the major point to be made in these matters is that trade and other economic relations are not in themselves critical to the establishment of either cooperation or conflictual international relations. No generalizations on the relationship of economic interdependence and political behavior appear possible.... In general, the character of international relations and the question of peace and war are determined primarily by the larger configurations of power and strategic interest among both the great and small powers in the system."

Through this channel, Rowe (2005) suggests that globalization may have helped to cause World War I, although McDonald and Sweeney (2007) strongly disputes this.[32]

Given the different perspectives on the determinants of conflict and the role of trade in influencing them, the relationship between trade and conflict is an empirical question. A large empirical literature in political science on this question starts from the pioneering work of Solomon Polachek (1980). Polachek found that greater trade was associated with lower incidence of conflict. Most subsequent empirical studies have tended to support the idea that there is a positive link between trade and peace. Indeed, in a recent survey of these studies, Mansfield and Pollins (2001, 837) conclude that "most such studies support the liberal hypothesis that heightened economic exchange inhibits conflict, although some research challenges these findings."[33]

However, as with most empirical relationships, establishing definitive causality is extremely difficult. In this case, trade may promote peace, but peace certainly promotes trade and the prospect of conflict reduces trade. Hence, states that are politically friendly are more likely to trade with one another, whereas trade may be low between states with a likelihood of conflict. This can account for the positive correlation between trade and peace, but in this case there is no causal relationship between trade and peace.

---

[32] Rowe argues that increased trade constrained domestic efforts to strengthen military forces, as the liberal idea suggests, but this heightened insecurity in Europe. By generating visible constraints on military force, Rowe argues that it weakened deterrence in prewar Europe because it made the threat of force less credible and states became less confident that they would deter rivals from aggressive policies: "the knowledge that other states confronted strong internal constraints on military force increased the probability of miscalculation by undermining the credibility of their threats to use force" (Rowe 2005, 438). As Rowe (2005, 445-446) concludes: "liberal theory correctly predicts that globalization generates substantial internal constraints on military force.... Where liberal theory errs, however, is in assuming that internal constraints on military force necessarily strengthen prospects for international peace. This overlooks the necessary role that the credible threat of force plays in protecting national interest and sustaining international order.... Europe did not go to war despite globalization's constraints on military force in pre-war Europe; Europe went to war because these constraints undermined the very foundations on which European peace rested." By contrast, McDonald and Sweeney (2007) argue that protectionist trade policies contributed to the outbreak of World War I.

[33] The one major dissenter from this conclusion is Barbieri (1996, 2002), who finds instead that economic interdependence, under certain circumstances, promotes conflict. However, her work has been criticized on several methodological grounds and is not widely accepted. Several studies have been able to replicate Barbieri's findings, but find that her conclusions are sensitive to the empirical specification. One major problem with her approach is that bilateral trade is measured as the share of a partner's trade in the country's total trade, rather than as a share of the economy, so that country size or dependence on trade is not accurately captured (Oneal and Russett 1999). In addition, Xiang, Xu, and Keteku (2007) find that including independent measures of country power reverses Barbieri's conclusions.

3.3 Foreign Policy Motivations for Trade Agreements

Indeed, recent work has cast doubt on the sweeping and unqualified conclusion that trade promotes peace. While finding clear evidence that conflict reduces trade, Glick and Taylor (2005) find no statistical evidence that trade reduces conflict. Kim and Rousseau (2005) investigate the problems of simultaneity bias and find that the trade-peace connection does not survive many alternative specification tests. Furthermore, Martin, Mayer, and Thoenig (2008) attempt to control more carefully for the endogeneity of war and trade. In their framework, an increase in bilateral trade reduced the probability of conflict between countries, but an increase in multilateral trade increases the likelihood of conflict. The latter reduces the costs of war with any given country, and thereby weakens the incentive to make concessions to avert escalation. Thus, an increase in trade between two countries reduces the likelihood of conflict between them, but increases the likelihood of trade with third countries. However, the authors also suggest that multilateral openness may increase the probability of local wars but decrease the risk of global conflict. Using data from the post-World War II period, they find empirical support for these conclusions.

These empirical weaknesses have led researchers to believe that the relationship between trade and peace may be a contingent one that is mediated by various factors that can affect the strength of the relationship. For example, there is evidence that while trade inhibits conflict between democracies, autocracies are insulated from popular pressure and hence rising trade has no impact on their propensities to initiate military conflict (Gelpi and Grieco 2007). Furthermore, some studies find that economic interdependence reduces conflict between high-income countries but has little impact on conflict between low-income countries (Hegre 2000). One of the most robust empirical relationships in political science is that democracies tend not to fight one another, so to the extent that more trade promotes political liberalization, it may indirectly promote peace.

Of course, trade was just one component of U.S. strategy of international engagement following World War II. The United States – chiefly, Cordell Hull and the State Department – sought to create a web of multilateral institutions, the centerpiece being the United Nations, that would support international cooperation and lead to conditions favoring peace. In his famous essay "Perpetual Peace," Immanuel Kant emphasized the pacifying effects of the triad of republican constitutions, cooperative international organizations, and economic interdependence. In work that is highly regarded by political scientists, Oneal and Russett (2001) find broad empirical support for Kant's proposition. Indeed, Oneal and Russett find that trade is the strongest part of the triad, although the other components of the triad matter as well. Of course, the major problem in formally testing the Kant hypothesis is that so many aspects of the triad are interrelated. For example, democratic governments tend to join cooperative institutions, tend to trade more, and tend to be more peaceful with respect to one another, but there are a wide variety of causal mechanisms at work, making it difficult to disentangle cause and effect and correlation from causation.

While the empirical relationship between trade and peace may never be determined precisely, Hull and many of his generation strongly believed that cooperation to establish more liberal trade policies would not only bring economic benefits, but would lay the groundwork for political cooperation in other areas and hence reduce the chances of military conflict. Indeed, if there was one overarching rationale for the GATT, as envisioned by its founders, it was simply one component of a broad effort to avoid the problems of the 1930s and establish conditions that might increase the chances for world peace after World War II.

One final, related political motivation for trade agreements is related to another noneconomic objective of governments: national security. Indeed, political scientists have also argued that international trade creates national-security externalities and this is the purpose of trade-liberalizing agreements among allies (Gowa 1989, Gowa and Mansfield 1993). The gains from trade strengthen the economies of countries that choose to liberalize their trade together, and therefore alter the power relationships between these partners and their rivals. Therefore, countries will prefer to liberalize trade with allies to internalize the security externalities arising from trade and restrict trade with adversaries. In addition, Gowa (1989) maintains that the evolution of alliances into free-trade coalitions is more likely in bipolar than in multipolar international systems, something that emerged after World War II.

The problem with the security-externality story as an explanation for the GATT is that the agreement had been envisioned far in advance of the outbreak of the Cold War. The United States invited the Soviet Union and others to participate in the GATT and ITO, although the Soviet Union declined to do so. Thus, it appears that the exclusion of the Soviet bloc from the GATT was more a choice made by the Soviets than a strategic decision on the part of the United States to exclude and thereby weaken them as rivals.[34] The planning for the Geneva conference occurred long before the breakdown in American-Soviet relations, although the conference opened a year after Winston Churchill gave his famous "Iron Curtain" speech in March 1946. Indeed, the formal Western military alliance – North Atlantic Treaty Organization (NATO) – was formed in 1949, long after steps had been taken to establish a new international trading system.

However, the security externalities identified by political scientists may be better at explaining the end-game of the Geneva conference. Recall from Chapter 1 that Will Clayton, the lead U.S. official at Geneva, was willing to break off the

---

[34] See footnote 95 in Chapter 1. The exclusion was not total: Czechoslovakia, which shifted to the Communist block halfway through the negotiations, remained a contracting party to the GATT.

negotiations due to British intransigence over imperial preferences. However, he was overruled by the State Department largely on foreign-policy grounds. After discussing the matter with President Truman, Acting Secretary of State Robert Lovett reported to Clayton:

> We are concerned over likelihood that USSR will exploit fully any such differences between US and UK just as they are now trying to capitalize on British weakness by increasing pressure throughout Eastern Europe and Near East. Consequently best course seems to be to get best agreement possible in present highly unfavorable circumstances and reserve part of our negotiating position for use at more propitious time by trimming our offers correspondingly. From standpoint of public and congressional opinion here thin agreement of this kind we believe better than none, especially if made clear that present agreement only an initial stage in dealing with this problem (FRUS 1947, I, 981).

Furthermore, the national-security rationale may help explain the domestic support for the GATT in the late 1940s and early 1950s when the Republican party, which had traditionally opposed trade agreements, gained more political power. Once the Cold War between the United States and the Soviet Union was a clear feature of the international political environment, then a strong trade relationship between the United States and Western Europe through the GATT took on greater importance. Certainly in terms of domestic U.S. politics, the GATT was considered important as much for its political symbolism of cooperation as for its economic effects. For example, Fordham (1998) finds that Congressional opposition to President Harry Truman's foreign policies came from states and districts with more import-competing producers, and support came from European-oriented trade and financial relationships. Thus, there was an economic basis for the foreign policy of the period.

3.4 Concluding Assessments

This brief Chapter has considered three approaches that explain the rationale for a trade agreement such as the GATT: to avoid terms of trade losses, to establish a commitment (both economic and political) against domestic interests, and to pursue foreign-policy objectives related to peace and security. The evidence that we presented in Chapters 1 and 2 provides *some* support for all three explanations for trade agreements, although the case for economic commitment emerges as the one with the weakest support. The negotiators appear to have been hopeful that the establishment of a multilateral trading system would contribute to world peace. But because the major parties did not want to have trade concessions go un-reciprocated, the multilateral approach is also consistent with the terms-of-trade type of reasoning (which is also related to the notion of market access and expanding the volume of goods traded).

The structure of the bargain suggests that terms-of-trade considerations were implicitly an important part of its rationale. Recall that negotiations would take place following the principal-supplier rule and that reciprocity was the guiding negotiating principle.[35] A focus on principal suppliers and reciprocal concessions hints that the arrangement was indeed focused on unraveling the damage done to the volume of trade by noncooperative tariffs, akin to the core problem in the terms-of-trade models. Moreover, provisions such as the safeguard option in GATT Article XIX, the re-negotiation of schedules permitted by Article XXVIII, and the NVC in Art. XXIII.1b, lend extra support to this thesis, since these instruments address the need for rebalancing of concessions following a deviation. Thus, it is plausible to argue that the actions of trade negotiators in 1947 were guided and shaped by terms-of-trade considerations. Even if terms-of-trade considerations were not at the forefront of the minds of the GATT founders or consciously articulated, the volume of trade (a notion intimately linked to terms of trade, as briefly alluded to) certainly was. And their actions were, certainly, consistent with the terms-of-trade view, that a multilateral tariff reduction would internalize an important international externality and be superior to countries setting their trade policies unilaterally.

Although some aspects of the GATT (such as the regulation of subsidies, or antidumping) cast doubt on the terms-of-trade theory, the most central motivation for the GATT seems to be along the lines of unwinding the retaliatory trade policies and other protectionist measures that had built up during the 1930s. In other words, terms of trade are useful in understanding the tariff bargain struck, but does not help us understand each and every provision of the GATT.

By contrast, the GATT negotiating history lends at best modest support to the domestic commitment theory. The economic commitments in the GATT were relatively weak, and many countries insisted upon provisions that would allow them to escape from international obligations in situations that they thought would be applicable to them (i.e., balance-of-payments difficulties, economic development, agricultural subsidies, etc.). Commitment theory might be more appropriately used to explain why, in modern day, *some* nations join the WTO, now that the WTO has a wider mandate and that the GATT *acquis* has completed the original contract. Even now, nonetheless, such a claim would rest on shaky grounds in light of the rather inefficient remedies built in the WTO legal system.

[35] The principal-supplier rule came out of the selective (bilateral, product-by-product) negotiating approach insisted upon by the U.S. Congress. As Chapter 1 noted, at the staff level, both U.S. and UK trade negotiators would have preferred an across-the-board horizontal reduction in import duties.

3.4 Concluding Assessments

There is somewhat more evidence in favor of political commitment. At least in the United States, the turn to trade agreements as a result of the 1934 Reciprocal Trade Agreements act took trade policy away from the legislature, which had proven to be highly sensitive to import-competing interests. Certainly within the American political system, so vividly described by Schattschneider (1935), a purpose of reciprocal trade agreements was to overcome a domestic political system that was hopelessly biased in favor of import-competing producers while neglecting the impact of trade policy on exporters and the nation's foreign-policy interests. The GATT helped to extend a multilateral setting to this bilateral-agreements approach, and reinforced the containment of domestic political interests that previously had proven adept at getting Congress to enact higher tariffs. There is some limited evidence that GATT was viewed as a "hands-tying" mechanism in relation to domestic interest groups, for example, by at least some of its signatories.

While economists sometimes tend to neglect the foreign-policy implications of trade policy, the State Department clearly saw trade agreements as part of a new postwar framework for the world. We also see in the history considerable desire to promote cooperation that was, in some ways, greater than the desire to promote a narrow conception of the national economic interest. For example, the most powerful country, the United States, did not insist upon complete reciprocity. This behavior arguably goes beyond that captured by the terms-of-trade models. In such models, governments have no regard for the welfare of other nations *per se*. Yet there is, as we saw, some historic evidence that the United States (and perhaps others) were prepared to sacrifice some national objectives in the narrow sense, if necessary, to achieve agreement because of the broader benefits that a more prosperous and stable world economy might bring. The overriding goal of U.S. foreign-policy makers was to create an international institutional framework that would secure conditions for world peace in contrast to the way things developed after World War I. There was a clear link between the negotiation of the GATT and the wider Bretton Woods institutions umbrella. What is less clear is the degree to which this "political" motivation for the GATT is analytically distinct from the traditional terms-of-trade account. We have speculated here on one consideration that might distinguish it – in the "political" account, there is some notion that nations, such as the United States, might have been willing to sacrifice (to a limited extent) the usual concerns about national income and domestic distribution in favor of policies that would ensure prosperity abroad and thereby reduce the future risks of political instability. And, given the incomplete indications that the United States made greater concessions at the Geneva conference in 1947 than other countries, there is some evidence to support this view.

By any account, however, the hope that international cooperation and lower trade barriers might improve the state of the world economy and foster conditions conducive to world peace was a central animating theme of Cordell Hull and others in the State Department.

In conclusion, we believe that these various theories are perhaps best understood as complementary, rather than competing, explanations for the remarkable achievements that led to the GATT in 1947.

Conclusion

In light of the difficulties that recent multilateral trade negotiating rounds have encountered, trade officials, sometimes with nostalgia, reflect back on the easier trade negotiations of the past. Yet, although the 1940s was a golden age of international institution building, the negotiations that led to the GATT were never easy. The path from James Meade's draft plan for an "International Commercial Union" in 1942 to the Geneva conference in 1947 was fraught with pitfalls, delays, and obstacles. The ambitious plans for an International Trade Organization were eventually abandoned. In its place remained a smaller and shorter agreement on commercial policy that had many weaknesses. Yet the GATT survived the test of time.

The delegates entrusted with the task of rebuilding the multilateral system of world trade and payments were a rare breed. It is unusual to see some of the greatest economic minds actively participate in national delegations, and work together with the political establishment towards the institutionalization of international cooperation and the constraint of economic unilateralism. It is to Henry Cabot Lodge that the phrase "the U.N. system is designed to avoid taking us to hell, but it cannot take us to heaven" is attributed. The Bretton Woods institutions and the GATT were designed as the first steps towards the other way.

The negotiating record amply supports the view that the GATT is very much the end product of a transatlantic negotiation. Other countries mainly reacted to a design that had already been largely agreed upon by U.S. and UK officials. This is not to say that they had no influence at all. Canada encouraged American officials to think multilaterally in scope and broadly in terms of trade liberalization, even though those civil servants had to scale back their initial hopes for wide tariff cuts and a strong trade agreement. Canada also suggested the "nuclear" approach in which the GATT was carved out of the larger ITO Charter on the correct presumption that the more inclusive meeting might fail.

Developing countries also intervened and shaped some provisions of the GATT, such as the introduction of a provision on infant-industry protection, and later Part IV. Nonetheless, the Anglo-American transatlantic partners came up with the basic GATT design, particularly the strict disciplines on trade combined with regulatory diversity cum nondiscrimination on domestic instruments. This basic approach has remained intact ever since.

The U.S. and the UK delegates can be credited with a document that fostered trade liberalization for the subsequent 60 years, and probably contributed to world peace. This was a time when leadership rose to the challenges that the world was facing. The institution they created helped solve the specific problem they confronted: the danger that postwar trade policy would remain plagued with high and discriminatory trade barriers that had stifled and compartmentalized world trade in the 1930s. Given the postwar record of expanding world trade and incomes, they succeeded perhaps beyond their wildest hopes. The question today is whether the problems currently facing the world trading system are pressing enough to demand that today's leaders also rise to the occasion and confront the challenge before us.

Annex A – Documents Relating to the Negotiations

1. General Provisions for Inclusion in Trade Agreements, as revised to December 13, 1941, National Archives II, Lot File 57D-284, Box 89.
2. A Proposal for an International Commercial Union (James Meade), July 25, 1942, Public Records Office, T 230/14.
3. Anglo-American Discussions under Article VII: Section on Commercial Policy, November 1943, Public Records Office, BT 11/2215.
4. Proposed Multilateral Convention on Commercial Policy: Summary of Significant Provisions, U.S. State Department, October 1944, National Archives II, Lot File 57D-284, Box 24.
5. Excerpts from "Proposals for Expansion of World Trade and Employment," State Department Publication No. 2411, December 1945.
6. Preparations for Preliminary International Meeting on Trade and Employment, February 6, 1946, FRUS (1946, I, 1280-1289).
7. U.S. Delegation Report on First Preparatory Meeting for an International Conference on Trade and Employment (London), December 27, 1946, FRUS (1946, I, 1360-1366).
8. Report on the Geneva GATT Negotiations, Memorandum from State Department to President Truman, October 17, 1947, FRUS 1947, I, 1015-1024.

ANNEX A-1

From National Archives II, Lot File 57D-284, Box 89

General Provisions for Inclusion in Trade Agreeements

As revised to December 19, 1941

Preamble

Provisions Relating to Treatment of Trade in General

(1) Most-favored-nation clause
(2) Internal taxes
(3) Quotas in general
(4) Exchange Control
(5) Monopolies and government purchases
(6) Customs administrative matters, advances in duties, and customs penalties

Provisions Relating to Concessions

(7) Duty concessions by foreign country
(8) Duty concessions by the United States
(9) Compensating taxes
(10) Dutiable value and conversion of currencies
(11) Quotas on scheduled products
(12) Withdrawal or modification of concessions
(13) General provision to safeguard concessions

General Provisions as to Application of Agreement

(14) Territorial application
(15) Exceptions to most-favored-nation treatment
(16) General reservations
(17) Consultation regarding technical matters; committee of sanitary experts
(18) Proclamation, ratification and definitive entry into force
(19) Provisional application
(20) Duration and termination

The President of the United States of America and the [*insert* head of state] of [*insert* country name], being desirous of strengthening the traditional bonds of friendship existing between the two countries by maintaining the principle of equality of treatment in its unconditional and unlimited form as the basis of commercial relations and by granting mutual and reciprocal concessions and advantages for the promotion of trade, have through their respective Plenipotentiaries arrived at the following Agreement:

Article (1)

1. The United States of America and will grant each other unconditional and unrestricted most-favored-nation treatment in all matters concerning customs duties and subsidiary charges of every kind and in the method of

levying duties, and, further, in all matters concerning the rules, formalities and charges imposed in connection with the clearing of goods through the customs, and with respect to all lams or regulations affecting the sale, taxation or use of imported goods within the country.
2. Accordingly, articles the growth, produce or manufacture of either country imported into the other shall in no case be subject, in regard to the matters referred to above, to any duties, taxes or charges other or higher, or to any rules or formalities other or more burdensome, than those to which the like articles the growth, produce or manufacture of any third country are or may hereafter be subject.
3. Similarly, articles exported from the territory of the United States of America or and consigned to the territory of the other country shall in no case be subject with respect to exportation and in regard to the above-mentioned matters, to any duties, taxes or charges other or higher, or to any rules or formalities other or more burdensome, than those to which the like articles when consigned to the territory of any third country are or may hereafter be subject.
4. Any advantage, favor, privilege or immunity which has been or may hereafter be granted by the United States of America or in regard to the above-mentioned matters, to any article originating in any third country or consigned to the territory of any third country shall be accorded immediately and without compensation to the like article originating in or consigned to the territory of or the United States of America, respectively.

Article (2)

Articles the growth, produce or manufacture of the United States of America or, shall, after importation into the other country, be exempt from all internal taxes, fees, charges or exactions other or higher than those imposed on like articles of national origin or of any other foreign origin.

Article (3)

1. No prohibition or restriction of any kind shall be imposed by the Government of either country on the importation of any article the growth, produce or manufacture of the other country or upon the exportation of any article destined for the other country, unless the importation of the like article the growth, produce or manufacture of all third countries, or the exportation of the like article to all third countries, respectively, is similarly prohibited or restricted.

2. No restriction of any kind shall be imposed by the Government of either country on the importation from the other country of any article in which that country has an interest, whether by means of import licenses or permits or otherwise, unless the total Quantity or value of such article permitted to be imported during a specified period, or any change in such Quantity or value, shall have been established and made public. If the Government of either country allots a share of such total Quantity or value to any third country, it shall allot to the other country, unless it is mutually agreed to dispense with such allotment, a share based upon the proportion of the total imports of such article supplied by that country in a previous representative period, account being taken in so far as practicable in appropriate cases of any special factors which may have affected or may be affecting the trade in that article, and shall make such share available so as to facilitate its full utilization. No limitation or restriction of any kind other than such an allotment shall be imposed, by means of import licenses or permits or otherwise, on the share of such total quantity which may be imported from the other country.
3. The provisions of this Article shall apply in respect of the quantity of any article permitted to be imported at a specified rate of duty.

Article (4)

1. If the Government of either country establishes or maintains any form of control of the means of international payment, it shall accord unconditional most favored-nation treatment to the commerce of the other country with respect to all aspects of such control.
2. The Government establishing or maintaining such control shall, impose no prohibition, restriction or delay on the transfer of payment for any article the growth, produce or manufacture of the other country which is not imposed on the transfer of payment for the like article the growth, produce or manufacture of any third country. With respect to rates of exchange and with respect to taxes or charges on exchange transactions, articles the growth, produce or manufacture of the other country shall be accorded unconditionally treatment no less favorable than that accorded to the like articles the growth, produce or manufacture of any third country. The foregoing provisions shall also extend to the application of such control to payments necessary for or incidental to the importation of articles the growth, produce or manufacture of the other country. In general, the control shall be administered so as not to influence to the disadvantage of the other country the competitive relationships between articles the growth, produce

or manufacture of the territories of that country and like articles the growth, produce or manufacture of third countries.

Article (5)

1. In the event that the Government of either country establishes or maintains a monopoly for the importation, production or sale of any article or grants exclusive privileges, formally or in effect, to any agency to import, produce or sell any article, it is agreed that the commerce of the other country shall be accorded fair and equitable treatment in respect of the foreign purchases of such monopoly or agency. To this end such monopoly or agency will, in making its foreign purchases of any article, be influenced solely by those considerations, such as price, quality, marketability and terms of sale, which would ordinarily be taken into account by a private commercial enterprise interested solely in purchasing such article on the most favorable terms,
2. The Government of each country, in the awarding of contracts for public works and generally in the purchase of supplies, shall accord fair and equitable treatment to the commerce of the other country as compared with the treatment accorded to the commerce of any third country.

Article (6)

1. Laws, regulations of administrative authorities and decisions of administrative or judicial authorities of the United States of America or, respectively, pertaining to the classification of articles for customs purposes or to rates of duty shall be published promptly in such a manner as to enable traders to become acquainted with them. Such laws, regulations and decisions shall be applied uniformly at all ports of the respective country, except as otherwise specifically provided in statutes of the United States of America relating to articles imported into Puerto Rico.
2. No administrative ruling by the Government of either country effecting advances in rates of duties or in charges applicable under an established and uniform practice to imports originating in the territory of the other country, or imposing any new requirement with respect to such importations, shall be effective retroactively or with respect to articles either entered, or withdrawn from warehouse, for consumption prior to the date of publication of notice of such ruling in the usual official manner. The provisions of this paragraph shall not apply to administrative orders imposing anti-dumping duties, or relating to regulations for the protection of human, animal or

plant life or health, or relating to public safety, or giving effect to judicial decisions.
3. Greater than nominal penalties shall not be imposed by the Government of either country in connection with the importation of articles the growth, produce or manufacture of the other country because of errors in documentation which are obviously clerical in origin or with regard to which good faith can be established.

Article (7)

1. Articles the growth, produce or manufacture of the United States of America enumerated and described in Schedule I annexed to this Agreement shall, on their importation into, be exempt from ordinary customs duties in excess of those set forth and provided for in the said Schedule, subject to the conditions therein set out. The said articles shall also be exempt from all other duties, taxes, fees, charges or exactions, imposed on or in connection with importation, in excess of those imposed on the day of the signature of this Agreement or required to be imposed thereafter under laws of in force on the day of the signature of this Agreement.
2. Schedule I and the notes included therein shall have full force and effect as integral parts of this Agreement.

Article (8)

1. Articles the growth, produce or manufacture of enumerated and described in Schedule II annexed to this Agreement shall, on their importation into the United States of America, be exempt from ordinary customs duties in excess of those set forth and provided for in the said Schedule e subject to the conditions therein set out. The said articles shall also be exempt from all other duties, taxes, fees, charges or exactions, imposed on or in connection with importation, in excess of those imposed on the day of the signature of this Agreement or required to be imposed thereafter under laws of the United States of America in force on the day of the signature of this Agreement.
2. Schedule II and the notes included therein shall have full force and effect as integral parts of this Agreement.

Article (9)

The provisions of Articles (7) and (8) of this Agreement shall not prevent the Government of either country from imposing at any time on the importation of any article a charge equivalent to an internal tax imposed in respect of a

Annex A-1

like domestic article or in respect of a commodity from which the imported article has been manufactured or produced in whole or in part.

Article (10)

In respect of articles the growth, produce or manufacture of the United States of America or of enumerated and described in Schedules I and II, respectively, imported into the other country, on which ad valorem rates of duty, or duties based upon or regulated in any manner by value, are or may be assessed, the general principles applicable in the respective countries for determining dutiable value and converting currencies shall not be altered so as to impair the value of any of the concessions provided for in this Agreement.

Article (11)

1. Subject to the provisions of the second paragraph of this Article and to the provisions of Article (12), no prohibition, restriction or any other form of quantitative regulation, whether or not operated in connection with any agency of centralized control, shall be imposed by on the importation or sale of any article the growth, produce or manufacture of the United States of America enumerated and described in Schedule I, or by the United States of America on the importation or sale of any article the growth, produce or manufacture of enumerated and described in Schedule II, [except as otherwise expressly provided for in the said Schedules.]
2. The foregoing provision shall not prevent the Government of either country from imposing quantitative regulations in whatever form on the importation or sale of any article in conjunction with governmental measures or measures under governmental authority operating to regulate or control the production, market supply, quality or prices of like domestic articles, or tending to increase the labor costs of production of such articles, or to maintain the exchange value of the currency of the country. Whenever the Government of either country proposes to impose or substantially alter any quantitative regulation authorized by this paragraph, it shall give notice thereof in writing to the other Government and Shall afford such other Government an opportunity to consult with it in respect of the proposed action; and if agreement with respect thereto is not reached the Government which proposes to take such action shall, nevertheless, be free to do so and the other Government shall be free with-7 in thirty days after such action is taken to terminate this Agreement in whole or in part on thirty days written notice.

Article 12

1. If, as a result of unforeseen developments and of the concession granted on any article enumerated and described in the Schedules annexed to this Agreement, such article is being imported in such increased quantities and under such conditions as to cause or threaten serious injury to domestic producers of like or similar articles, the Government of either country shall be free to withdraw the concession, in whole or in part, or to modify it to the extent and for such time as may be necessary to prevent such injury. Accordingly, if the President of the United States of America finds as a fact that imports of any article enumerated and described in Schedule II are entering the United States of America under the circumstances specified in the preceding sentence, he shall determine whether the withdrawal, in whole Or in part, of the concession with regard to the article, or any modification of the concession, by the imposition of quantitative regulations or otherwise, is necessary to prevent such injury, and he shall, if he finds that the public interest will be served thereby, proclaim such finding and determination, and on and after the effective date specified in such proclamation, and so long as such proclamation remains in effect, imports of the article into the United States of America shall be subject to the customs: treatment so determined to be necessary to prevent such injury. Similarly, [insert similar provision for other country]
2. Before the Government of either country shall withdraw or modify a concession pursuant to the provisions of paragraph 1 of this Article, it shall give notice in writing to the Government of the other country as far in advance as may be practicable and shall afford such other Government an opportunity to consult with it in respect of the proposed action; and if agreement with respect thereto is not reached the Government which proposes to take Such action shall, nevertheless, be free to do so and the other Government shall be free within thirty days after such action is taken to terminate this Agreement in whole or in Part on thirty days' written notice.

Article (13)

If the Government of either country should consider that any measure adopted by the other Government, even though it does not conflict with the terms of this Agreement, has the effect of nullifying or impairing any object of the Agreement, such other Government shall give sympathetic consideration to such written representations or proposals as may be made with a view to effecting a mutually satisfactory adjustment of the matter.

If agreement is not reached with respect to the matter within thirty days after such representations or proposals are received, the Government which made them shall be free, within fifteen days after the expiration of the aforesaid period of thirty days, to terminate this Agreement in whole or in part on thirty days' written notice,

Article (14)

1. The provisions of this Agreement relating to the treatment to be accorded by the United States of America and, respectively, to the commerce of the other country shall apply to the respective customs territories of the two countries.
2. Furthermore, the provisions of this Agreement relating to most – favored – nation treatment shall apply to all territory under the sovereignty or authority of the two countries, except that they shall not apply to the Panama Canal Zone.

Article (15)

1. The advantages now accorded or which may hereafter be accorded by the United States of America or to adjacent countries in order to facilitate frontier traffic, and advantages accorded by virtue of a customs union to which, either country may become a party, shall be excepted from the operation of this Agreement.
2. The advantages now accorded or which may hereafter be accorded by the United States of America, its territories or possessions or the Panama Canal Zone to one another or to the Republic of Cuba shall be excepted from the operation of this Agreement. The provisions of this paragraph shall continue to apply in respect of any advantages now or hereafter accorded by the United States of America, its territories or possessions or the Panama Canal Zone to one another, irrespective of any change in the political status of any of the territories or possessions of the United States of America.

Article (16)

1. Nothing in this Agreement shall be construed to prevent the adoption or enforcement of measures:
   (a) imposed on moral or humanitarian grounds;
   (b) designed to protect human, animal or plant life or health;
   (c) relating to prison-made goods;
   (d) relating to the enforcement of police or revenue laws;
   (e) relating to the importation or exportation of gold or silver;

(f) relating to the control of the export or sale for export of arms, ammunition, or implements of war, and, in exceptional circumstances, all other military supplies;

(g) relating to neutrality;

(h) relating to public security, or imposed for the Protection of the country's essential interests in time of war or other national emergency.

2. The provisions of this Agreement relating to the sale, taxation or use of imported articles within the United States of America are understood to be subject to the constitutional limitations on the authority of the Federal Government.

Article (17)

1. The Government of each country will accord sympathetic consideration to, and will afford adequate opportunity for consultation regarding, such representations as the other Government may make with respect to the operation of customs regulations, quantitative regulations or the administration thereof, the observance of customs formalities, and the application of sanitary laws and regulations for the protection of human, animal or plant life or health.

2. If the Government of either country makes representations to the Government of the other country in respect of the application of any sanitary law or regulation for the protection of human, animal or plant life or health, and if there is disagreement with respect thereto, a committee of technical experts on which each Government shall be represented shall, on the request of either Government, be established to consider the matter and to submit recommendations with respect thereto.

Article (18)

This Agreement shall be proclaimed by the President of the United States of America and shall be ratified by the. It shall enter definitively into force on the day of the exchange of the proclamation and the instrument of ratification, which shall take place in Washington as soon as possible.

Article (19)

Pending the definitive entry into force of this Agreement as provided in Article (18), the provisions thereof shall be applied provisionally on and after, subject to a right to terminate the provisional application of the Agreement pursuant to the Provisions of Article (11), Article (12), and Article (13), or upon six months' written notice.

Article (20)

>Subject to the provisions of Article (11), Article (12), Article (13), and Article (19), this Agreement shall remain in force until 194X, and, unless at least six months before that date the Government of either country shall have given notice in writing to the other Government of intention to terminate the Agreement on that date, it shall remain in force thereafter until the expiration of six months from the date on which such notice shall have been given.
>
>In witness whereof the respective Plenipotentiaries have signed this Agreement and have affixed their seals hereto. Done in duplicate, in the English and languages, both authentic, at the City of [insert name] this day of [insert date] 194X. For the President of the United States of America:
>
>For the of [insert foreign representative]

ANNEX A-2

From Public Records Office, T 230/14

A Proposal for an International Commercial Union

I Our Post-War Commercial Problem

1. The United Kingdom will be in a difficult commercial position after the war. As a community we depend upon imports of essential foodstuffs and raw materials, which we must purchase by the export of manufactured goods. Developments during the war, such as the loss of income from foreign investments, will have increased our need for an expanded export trade, while at the same time the industrialisation which has taken, or is likely to take, place in certain overseas territories may well have restricted some of our export opportunities. We import essentials; we export goods with which our customers can more easily dispense. If ever there was a community which had an interest in the general removal of restrictions to international commerce, it is the United Kingdom.
2. Our trade in the past has been very largely of a multilateral character. We have bought goods from the United States with income obtained from the sale of our produce in other less well developed territories. If many of our most readily available sources of supply of essential imports are not to be closed to us, it is important that the opportunities for beneficial multilateral trade should be preserved to their fullest extent.
3. Our export possibilities would thus be directly and indirectly greatly improved, if we could obtain the agreement, for example, of the United

States to modify its pre-war excessive tariff barriers and of Germany to give up its pre-war policy of bilateralism and trade discrimination. These considerations suggest that we, above all other countries, stand to gain (i) from a policy of general world economic and financial expansion which will maintain a high level of buying power in export markets, (ii) from a general reduction of barriers and restrictions in international markets and (iii) from a removal of those discriminations and rigidly bilateral bargains which remove the opportunities for multilateral trading.

4. Multilateral trading the removal of trade restrictions do not, however, imply laissez-faire, and are in no way incompatible with a system of state trading. We shall wish to co-operate with the United States, on the basis of Article VII of the Mutual Aid Agreement of 23 February 1942, on 'action by the United States of America and the United Kingdom, open to participation by all other countries of like mind, directed to . . . the elimination of all forms of discriminatory treatment in international commerce, and to the reduction of tariffs and other trade barriers . . . ' At the same time we must aim at the formulation of such action by means, which do not automatically preclude countries such as the USSR which may be assumed to desire to continue a system of state trading nor prevent us, if we so desire, from continuing a system of state importation for certain products.

5. After the war we shall not be in a good position in which we can afford <u>unconditionally</u> to abandon all protective devices. We cannot readily indulge in a unilateral policy of removing our protective armour and shall thus desire to retain the right to restrict purchases from, and to discriminate against, those countries which themselves retain highly protective commercial policies or which discriminate against ours. We shall, moreover, need to retain the right to impose more general restrictions on purchases of inessential goods or on unnecessary payments abroad so long as we are faced with an acute problem of restoring equilibrium to our international balance of payments.

6. The essential features of our post-war commercial problem may, therefore, be summarised as follows:
    (i) We shall need a large expansion of our export trade and shall stand to gain very greatly from a general world system in which there is a general expansion of world purchasing power and in which restrictions and discriminations on foreign trade are reduced or removed.
    (ii) Apart from our interests we are committed under Article VII of the Mutual Aid Agreement to such a policy, and the future of our relations with the United States requires that we should implement this undertaking.

(iii) We need, however, to implement these undertakings in a way which leaves room for state trading and which does not preclude us (a) from imposing restrictions or discriminations against those countries which impose severe restrictions or discriminations against us or (b) from restricting our payments to other countries if and when balance-of-payments difficulties make such action inevitable.

II The Contribution of Other Proposed Institutions to the Solution of the Commercial Problem

7. The proposals which have already been made (RP(42)2, paragraphs 51-3, 61-134) for the institution of an International Clearing Union, if they are adopted, should much simplify our tasks in formulating far-reaching and imaginative proposals for the reduction of restrictions to international commerce.
8. In the first place, these and similar proposals would greatly help – indeed this is the essence of the proposals – to adjust the balance of payments without undue strain on the debtor countries. Since a large number of protective devices are in origin essentially weapons of defence of countries which are faced with an undue pressure on their balances of international payments, an effective mechanism which makes the creditor nations responsible for a due part, if necessary, of adjustments of international payments should clear the way for attempts to mitigate protectionism.
9. But, in the second place, the machinery of the Clearing Union, through the debit and credit balances of its members, provides an effective and automatic measurement of existing maladjustments in balances of payments. A country which claims that it must be permitted to impose certain protective restrictions as a result of a serious maladjustment in its balance of payments can appeal to (or to be referred to) a reasonably unambiguous index – its debit balance with the Clearing Union. It should, for example, be possible for a country to commit itself in commercial agreements to remove various protective devices but, at the same time, to reserve the right to reimpose some of these devices when and for as long as its debit with the Clearing Union was in excess of a certain figure.
10. Thirdly, the Clearing Union may be expected to aid in promoting that general expansion of demand in world markets which, in Article VII of the Mutual Aid Agreement itself, comes before the removal of trade restrictions and discriminations as an objective of international cooperative action. Indeed, it is only in a general milieu of economic expansion that the pressure on the balances of payments of debtor countries is likely to be sufficiently relieved to make possible a really effective lowering of protective devices.

There are other proposals under consideration which will help towards the same purpose of economic expansion. In particular, the proposals for the development of international investment (RP(42)2 paragraphs 36-50) and the proposals for a systematisation of buffer stock arrangements for primary products (USE (42)15) should provide effective support to an expansive international policy.

III Outline of a Possible Commercial Union

11. It is suggested, therefore, that the United Kingdom should propose the formulation of an International Commercial Union for the purpose of achieving a general reduction of restrictions on international commerce. The Commercial Union would be founded on the following principles:
    i. Membership of the Union would be open to all states which applied for membership and which were willing to carry out the obligations of membership. Membership of the Commercial Union would not be confined to members of the Clearing Union (just as membership of the Clearing Union would in no way be confined to members of the Commercial Union); but, as is indicated in (iv) below, members of the Commercial Union who were also members of the Clearing Union would obtain certain privileges in the Commercial Union.
    ii. Members of the Commercial Union would undertake not to grant preferences or other price advantages to any other member of the Union without extending it to all members, except that certain moderate and defined degrees of preference might be given as between members of a recognised political or geographical group of nations. A clause of this kind would permit discrimination of any degree desired against countries which were not members of the Commercial Union and which had not, therefore, pledged themselves in turn not to discriminate. It would also permit discrimination of a defined and moderate degree in favour of a recognised political or geographical grouping of states, and would thus permit the continuation of a moderate degree of Imperial Preference.
    iii. Members of the Commercial Union would undertake to remove altogether certain protective devices against the commerce of other members of the Union and to reduce to a defined maximum the degree of protection which they would afford to their own home producers against the produce of other members of the Union. A clause of this type would pledge members to eliminate or to limit their protective devices against other members of the Union who had undertaken a similar pledge, but would leave them free to introduce what protective measures they desired

against non-members. Such an arrangement would be safeguarded by the right of any non-member state to join the Commercial Union.

iv. Members of the Commercial Union, who were also members of the Clearing Union and whose accounts with the Clearing Union were in deficit by a certain defined amount, would be permitted to impose certain protective devices so long as their debt remained in excess of the prescribed amount.

v. The Charter of the Commercial Union would expressly state that state trading by members of the Union was not precluded. An indication should be given of the way in which the provisions of the Charter of the Commercial Union should be applied both in the case of competitive trading and in the case of state trading.

vi. The Charter of the Commercial Union would provide for the institution of an International Commerce Commission of a semiarbitral semi-judicial nature. Members could refer complaints to this body in order to obtain an opinion on whether the Charter of the Union was being broken by any particular action of a particular member of the Union.

vii. Membership of the Commercial Union would in no way preclude any member from concluding any type of commercial treaty or agreement with any other state – whether a member of the Union or not – provided only that the terms of the treaty or agreement were not incompatible with its obligations as a member of the Union.

12. If an attempt were made to draft a Charter for a Commercial Union of this type, one of the most important questions would be how precisely worded should be the definition of the discriminations and degrees of protection that would be disallowed to members of the Union and of the actions which would be permitted or disallowed to state trading organisations. It is in this connection that the major dilemma is to be faced. If an attempt is made to define very rigidly and precisely exactly what any member may or may not do in all possible circumstances, it is probable that as circumstances change and as states introduce new methods of trading organisation certain state measures may be precluded which it is not in the general intention of the Charter to disallow and certain other measures may be allowed which it is in the intention of the Charter to forbid. On the other hand, if the Charter is drawn up in much less precise terms and expresses only in the most general terms the types of protective device which it is intended to forbid and the general maximum degree of protection which it is intended to allow, then very great responsibility will rest upon the International Commerce Commission or similar body whose duty it was to interpret the Charter. The success of the Union will depend upon the formulation of the Charter in

terms which, on the one hand do not attempt to put international trade into an impossible straitjacket and, on the other hand, do not impose upon the International Commerce Commission such a burden of semi-legislative duties that it could not bear.
13. The following clauses are intended merely as an illustration of one possible set of conditions which might be included in that section of the Charter of the Commercial Union in which the limitations on members' discriminatory or protective policy are defined:
   i. Members would be forbidden to discriminate (whether by means of taxes, subsidies, preferential prices offered by state organisations, or other means) in the prices offered for the produce of other members of the Union.
   ii. Members would be bound to give other members of the Union as favourable prices for their produce as they gave for the similar produce from any non-member state.
   iii. As exceptions to clauses (i) and (ii) above members could give price preferences up to a maximum of, say, 10 per cent to the produce of another state with which it formed a special recognised geographical or political union.
   iv. Members would be forbidden to give a preference (whether by tax, subsidy, price offered by state trading body or other means) in price to their home producers which was more than, say, 25 per cent greater than the price offered for similar goods produced by other members of the Union.
   v. Members would be forbidden to impose quantitative restrictions or prohibitions, other than for reasons of public health or public safety, on the import of goods from other members of the Commercial Union.
   vi. Members would undertake not to impose restrictions on payments for current (as opposed to capital) transactions to other members of the Union, except that a country which was also a member of the Clearing Union and was a 'deficiency' country with the Clearing Union would be permitted to impose restrictions on current payments for as long as it remained a 'deficiency' country.
   vii. Members would undertake not to impose quantitative restrictions or prohibitions on exports except as part of a recognised international regulation scheme for primary products (as arranged for in the scheme outlined in U.S.E. (42)15).
   viii. Members would undertake not to impose open or hidden taxes or subsidies of more than, say, 10 per cent on exports to any country whether a member of the Commercial Union or not.

14. The purpose of these various provisions is clear. Clauses (i) to (iii) in the, preceding paragraph would limit price discriminations for imports; clause (iv) would limit the degree of price protection which could be given to home production; clauses (v) and (vi) would prevent quantitative or value restrictions on imports, except in the case of countries in a 'deficiency' position with the Clearing Union; and clauses (vii) and (viii) would cover export policy, preventing both undue restriction of export and export dumping, – the latter of which may be equally obnoxious whether it be to other member states or to non-member states.

IV The Problem of State Trading

15. The general principles of the application of these clauses to countries adopting a competitive trade organisation are clear, although there would, no doubt, be many difficult technical problems to be determined in borderline cases by the International Commerce Commission, as to what exactly did or did not constitute a price preference or a restriction on payments. The problem of applying these clauses to cases of state trading would probably in practice present more difficulties since it is as yet a less familiar problem; but in principle it should be no less capable of satisfactory solution.

16. It resolves itself into a two-fold problem:
    i. that of determining the degree of price preference or protection which is being offered by the state trading organisation and
    ii. that of deciding whether a quantitative restriction on imports (or on exports) is being imposed.

    In the case of a state which, while its trading system is mainly competitive, monopolises for itself the trade of a limited number of commodities, the problem of judging the degree of price discrimination or of price preference given as between one source of supply and another or as between one market and another does not present any additional difficulties of principle. This problem may become somewhat more complicated in practice, but it still remains in essence the same, even in the case of a country which has socialised trade in all or the majority of products; such extreme cases are, however, in the post-war world likely to be relatively few in number; and they will be still less important from the point of view of their share in the total of international trade.

17. The regulation of price preferences is not, however, sufficient to prevent discrimination or protection. A state trading organisation might, for example, discriminate in favour of one source of supply as opposed to another by

buying much in the first and little in the second, even though it paid a non-discriminatory price. It is necessary to determine what corresponds in the case of state trading to the obligations (suggested in clauses (v)–(vii) of paragraph 14 above) not to impose quantitative restrictions on imports or exports except in certain clearly defined cases. This limitation corresponds in the case of state trading to an obligation (i) to take from each foreign market as much imports as each such market would wish to supply at the price which the importing state organization is offering and (ii) to sell in all foreign markets as much foreign exports as each such market would wish to purchase at the price at which the goods are offered by the state exporting organisation.

18. These considerations suggest that the principles of membership of the Commercial Union should be applied in such a way as (i) to impose the same obligations both to competitive and to state trading in all matters of price discrimination and price preference, (ii) to forbid in the case of competitive trading quantitative restrictions on imports and exports and on current payments, and (iii) to impose in the case of state trading obligations to purchase from, or to sell to, each foreign market as much as that foreign market wishes to sell, or to purchase, at the prices offered by the state trading organisation. It would, however, be a matter for detailed consideration to determine the extent to which, and the conditions on which long forward contracts could be entered into by state trading organisations within the framework of these principles. Such contracts should not be excluded; but they should be undertaken in such a way as to maintain a reasonable approximation to the principles outlined above.

V The International Commerce Commission

19. The existence of some international body which had the competence to interpret the Charter of the Commercial Union, and to arbitrate or to give decisions in case of disputes among its members would be an essential part of the mechanism of such a Union. It would, however, be premature at this stage to make detailed suggestions about the constitution of such a body. Its members should, no doubt, be appointed by the governments of the states making up the Commercial Union. It should, no doubt, have the power of expressing an opinion upon any complaint brought to its notice by one member of the Union against another member, and of requiring members of the Union to provide it with the statistical and other information necessary to form a judgement in such cases. It might well be ruled that, in such cases, its findings – both its majority and minority findings – should be published.

Annex A-3

But it is a matter for further consideration how such findings should be binding on members of the Union. It might, for example, be provided, as a sanction against breaches of the Charter of the Union, that any member of the Union which refused to accept a majority finding of the Commission could be treated by other members as if it were no longer a member of the Union, in so far as the clauses prohibiting discriminatory practices were concerned. This, however, is a question which is probably best answered at a much later stage.

VI The Problem of the Transition

20. Membership of the Commercial Union (at any rate on anything like the terms suggested above for illustrative purposes) would require an extensive readjustment of commercial policy in the case of a number of countries. If such major readjustments are desirable, there is much to be said for undertaking them after the cataclysm of a major war; for serious readjustments will be inevitable in such a period in any case, and it is surely better to readjust then to the conditions which are most desired than to rebuild to an ancient plan which it is intended in any case to reconstruct sooner or later. Nevertheless, it would be out of the question to suggest this or any other country should commit itself to an immediate acceptance of all the principles of the Commercial Union immediately after the war. What is required is some transitional arrangement whereby countries can become members of the Commercial Union during a period of, say, five years after the close of hostilities on condition:
   i. That they undertake to fulfil some of its obligations, such as the removal of quantitative import restrictions and prohibitions, within a short period of a year or two, and
   ii. That they undertake to fulfil the remaining obligations within a period of not less than, say, five years. Such an arrangement might serve to secure that certain protective devices were quickly eliminated, that a more gradual movement was initiated for the removal or reduction of others, and – most important of all – that each member could plan its economic development on the assumption that within a specified number of years other members would have contracted their protective and discriminatory devices within reasonably precise and clearly defined limits.

[James E. Meade]

25TH July, 1942.

ANNEX A-3

From Public Records Office, BT 11/2215

Anglo-American Discussions Under Article VII: Commercial Policy

Informal Exploratory Conversations Between Officials of the United States and the United Kingdom Regarding the Formulation of an Agenda for Discussions Looking Toward the Implementation of article VII of the Mutual-Aid Agreement Between the United States and the United Kingdom

SECTION ON COMMERCIAL POLICY
1. TARIFFS.
   1. Multilateral tariff action

There are set forth below for further study tariff-reduction provisions for possible inclusion in a general multilateral convention on commercial policy. All of these are multilateral tariff-reduction formulas except the last (see E, below), which is e proposal for multilateral Provisions embodying an undertaking to negotiate bilateral tariff agreements.

It is the view of both the United States and United Kingdom groups that if a workable multilateral tariff-reduction formula acceptable to a large number of nations providing for a drastic reduction of tariffs without nullifying exceptions and reservations can be found, it would be superior. It would be superior because it would accomplish tariff reductions more quickly and because it would make it easier to accomplish the elimination of quotas and other non-tariff trade restrictions. The spirit of close international cooperation engendered by the war provides a favourable atmosphere for multilateral action now; as the end, of the war approaches the atmosphere for such action may be expected to become less favourable; after the war it may be too late for such action.

In the view of the United Kingdom group, it will not be possible to obtain adherence to a multilateral convention prohibiting quantitative import restrictions and limiting the use of other protective devices unless it includes a satisfactory formula for multilateral tariff reduction. It is their view that a precise obligation to limit the use of other protective devices would be impossible without an equally comprehensive and closely defined obligation covering tariffs, and that this could be achieved only if the convention provides for simultaneous multilateral action to reduce tariffs. Otherwise countries will be required to abandon the use of quantitative import restrictions and other instruments of protection in conditions in which the extent of the tariff benefits to be enjoyed later must inevitably be problematical. Moreover, in their view, the 'justifiable anxieties which will exist in many countries with serious balance-of payments problems will make it impossible to proceed sufficiently far and fast by bilateral negotiations

Annex A-3   223

under most-favored-nation rules, which would involve giving concessions to third parties without the assurance of corresponding counter-concessions.

The United States group does not associate itself with the views set forth in the paragraph above.

2. Alternative provisions for the implementation of tariff reduction.
   A. The reduction of all duties by X percent of their height at a given time, or to Y percent ad valorem (or its equivalent in the case of specific duties), whichever may result in the lower duty, but no duty need be reduced below Z percent ad valorem (or its equivalent in the case of specific duties)
   Advantages
   One of the principal advantages of formula 4% appears to be that it would bear more heavily on the higher duties and less heavily on the lower duties, Countries with low tariffs would not be required to make the same total percentage reduction as countries with high tariffs.
   Disadvantages
   Some of the principal disadvantages of formula A seem to be:
   1) It would tend to destroy the tariff structure, i.e. the relationships between the tariffs on different commodities of countries having a large number of duties in excess of Y percent; however, such countries might make proper adjustment through downward revision of the related duties.
   2) It would require the establishment of a relatively uniform system of tariff valuation among the various countries (and the conversion of ad valorem duties to the new basis) in order that Y percent and Z percent might mean approximately the same thing in all countries;
   3) It would required the determination of the ad, valorem equivalents of specific duties. This would not be so difficult in countries which have a system of tariff valuation; but would present a problem for the countries which have adopted general systems of specific duties or systems of arbitrary valuation.
   B. The uniform reduction of all duties in all countries by a given percentage of their height en a given date.
   Advantages
   Some of the advantages of formula B appear to be its simplicity and ease of administration in all countries, its appearance of treating all countries alike, and the fact that it would to a considerable extent preserve the relationships between the tariffs on different commodities.
   Disadvantages
   The main disadvantages of formula B appears to be that it would reduce low tariffs to the same relative extent as high tariffs, and therefore

would almost certainly be considered as inequitable by low-tariff countries, particularly those having specific duties the protective incidence of which has declined because of increased prices. This disadvantage might be remedied by providing for the reduction of the higher duties by a greater percentage than the lower. However, this would introduce technical difficulties of the kind indicated under A, above.

C. The reduction of all duties by a given percentage, except than no duty need be reduced below a specified ad valorem rate.

Advantages

The advantages of formula C are that: 1) it would permit the application to high-tariff and low-tariff countries of a uniform tariff reduction in a manner equitable to both; and 2) it would preserve to a considerable extent the tariff structures of the various countries.

Disadvantages

The main disadvantages of formula t is that, like formula C is that, like formula A, it presents technical difficulties of tariff valuation and the conversion of specific duties, although on a lesser scale.

D. The uniform reduction by a given percentage of the overall ad valorem equivalent of each country's entire tariff calculated in comparison with its total imports. It is assumed that there would be provision preventing any increase in duties.

Advantages

The chief advantages of formula D appear to be that it would permit tariff reduction on a highly selective basis, would be free from technical problems of customs enforcement and would interfere to a relatively small degree with the tariff autonomy of the various countries. For these reasons, formula D might be more attractive to a large number of countries than the other formulas considered. This formula would raise some technical questions, e.g. whether revenue duties should be included, et cetera.

Disadvantages

Some of the major disadvantages of formula D appear to be:-

1) Existing methods of tariff measurement involve the use of the volume of imports as weights, and since protective duties, especially highly protective duties, curtail imports the moderate duties receive in general the greatest weight. Therefore, under existing methods of tariff measurement, formula D might cause countries to bring about the required reduction in the overall ad valorem level by reducing the moderate duties, and there would be little or no incentive to reduce the highly protective or prohibitive duties. On the other hand, this

formula would give no weight to reductions of superfluous duties on products of which there is little or no actual or potential importation.

2) Formula D would not require any greater proportionate tariff cut by high-tariff countries than by low-tariff countries.

E. The inclusion in the proposed commercial policy convention of a provision whereby each country would agree to negotiate with its principal suppliers bilateral agreements providing for tariff reductions on its major dutiable imports. This would of course involve dealing by the same method with preferences heretofore regarded as exceptions from the most-favoured-nation clause.

Advantages

The advantages of proposal E are that it would be technically sound and relatively free from problems of equity as between high-tariff and low-tariff countries.

Disadvantages

Disadvantages of this method of approach as compared with multilateral formulas are indicated under 1 above.

3. Revenue duties

It is assumed that any provisions for the simultaneous reduction of tariffs in all countries would not apply to revenue duties, which could be increased. Revenue duties might include the following:-

(a) Duties which compensate for taxes imposed on the like domestic articles or ingredients thereof.

(b) Duties which are imposed on imports of products not produced domestically, with provision, if possible, for guarding against the non-reduction or increase of duties which are clearly designed to protect domestic production of a closely competitive product.

(c) Ancillary charges on imports commensurate with the cost of services rendered.

4. Infant industries and security industries

There are strong arguments against permitting exceptions for the protection of national defense or "infant" industries, in view of other methods, less objectionable than tariffs, available for this purpose. But in order to obtain the adherence of countries which are industrially undeveloped and .which have difficulty in raising funds for the payment of subsidies, it may be necessary to contemplate some modification of this rule. (see III, Quantitative Import Restrictions, point I; and. V, Subsidies, point 4).

5. Other tariff measures

It is believed that the problem of antidumping and countervailing duties, multi-column tariffs, tariff quotas, and other similar tariff measures, questions regarding which would arise in connection with any multilateral convention regarding tariffs, should be explored later, in the light of the particular tariff-reduction proposal selected as most feasible.

6. Comments

It is believed that a major obstacle to the application of an equitable multilateral tariff-reduction formula is the technical problem of uniform tariff valuation and conversion of duties involved in the application to the tariffs of all countries of uniform ad valorem "floors" or "ceilings", and that further investigation of methods to overcome this obstacle might be useful, In this connection, the practicability of the fallowing suggestions might be investigated.

(d) The necessity for drastically changing the tariff valuation systems of many countries to a single basis, and for the consequent recomputation of the existing ad valorem duties of those countries, might be avoided by providing for a different ad valorem "floor" or "ceiling" for the two principal valuation systems now used, namely, landed value and foreign value. Thus, the ad valorem tariff "floor" for countries having a non-arbitrary valuation system based on landed value might be X percent, whereas the "floor" for countries having a non-arbitrary valuation system based on foreign value might be X plus Y percent.

(e) Countries having some system of non-arbitrary tariff valuation might, with relatively little difficulty, be able to modify it so as to conform to either a standard landed-value system or a standard foreign value system, which might be described in the multilateral convention. Each standard system might be loosely described so as to require merely a rough uniformity among countries adhering to it.

(f) A study might be undertaken of ways in which countries having primarily specific rates of duty, or having purely arbitrary valuation systems, might be assisted in establishing a satisfactory system of tariff valuation.

7 Conclusions

Further study would appear to be required before even tentative conclusions can be reached as to which one of the tariff proposals outlined above would prove suitable for inclusion in the proposed general multilateral convention on commercial policy.

II. PREFERENCES

1. Article VII of the Mutual-Aid Agreement between the United States and the United Kingdom provides for agreed action looking not only toward the reduction of tariffs but also toward the elimination of all forms of discriminatory treatment in international commerce, No convention of the

kind proposed would give final effect to these obligations unless it makes definite provision both for an adequate reduction of tariffs and for the ultimate substantial abolition of preferences. There remains for determination at the proper time the difficult question of what reduction of tariffs, at one step or by stages, would be adequate to make possible the substantial abolition of preferences. It has become clear in the course of the discussions that United. States opinion would not consider it equitable or reasonable to contemplate drastic and comprehensive reduction of tariffs (assuming this to be feasible) if it were not accompanied by the simultaneous substantial abolition of preferences.

2. It would seem desirable and necessary to provide in the proposed commercial policy convention for the following exceptions from the provisions for equality of tariff treatment:
   (a) Preferences granted in order to facilitate frontier traffic (i.e. within a zone not exceeding, say, 15 kilometers on each side of the frontier).
   (b) Preferences granted as a transitional stage of an approved customs union, Such preferences should be excepted only if the attainment of the full customs union is scheduled to be achieved within a fixed and reasonable period of years at a predetermined rate of moderation and final elimination of the internal duties.

3. The provisions of the proposed commercial policy convention looking toward the abolition of tariff preferences would not apply to customs unions which already exist. However, future customs unions between any two or more customs areas should be reviewed by the proposed international commercial policy organization (see VII, International Commercial Policy Organization). In so far as economic criteria are concerned, it is suggested that future customs unions should not be favorably viewed which failed to meet certain specified requirements) among which might be the following:-
   (a) In general, a union between two or more customs areas should be such as would promote the economic selection and location of industry and afford in time the benefits of larger-scale and more specialized production.
   (b) The customs union should be effected by applying to the whole of the proposed new customs territory external rates of duty not in excess of the average of the corresponding rates previously applicable in the constituent areas.

There may be overriding political factors and considerations which might render certain proposed customs unions unacceptable even if they meet fully the test of the economic criteria suggested above; on the other hand such considerations might impel the acceptance of certain customs unions which did not meet all the desirable economic criteria.

III. PROHIBITIONS AND QUANTITATIVE RESTRICTIONS ON IMPORTS
1. General aspects

    Absolute import prohibitions and import restrictions such as quotas and licensing systems are among the devises most destructive of international trade. They introduce an element of rigidity into trade relationships which frequently lends itself to speculative manipulations and erratic price fluctuations. They almost inevitably result in discrimination among suppliers, uneconomic diversion of trade, international friction and ill will.

    As part of a multilateral convention the use of prohibitions or quantitative restrictions except in certain special cases should be prohibited. Their use for the purpose of protecting home industries, including infant industries and industries deemed necessary on grounds of national security, would be proscribed (see I, Tariffs, point 4; and V, Subsidies, point 4). Existing import prohibitions and restrictions would be abolished subject to specified exceptions. These exceptions would be held to a minimum and defined as closely as possible in order to avoid loopholes through which the purses of the convention would be impaired.

2. Exceptions
    (a) Balance-of-payments difficulties. The use of quantitative restrictions to safeguard a country's balance of payments would be permissible, provided no preferable means which would render unnecessary the imposition of quantitative restrictions were found. Any such restrictions would be applied only to the extent and so long as the country's balance-of-payments position required, and would be subject to approval by the proposed international commercial policy organization and to an objective test. A suggested procedure is as follows:
    1) The imposition of quantitative restrictions on imports for balance-of-payments reasons should be based on objective criteria. Account should be taken of the balance of payments of the country in question with the rest of the world. The imposition of appropriate restrictions on imports, on a non-discriminatory basis between countries, should be permitted if its balance on current account, together with inward long-term capital transactions, had been seriously adverse over a specified period, or if the country's holdings of liquid reserves is inadequate. The deficit on balance of current account in the former alternative might be measured as a percentage of a country's foreign trade; and the adequacy of the liquid reserves by a similar test or by reference to tests provided under any monetary scheme.

2) If in the light of those criteria a country concluded that action was necessary on its part, it would be entitled unilaterally to impose a temporary stoppage on any increase in its imports above those in the most recent twelve months period, but should be bound to obtain the subsequent approval of the proposed international commercial policy organization for its action. Any more drastic action on its part would require the prior approval of such an organization. The organization should base its decision upon the objective criteria mentioned in (1) above.

3) Unless contrary arrangements were approved by the international commercial policy organization, a country which imposed quantitative restrictions on imports under the foregoing rule would be required to complete their removal within twelve months if (on objective criteria corresponding to those outlined in (1) above) its balance of payments on current account had been sufficiently favorable over a period and its holdings of liquid reserves had been restored to an adequate level.

4) If quantitative restrictions on imports imposed under these rubs continue for more than two (or perhaps three) years the country in question undertakes to consult with the international commercial policy organization and with other appropriate international institutions in order to determine whether some other action (such as an adjustment of exchanges alterations in the flow of international long-term capital or an expansion of money incomes in other countries) could not be appropriately taken.

    It may be necessary to consider a special supplementary provision if arrangements are made under the proposed international monetary institution for special measures to deal with scarce currencies.

(b) <u>Commodity agreements</u>. The use of quantitative restrictions when necessary to implement a recognized international commodity agreement would be allowed.

(c) <u>Other exceptions</u>. The convention would provide for necessary and legitimate exceptions in regard to such matters as sanitary regulations, et cetera. If application is given to the principles laid down in the section on subsidies, it would be unnecessary to have any exception with respect to the imposition of quantitative restrictions in connection with domestic production control measures.

3. <u>Temporary emergency exceptions</u>

    In the emergency period during and immediately following the war import prohibitions and quantitative limitations would be permitted when necessary to meet emergencies arising from (a) the necessity of rationing imports because of shortages of supplies, shipping or foreign exchange and (b) a temporary surplus of stocks of the commodity to which the restriction applies. These temporary exceptions would be applicable for a specified limited period after the cessation of hostilities unless the period of their application were further extended by action of the proposed international commercial policy organization.

4. Rules of fair conduct

The provisions in the multilateral convention with respect to import prohibitions and restrictions would include provisions designed to minimize discriminatory and other objectionable practices in the administration of such prohibitions and restrictions as were not proscribed. These rules would embody principles such as those which have been included in the pertinent provisions of trade agreements concluded by the United States, (See, for example, Article V of the United Kingdom-United Stator trade agreement and Article III of the United States Mexico trade agreement.)

5. Exchange restrictions

Exchange restrictions should not be applied in a manner inconsistent with the above provisions for the use of quantitative import restrictions.

IV. EXPORT TAXES AND RESTRICTIONS

1. There should be agreed action looking toward the abolition of export taxes and restrictions.
2. Provision in a general multilateral commercial policy convention for the abolition of quantitative restrictions on exports, including prohibitions, would in general be subject to the same carefully safeguarded exceptions as may be agreed upon in respect of quantitative restrictions on imports, in so far as they may be pertinent (e.g. quantitative regulations imposed pursuant to recognized international commodity agreements, et cetera). In addition, it probably would be necessary to provide for exceptions in respect of quantitative export restrictions which are: (1) imposed under conditions of famine or severe domestic shortage in the exporting country, and (2) designed to regulate the trade in, military supplies-under specified conditions,
3. Export taxes and other forms of government action which result in the sale of goods in foreign markets at prices higher than those corresponding to the domestic prices would be banned, subject to an exception for export taxes imposed for purposes of revenue. A revenue tax might be defined as one which does not result in the sale of a product for export at a price higher than that corresponding to the price charged in the home market. Examples of revenue taxes might be the following:

Annex A-3

(a) A tax on the export of a manufactured product which is compensated for by an equivalent tax on the domestic consumption of that product,
(b) A tax cm the export of a raw material which is compensated for by an equivalent tax on the raw material consumed by a domestic manufacturing industry, whether for home consumption or export.
(c) A tax on the export of a raw material which is not consumed domestically as a raw material by a manufacturing industry.

It should be noted that in cases in which a country exports the whole or a substantial part of the worlds supply of a scarce commodity, and has no substantial home consumption of that commodity, compliance with the above definition of revenue export taxes would not serve as a check on the height of the tax. Moreover, under such conditions importing countries would be forced to pay a tax of almost any height because of the absence of adequate alternative sources of supply. In such cases importing countries should be enabled to refer the matter to the proposed international commercial policy organization.

4. The convention would provide that revenue taxes, and, under like circumstances and conditions, permissible quantitative restrictions, imposed on exports from any area, would be applied uniformly irrespective of destination.

V. SUBSIDIES

1. Subsidies are preferable to tariffs and other import restrictions as a means of protecting domestic industries because (a) they do not impose burdens on consumers, and (b) being visible, they are likely to be employed less frequently and for shorter duration than tariff and other import restrictions,
2. However, export subsidies and other government action which results in the sale of goods in foreign markets at prices lower than those corresponding to the prices charged for like products in the home market (hereinafter referred to as export subsidies) are objectionable from the standpoint of commercial policy. In so far as they are effective, they cause uneconomic diversions of trade, work unjust hardships on competitors and engender international ill will.
3. In any comprehensive international convention with respect to commercial policy that may be concluded, provision should be made looking to the elimination of export subsidies, including all forms of the two-price system, as soon as practicable. Efforts would be made to induce countries parties to such a convention to adopt less objectionable methods of assisting industries which they deem require state aid.

4. Programs for the subsidization of products which do not result in selling for export at prices less than those corresponding to the domestic prices would not be banned, Further consideration should be given to the question of insuring that such subsidization is kept within moderate limits and, in particular, to the question of setting a limit to the subsidization of the production of goods of which world surpluses exist. The discussions have shown clearly that the possibility of obtaining adherence to any rule prohibiting, in surplus areas, export subsidies on certain agricultural products in excess world supply will depend upon the possibility of setting definite limits to the subsidization of production in deficit areas (see also Section (12 Commodity Policy, IV, Subsidies). There would probably have to be appropriate agreed exceptions for infant industries, security measures, et cetera (see I, Tariffs, point 4; and III, Quantitative Import Restrictions. point 1).
5. Consideration probably should be given to the desirability of including, at the appropriate place in any commercial policy convention, provisions with respect to export dumping by individual producers and associations of producers see L Tariffs, point 5).
6. Provision would be made for review by the proposed international commercial policy organization in cases where a country believed that domestic subsidies were in effect concealed or indirect export subsidies and that its interests were injured. The remission of taxes on exported goods probably should not be considered as an export subsidy within the meaning of this provision.

VI. STATE TRADING

1. Prior to the war one government, the Soviet Union, had a monopoly of the country's entire foreign trade and in other countries governmental trading was practiced to some extent. It is not unlikely that conditions created by the war will tend to result in state trading on a more extensive scale than theretofore.
2. It is necessary, therefore, that methods and arrangements for trading between private-enterprise countries and state- trading countries, whether bilateral or multilateral, be such as to take account of this situation in order that the interests of both may be harmonized.
3. The general objective of such methods and arrangements should be to maximize the economic use of resources by:
   (a) elimination of discrimination; and
   (b) expansion of trade.

Annex A-3

4. Any Principles that may be adopted by private-enterprise countries with respect to trade relations with state-trading countries must cover satisfactorily the three general types of state trading, as follows:
   (a) complete state monopoly of a country's foreign trade;
   (b) state or state-sponsored monopoly of the trade in particular. products only; and
   (c) nonmonopolistic state trading.
5. <u>Creation of government-trading organizations by private enterprise countries to deal with state-trading countries</u>. Private-enterprise countries might be disposed to adopt the policy of creating state, or state-sponsored, trading organizations to handle their trade with state-trading countries with a view to improving their bargaining power and thereby obtaining better terms of trade. Such a course would be open to the following objections:
   (a) Discrimination against other countries is likely to result from such practices. The creation of a government-trading organization in a private-enterprise country to deal with a state-trading country might lead to barter-type arrangements between the two countries, with resulting discrimination usually associated with such arrangements. Large purchases by the private-enterprise country, induced by the opportunity for large sales, might reduce the market for competing products of third countries.
   (b) If private-enterprise countries were to adopt state trading to deal with state-trading elsewhere, there might be a progressive substitution of state-trading for private enterprise.
   (c) Moreover, it is questionable whether the difficulty such arrangements would be designed to meet will in reality prove a very serious one. Available evidence based on past experience does not suggest that state-trading countries have in fact taken advantage of their strong negotiating position to the real detriment of competing individual traders in other countries.

   Consequently, it is suggested that government action in private-enterprise countries should be confined to ordinary trade control measures, within the limits set by the general commercial policy convention, which set the conditions under which private traders can conduct business with the foreign state-trading country, just as they do in the case of trade with private-enterprise countries. In that case, in any agreements between governments of state-trading countries and private-enterprise countries, the concessions made by the latter would be of exactly the same kind as those made to private-enterprise countries, i.e. concessions designed to improve

the opportunities for trade by the state-trading country with private traders in the private-enterprise country.
6. <u>Bilateral minimum purchase commitments from particular supplying countries</u>. A possible type of agreement would be one whereby a state-trading country undertakes a minimum purchase commitment, of all products or specified products, such purchases to be made in the supplying country partly to the arrangement as a *quid pro quo* for relaxation of barriers to trade with private interests in the supplying country.

   Such an arrangement is objectionable because it tends to discriminate among supplying countries; i.e. comparative costs and competitive market conditions might exist or develop whereby the state-trading country would be compelled, if it complied with the specified minimum purchase commitment, to purchase goods from the other country party to the arrangement which could be purchased more economically elsewhere. The same objection does not apply to long-term contracts made by state-trading organizations on terms based solely on commercial considerations.
7. <u>Purchases allocated in consultation with suppliers</u>. Under such an arrangement the state-trading country desiring to purchase specified commodities would allocate them in a nondiscriminatory manner among the supplying countries on the basis of multilateral consultation and agreement between the interested governments.

   Such an arrangement might in some cases be impracticable because of the time consumed in making arrangements for numerous specific transactions and the possibility of disputes among sellers. It would presumably require continuous and active participation by the Governments concerned with respect to particular commercial transactions. There may be cases in which such negotiated arrangements may prove the least objectionable method of allocating markets.
8. <u>Purchases solely on basis of commercial considerations</u>. Under such an arrangement the state-trading country might purchase any commodity abroad either from private traders or the government of any supplying country without prior consultation with the governments of countries which were alternative sources of supply, subject merely to the general undertaking that such purchases shall be governed solely by commercial considerations (e.g. Article VIII, United Kingdom United States trade agreement) and with possible Provision for appeal by an interested government to, and review by, the proposed international commercial policy organization,

   Such an arrangement would provide a general basis for assuring nondiscriminatory treatment without, however, imposing any contractual limitation on the degree of protection of domestic industry by the state-trading country. Such assurances of nondiscriminatory treatment, however, are essential to any international arrangements for dealing with state trading.

9. <u>Provisions to limit the use of state monopolies in giving excess protection to home production.</u> Countries might undertake not to give greater protection by means of state trading than they would be permitted to do under the other clauses of the general commercial convention. (1) The relationship between the price paid to the foreign supplier and the price charged to the home consumer, and (2) the question whether the monopoly was satisfying the full domestic demand for the foreign product, might help to determine whether the degree of protection exceeded that allowed by any maximum specified in the section dealing with tariff policy, These criteria would be applied in combination with provisions for nondiscriminatory treatment as in point 8, above.

These criteria would not preclude such direct subsidies as may be permitted in the case of nonmonopolized goods to either domestic producers or consumers in respect of like or similar domestic products (see V, Subsidies, above). Also, if revenue tariffs are to be excepted from any rule limiting the height of tariffs, a corresponding exception will probably have to be made in the case of products monopolized and sold at a high price domestically primarily for revenue rather than protective purposes. If in the case of state-trading monopolies an appropriate limit could be set between, on the one hand, the price paid to the foreign supplier and on the other hand, the price paid to the domestic producer or that charged to the domestic consumer (whichever is the lower), suitable allowance will have been made both for subsidies on domestic, production and for the use of monopolized trading for revenue purposes.

The utility of any such price criterion is necessarily limited. It is likely to be readily applicable only to single product monopolies in private-enterprise countries, Moreover, certain administrative problems would arise in connection with such a rule; e.g., the problem of determining equitable processing and distribution costs. This would involve the problem of defining and determining the price paid the foreign supplier, and of defining the selling price, particularly in the case of products not ready for direct consumption including, when the monopoly sold domestic as well as foreign goods, the allocation of processing and distribution costs between foreign and domestic supplies.

For these reasons a price criterion of this kind cannot be used as a precise and arithmetical rule. Nevertheless, if countries adopting state-trading monopolies were to undertake not to use such monopolies to give protection to their domestic production in excess of the amount of protection permitted under the other clauses of the multilateral commercial policy convention;

these price relationships might be used as a general guide in considering any complaint that a particular country is using a trading monopoly to provide excessive protection to its domestic production.

10. <u>Minimum global purchase commitment by a state-trading country unallocated by countries</u>. Under such an arrangement the state-trading country, in return for tariff and other trade concessions from private-enterprise countries, would undertake to purchase abroad not less than specified amounts either of particular products or of total imports, depending on whether the commitment is made in bilateral agreements or in a multilateral convention.

Reasonable flexibility in regard to such minimum purchase commitment might be provided by an escape clause relating to the country's foreign exchange availabilities.

Such arrangements should include provisions assuring nondiscriminatory treatment

The countries negotiating bilateral agreements with state-trading countries on this basis could, as compensation for tariff or other trade concessions to the latter, select products of particular export interest to them in respect of which minimum purchase commitments unallocated among supplying countries would be made by the state-trading country. In this way they could negotiate agreements for bringing about an expansion of their trade with the state-trading country without causing the latter to discriminate against the trade of any other country, since in this as in other cases there would be a general commitment on the part of state-trading countries to buy always in the best market.

Similarly, in a multilateral convention a country with a complete state monopoly of foreign trade might equitably be asked to give a commitment with respect to its total imports in view of the fact that the multilateral convention would be conferring benefits on the state-trading country in the form of relaxation of trade barriers by all of the other parties to the convention.

Undertakings of the sort above indicated might well foster increasing participation in world trade on the part of state-trading countries such as the Soviet Union; on the basis of productive aptitudes.

11. <u>Conclusions</u>
   (a) A general multilateral commercial policy convention for the expansion of international trade on a nondiscriminatory basis which should be so devised that countries having a complete state monopoly of foreign trade can associate themselves with it might contain a commitment whereby such countries would agree to purchase from outside sources goods to a total specified value, without specifying particular countries or products. Such a commitment on the part of a country having a complete

state monopoly of foreign trade could be considered a counterpart to measures for the relaxation of trade barriers which private-enterprise countries would be undertaking to make effective pursuant to such a convention.

(b) A country having a monopoly for the whole or part of its foreign trade might be asked to agree not to use such a monopoly so as to give protection to its domestic producers in excess of that which would be permitted under other clauses of the convention. The relation between the prices paid to foreign suppliers and the prices paid to domestic producers or charged to domestic consumers might in some cases help to determine whether state-trading monopolies were being misused for the purpose of giving excessive protection. This criterion is likely to be effectively applicable only to single product monopolies in private-enterprise countries.

(c) Such a general multilateral commercial policy convention should also lay down the general principles to govern the practices of state-trading countries, partial or complete, and the principles to govern the negotiation of agreements with such countries, including the following:-

1) that purchases and sales by governments shall conform to the principle that they shall be made in accordance solely with commercial considerations, as provided in Article VIII of the United States-United Kingdom trade agreement; and accordingly,

2) that purchases of specified quantities of goods by any state-trading country, provided for in any intergovernmental agreement, shall not be limited to purchases in the other country or countries participating in the agreement, but shall be global purchases to be made in the country or countries best able to supply the goods, except possibly countries not participating in the general multilateral convention. A further exception might be made in cases where purchases are allocated in accordance with an agreement among the principal countries supplying and consuming the goods in question (see point 7, above). This clause is not intended to preclude contracts for purchases by state-trading organizations provided that they do not conflict with the principle laid down in point c(1), above.

d) It is suggested that government action in private-enterprise countries in trading with state monopolies in other countries should be confined to their normal trade control measures (such as adjustment of tariffs) exercised within the limits set by the general commercial policy convention rather than that they should institute special countermonopolies.

e) During a temporary period after the cessation of hostilities, the length of which should be laid down in the multilateral commercial policy convention, member countries might be excused from the strict application of the foregoing rules to their trading monopolies in those cases in which emergency conditions (such as shortages of supplies, of shipping or of foreign exchange, or the need to dispose of temporary surplus stocks) necessitate exceptional action.

VII. INTERNATIONAL COMMERCIAL POLICY ORGANIZATION

1. The creation of an appropriate international commercial policy organisation seems essential to the successful operation of any general multilateral commercial policy convention. Discussions regarding the possible subject-matter of such a convention have disclosed that it would be desirable to include therein several provisions, some of vital importance, which could be made workable only with the assistance of some organization representing all the member countries. Among these would be provisions for the application by the organization of stated criteria to: a) future customs unions; b) quantitative import regulations imposed on grounds of balance-of-payments difficulties; c) state-trading operations; d) revenue tariffs; e) subsidy programs; and f) export restrictions imposed on grounds of severe domestic shortage.

2. In general, the purposes of the proposed international commercial policy organization would be as follows:-
    a) To provide information to member countries regarding the implementation of the convention by other member countries.
    b) To afford a source of consistent interpretation regarding the provisions of the convention.
    c) To carry out investigative and fact-finding functions required or permitted by the provisions of the convention.
    d) To provide a mechanism for the consideration of complaints the adjustment of differences, and appropriate action in oases of nonobservance of the convention.
    e) To recommend to member countries any amendments to the convention which appear desirable in the light of experience.

3. Further consideration might show the desirability, for administrative reasons, of providing within the proposed commercial policy organization for: 1) a Council, or supervisory body, representing all member countries, to which would be referred important policy matters; and 2) a Commission, or operating body preferably a small group assisted by a staff of experts, which would carry out investigative and fact-finding functions and consider minor complaints, et cetera, subject to periodic review by the Council. It is believed the organisation should be guided by a set of general rules, made as precise as possible, which would be included in the convention, in order to avoid burdening it with too great a measure of responsibility.

4. In addition to the proposed international organisation on commercial policy, consideration is being or may be given to the creation of separate international organizations to deal with problems of currency stabilization, commodity agreements, and possibly others such as international investment and cartels, the membership of which, may not be identical. In view of the closely related character of these fields, and the possibility that measures might be taken by one organization which would be inconsistent with measures taken by the others, it is suggested that consideration be given to some form of economic organization to coordinate their activities (see also Section on International Coordination of Measures for the Maintenance of High Levels of Employment, below).
5. It is believed that the convention should be so drawn as to be open to adherence by all nations. Ex-enemy countries should of course be allowed to become members of the proposed convention. In view of their recent commercial history, and for reasons of security they might well be compelled to join, if it should prove necessary.
6. Parties to the convention should be required to give each other most-favoured-nation treatment. Nations which, after invitation, have refused to participate in the proposed convention, should be denied its benefits. Unless member nations are required to deny such benefits, for example their tariff reductions, to the trade of nonmembers, there might be a strong tendency on the one hand for nations to remain outside the convention and bargain individually with member nations, and on the other hand for member nations to compete with each other in obtaining special favors from nonmember nations. It is proposed that the general rule against granting the benefits of the convention to nonmember nations might be relaxed by empowering the international commercial policy organization to recommend exceptions in justified cases.

ANNEX A-4

From National Archives II, Lot File 57D-284, Box 24
October 6, 1944

Proposed Multilateral Convention on Commercial Policy:
Summary of Significant Provisions

A. General Commercial Provisions
   Provisions are included in this section (Article II, paragraph 1) which would require the repeal of the Buy-American Act and similar laws. In considering the political feasibility of these provisions, attention should be given to their economic significance in connection with domestic full employment

programs and the principles set forth in the preamble regarding the contribution of full employment measures to international trade.

B. Tariffs

This section would involve:

1. The reduction of tariffs by 50 percent (on the basis of rates in effect on July 1, 1939) subject to a floor of 10 percent ad valorem below which no duty need be reduced. The effect on existing United States tariffs, in terms of trade, would be about as follows:

   60 percent would be reduced by one-half
   15 percent would be reduced by less than one-half
   25 percent would not be reduced.

   There are emergency provisions whereby an absolute import quota equal to past imports can be unilaterally imposed for 5 years after the Convention comes into effect in case of serious injury to any industry caused or threatened by increased imports resulting from the tariff reduction or otherwise, A quota can be continued beyond the 5-year period, or a new quota can be established thereafter, if the International Trade Organization approves. The Organization is required to approve if there is a definite program for the relaxation and removal of the quota "within a reasonable period".

2. The elimination of most tariff preferences and the reduction of the rest in varying degrees. All preferences would be subject to a ceiling of one-quarter of the margin in effect on July 1, 1939, except that the ceiling would not apply in cases in which the most-favored-nation rate is not over 10 percent ad valorem. All preferences, whether Empire, regional, Cuban-American, etc., would be treated alike. Preferences granted by the United States to Cuba would be largely eliminated by the tariff-reduction provisions alone, except in the important cases of sugar and copper, which present special problems.

C. Quantitative restrictions

This section would abolish quotas, subject to a) permanent exceptions and b) temporary exceptions.

Of the permanent exceptions, the following are important:

a) quotas imposed under commodity agreements
b) import quotas required in conjunction with measure operating to restrict the quantities of like domestic products marketed or produced.

Quotas imposed under (b) may not be more restrictive than necessary must be removed as soon as possible, and must be made the subject of yearly consultation with the International Trade Organization. The Organization may make representations for the removal of the quotas at any time.

The principal temporary exception (others relate to products in short supply) permits quotas necessary to the orderly liquidation of government surpluses. Such quotas may be imposed unilaterally, but only after an effort has been made to obtain appropriate international action.

1. Quotas imposed under temporary exceptions must be removed as soon as the wartime or transitional conditions justifying them have ceased, and in any event not later than 3 years after the war. The International Trade Organization may extend this period.

D. Exchange Control

1. These provisions parallel the provisions of the Monetary Fund Agreement. The following are the principal differences between the two:
   a) Whereas the commitment in the Fund Agreement for the abolition of exchange control is indefinite (consultation with the Fund after 5 years), the commitment in the Convention is fixed at 5 years after the Fund begins operations. If necessary, however, the period may be extended by the International Trade Organization.
   b) Whereas the Fund Agreement prohibits discriminatory exchange treatment (after the transitional period), without further definition of what constitutes discrimination, the Convention contains detailed provisions for non-discriminatory treatment
   c) Whereas the Fund Agreement permits discriminatory exchange treatment during the transitional period, without important qualifications, the Convention prohibits discrimination except to the extent necessary in connection with the settlement of international indebtedness arising out of the war (principally blocked sterling balances in London), and requires that the discriminatory features of such settlements be made the subject of prior consultation with the International Trade Organization. The transitional exception in respect of discriminations provided for in the Convention is proposed tentatively. In the analysis of the draft text, the Trade Barriers Committee recommends that this government encourage and assist the British to find a solution to the blocked-balance problem which will reduce to a minimum the need for discriminatory exchange measures.
   d) The Convention would prohibit the further blocking of foreign exchange by requiring that exchange be made available for all products permitted to be imported in the future. There is no provision of this kind in the Fund Agreement.

2. The exchange control section includes provisions permitting countries to meet serious balance of payments difficulties. The important points in connection with these provisions are:

> Restrictions on imports may be imported by any country during any period in which the Monetary Fund determines that it is confronted with serious balance-of-payments difficulties.
> The restrictions may be in the form of a) import quotas alone, or b) exchange quotas accompanied by equivalent quantitative restrictions (in the form of prior import licenses).

E. State Trading

This section provides for a) equality of treatment with regard to all forms of State trading (i.e., the standard trade-agreement provisions expanded to cover unmonopolistic state trading); b) a global purchase commitment for the Soviet Union, and for any other completed state-trading; countries which would be subject to the same balance-of payments escape provisions applicable to other countries; and e) a set of general principles designed to encourage the reduction of the prices at which single-product government monopolies sell imported products in their home markets and to stimulate imports in response to such reduced prices.

The Trade Barriers Committee does not consider the global purchase commitment as essential. It points out that the value of the commitment is its visibility to the public, and that the Soviet Union might well be prepared to make a unilateral declaration as to prospective purchases which would be substantially greater than the amount it would be prepared to subscribe to in the form of a commitment.

F. Subsidies (Not yet approved by the Trade Barriers Committee)

1. Subsidies would be prohibited, subject to the following exceptions:
   a) export subsidies employed during a transitional period of three (or five) year after the effective date of the Convention (with provisions for abolition of the subsidies "at the earliest practicable date").
   b) Export subsidies granted in a product during any period in which such product is determined to be in chronic world surplus by an [international commodity organization]. The criteria in accordance with which such a determination must be under have been worked out by the Commodity Agreements Committee. These criteria would appear to provide adequate safeguards against the abuse of the exceptions.

   It should be noted that while the exceptions described above would permit subsidies on any product during a transitional period, and or any-product in chronic world surplus, such subsidies would, as a practical matter, have to be restricted to a) products on which there are domestic production or marketing restrictions and for which quantitative import restriction are permitted under section c) and b) products in respect of which either tariffs or transportation costs are high enough to provide an effective bar to reimports and imports of like foreign products.

2. "Domestic" subsides (i.e., any subsidy not an export subsidy) would be expressly permitted. Any country granting domestic subsidies in excess of those granted on July 1, 1939 would be required to keep the International Trade Organization informed as to the extent and the effect on trade of the subsidization, the reasons for the subsidization, and the measures being taken to make the subsidization unnecessary. However, these reporting requirements would not apply to products determined to be in chronic world surplus.

With regard to products determined to be in chronic world surplus, the Convention would require that if any such product is subject to governmental subsidization of any kind (export or domestic) affecting a material portion of the world supply, the countries which are important producers or consumers of the product will: a) promote consumption increases and the diversion of uneconomic production, b) seek the conclusion of an international commodity arrangement to limit the subsidization, promote expansion of trade, etc., and c) pending the conclusion of a commodity arrangement report annually to the International Trade Organization.

G. Exceptions – Territorial Application Non-contracting States

1. General exceptions

   The most important of the exceptions is that permitting any country to take any measure authorized by the International Trade Organization.

   a) The exception is designed (1) to provide flexibility in general, and (2) to afford a means whereby certain of the less developed countries may be permitted to adhere to the Convention on less exacting terms.

   b) The exception will need to be safeguarded against abuse by appropriate provisions in the constitution of the International Trade Organization.

2. Territorial Application

   The provisions on customs unions depart from past policy, which has been unqualified approval of all customs unions. These provisions would prohibit unions for customs purposes between metropolitan areas and colonies, and would prevent the formation of customs unions which result in an increase in the average level of protection. Details regarding proposed customs unions would be required to be transmitted to the International Trade Organization.

3. Relations with noncontracting States

These provisions would require discrimination against nonmembers. While they are considered essential to the successful negotiation of the Convention, they may not result in any substantial degree of discrimination. To the extent that they do, they may require termination of existing treaties or agreements.

ANNEX A-5

Excerpts from "Proposals for Expansion of World Trade and Employment," State Department Publication No. 2411, December 1945.

Proposals for Expansion of World Trade and Employment

Developed by a Technical Staff within the Government of the United States in Preparation for a International Conference on Trade and Employment and Presented for Consideration by the Peoples of the World

Department of State
Washington

November 1, 1945.

Mr. Secretary:

I hand you herewith "Proposals for Consideration by an International Conference on Trade and Employment", together with a statement of their purpose.

These proposals have been developed over many months by a group of experts drawn from all the interested departments and agencies of the government. They are intended to suggest a way in which the United States and other countries may concert their policy and action in the field of international trade so that the enormous productive powers which lie all about us may be released to operate fully for the general benefit. They are not regarded as final and perfect, but as a working basis for discussion and, I hope, for international action in the near future.

It is important that international agreement on the range of questions covered by these proposals be reached soon. All countries are faced by serious commercial problems and are taking action on them every day. Unless they act together, they will act at cross purposes and may well do serious damage to each other. But if they do act together, there is every possibility that the peoples of the world may enjoy, in our lifetime, a higher degree of prosperity and welfare than they have ever had before. Powers of production are now the greatest that the world has known. To bring them into play requires agreement on principles of exchange and distribution which will permit trade, production, employment, and consumption all to expand together.

I therefore recommend that these proposals be published as a basis of discussion and I would hope that such discussion might lead to an International Conference on Trade and Employment, to meet under the sponsorship of the United Nations, not later than the summer of 1946.

Respectfully,
WILLIAM L. CLAYTON
Assistant Secretary of State

Expansion of World Trade and Employment-Analysis of the Proposals

The main prize of the victory of the United Nations is a limited and temporary power to establish the kind of world we want to live in.

That power is limited by what exists and by what can be agreed on. Human institutions are conservative; only within limits can they be moved by conscious choice. But after a great war some power of choice exists; it is important that the United Nations use it wisely.

The fundamental choice is whether countries will struggle against each other for wealth and power, or work together for security and mutual advantage. That choice was made in principle at San Francisco and has since been ratified by the overwhelming majority of the governments concerned. The business of the immediate future is to give that decision the necessary body of common institutions and so to support those institutions that the experiment may succeed.

Success requires that the United Nations work together in every field of common interest, in particular the economic. The experience of cooperation in the task of earning a living promotes both the habit and the techniques of common effort and helps make permanent the mutual confidence on which the peace depends. The United Nations have therefore created not only an Economic and Social Council but special bodies to help them work together on many practical matters. Already there exist, or are in process of creation, agencies to deal with emergency relief, with currency, with international investment, with civil aviation, with labor, and with food and agriculture.

The United Nations should also endeavor to harmonize their policies with respect to international trade and employment. An International Trade Organization is still to be created. To this end, it is now proposed that an International Conference on Trade and Employment should be called by the United Nations, to meet not later than the summer of 1946.

The common interests of countries in world trade are obvious. Science and technology have enormously increased the productive powers of man. Limits upon human welfare are imposed today, not by the ultimate poverty of nature's resources, but by failure to use human powers to the full. Among the factors which obstruct our march toward the 'goal of freedom from want are excessive restrictions on exchange and distribution. Progress requires release from these restrictions.

Every country has its arrangements for the organization of production and distribution within its borders. To make the best use of these arrangements, countries must exchange their products. World trade is not only the device through which useful goods produced in one country are made available to consumers in another; it is also the means through which the needs of people in one country are translated into orders and therefore into jobs in another. Trade connects employment, production and consumption and facilitates all three. Its increase means more jobs, more wealth produced, more goods to be enjoyed.

Countries should therefore join in an effort to release trade from the various restrictions which have kept it small. If they succeed in this they will have made a major contribution to the welfare of their peoples and to the success of their common efforts in other fields.

International trade is kept small by four things:

(1) Restrictions imposed by governments;
(2) Restrictions imposed by private combines and cartels;
(3) Fear of disorder in the markets for certain primary commodities;
(4) Irregularity, and the fear of irregularity, in production and employment.

The Proposals which are herewith published deal with each of these problems.

I. Release from Restrictions Imposed by Governments

Governments have restricted the freedom of traders by many measures and for many reasons. They will continue to do so. No government is ready to embrace "free trade" in any absolute sense. Nevertheless, much can usefully be done by international agreement toward reduction of governmental barriers to trade.

These barriers take many forms. A transaction between a willing buyer in one country and a willing seller in another may be prevented because the tariff of the buyer's country creates an added cost too great to be borne; or because the paper-work required for export or import is so burdensome that the deal is not worth while; or because the seller cannot get an export license; or because the buyer cannot acquire the seller's currency to make a payment; or because importation is restricted by the buyer's country to a quota which has been exhausted; or because it is forbidden altogether. Or the seller may discover that the tariff of the buyer's country discriminates against him in favor of sellers located elsewhere.

All these restrictions and the red tape connected with them have undoubtedly prevented many business transactions, cut down the total of world trade, and reduced to that extent the benefits which trade might bring to all the parties concerned.

Barriers of this sort are imposed because they serve or seem to serve some purpose other than the expansion of world trade. Within limits they cannot be forbidden. But when they grow too high, and especially when they discriminate between countries or interrupt previous business connections, they create bad feeling and destroy prosperity. The objective of international action should be to reduce them all and to state fair rules within which those that remain should be confined.

This has often been attempted between two countries at a time or among several countries with respect to a single problem. These attempts have not been adequate because the many barriers are interdependent. Every country has its own kind of restriction, adapted to its own situation, and can hardly be expected to throw off its peculiar armor unless the other kinds of armor, employed by other countries, are thrown off at the same time. What is needed is a broad and yet detailed agreement, among many nations, dealing at one time with many different sorts of governmental restrictions upon trade, reducing all of them at once on a balanced and equitable basis, and stating rules and principles within which the restrictions permitted to remain should be administered. To prepare such an agreement should be one of the main tasks of the International Conference on Trade and Employment.

The Proposals now published afford a basis on which agreement might be reached. Rules are suggested to limit quotas and embargoes to carefully defined cases and to avoid discrimination in their application. Provision is made for the substantial reduction of tariffs and the elimination of tariff preferences. Subsidies, especially subsidies on exports, would be brought under supervision. Local taxes on imported products would be limited to rates no higher than those levied on like products produced at home. Agencies of governments conducting foreign trade would be asked to give fair treatment to the commerce of friendly states, to make their purchases and sales on economic grounds, and to avoid using a monopoly of imports to afford excessive protection to domestic producers. On these and other points the Proposals try to state fair principles acceptable to all and of benefit to all.

The proof of any principle is in its application. Therefore, effective preparation for the Conference must include detailed negotiations on trade barriers to commence as soon as possible. These negotiations should get down to cases, seeking to reduce tariffs, to eliminate preferences, and to lighten or remove other barriers to trade, whatever they may be.

In the United States, such negotiations are conducted under the Reciprocal Trade Agreements Act, which was renewed by Congress in June 1945 with an increase of the authority conferred upon the President. The use of that authority is one of the most important contributions which the United States can make to the success of the Conference.

Accordingly, this country should undertake negotiations under the Trade Agreements Act with several other governments as soon as a mutually satisfactory basis can be found, the required notices published, the statutory public hearings held, and their results considered. These negotiations cannot practicably be conducted with all countries at the same time, but the effort should be to get forward with the work, commencing before the general Conference convenes and continuing until every friendly country has participated in the enterprise.

Together, if they will, the countries of the world now have it in their power to free their trade from excessive governmental barriers. When that happens and to the extent that it happens, more ships will sail with fuller cargoes, more men will be employed, more goods will be produced, and more people will have better things to eat and wear and otherwise consume.

II. Release From Restrictions Imposed by Private Combines and Cartels

Trade may also be restricted by business interests in order to obtain the unfair advantage of monopoly.

In many lines this has not happened, but in others, as experience discloses, firms have banded together to restrain competition by fixing common selling prices, by dividing the world into exclusive markets, by curtailing production, by suppressing technology and invention, by excluding their rivals from particular fields, and by boycotting outsiders. These practices destroy fair competition and fair trade, damage new businesses and small businesses, and levy an unjust toll upon consumers. Upon occasion, they may be even more destructive of world trade than are restrictions imposed by governments.

Goods can surmount a tariff if they pay the duty; they can enter despite a quota if they are within it. But when a private agreement divides the markets of the world among the members of a cartel, none of those goods can move between the zones while the contract is in force. Clearly, if trade is to increase as a result of the lightening of government restrictions, the governments concerned must make sure that it is not restrained by private combinations.

The Proposals therefore contemplate that countries will act, individually and cooperatively, to curb those restrictive business practices in international trade which interfere with the objectives of increased production and trade, access on equal terms to markets and raw materials, and high levels of employment and real income.

To this end, it is suggested that a special agency be established within the International Trade Organization to receive complaints concerning restrictive practices of international combines and cartels, to obtain and examine the facts which are relevant to such cases, and to advise the Organization as to the remedies that may be required.

Enforcement against private violators necessarily rests with member governments. It will be the function of the Organization to recommend to these governments that they take action under their own laws and procedures. In the United States, enforcement would continue to be by judicial proceedings under the antitrust laws.

III. Release From Fear of Disorder in the Markets for Primary Commodities

After a great war there is danger of violent and rapid movement in the markets for primary commodities. The production of some things has been increased enormously to meet a war demand or to replace sources of production cut off by enemy action. Some time after the end of the fighting, the war demand subsides, goods held by the armies are returned to normal channels, and old sources of production come back into the markets and add to supplies. There is suddenly too much of some commodities and the prices react accordingly. Many countries learned after the last war that such changes can be devastating.

If the Proposals so far discussed can be put into effect, a great advance will have been made toward increasing trade and business activity. The resulting expansion of incomes and consumption should go a long way toward enlarging the demand for primary commodities. The best cure for any surplus is more money in the pockets of consumers. And general prosperity will make it easier for people caught by a particular failure of demand to shift to other lines where opportunities are better.

Such shifts are occurring all the time in any progressive society, Public policy should not seek to prevent them, for they are a necessary part of the process by which the economy meets the changing needs of the people. But if the changes come too fast they may bring serious distress to many small producers and to their communities. It is important that the needed changes be made gradually.

When excess supplies threaten, the first effort obviously should be to increase consumption. But if study discloses that that cannot be done rapidly enough to be effective, other measures may be needed. And since action by one country is quite likely to affect producers and consumers in another, there should be consultation between governments.

Consultation may result in a proposal for an intergovernmental commodity agreement. Such agreements are not intended to freeze existing patterns of production, but rather to provide a program of adjustment and a period of time within which the essential changes can be made without undue hardship.

During the transition, it may be necessary to restrict production or exports, to fix prices, or to allocate shares of markets among producing countries. Controls of this sort should not be applied in any case unless the need is real and serious, affecting many people, and not curable by the, normal process of competition. And when they are set up they should be strictly temporary, lasting no longer than required to carry out the necessary shifts. Their purpose is not to protect vested interests, but to prevent widespread distress during the course of necessary change.

Intergovernmental restrictions on production or on exports might be used – like international cartels – to take unfair advantage of consumers. Therefore the Proposals recommend adherence to the rule that consuming countries be entitled to participate along with producers in the original consideration of such agreements and be entitled also to an equal voice in their administration. Furthermore, there should be full publicity about each scheme and all its operations, in order that the world may make sure that it is managed in the general interest.

IV. Release From Fear of Irregularity in Production and Employment

Every country will seek so to manage its own affairs that its business life will be free from violent depressions. The object of international action should be to insure that these national efforts reinforce each other and do not cancel out.

The industrial activity of every country is affected by the size and the regularity of its orders from abroad. When industry in any country slows down and its purchases of foreign materials are cut, the effects are felt in every corner of the globe. Full and regular production at home, with increased participation in world trade, is the greatest boon which any people can confer upon producers throughout the world.

It is important, however, that nations should not seek to obtain full employment for themselves by exporting unemployment to their neighbors. To seek employment by prohibiting imports or by subsidizing exports would be harmful and self-defeating. The business of the Conference, therefore, should be to establish general agreement that each country will seek, on its own account, to maintain full and regular production, that it will not do so by using measures which would damage other countries or prevent the expansion of world trade, and that all countries will cooperate in exchanging information and participate in consultations with respect to anti-depression policies.

V. An International Trade Organization

Arrangements on this scale clearly require, for their successful operation, both an international forum where they may be discussed and improved and an international staff to assist in their administration.

The Proposals therefore suggest that an International Trade Organization be created, to stand beside the existing international agencies dealing with currency, investment, agriculture, labor, and civil aviation. It should have a constitution much like those of the other agencies set up by the United Nations, with enough internal specialization to enable it to perform the tasks assigned to it in dealing with trade barriers, restrictive business practices, and international commodity arrangements. Detailed suggestions on this matter are contained in the Proposals.

The Organization should be designed as the central international agency to deal with trade. It should be brought into relation with the Economic and Social Council in the manner provided in the Charter of the United Nations.

The Proposals reflect awareness that we live in a world of many countries with a variety of economic systems. They seek to make it possible for those systems to meet in the market-place without conflict, thus to contribute each to the other's prosperity and welfare. In no case do they impinge upon sovereign independence, but they do recognize that measures adopted by any country may have effects abroad and they suggest for general adoption fair rules of mutual tolerance.

The purpose is to make real the principle of equal access to the markets and the raw materials of the world, so that the varied gifts of many peoples may exert themselves more fully for the common good. The larger purpose is to contribute to the effective partnership of the United Nations, to the growth of international confidence and solidarity, and thus to the preservation of the peace.

PROPOSALS FOR CONSIDERATION BY AN INTERNATIONAL CONFERENCE ON TRADE AND EMPLOYMENT
A. NEED FOR INTERNATIONAL ECONOMIC COOPERATION

1. Collective measures to safeguard the peoples of the world against threats to peace and to reach just settlements of disputes among nations must be based not only on international machinery to deal directly with disputes and to prevent aggression, but also on economic cooperation among nations with the object of preventing and removing economic and social maladjustments, of achieving fairness and equity in economic relations between states, and of raising the level of economic well-being among all peoples.

2. Important contributions have already been made toward the attainment of these objectives. The Food and Agriculture Organization of the United Nations has been established. An International Monetary Fund to maintain reasonable exchange stability and facilitate adjustment in the balance of payments of member countries, and an International Bank for Reconstruction and Development to provide financial resources on a cooperative basis for those purposes are awaiting the action of governments required for their establishment.
3. In order to reach the objectives of the Atlantic Charter and Article VII of the mutual-aid agreements, it is essential that the cooperative economic measures already taken or recommended be supplemented by further measures dealing directly with trade barriers and discriminations which stand in the way of an expansion of multilateral trade and by an undertaking on the part of nations to seek full employment.
4. Cooperative action with respect to trade and employment is indispensable to the success of such other measures as those dealing with monetary and exchange stability and the flow of, investment capital. Effective action in regard to employment and to trade barriers and discriminations must, therefore, be taken or the whole program of international economic cooperation will fail, and an economic environment conducive to the maintenance of peaceful international relations will not be created.

B. PROPOSALS CONCERNING EMPLOYMENT

. . . . . .

C. PROPOSALS CONCERNING AN INTERNATIONAL TRADE ORGANIZATION

Need for an International Trade Organization

1. Measures designed to effect an expansion of trade are essential because of their direct contribution to maximum levels of employment, production and consumption. Since such expansion can only be attained by collective measures, in continuous operation and adaptable to economic changes, it is necessary to establish permanent machinery for international collaboration in matters affecting international commerce, with a view to continuous consultation, the provision of expert advice, the formulation of agreed policies, procedures and plans, and to the development of agreed rules of conduct in regard to matters affecting international trade.
2. It is accordingly proposed that there be created an International Trade Organization of the United Nations, the members of which would undertake to conduct their international commercial policies and relations in accordance

with agreed principles to be set forth in the articles of the Organization. These principles, in order to make possible an effective expansion of world production, employment, exchange, and consumption, should:
a) Provide an equitable basis for dealing with the problems of governmental measures affecting international trade;
b) Provide for the curbing of restrictive trade practices resulting from private international business arrangements; and
c) Govern the institution and operation of intergovernmental commodity arrangements.

Proposed International Trade Organization

There follows an outline of the principles which it is proposed should be incorporated in the articles of the Organization.

CHAPTER I

PURPOSES

The purposes of the Organization should be:

1. To promote international commercial cooperation by establishing machinery for consultation and collaboration among member governments regarding the solution of problems in the field of international commercial policies and relations.
2. To enable members to avoid recourse to measures destructive of world commerce by providing, on a reciprocal and mutually advantageous basis, expanding opportunities for their trade and economic development.
3. To facilitate access by all members, on equal terms, to the trade and to the raw materials of the world which are needed for their economic prosperity.
4. In general, to promote national and international action for the expansion of the production, exchange and consumption of goods, for the reduction of tariffs and other trade barriers, and for the elimination of all forms of discriminatory treatment in international commerce; thus contributing to an expanding world economy, to the establishment and maintenance in all countries of high levels of employment and real income, and to the creation of economic conditions conducive to the maintenance of world peace.

CHAPTER II

MEMBERSHIP

The original members of the Organization should be those countries participating in the Conference on Trade and Employment which accept membership.

CHAPTER III

GENERAL COMMERCIAL POLICY

Section A. General Commercial Provisions

Members should undertake:

1. To accord to products imported from other members treatment no less favorable than that accorded to domestic products with regard to matters affecting the internal taxation and regulation of the trade in goods.
2. To provide, for products in transit through their territories, corning from or going to other members, freedom from customs and transit duties, from unreasonable transit charges, and from discriminatory treatment of all kinds.
3. To subscribe to a general definition of the circumstances under which antidumping and countervailing duties may properly be applied to products imported from other members.
4. To give effect, as soon as practicable, to agreed principles of tariff valuation designed to assure the use of true commercial values as a basis for assessing duties, and to cooperate with other members and with the Organization in working out internationally acceptable valuation procedures of a standardized character.
5. To give effect, as soon as practicable, to agreed principles looking toward the simplification of customs formalities with a view to eliminating unnecessary requirements which afford an indirect protection to domestic products.
6. To eliminate excessive requirements regarding marks of origin in so far as they affect products imported from other members.
7. To refrain from governmentally financed or organized boycotts or campaigns designed to discourage, directly or indirectly, importation or consumption of products of other members.
8. To provide for adequate publicity regarding laws and regulations affecting foreign trade, and to maintain or establish national tribunals of an independent character to review and correct administrative customs action.
9. To transmit to the Organization appropriate trade information and statistics.
10. To cooperate with the Organization and with other members in carrying out or implementing the articles of the Organization.

Section B.. Tariffs and Preferences

1. *Import tariffs and preferences.* In the light of the principles set forth in Article VII of the mutual aid agreements, members should a enter into arrangements for the substantial reduction of tariffs and for the elimination of tariff preferences, action for the elimination of tariff preferences being

taken in conjunction with adequate measures for the substantial reduction of barriers to world trade, as part of the mutually advantageous arrangements contemplated in this document.

As an initial step in the process of eliminating tariff preferences it should be agreed that:
  a) Existing international commitments will not be permitted to stand in the way of action agreed upon with respect to tariff preferences.
  b) All negotiated reductions in most-favored-nation tariffs will operate automatically to reduce or eliminate margins of preference.
  c) Margins of preference on any product will in no case be increased and no new preferences will be introduced.
2. *Export tariffs and preferences.* Export duties should be open to negotiation in the same way as import duties. Members should undertake not to impose or maintain export duties which differentiate by reference to the destinations to which the goods are exported.
3. *Emergency action.* Commitments with regard to tariffs should permit countries to take temporary action to prevent sudden and widespread injury to the producers concerned. Undertakings for reducing tariffs should therefore contain an escape clause to cover such contingencies.

Section C. Quantitative Trade Restrictions

1. *General elimination of quantitative restrictions.* Except as provided for elsewhere in this Chapter, members should undertake not to maintain any quotas, embargoes, or other quantitative restrictions on their export or import trade with other members. This undertaking should not, however, apply to the following:
  a) Import and export prohibitions or restrictions, imposed during the early postwar transitional period, which are essential to (a) the efficient use of shipping space in short supply, (b) the equitable international distribution of products in short supply, or (c) the orderly liquidation of temporary surpluses of government stocks accumulated as a result of the war. Such prohibitions and restrictions should be removed not later than three years after the close of hostilities, but provision should be made whereby this period may be extended with the concurrence of the Organization.
  b) Export prohibitions or restrictions temporarily imposed to relieve conditions of distress in the exporting country caused by severe shortages of foodstuffs or other essential products.
  c) Export prohibitions or restrictions necessary to the application of suitable standards for the classification and grading of commodities in international commerce.

d) Export or import quotas imposed under intergovernmental commodity agreements conforming to the principles set forth in Chapter V.
e) Import quotas on agricultural products, imported in any form, necessary to the enforcement of governmental measures which operate (a) to restrict the quantities of like domestic products which may be marketed or produced, or (b) to remove a temporary surplus of like domestic products by making such surpluses available to certain groups of domestic consumers free of charge or at prices below the current market level. Such quotas should not be more restrictive than necessary, should be removed as soon as they cease to be necessary for the purposes of this subparagraph, and should be made the subject of periodic consultation with the Organization. V such quotas are allocated among sources of supply, they should be allocated fairly, on the basis of. imports during a previous representative period, account being taken in so far as practicable of any special factors which may have affected or which may be affecting the trade in the product concerned. Import quotas imposed under (a) of this subparagraph should not be such as would reduce imports relatively to domestic production as compared with the proportion prevailing in a previous representative period, account being taken in so far as practicable of any special factors which may have affected or which may be, affecting the trade in the product concerned.
2. *Restrictions to safeguard the balance of payments.* Members confronted with an adverse balance of payments should be entitled to impose quantitative import restrictions as an aid to the restoration of equilibrium in the balance of payments. This provision should be operative under conditions and procedures to be agreed upon. These conditions and procedures
   a) should set forth criteria and requirements in the light of which balance-of-payments restrictions might be imposed;
   b) should, as regards the use of such restrictions in the post-war transitional period, be framed on principles which would be designed to promote the maximum development of multilateral trade during, that period and which in no event would be more restrictive of such trade than the principles applicable, under Article XIV of the International Monetary Fund Agreement, to the use of exchange restrictions in the transitional period;
   c) should provide for the determination of the transitional period for the purposes of subparagraph b, above, by a procedure analogous to that contained in Article XIV of the International Monetary Fund Agreement;
   d) should provide for the full application of nondiscrimination in the use of such restrictions after the transitional period; and

e) should make appropriate provision for international consultation regarding balance-of-payments restrictions, whether imposed during the transitional period or thereafter.
3. *Equality of treatment.* Quantitative restrictions imposed on balance-of-payments grounds should be deemed nondiscriminatory if they are administered on a basis which does not discriminate among sources of supply in respect of any imported product.
   a) In the case of restrictions imposed in the form of quotas, members imposing such quotas should publish the global amounts or values of the various products which will be permitted to be imported during *a* specified future period. Any allocation of such quotas among sources of supply should be based in so far as practicable upon the proportion of the total imports of the product in question supplied by the various member countries in a previous representative period, account being taken of any special factors which may have affected or which may be affecting the trade in that product.
   b) In the case of restrictions not imposed in the form of quotas, the member imposing the restrictions should undertake to provide, upon the request of any other member having an interest in the product concerned, all relevant information as to the administration of the restriction, including information as to the import licenses granted over a past period and the distribution of such licenses among sources of supply.
   c) Any member should be entitled to raise with the Organization the question as to whether another member was imposing balance-of-payments restrictions, whether in the form of quotas or otherwise, in a manner not in harmony with the guiding principles stated above or in a manner which unnecessarily injured its commerce, and the member imposing the restrictions should undertake in these circumstances to discuss the grounds on which it had acted.
4. *Inconvertible currencies.* The undertakings *set* forth in paragraph 3, above, should not apply in cases in which their application would have the effect of preventing a member from utilizing inconvertible currencies for buying needed imports.
5. *Scarce currencies and currencies of territories having a common Quota in the Monetary Fund.* Members should not be precluded by this Section from applying quantitative restrictions a) in pursuance of action which they may take under Article VII of the International Monetary Fund Agreement, relating to scarce currencies, or *b)* in a manner designed to maintain the par value of the currencies of territories having a common quota in the Monetary Fund, in accordance with Article XX, Section 4 (g) of that Agreement.

6. *Application of quantitative restrictions by state-trading organizations.* The provisions of this Section relating to quantitative restrictions on imports for balance-of-payments reasons should apply equally to the restriction of imports by state-trading organizations for the same reasons.

Section D. Subsidies

1. *Subsidies in general.* Subject to the provisions of paragraphs 2 and 3, below, members granting any subsidy which operates to increase exports or reduce imports should undertake to keep the Organization informed as to the extent and nature of the subsidy, as to the reason therefore and as to the probable effects on trade. They should also be prepared, in cases where, under procedures approved by the Organization, it is agreed that serious injury to international trade threatens to result from the operation of the subsidy,' to discuss with other members or with the Organization possible limitations on the quantity of the domestic product subsidized. In this paragraph, the term "subsidy" includes any form of internal income or price support.
2. *Export subsidies.* Subject to the provisions of paragraph 3, below, members should undertake not to take any action which would result in the sale of a product in export markets at a price lower than the comparable price charged for the like product to buyers in the home market, due allowance being made for differences in conditions and terms of sale, for differences in taxation, and for other differences affecting price comparability. This undertaking should take effect, at latest, within 3 years of the establishment of the Organization. If at the end of that time any member considers itself unable to comply with the undertaking in respect of any particular commodity or commodities, it should inform the Organization, with an explanation of the reasons. It should then be decided by consultation among the interested members under procedures approved by the Organization whether there should be some further extension of time for the member desiring it in respect of the commodity or commodities concerned.
3. *Commodities in surplus supply.*
    a) When it is determined, in accordance with procedures approved by the Organization, that a commodity is, or is likely to become in burdensome world surplus, the members which are important producers or consumers of the commodity should agree to consult together with a view to promoting consumption increases, to promoting the reduction of production through the diversion of resources from uneconomic production, and to seeking, if necessary, the conclusion of an intergovernmental commodity arrangement in accordance with the principles of Chapter V.

b) If, however, within a reasonable time to be agreed upon, such steps should fail of their object, the provisions of paragraphs 1 and 2, above, should cease to apply to such product until such time as it has been agreed under procedures approved by the Organization that those provisions should be reapplied to it.

c) With regard to any export subsidies which may be imposed under sub-paragraph (b), no member should employ such subsidies so as to enlarge its share of the world market, as compared with the share prevailing in a previous representative period. The question as to what period would be representative in respect of the particular product concerned should be a subject for international consultation through the Organization.

Section E. State Trading

1. *Equality of treatment.* Members engaging in state trading in any form should accord equality of treatment to all other members. To this end, members should undertake that the foreign purchases and sales of their state-trading enterprises shall be influenced solely by commercial considerations, such as price, quality, marketability, transportation and terms of purchase or sale.

2. *State monopolies of individual products.* Members maintaining a state monopoly in respect of any product should undertake to negotiate, in the manner contemplated for tariffs, the maximum protective margin between the landed price of the product and the price at which the product (of whatever origin, domestic or foreign) is sold in the home market. Members newly establishing such monopolies should agree not to create protective margins greater than these tariffs which may have been negotiated in regard to those products. Unless the product is subject to rationing, the monopoly should offer for sale such quantities of the product as will be sufficient to satisfy the full domestic demand.

3. *Complete state monopolies of foreign trade.* As the counterpart of tariff reductions and other actions to encourage an expansion of multilateral trade by other members, members having a complete state monopoly of foreign trade should undertake to purchase annually from members, on the nondiscriminatory basis referred to in paragraph 1, above, products valued at not less than an aggregate amount to be agreed upon. This global purchase arrangement should be subject to periodic adjustment in consultation with the Organization.

Section F. Exchange Control

1. *Relation to the International Monetary Fund.* In order to avoid the imposition of trade restrictions and discriminations through exchange techniques, the

members of the International Trade Organization should abide by the exchange principles established pursuant to the Articles of Agreement of the International Monetary Fund and for this reason it should be required that the Organization and the Fund have a common membership.
2. *Equality of exchange treatment.* Members maintaining or establishing exchange restrictions should undertake to accord to the trade of other members the equality of treatment with respect to all aspects of such restrictions required under the provisions of the Articles of Agreement of the International Monetary Fund or, in cases where the approval of the Fund is required, the equality of treatment prescribed by the Fund after consultation with the International Trade Organization.

Section G. General Exceptions

The undertakings in this Chapter should not be construed, to prevent members from adopting or enforcing measures:

1. necessary to protect public morals;
2. necessary to protect human, animal or plant life or health;
3. relating to the traffic in arms, ammunition and implements of war, and, in exceptional circumstances, all other military supplies;
4. relating to the importation or exportation of gold or silver;
5. necessary to induce compliance with laws or regulations, such as those relating to customs enforcement, deceptive practices, and the protection of patents, trademarks and copyrights, which are not inconsistent with the purposes of the Organization;
6. relating to prison-made goods;
7. imposed for the protection of national treasures of artistic, historic or archaeological value;
8. undertaken in pursuance of obligations for the maintenance of peace and security; or
9. imposed in exceptional cases, in accordance with a recommendation of the Organization formulated in accordance with criteria and procedures to be agreed upon.

Section H. Territorial Application of Chapter III

1. *Customs territories.* The provisions of Chapter III should apply to the customs territories of the members. If any member has more than one customs territory under its jurisdiction, each customs territory should be considered a separate member for the purpose of applying the provisions of Chapter III.
2. *Frontier traffic and customs unions.* The provisions of Chapter III should not prevent any member a) from according advantages to adjacent countries

in order to facilitate frontier traffic or b) from joining a customs union, provided that such customs union meets certain agreed criteria. Members proposing to join a customs union should consult with the Organization and should make available to it such information as would enable it to make appropriate reports and recommendations.

. . . .

ANNEX A-6

From FRUS (1946, I, 1280-1289)
Memorandum Prepared in the Division of Commercial Policy

Preparations for Preliminary International Meeting on Trade and Employment

CONFIDENTIAL
[WASHINGTON,] February 6, 1946.

The Government of the United States published, on December 6, 1945, a document entitled "Proposals for Expansion of World Trade and Employment," copies of which were transmitted to other governments of the world for their consideration.

These *Proposals* urged the view that world security and well-being require the adoption by all countries of a code of commercial conduct embracing the fields of governmental barriers to trade, cartels, inter-governmental commodity agreements, and permanent international machinery to deal with these matters on a continuing basis. Recognizing the close relationship between levels of trade and conditions of employment, the *Proposals* also made clear the importance of domestic measures to maintain employment and the need for continuing international consultation on employment policies.

With a view to bringing about the implementation of the *Proposals*, the Government of the United States suggested that the United Nations Organization convene a general world conference for this purpose. At the same time, in order to assure adequate preparation for the world conference, the Government of the United States extended invitations to the governments of fifteen other countries to participate in a preliminary meeting on the subject.

The purpose of the present memorandum is to indicate the views of the Government of the United States regarding a) the objectives which should be sought at this preliminary meeting, b) the procedures which appear to be necessary before and at the meeting in order to achieve these objectives, and c) the methods whereby the results of the preliminary meeting can be broadened internationally at the general world conference on trade and employment which it is hoped the United Nations Organization will convene later on.

Objectives of the Preliminary Meeting

It is considered that the best means of preparing for the general world conference would be to develop in advance a body of definite and concrete international commitments on the various aspects of the Proposals which a broadly representative group of nations, including the major trading nations, would be prepared to support and adopt. Accordingly, it is believed that the objective of the preliminary meeting should be to negotiate, and reach substantial agreement upon, a detailed international instrument incorporating such commitments. It is suggested that this multilateral instrument should be called the Charter of the International Trade Organization of the United Nations. This Charter, like the Articles of Agreement of the International Monetary Fund, would contain not only provisions relating to the machinery of the Organization but also provisions embodying positive and substantive commitments as to the reduction of trade barriers of all kinds, as to the procedures to be followed in dealing with cartels, as to the principles and procedures which would govern the negotiation and operation of intergovernmental commodity arrangements, and as to the international aspects of domestic employment policies in the member countries. As explained below, the provisions of the Charter dealing with trade barriers would have a more definitive status (in respect of the countries participating in the preliminary meeting) than would the remainder of the Charter.

As an essential part of the undertakings for the reduction of trade barriers, provision must be made for the reduction of tariffs. However, in view of the thousands of tariff items involved, and the need for proceeding with tariff reduction on a selective, product-by-product basis, provisions effectuating actual tariff reductions cannot be incorporated in the Charter itself. It is proposed, therefore, that to the Charter there be appended a Protocol in which each country participating in the preliminary meeting (except, of course, countries having a complete state monopoly of foreign trade[1]) would agree to reduce individual import tariffs, or bind them against increase, in accordance with a, schedule setting forth and describing the various products on which that country

---

[1] With regard to such countries, it is suggested that, in lieu of reducing its tariffs, the country having a complete or substantially complete state monopoly of foreign trade might agree to purchase annually from the other countries concerned products valued at not less than an agreed amount. This commitment would be the subject of negotiations at the preliminary meeting and would, like the tariff schedules, be provided for in the Protocol.

would grant tariff concessions and the agreed maximum rate of duty for each such product.

It has been the past international practice, with few exceptions, to confine negotiations on tariffs to agreements between two countries. In these bilateral agreements, such as those heretofore concluded by the United States under the reciprocal trade-agreements program, each of the two countries parties to the agreement granted reductions or bindings of its import tariffs on products of which the other was a principal or important supplier. While these concessions were as a rule generalized to third countries, either by virtue of most-favored-nation obligations or as a matter of policy, third countries had no contractual right to them independently of the existence of the bilateral agreement in which they were embodied. In other words, tariff reductions have been effected in the past either unilaterally or by means of a network of bilateral instruments, each separate from the other and dependent for its existence and continuation in force upon the policies and decisions of the particular pair of countries concerned.

It is now suggested that the purely bilateral method of negotiating tariff concessions should be modified in connection with the proposed negotiations relating to the Charter of the International Trade Organization, and that a multilateral procedure be developed under which tariff reductions effected in conjunction with these negotiations may stand on all fours with the multilateral commitments relating to other trade barriers which would be incorporated in the Charter itself. In this way each country subscribing to the relaxation of trade barriers other than tariffs under a multilateral plan affecting many products and many countries, would also be assured that equally broad and precise action would be taken with regard to tariffs.

It is proposed, therefore, that the tariff schedules which it is envisaged would result from the negotiations at the preliminary meeting would be multilateral, both in scope and in legal application. Under this plan, there would result from the negotiations a total of 14 schedules of tariff concessions, each schedule setting forth a description of the products and of the concession rates of duty thereon which would be applicable in respect of the imports into a particular country. The products listed in the schedule pertaining to the imports into each country would include those of which the other countries are or are likely to become, principal suppliers, individually or in combination. Each country participating in the arrangement would be contractually entitled, in its own right and independently of the most-favored-nation clause, to the concessions in each of the schedules of the other countries.

It is clear from the foregoing that the negotiations contemplated with regard to tariffs represent an undertaking of considerable magnitude and will constitute a main task of the preliminary meeting. The tariff aspect of the negotiations will accordingly require particularly careful and extensive preparation in advance of the meeting. Suggestions as to certain preparatory steps which might be taken are set forth elsewhere in this memorandum. The Government of the United States hopes that within the next six or eight weeks it will be able to transmit to the other governments intending to participate in the preliminary meeting, for their study and consideration, a detailed draft text of the proposed Charter of the International Trade Organization 36 and of the general provisions of the Protocol. Meanwhile, it may be noted that under the Protocol certain Articles of the Charter (e.g. those relating to most-favored-nation treatment, quantitative restrictions, national treatment in respect of internal taxes, et cetera) would be susceptible of being brought into force independently of the remainder of the Charter and in conjunction with the entry into force of the tariff schedules. The purpose of this arrangement is to assure that the tariff schedules, together with those related trade-barrier provisions of the Charter which are designed to safeguard the value of the tariff concessions and which have customarily been included in trade agreements in the past, can be made effective as a separate international instrument in the event of any delay in the general acceptance by the legislatures of the various countries of the Charter as a whole.

The procedures for conducting the tariff negotiations at the preliminary meeting should be such that failure of any pair of countries to reach satisfactory agreement on particular tariff rates would not obstruct the completion of a broad multilateral agreement. In such cases provision might be made for continuing or supplementary negotiations between the countries concerned.

Preparatory Steps in Advance of the Meeting

The following suggestions are made as to the steps which it is believed should be taken to assure adequate preparations for the preliminary meeting:

1. Each Government should endeavor to formulate, with a view to definitive discussion at the meeting, its position and views as to the various principles set forth in the Proposals published by the United States and as to the provisions of the detailed draft Charter, referred to above, in which these principles would take concrete form. The Government of the United States would be glad to receive, in advance of the meeting, the views of any of the other Governments regarding any aspect of the *Proposals* or the draft Charter.
2. The Government of each country should transmit to the Government of each other country from which it wishes to receive tariff concessions a statement setting forth (1) a list of the products on which it will request concessions of that country, and (2) the actual reductions or bindings of tariff rates which it

plans to request in respect of such products. This statement containing both types of information should be transmitted as soon as possible. However, since it is relatively easy to prepare a list of products alone, without an indication of the tariff concessions to be requested, and since even such a list would provide some assistance to the various countries in preparing for the negotiations, it is suggested that a list of this kind might well be sent in advance of the more complete statement containing detailed requests for tariff concessions. The work of all concerned would be facilitated if, in preparing the list of products and the concessions to be asked, use would be made of the statistical or tariff nomenclature of the country of which the concessions are requested.

3. In preparing requests for tariff concessions, it is suggested that the participating Governments may wish to apply the principles outlined in the *Proposals* relating to cases in which there is a state monopoly of the trade in an individual product (Chapter III, Section E, paragraph 2 of the Proposals). These principles suggest that, in the case of such monopolies, the protection afforded domestic producers by means of price disparities similar to those caused by import tariffs can be effectively reduced or bound against increase by negotiating a maximum margin between the landed price at which the monopoly can buy the foreign product and the price at which the monopoly sells the product in the home market. Such negotiated margins would be set forth and provided for in the tariff schedules along with the negotiated rates of customs duty. These margins would, of course, be exclusive of transportation, distribution and other expenses incident to the sale of the imported product.

4. In addition to import tariffs, each Government should also examine the export tariffs or taxes which may be maintained by certain of the other governments participating in the meeting with a view to determining whether it wishes to request concessions on individual export tariffs affecting its sources of supply. As in the case of import tariffs, requests for concessions on export tariffs should be communicated to the appropriate government or governments in advance.

5. The requests for tariff concessions which each Government would have made of the others, and the requests which each Government would have received from the others, should make it possible for each Government to have formulated, by the time the meeting begins, a schedule of the offers which it would be prepared to make to all of the other governments as a group in the light of what it would expect to receive from each of them. It is suggested that, for convenient reference in transmitting requests for tariff concessions prior to the opening of the preliminary meeting, the

Schedules which would pertain to the various countries might be numbered in alphabetical order, as follows:

Name of Country	
Australia	Schedule I
Belgo-Luxembourg Economic Union and Belgian Congo	Schedule II
Brazil	Schedule III
Canada	Schedule IV
China	Schedule V
Cuba	Schedule VI
Czechoslovakia	Schedule VII
France and French Empire	Schedule VIII
India	Schedule IX
Netherlands and Empire	Schedule X
New Zealand	Schedule XI
Union of South Africa	Schedule XII
Union of Soviet Socialist Republics	Schedule XIII
United Kingdom, Newfoundland, Southern Rhodesia, Burma and colonial dependencies	Schedule XIV
United States	Schedule XV

Procedures for Conducting Negotiations at the Preliminary Meeting

In order that the work of negotiating arrangements of the complexity and scope of those under consideration may proceed in an orderly and expeditious fashion, it is essential that the preliminary meeting be well organized. The following suggestions bearing upon the make-up of the delegations and the committee structure of the meeting are advanced for consideration:

1. Make-up of the Delegations. It is believed that the main considerations to be borne in mind with regard to the make-up of the delegations are that a) the meeting is intended to be preliminary to the world conference on trade and employment and would not therefore be of the same order of importance as the world conference, and b) the primary work of the meeting would be highly technical in character, requiring the services of persons competent in the various specialized fields embraced under the following headings:
    i) Employment policies;
    ii) Tariffs (including tariff policies in respect of individual products as well as technical tariff, tariff nomenclature, and customs administrative problems);
    iii) Exchange and international financial controls;
    iv) Agricultural policies bearing on international trade;

Annex A-6

- v) Policies in respect of intergovernmental controls over the production of, or trade in, primary commodities;
- vi) Cartels;
- vii) Commercial policy in general (including broad questions of tariff policy such as most-favored-nation treatment, generalization of duties, et cetera); and
- viii) International organizational problems.

2. Organization of the Meeting. The first task of the meeting will be to agree upon the committees or other groups which will need to be established in order to conduct the negotiations on substantive matters. In the light of the various subjects to be discussed, and the need for proceeding more or less simultaneously over a broad field, it is suggested that committees consisting of representatives from each of the participating governments may need to be established to cover the areas indicated below. The outline which follows is intended to be tentative and suggestive only, and is merely put forward for the purpose of indicating the organizational problems involved.

   A. Committee on Employment Policies. (This Committee would deal with provisions relating to the international aspects of domestic employment policies.)

   B. Committee on Tariffs. (This Committee might deal with questions of most-favored-nation treatment and generalization of duties as well as with the broad aspects of the detailed negotiations for the reduction of tariffs. Since the matter of a particular tariff concession, offered by one country in respect of a product of which another is the principal supplier, is not usually of primary interest to countries other than the two countries immediately concerned, it is probable that the detailed negotiations for tariff concessions would be very largely conducted in the groups representing pairs of countries. In other words, although the tariff schedules, as finally worked out, would be multilateral in scope and would be subject to general approval by the Committee on Tariffs, decisions as to the particular concessions on particular commodities would be taken in the small negotiating groups, which would usually be of a bilateral character.)

   C. Committee on Non-Tariff Trade Barriers. (This Committee might deal with quantitative restrictions, exchange controls, and subsidies.)

   D. Committee on General Commercial Provisions. (This Committee might deal with such questions as customs formalities, marks of origin, tariff valuation, freedom of transit, and miscellaneous commercial provisions.)

   E. Committee on Cartels. (This Committee would deal with provisions relating to the curbing of restrictive business practices.)

F. Committee on Commodity Policy. (This Committee would deal with provisions relating to the principles and procedures which should govern the negotiation and operation of intergovernmental agreements which restrict the production of, or trade in, primary commodities.)

G. Organization. (This Committee would deal with provisions relating to the functions and structure of the International Trade Organization.)

In addition to the foregoing, there would appear to be need for 1) a legal and drafting committee, and 2) a general committee, consisting of the heads of delegations, to pass upon the work of the meeting as a whole.

Relation Between Preliminary Meeting and Proposed World Conference on Trade and Employment

If the negotiations at the preliminary meeting are successfully carried forward along the lines indicated above, there would emerge from the meeting the draft Charter of the ITO and the Protocol. It is proposed that the draft Charter should be submitted to the world conference on trade and employment for its consideration and that the provisions of the Charter should be open to amendment at that conference in the light of the new considerations introduced as a result of the larger number of countries participating.

With regard to the tariff schedules provided for under the Protocol, however, it seems clear that these cannot practicably be reopened, as among the countries participating in the preliminary meeting, for consideration and possibly renegotiation at the general world conference. Nor would such action seem to be required or appropriate on grounds of equity. It is proposed, therefore, that the Protocol, consisting of the tariff schedules and of the non-tariff trade barrier provisions of the draft Charter which it may be agreed to incorporate in the Protocol by reference, should, at the close of the preliminary meeting, be signed and published by the countries participating in that meeting and should come into force, independently of the Charter, in accordance with provisions to be worked out. In order to make perfectly clear the relationship between the Protocol and the Charter, provision might be made whereby the Protocol could later be adapted to any changes in the provisions of the Charter relating to non-tariff trade barriers which might result from the action of the world conference.

The question will arise at the preliminary meeting, and later at the world conference, as to what treatment should be accorded to the commerce of countries which fail to adhere to the Charter of the ITO or which, having adhered, fail to carry through tariff reductions comparable in scope to those which it is expected the countries participating in the preliminary meeting will have effected as a result of the prior negotiations.

Related to the foregoing is the question as to what procedure should be followed in conducting tariff negotiations a) between those countries which have participated in the preliminary meeting (and which have, therefore, already agreed upon tariff concessions over a wide range of products) and newly adhering countries, and b) between the newly adhering countries themselves.

With regard to the first question, it is suggested that any final decision involving the concerted withholding from the trade of non-adhering countries of the benefits of the provisions of the charter relating to non-tariff trade barriers, or involving the denial of tariff concessions to the trade of countries which, having adhered to the Charter, fail to carry out adequate tariff reductions, can only be taken at the general world conference in the light of the views of all interested countries. It is clear, however, that the countries participating in the preliminary meeting should formulate and make recommendations to the world conference on this point. The following suggestions are put forward as to the policy which these recommendations might urge for adoption:

1. The members of the ITO, i.e. those countries which adhere to the Charter, should pursue a common policy regarding the generalization to the trade of non-members of the benefits of the trade provisions of the Charter, including tariff concessions granted pursuant to the Charter.
2. In order to facilitate the foregoing, the countries participating in the world conference should agree, at the conference, that they will not invoke prior most-favored-nation obligations for the purpose of obtaining the benefits under reference.
3. Subject to exceptions authorized by the International Trade Organization, and to any temporary or conditional exceptions which the world conference may agree to make in respect of countries that may not have had an opportunity to participate in the formulation of the Charter, countries adhering to the Charter should, after a reasonable period, withhold the benefits of the Charter from the trade of countries which refuse to adhere to it. Similarly, and subject to exceptions authorized by the ITO, those countries adhering to the Charter which have completed adequate tariff negotiations might, after a reasonable period, become entitled to withhold the tariff concessions resulting from such negotiations from the trade of countries which, although having adhered to the Charter, fail to negotiate tariff reductions judged by the ITO to be in conformity with the spirit of the commitments to negotiate tariff reductions contained in the Charter.
4. The policy suggested in 2 and 3, above, should also apply, of course, in respect of member countries which withdraw from the ITO or which terminate the tariff concessions they have made. With regard to the related question of the procedure for assuring, by negotiation, the reduction of (tariffs on the part of adhering countries other than those which have reduced their tariffs in

connection with the preliminary meeting, the following possibilities occur to the Government of the United States:

A. Countries which have completed tariff negotiations among themselves at the preliminary meeting would negotiate separate bilateral tariff-reduction agreements with adhering countries not present at that meeting, and the latter would negotiate such agreements between themselves. The requirement would be made that these negotiations must proceed as soon as practicable upon the request of either party.

B. It may be possible to establish within the ITO a mechanism whereby the multilateral tariff negotiations initiated at the preliminary meeting may be continued on a multilateral basis with adhering countries not present at that meeting. Under this procedure, each adhering country which had not yet undertaken tariff negotiations would offer to negotiate with those that had, a multilateral schedule of concessions similar in scope and legal application to the schedules emerging from the preliminary meeting; and the countries already having such multilateral schedules in effect would offer to amend them to the extent necessary to assure appropriate concessions on products of which the newcomer was a principal supplier.

Whatever procedure is adopted, due weight should be given in the negotiating process to concessions already made as a result of prior negotiations.

ANNEX A-7

U.S. Delegation Report on First Preparatory Meeting for an International Conference on Trade and Employment

From FRUS (1946, I, 1360-1366)
The Director of the Office of International Trade Policy (Wilcox) to the Secretary of State

[WASHINGTON,] December 27, 1946.

CONFIDENTIAL REPORT TO THE SECRETARY OF STATE FROM THE CHAIRMAN OF THE UNITED STATES DELEGATION TO THE FIRST MEETING OF THE PREPARATORY COMMITTEE FOR AN INTERNATIONAL CONFERENCE ON TRADE AND EMPLOYMENT

London, England, October 15-November 26, 1946

This Confidential Report is supplementary to the formal Report of the United States Delegation to the First Meeting of the Preparatory Committee for an International Conference on Trade and Employment. It sets forth (1) the principal issues considered at the meeting, (2) the attitudes of other countries toward the American proposals, (3) the strategy adopted by the United States delegation, (4) the outcome of the negotiations, and (5) the prospects of the program for international trade.

It should be emphasized that the work of the meeting was carried on at the expert level, that the negotiations were preparatory rather than conclusive, and that the positions taken involve no final commitments. It is nonetheless true that the Committee has carried the work of drafting a world trade charter to a stage that should make possible its approval without major changes in form or substance.

(1) The Principal Issues
The major objective of the United States was the adoption of a rule that would outlaw the use of *import quotas* and other quantitative restrictions as a matter of principle, permitting them only with international approval in exceptional cases and requiring that they be administered, in such cases, without discrimination. In the absence of such a rule, it is virtually certain that all other nations will impose quotas on imports and that many nations will so administer these quotas as to discriminate against American goods.

A second objective was an agreement to reduce *tariffs* and a rule that such reductions would operate automatically to reduce or eliminate *margins of preference*.

Other nations would like to require us to purchase larger import quotas and narrower margins of preference by reducing our tariffs. We insisted that import quotas be outlawed by rule and preferences be cut automatically so that we could use our tariff concessions to purchase equivalent tariff concessions abroad. On both of these points, we were successful.

The Australians argued that our *Proposals* were negative rather than affirmative, consisting of prohibitions rather than positive measures to expand trade. They and the British emphasized the importance of *employment policy*. Superficially this appeared to be a major issue. Actually no delegation proposed any positive international measures to expand or maintain employment. The opposition on this point was satisfied with recognition of the fact that a persistent export surplus in the United States or a sudden, sharp decline in our demand for their foods would put them in balance-of-payment difficulties and with a provision permitting countries in such difficulties to use quantitative restrictions to protect their monetary reserves. Such a provision had been included in our original proposals. On this point, we made no concession of substance.

The Australians, with the support of the Indians, Chinese, Lebanese, Brazilians, and Chileans, urged that affirmative provision be made for the *industrialization* of undeveloped areas. It was the real purpose of this drive to obtain freedom to promote industrialization by using import quotas. Initially this appeared to be the most difficult problem before the Committee. It was resolved, however, when the United States delegation drafted and introduced a new chapter on economic development. In the course of this chapter a procedure is provided whereby the International Trade Organization can grant an undeveloped country, in a particular case, permission to make a limited use of import quotas. This was the only important concession made by the United States during the meeting and it was this that brought about the virtually unanimous acceptance of the charter as a whole.

On *cartel policy*, our whole position was opposed by the Belgians and the Dutch and the formulation set forth in our Suggested Charter was opposed by the British. Our only real support came from the Canadians. With their help, however, we obtained a revised chapter that is stronger than our original proposals and far stronger than we had thought was possible.

On *commodity policy* the Committee was confronted with the effort of the FAO to separate agricultural commodities from other commodities and to separate agricultural commodity policy from trade policy by setting up a comprehensive buffer-stock, surplus-disposal, and relief operation under a World Food Board. The U.S. delegation insisted that a common policy apply to agricultural and non-agricultural commodities and that commodity policy be kept in relation with commercial policy under the International Trade Organization. We succeeded in obtaining general support for this position. We defeated a British drive to obtain specific endorsement for buffer stocks as a preferred device. And we came out with a revised chapter that retains all of the safeguards contained in our original proposals.

With respect to *organization*, the only important issues related to weighted voting and to the membership of the Executive Board of the ITO. These issues were not resolved.

(2) Attitudes of Other Countries
The *Russians* did not attend. They consistently attributed their absence to a shortage of trained personnel. This would indicate, at least, that they are not ready to oppose the program. Their absence was fortunate, since it made it possible for us to organize the meeting promptly and to devote our attention almost exclusively to issues with which they would have had little concern. Klentzov, head of the USSR trade mission in London, had Kunoci, vice-chairman of the Czech delegation, invite me to lunch and then suggested a subsequent lunch where I outlined the American program and the progress of the London meeting. He said that the USSR would have to study the program carefully and determine whether it was in their interest to participate.

The *Czechs* were the only eastern Europeans at the meeting. They were well represented, entirely cooperative, and gave every evidence of a sympathetic interest in the American program and a desire to see the negotiations succeed. We avoided embarrassment for them and others, in their relations with Russia, by postponing consideration of the articles of the Charter dealing with complete state monopoly of foreign trade and with relations with non-members. They were plainly grateful.

The most striking development at the meeting was the unexpected vigor of the support given us by the countries of western Europe: *Norway, The Netherlands, Belgium,* and *France.* They appear to be motivated by a strong desire to follow the U. S. line on trade policy. Aside from these countries, our most helpful support came from *Canada* and *Cuba.*

Our strongest opposition came from India and Australia. These countries had two of the most effective delegations at the meeting. The *Indians* came with a chip on their shoulder. They regarded the *Proposals* as a document prepared by the U. S. and the U. K. to serve the interest of the highly industrialized countries by keeping the backward countries in a position of economic dependence. They left the meeting in a much better frame of mind. But it is clear that they feel themselves under pressure to push their industrialization by all possible means and with the utmost possible speed.

The *Australians* were able, intelligent, and reasonable. The head of their delegation, Dr. Coombs, displayed a real capacity for economic statesmanship. The differences between us were more a matter of emphasis than of substance and we succeeded in meeting their political necessities without surrendering anything that we regarded as a matter of fundamental principle. We were fortunate that the nominal leadership of the opposition was in such good hands.

The *United Kingdom* lived up to the letter of its commitments to us and was scrupulously correct in its public statements of formal support. In the closed negotiations, however, it did not assume a role of leadership in support of our program, but took a fairly independent line, supporting us on some issues, opposing us on others, and acting as a mediator between us and our opponents on still others. It had an able delegation and made a major contribution to the outcome of the meeting. One gets the impression that the commitments which the United Kingdom has made to us are highly unpalatable to important segments of British opinion and that the Government, in living up to these commitments, is having to swim against a strong current of public sentiment.

(3) Delegation Strategy
It was the purpose of the United States to advance as far as possible the project of drafting a charter for an international trade organization and promoting

definitive negotiations for the reduction of barriers to trade. To this end we had prepared a *Suggested Charter* elaborating our original *Proposals*, circulated it to the other members of the Committee, discussed it with all of them (except the Russians), and published it on September 20, 1946. In the meeting our *procedural objectives* were: (1) acceptance of the American draft as the basis of the Committee's deliberations, (2) completion and publication of as large a part as possible of a revised draft, (3) appointment of an interim drafting committee to carry the drafting work forward between the first and second meetings of the Preparatory Committee, and (4) sponsorship by the Preparatory Committee of the reciprocal trade agreement negotiations projected in December 1945 by the United States.

The British and French had strongly opposed the publication of our Charter. The Australians took the position that it was too early to draft detailed provisions for a charter; that the first meeting of the Committee should produce a more tentative document, similar in character to our original *Proposals*. We made it clear at the outset that we would not insist upon our particular formulation of the articles in the Charter and that we were prepared sympathetically to consider the proposals made by other countries. The Norwegians and the Dutch then urged the adoption of our Charter as the basis for the Committee's work and the Committee accepted their proposal, set up a series of subcommittees, one to deal with each of our chapters, and took the articles of the relevant chapter as the agenda of each subcommittee.

From then on all of the work of the Committee was directed toward our document. This gave us a great advantage in the negotiations. We had stated the problems, suggested the solutions, established the general pattern of the charter, and provided large sections of text that have not been and will not be altered in any way. Our careful preparation had built up a momentum that carried through the meeting. Our open-minded attitude in the opening sessions allayed the fears of our opponents. The willingness of sixteen other nations to accept a purely American draft as the basis of their work indicates their confidence in our fairness and objectivity and is a tribute that could scarcely have been paid to any other power.

There was considerable reluctance among other delegations concerning the publication of revised texts, the appointment of an interim drafting group, and Committee sponsorship of the tariff negotiations. In each of these cases we waited until the progress of the negotiations had reached a point sufficiently encouraging to indicate a favorable outcome and then proposed the procedure we desired. In each case we obtained unanimous support.

The key to general *agreement on substance* was an understanding between the heads of the U. S. delegation and the Australian delegation. It became clear that some expansion of the Employment Chapter and the insertion of an Economic Development Chapter would suffice to satisfy Dr. Coombs and that the other members of the undeveloped-nations bloc, with the possible exception of India, would follow his leadership. Coombs finally accepted a radically modified version of his proposals on employment and industrialization and, in return, acquiesced to our insistence on the general rule against import quotas and the automatic reduction of margins of preference. This was the basic bargain in the meeting. The other agreements were collateral.

(4) The Outcome of the Negotiations
Among the 89 articles for the trade charter proposed and discussed, the Committee reached general agreement on 74. These included all substantive issues of major importance. Reservations as to eleven of these articles were recorded by one, two, or three delegations. Each of the present articles thus has the approval, at the expert level, of 14, 15, 16, or 17 countries. The Committee divided on only two articles – those relating to voting and to membership on the Executive Board of the ITO. It failed to complete its work on 11 articles, dealing mainly with customs administration and formal matters, and referred them to the Interim Drafting Committee. It took no action on two articles – state monopoly of foreign trade and relations with non-members – postponing consideration of these issues until its second meeting.

The Committee approved some 200 pages of subcommittee reports reviewing the questions discussed, outlining the positions taken, and explaining the agreements reached. It also approved a memorandum setting forth in elaborate detail the procedures to be followed in the forthcoming reciprocal trade agreement negotiations. And it adopted a series of resolutions relating to the future phases of its work.

It should be recorded that the Committee carried the project of writing a world trade charter much farther than any of its members had believed possible when it met. It completed its work within the six weeks originally assigned to it. And it carried on its deliberations throughout in an atmosphere of cordial cooperation without a bitter exchange or a major division on any matter of substance.

The resulting draft is, in many respects, an improvement on the Charter suggested by the United States. But it closely follows the pattern of that document, making no important concessions on any matter of fundamental principle.

(5) The Prospects of the Program
The success of this project will depend (1) upon the attitude of the USSR, and (2) upon the future attitude of the other countries on the Preparatory Committee,

but, most importantly, (3) upon the support that it receives within the United States.

If the Russians stay away from the second meeting of the Committee, or if they attend the meeting and fight the program, it will be difficult if not impossible to persuade many neighboring states both in Europe, and in Asia to go along with plans establishing an effective ITO. It is therefore desirable that they be persuaded to attend the next meeting and that the substantive matters covered in the first meeting be explained to them in detail. The ITO could function effectively without Russian participation. But an ITO opposed by the USSR might draw an economic line farther to the west than would otherwise be necessary.

The other nations on the Committee have their fingers crossed. They will go along with our program if we give evidence that we are prepared to practice what we preach. They will abandon it if we don't.

The outcome of the whole enterprise will depend upon the sort of offers that we make at the trade agreement negotiations beginning in Geneva in April 1947. If they are adequate, the rest of the world will follow our leadership. If they are not, our program will be lost. The success or failure of our international trade policy thus depends less upon the attitude of other countries than it does upon the sort of support that is forthcoming within the United States. If that support is to be effective, it must be vigorous, widespread, and bipartisan. To this end, the Department must be prepared, during the coming months, to devote a considerable part of its time and energy to a program of public information and Congressional relations.

The program to which sixteen other nations have now tentatively agreed is an American program. It was at our insistence that a commitment with respect to trade policy was written into the Atlantic Charter in 1941 and that Article VII was written into the lend lease agreements in 1942. It was the United States that published the *Proposals for Expansion of World Trade and Employment* in December 1945 and persuaded the Governments of the United Kingdom and France to go on record in support of these Proposals. It was the United States that invited seventeen [15] other nations, in December 1945, to enter into definitive negotiations for the reduction of tariffs and other barriers to trade. It was at our initiative that the Economic and Social Council of the United Nations set up the Preparatory Committee and agreed to call an International Conference on Trade and Employment. It was our Government that published and circulated *The Suggested Charter*, sent its representatives to sell the *Charter* to fifteen other nations in the summer of 1946, and urged the adoption of its provisions upon the Preparatory Committee in the fall of that year. If we do not now go through with the program that we have proposed, we cannot again, in this generation, expect any other proposal that we may make to be considered seriously by the other nations of the world.

Respectfully submitted,
CLAIR WILCOX

ANNEX A-8

U.S. Report on the Geneva GATT Negotiations

From FRUS 1947 I, 1015-1024.

Lot 65A987, Box 98

Memorandum by the Acting Secretary of State to President Truman
WASHINGTON, October 24, 1947.

I take pleasure in submitting the recommendations of the Interdepartmental Committee on Trade Agreements with respect to the General Agreement on Tariffs and Trade which has now been completed at Geneva by negotiators representing the United States and twenty-two other countries belonging to fifteen other customs areas.

The proposed agreement is the result of fifteen negotiations between the United States and other countries and more than ninety negotiations between other pairs of countries carried on simultaneously over the past six months. It covers countries that handled three-quarters of the world's trade before the war and represents the most extensive action been undertaken for the reduction of barriers to trade.

This agreement has been concluded in the face of great difficulties. Our representatives are to be congratulated on what they have achieved.

I join in the request of the Committee on Trade Agreements that you approve its recommendations.

Robert A. Lovett

[Enclosure]

Memorandum by the Chairman of the Committee on Trade Agreements (Brown) to President Truman

SECRET [GENEVA,] October 17, 1947.

Subject: Request for Approval of Results of Geneva Trade Agreement Negotiations

(a) Tariff Concessions

On April 5, 1947, you approved a schedule of offers of tariff concessions to be made to, and requests for concessions to be made of, the seventeen (now twenty-two)[2] countries with which we have been conducting trade-agreement negotiations at Geneva.

The negotiations have now been concluded. Schedules setting forth the concessions offered by other countries and certain changes in the concessions originally offered by the United States which are necessary to obtain these concessions are attached. The Committee on Trade Agreements recommends that both be approved.

A summary table showing the volume of United States trade covered by the modified concessions now recommended, and their general nature, as compared with the original United States offers, is attached as Annex A.

A summary table showing the trade coverage of offers by other countries is attached as Annex B.

The improvements recommended in the United States offers are for the most part of minor significance. Exceptions are the recommended new offers on wool, which you have already approved, and on beef, butter, rayon filament yarns, rayon staple fiber, seed potatoes, coarse grains, apples and lace. A brief memorandum with respect to each of these offers is attached as Annex C.

The concessions of other countries which it is recommended that we accept cover less of our trade than our original requests, and in many cases cover different products. This was expected, as our strategy was to ask for more than we expected to obtain and to bargain in the area of our requests rather than in the area of our offers. The concessions in question, however, in the opinion of the Committee on Trade Agreements, represent substantial advantage for the United States and a satisfactory *quid pro quo* for the concessions which it is recommended that we make.

With only four exceptions, recommendations of the Committee on Trade Agreements for improvements in our offers are unanimous.

In five cases there was dissent from our acceptance of offers made by other countries. In one case, that of the United Kingdom, a member of the Committee abstained on the issue of whether the bilateral balance between the direct offers made to and received from the other country was satisfactory.

Annex C attached includes the reasons for dissents and abstentions and a summary of the majority view in each case.

The Brazilian concessions present a special problem, as Brazil, during the course of negotiations, proposed an upward adjustment of almost all of its specific tariff rates to take account of a depreciation in the value of its currency. Since most of the concessions offered by Brazil are bindings of low specific

---

[2] Pakistan, Burma, Ceylon, Southern Rhodesia, and Syria are now counted as separate countries.

rates, this would involve increases in the absolute amount of the majority of the rates appearing in our 1935 agreement with Brazil. The ad valorem incidence of the adjusted rates in question, however, is in all cases substantially below that prevailing when the 1935 agreement was signed. The Committee recommends that the Brazilian concessions be accepted:

(a) Because the adjustment upwards is 40 percent, whereas the currency depreciation involved was 47 percent and there has been serious price inflation in Brazil;
(b) Because the ad valorem incidence of the adjusted rates is still very low – 65 percent of United States trade covered enters at rates of 10 percent ad valorem or less, and 80 percent at rates of 20 percent or less;
(c) Because the rates would almost certainly be increased more than 40 percent if Brazil made no agreements at Geneva; and
(d) Because the coverage of the concessions now offered by Brazil is substantially greater than that in the 1935 agreement, whereas the additional coverage offered by the United States is not substantial.

The representative of the Department of Agriculture, though feeling that the adjusted rates offered by Brazil were generally satisfactory, abstained from voting on the ground that the adjustment would involve an increase in the specific rates on some agricultural products.

(b) General Provisions

The tariff concessions to be granted by each of the countries negotiating at Geneva will be embodied in a General Agreement on Tariffs and Trade, the text of which, together with the texts of related documents, is herewith submitted for your approval. The General Agreement is, for the most part, an elaboration of familiar-provisions of our trade agreements, adapted to the economic conditions of today and to the fact that it will be a multilateral agreement among twenty-three countries. Its provisions have been approved by the Committee on Trade Agreements and by the legal staff of the Department of State.

A memorandum briefly describing the Agreement and related documents is attached as Annex D.

(c) Procedure for Making the General Agreement Effective

It is proposed that the United States make the General Agreement provisionally effective on January 1, 1948, provided that Australia, Canada, Belgium-Netherlands-Luxembourg Customs Union (known as Benelux), Brazil, France and the United Kingdom, who account for 85 percent of the trade of the parties to the Agreement and over 50 percent of world trade, also make it provisionally effective on that date. The rest of the Geneva countries will make the Agreement provisionally effective as soon as they can constitutionally do so. The Agreement would be made definitively effective after the Charter of the International Trade Organization has been approved by the Havana Conference and by the Congress. Details of the proposed procedure are set forth in Annex D.

It is proposed to publish the text of the General Agreement and tariff schedules on November 18, 1947.

(d) General Comment

The General Agreement on Tariffs and Trade represents the most extensive action ever taken with respect to trade barriers. It embodies the results of 106 separate bilateral tariff negotiations and establishes trading rules for countries which accounted in 1938 for 70 percent of total world trade. It is the culmination of more than two years of intensive work by the United States Government. I cannot praise too highly the devoted and effective work of the men and women of the United States Government agencies who have made this Agreement possible.

The Agreement is the first major step to be taken by important nations to reverse the trend toward trade restriction and economic isolation which has persisted throughout the world since the first world war. It establishes liberal commercial policies for all of the leading trading nations. Announcement of this Agreement should create an auspicious atmosphere for the opening of the United Nations Conference on Trade and Employment scheduled for Havana on November 21, and, within the long-term framework which it establishes, it should be possible for the reconstruction of Europe under the Marshall plan to proceed with more confidence that efforts to restore world economy will not again be defeated by commercial warfare between the great trading powers.

WINTHROP G. BROWN

Annex D

THE GENERAL AGREEMENT ON TARIFFS AND TRADE AND RELATED DOCUMENTS
SUMMARY AND COMMENTS

1. *The Final Act.* The "Final Act adopted at the conclusion of the Second Session of the Preparatory Committee of the United Nations Conference on Trade and Employment" authenticates the text of the General Agreement on Tariffs and Trade and the Protocol of Provisional Application. Signature carries no commitment beyond such authentication. It will be signed by all countries negotiating at Geneva.
2. *The General Agreement.* The General Agreement on Tariffs and Trade is divided into three parts.

Part I contains the schedules of tariff concessions. It also binds all margins of tariff preference against increase. This binding represents a far-reaching commitment on the part of the British and other preference-granting areas which the United States has not been able to obtain in any previous trade-agreement negotiation.

Part II reproduces many of the commercial-policy provisions of the draft Charter for an International Trade Organization, which in turn have been largely drawn from, or developed on the basis of, provisions customarily included in past United States trade agreements.

Among the more significant provisions in Part II, insisted upon by the United States as necessary either to safeguard the tariff concessions, or to provide an adequate quid pro quo for tariff concessions, are the following:

a) Provision for equal treatment as between foreign and domestic products in the matter of internal taxation and regulation (Article III). These provisions are so drawn as to permit the continuation of United States mixing regulations on rubber at the level in effect on April 10, 1947.[3] [Here follows a statement by the Navy Department representative.]

b) A special Article (Article IV) which will afford protection to United States exports of motion-picture films. The inclusion of this Article, which operates almost entirely to the benefit of an American industry, is a source of great satisfaction to the United States delegation.

c) Provisions confining the use of antidumping and countervailing duties to their proper scope (Article VI) and looking toward the use of true commercial values in assessing ad valorem duties (Article VII).

d) Provisions designed to bring about the elimination of protective quotas on imports and exports and to assure their nondiscriminatory application (Articles XI through XIV). Since quotas rigidly limit the amount of trade that can be carried on, these provisions are of critical significance to the United States in the years ahead. It has been necessary to make substantial exceptions to the rule against quotas and against discrimination, in view of the special economic problems created by the war, particularly those involving important trading countries, such as the United Kingdom and France, in acute balance-of-payments difficulties. As these problems are met, however, the operation of the provisions against quotas will come into play to the benefit of the long-run export trade of the United States.

---

[3] Mixing regulations required manufacturers of rubber products to mix a specified percentage of synthetic rubber into their final product. These rules were designed to insure that the synthetic production capacity built up in the United States during the Second World War did not atrophy.

e) Provisions which extend the principles of nondiscrimination to state-trading and assure private traders an adequate opportunity to participate in purchases or sales by state-trading enterprises.
f) Provisions which would permit the United States, or any other party to the Agreement, to withdraw or modify the tariff or other concessions it has made to the extent and for the time necessary to prevent serious injury to domestic producers (Article XIX). These provisions conform to Executive Order No. 9832 which requires the inclusion of such provisions in trade agreements and sets forth the procedure for administering them.
g) Provisions designed to cover the eventuality that some situation may arise, or that some party to the Agreement may violate the Agreement, directly or indirectly, which would have the effect of nullifying or impairing the Agreement. In serious cases of this kind, the other parties to the Agreement could agree that they, or any of them, would be free to suspend the concessions they have made under the Agreement. Any party affected by such suspension could then withdraw from the Agreement on short notice 60 days.

In addition to the foregoing, Part II contains provisions relating to such trade matters as freedom of transit, marks of origin, publication of trade regulations and customs formalities. A special Article on economic development (Article XVIII) provides a carefully safeguarded method of adjusting tariff concessions and other obligations where additional protection is necessary for economic development.

Certain of the provisions of Part II of the Agreement cannot be made fully effective without changes in existing United States laws. These changes, mostly of a minor nature, include the elimination of certain existing discriminations in internal taxes, the amendment of our countervailing-duty legislation so as to make countervailing duties discretionary rather than mandatory, and the adaptation of United States tariff valuation methods. Since these changes cannot be effected by the Executive under the authority of the Trade Agreements Act or other executive powers, it is provided, under the Protocol of Provisional Application (see below), that, Part II of the General Agreement need be applied, during the period of provisional application, only "to the fullest extent not inconsistent with existing legislation". Part II will be given full force and effect only after the United States and other large trading countries formally deposit an instrument of acceptance of the Agreement with the Secretary-General of the United Nations (Article XXVI). It is contemplated that such an instrument will not be deposited by the United States until after Congress has acted on the Charter for an International Trade Organization or has otherwise passed the necessary legislation to bring United States laws into conformity with all of the provisions of the Agreement.

Since the provisions of Part II of the Agreement (as well as Article I relating to most-favored-nation treatment) are identical with corresponding provisions in the Draft Charter, provision is made whereby these provisions of the Agreement may be superseded by the provisions of the Charter if the parties agree. If this is done, as it presumably will be, no separate legislative action relating to the General Agreement will be necessary in order for the United States formally to accept the agreement and thus bring it into full force and effect.

Part III of the Agreement deals with matters common to the whole of the: Agreement, such as general exceptions (sanitary regulations, security exceptions and other matters customarily excepted from commercial agreements); amendments; territorial application; modification of concessions after the Agreement has run for three years (the Statutory limit for the initial period of trade agreements concluded by the United States); and the like. Part III also includes the provisions relating to formal acceptance of the Agreement and its entry into full force, referred to above, and for the supersession of Part II by the corresponding provisions of the Charter, also referred to above.

In view of the importance attached by many countries to provisions of the Charter for an International Trade Organization which are not incorporated in the Agreement, a paragraph has been included (paragraph 1 of Article XXIX) under which the contracting parties undertake, "pending their acceptance of a Charter in accordance with their constitutional procedures, to observe to the fullest extent of their executive authority the general principles" of the Charter recommended to the Havana conference by the Preparatory Committee. This undertaking does not in any way tie the hands of Congress or prejudice the freedom of action of the United States or of other countries at the Havana conference.

An important Article of Part III relates to joint action by the contracting parties (Article XXV). An earlier draft of the General Agreement, which was discussed during the hearings held by the Senate Finance Committee in March and April of this year, provided for the establishment of an Interim Trade Committee among the parties to the General Agreement. This provision was criticized by Senator Millikin as an attempt to set up a provisional International Trade Organization without Congressional approval. It has been omitted from the text for which approval is now sought. Instead, arrangements are made for meetings of representatives of the contracting parties in order to give effect to those substantive provisions of the Agreement where decisions must be taken by the contracting parties acting jointly. Such an arrangement is clearly necessary because of the multilateral character of the Agreement, and the functions of the contracting parties are confined to those necessary to carry out the Agreement.

3. Protocol of Provisional Application. The Protocol of Provisional Application, which will bind each country upon its signature by that country, provides that if Australia, Brazil, Belgium-Luxembourg, Canada, France, the Netherlands, the United Kingdom and the United States have signed the Protocol by November 15, 1947, the signatory countries will give provisional effect, on January 1, 1948 to a) Parts I and III of the General Agreement on Tariffs and Trade (relating to tariff concessions, the most-favored-nation clause and matters common to the whole agreement) and b) Part II of the General Agreement (other trade barriers) "to the fullest extent not inconsistent with existing legislation". Any signatory would be free to withdraw this undertaking on short notice – 60 days. It is anticipated that all "key" countries except Australia will sign the Protocol of Provisional Application at Geneva on or about October 30, and that Australia will sign at New York by November 15.

4. Supplementary Agreements. The General Agreement on Tariffs and Trade will replace our existing trade agreements with Brazil, Belgium-Luxembourg, Canada, Cuba, France, the Netherlands and the United Kingdom. It is accordingly proposed to sign with each of these countries, at Geneva and in conjunction with the signature of the Protocol, a supplementary agreement making it clear that the existing trade agreement concerned will be inoperative for such time as the United States and the other country concerned are both parties to the General Agreement (whether pursuant to the Protocol of Provisional Application or otherwise). If either country should withdraw from the General Agreement, the existing trade agreement would then come back into operation.

In the special case of Cuba, with which the United States has preferential relations, provisions have been included dealing with certain preferential matters not dealt with in the General Agreement.

Annex B – Negotiating Committees and Subcommittees

1. London Conference

The *Preparatory Committee* established the following working committees:

(f) Committee I: *Employment and Economic Activity*;
(g) Committee II: *General Commercial Policy*;
(h) Committee III: *Restrictive Business Practices*;
(i) Committee IV: *Intergovernmental Commodity Arrangements*;
(j) Committee V: *Administration and Organization*;

A sixth committee, the *Joint Committee on Industrial Development*, was established following a joint meeting of Committees I and II. During the First Session, Mr. Suetens (Belgium) was elected as Chairman of the Preparatory Committee, with Mr. Augenthaler (Czechoslovakia) as first, and Mr. Alvarez (Cuba) as second vice-chairman.[1] The Chairman of Committee II was Coombs (Australia), with Speekenbrink (Netherlands) acting as vice-chairman.[2] Committee II established a series of Sub-committees that were requested to report their findings to the main Committee (II): the single most important of all Sub-committees established is the *Technical Sub-committee*, which dealt with the following issues:

a. national treatment on internal taxation and regulation;
b. freedom of transit;
c. antidumping and countervailing duties;
d. tariff valuation;
e. customs formalities;
f. marks of origin;

---

[1] See E/PC/T/33 at p. 3.   [2] Id.

g. publication and administration of trade regulations – advance notice to restrictive regulations information, statistics, and trade terminology;
h. boycotts;
i. general exceptions.[3]

Participation to the *Technical Sub-committee* was open to delegates for all the countries represented on the *Preparatory Committee*. Mr. Videla (Chile) acted as Chairman, and delegates of six different nationalities acted as rapporteurs.[4] The choice of six rapporteurs was justified by the wish to accelerate the process. The six rapporteurs were chosen from the Belgian (Luxembourg), Canadian, French, Dutch, UK, and U.S. delegations.[5] The U.S. rapporteur was Mr. Leddy who served as rapporteur for the *Sub-Committee on Procedure* as well, and emerges as the key rapporteur in this process.[6]

The other Sub-committees were drafting committees: issues were first negotiated in detail within Committee II, and were then referred to them so that they were put in a form that would be acceptable to the *Preparatory Committee*:

a. The *Sub-Committee on Procedure* was originally asked to deal with matters relating to the proposed negotiations. It was further asked to deal with issues relating to MFN, tariffs (and tariff preferences), emergency provisions (safeguards), consultation, and territorial application. Speekenbrink (Netherlands) acted as Chairman, whereas Leddy (United States) acted as rapporteur. Brazil, Canada, Chile, Cuba, France, India, the United Kingdom, and the United States participated in this committee;[7]
b. The *Drafting Sub-committee on Quantitative Restrictions and Exchange Control* operated under the chairmanship of Coombs (Australia), and Meade (United Kingdom) and Gunter (United States) functioned as rapporteurs. It dealt with questions relating to quantitative restrictions and exchange controls and was composed of delegates from Australia, Brazil, France, India, the United Kingdom, and the United States, in addition to IMF representatives;[8]
c. A joint sub-committee of Committees II and IV, consisting of delegates from Australia, Brazil, Canada, the Netherlands, the United Kingdom, and the United States, dealt with questions relating to subsidies of primary

---

[3] See Report of Committee II, E/PC/T/30 of November 24, 1946, pp. 3–4.
[4] Id. at p. 4.
[5] See E/PC/T/C.II/54 of November 16, 1946 at p. 1.
[6] See E/PC/T/C.II/46 of November 8, 1946 at p. 1.
[7] See Report of Committee II, E/PC/T/30 of November 24, 1946, p. 3.
[8] Id. at p. 4.

products. McCarthy (Australia) acted as Chairman, and Schwenger (United States) acted as rapporteur;[9]

d. Another sub-committee comprising delegates from India, the United Kingdom, and the United States discussed subsidies on manufactured articles;[10]

e. A *Sub-committee on State Trading* comprised delegates from China, Czechoslovakia, New Zealand, the United Kingdom, and the United States. It was chaired by Shackle (United Kingdom), and Johnson (New Zealand), whereas Armstrong (United States) and Young (United Kingdom) functioned as rapporteurs. It was aided by a smaller *Sub-committee on Marketing Boards* comprising delegates from the Netherlands, South Africa, and the United States;[11]

f. Matters concerning preferences in the form of quotas were considered first by those primarily concerned, that is, Australia, Canada, New Zealand, the United Kingdom, and the United States, before they advised Committee II.[12]

2. New York Conference

The *Drafting Committee* prepared the *New York Draft* (the redraft of the ITO Charter, and the first GATT text). Colban (Norway) was appointed Chairman, and Adarkar (India) as vice-chairman. The agreed bifurcation (ITO text, GATT text) led to the establishment of a *Sub-committee on Tariff Negotiations*, the mandate of which was to decide which articles of the ITO should be included in the GATT. It was further decided that a small group would eventually be established to do the edit and put, in proper legal language, the outcome of the negotiations.[13] The group would be called *Legal Drafting Sub-committee*, and be comprised of delegates from Belgium, Cuba, France, the United Kingdom, and the United States. M. Kojève (France) served as Chairman.[14] The delegates were all in agreement that this Sub-committee would "put agreed ideas into appropriate words," and that "where any disagreement as to principle is left, the matter should not be referred to the *Legal Drafting Sub-committee*, but rather to an *ad hoc* drafting sub-committee."[15]

Two sub-committees were immediately established:

(a) the first to deal with Arts. 15–23 of the *London Draft*, that is, the provisions where no agreement could be reached during the *London Conference*. Delegates from Australia, Belgium, Czechoslovakia, France, the Netherlands, the

[9] Id.
[10] Id.
[11] Id. at p. 5.
[12] Id.
[13] See E/PC/T/C.6/2 at pp. 2–3.
[14] See E/PC/T/34 of March 5, 1947 at p. 2.
[15] See E/PC/T/C.6/17 of January 27, 1947.

United Kingdom, and the United States participated in this group, which kept the name (already granted during the *London Conference*) *Technical Sub-committee*. Shackle (United Kingdom) was elected Chairman.[16] Eventually, new members were added: Brazil, Canada, Cuba, New Zealand, and South Africa.[17] This group met 13 times within one month;[18]

(b) the second (comprising originally delegates from Belgium, Brazil, Cuba, the Netherlands, South Africa, the United Kingdom, and the United States) would focus on membership for the Executive Board of the ITO, and was appropriately named *Sub-committee on Voting and Executive Board Membership* (*Sub-committee on Administration*, or *Administrative Sub-committee*).[19] Alamilla (Cuba) was elected Chairman.[20] Chile and France joined ranks at a later stage.[21]

Eventually, as briefly alluded to above, a third sub-committee convened during the *New York* Conference, the *Sub-committee on Tariff Negotiations*. Mr. Adarkar (India) was elected as Chairman.[22] Recall that this group was requested to discuss the provisions of the ITO Charter that should find their way into the GATT. Although the sub-committees were of restricted membership, all delegates to the *Drafting Committee* were accorded the right to participate in the proceedings of the sub-committees at any time, and frequently availed themselves of this facility.[23]

3. The Geneva Conference

Negotiations in Geneva started on April 10, more or less on the date originally suggested by the U.S. delegation (April 8),[24] and agreed by the participants in the *London Conference*.[25] Since the mandate covered both the wrap up of the GATT

---

[16] See E/PC/T/C.6/6 of January 22, 1947; see also E/PC/T/C.6/55 of February 5, 1947.
[17] See E/PC/T/C.6/18 of January 27, 1947 at p. 1.
[18] See E/PC/T/C.6/55/Rev. 1 of February 11, 1947.
[19] See E/PC/T/C.6/4 at p. 3. This Sub-committee dealt with Arts. 1, 2, 64, 68, and 72–77 of the ITO Charter (*London Draft*), see E/PC/T/C.6/102 of February 24, 1947 at p. 3.
[20] See E/PC/T/C.6/5 of January 21, 1947 at p. 1. The first meeting of the Sub-committee was opened by Julio Lacarte (Uruguay) who, at that time, was acting as Executive Secretary. Mr. Lacarte has been ever-present in the evolution of the GATT, from its birth to modern day.
[21] See E/PC/T/C.6/62 of February 10, 1947.
[22] See E/PC/T/C.6/67 of February 11, 1947. This Sub-committee is occasionally referred to as *Sub-committee on Tariff Procedures* as well, see, for example, E/PC/T/C.6/102 at p. 4.
[23] See E/PC/T/C.6/102 at p. 4.   [24] See E/PC/T/C.6/53 of February 8, 1947.
[25] See E/PC/T/33, Annexure 10.

3. The Geneva Conference

and the first multilateral round of tariff negotiations, institutional arrangements were made to ensure the smooth organization of negotiations under both pillars.

During the first *Heads of Delegations* meeting,[26] it was decided that the five most experienced delegates (from China, Cuba, Czechoslovakia, India, and Norway) would be acting as vice-chairmen in order to assist with the negotiation.[27] Two Commissions were established (Commission A, and Commission B) and distributed the negotiated subject matter. Commission A dealt with commercial policies and restrictive business practices (RBP), whereas Commission B would focus on international commodity agreements, subsidies, and the institutional aspects of the ITO.[28] These Commissions were further in charge of appointing Committees, Sub-committees, and Working Parties that dealt with specific issues. To this effect, they appointed:

(a) the *Committee on Chapters I, II, VIII*: this Committee was dealing with the purposes, the membership, and other organizational issues. The Chairman was Naude (South Africa) and it comprised delegates of Australia, Belgium-Luxembourg, Brazil, China, France, South Africa, the United Kingdom, and the United States; [29]
(b) the *Sub-committee on Subsidies*: Hakim (Lebanon) was elected Chairman. Delegates of Australia, Lebanon, the Netherlands, New Zealand, the United Kingdom, and the United States participated as members of the sub-committee, whereas delegates of Canada, Chile, Czechoslovakia, and France took an active part in the discussions;[30]
(c) the *Sub-committee on STE*, where delegates of Australia, Belgium, Canada, Czechoslovakia, New Zealand, South Africa, the United Kingdom, and the United States participated;[31]
(d) *the Working Party on Technical Articles* (15–23 and 37)[32] under the Chairmanship of Colban (Norway);

---

[26] The *Heads of Delegations*, by now a GATT/WTO tradition, played a very active role during the *Geneva Conference*. It was essentially the bottleneck through which all technical negotiations would acquire legitimacy. A series of documents officially circulated during the *Geneva Conference* were dedicated to its meetings (E/PC/T/Del.), see, for example, E/PC/T/Del./22 of April 23, 1947.

[27] See E/PC/T/DEL/20 at p. 2.

[28] See E/PC/T/72 of May 19, 1947. The Chairman of Commission A was Suetens (Belgium), and the vice-chairmen were Colban (Norway) and de Vilhena Ferreira Braga (Brazil); Wilgress (Canada) acted as Chair for Commission B, whereas Royer (France) acted as vice-chair, see E/PC/T/180.

[29] See E/PC/T/139 of July 31, 1947.   [30] See E/PC/T/124 of July 10, 1947.

[31] See E/PC/TW.240 of July 11, 1947.

[32] See E/PC/T/66 of May 8, 1947 and E/PC/T/103 of June 19, 1947.

(e) the *Sub-committee on Arts. 25 and 27* under the chairmanship of Melander (Norway), where delegates of Brazil, China, Czechoslovakia, the Netherlands, Norway, the United Kingdom, and the United States participated;[33]

(f) *the Sub-committee on Infant Industry*, under the Chairmanship of Adarkar (India), and the participation of delegates from India, the Netherlands, Norway, the United Kingdom, and the United States;[34]

(g) *the Sub-committee on Arts. 14, 15 and 24* with Coombs (Australia) acting as Chair and delegates from Australia, Belgium, China, Cuba, Norway, the United Kingdom, and the United States;[35]

(h) *the Sub-committee on Arts. 26, 28 and 29*, with Phillips (Australia) acting as Chair, and delegates from Australia, Canada, Cuba, Czechoslovakia, France, the United Kingdom, and the United States.[36]

A number of *ad hoc* groups were established in order to address specific issues:

(a) a group was established to renegotiate marks of origin with the participation of representatives from Australia, Belgium, Cuba, Czechoslovakia, France, South Africa, the United Kingdom, and the United States. Shackle (United Kingdom) was the chosen head of this group;[37]

(b) a group was established to discuss Art. 17 of the *New York GATT Draft*. The Chairman was Shackle (United Kingdom), and the group comprised delegates from Australia, Belgium-Luxembourg, Cuba, France, India, Lebanon-Syria, the Netherlands, the United Kingdom, and the United States; a group was established to discuss Art. 18 of the *New York GATT Draft*, with Holloway (South Africa) acting as Chair, and delegates from Australia, Canada, China, France, the Netherlands, South Africa, the United Kingdom, and the United States;

(c) a group was established to discuss Art. 19 of the *New York GATT Draft*. The group elected as Chairman Shackle (United Kingdom), and included delegates from Australia, France, New Zealand, the United Kingdom, and the United States;

(d) a group was established to discuss Art. 21.3 of the *New York GATT Draft* with Shackle (United Kingdom) acting as Chair, and delegates from Canada, the Netherlands, the United Kingdom, and the United States;[38]

(e) a senior U.S. negotiator, Brown, chaired a group on safeguards.[39]

---

[33] See E/PC/T/141 of August 1, 1947.
[34] See E/PC/T/197 of September 15, 1947.
[35] See E/PC/T/174 of August 15, 1947.
[36] See E/PC/T/A/PV/41 at p. 2.
[37] See E/PC/T/WP.1/SR.3 of May 12, 1947.
[38] See E/PC/T/103 of June 19, 1947.
[39] See E/PC/T/146.

The study of the different proposals was streamlined by the *Working Party on Tariff Negotiations*, which operated under the Chairmanship of Wilgress (Canada), and comprised representatives of Canada, France, the Netherlands, the United Kingdom, and the United States. This group also received suggestions from nonparticipating delegations, and produced the first draft of the GATT that closely resembles the modern GATT text. The *Legal Drafting Committee* reconvened during the *Geneva Conference* and, as before, did not undertake any substantive discussions except when strictly necessary; it did, however, undertake a revision of agreed texts to ensure that the legal expression was appropriate, and also to ensure consistency across the English and the French versions of the various texts.[40] The first comprehensive draft was circulated as document E/PC/T/135 (July 24, 1947) and includes a very helpful comparative table that shows the changes in the numbering of the various provisions from the *New York GATT Draft* and the *New York Draft ITO Charter* to the *Geneva Draft*.[41]

Since the *Geneva Conference* also provided the forum for the first multilateral trade negotiations, a *Tariff Steering Committee* was established in accordance with § 2, Section F of the *Memorandum on Multilateral Trade Agreement Negotiations* (E/PC/T/33, Annexure 10), which would guide the work on tariff negotiations.[42] It was thought that negotiations should go on for at least three months, and thus the life of this Committee should be coextensive to that of negotiations.[43] The *Working Party on Tariff Negotiations* was established in order to arrange as many negotiations as possible.[44]

4. The Havana Conference

Various committees were established during the *Havana Conference* in order to honor the mandate. Of interest to this volume is the *Third Committee*, which focused on commercial policy, that is, essentially, the overlap between the GATT and the ITO Charter. Wilgress (Canada) acted as Chair for this committee, which also comprised delegates Muller (Chile) who acted as vice-chairman, and Puig Arosemena (Ecuador). Muller could not accept the post and was eventually

---

[40] Chair: Guttierez (Cuba). The other members were: van Tilchelen, Count de Liedekerke (Belgium), Monteiro de Barros-Filho (Brazil), Dorn (Cuba), Royer and Dieterlen (France), Fawcett (UK), and Catudal (U.S.), see E/PC/T/185 of August 25, 1947.
[41] A comparative table also exists in E/PC/T/180 of August 19, 1947.
[42] E/PC/T/C.6/88/Rev. 1 of February 17, 1947 at p. 5. See also E/PC/T/C.6/88, which provides additional information as to the planning of the Geneva-held negotiations.
[43] E/PC/T/C.6/88/Rev. 1 of February 17, 1947 at p. 6.
[44] See E/PC/T.47/Rev. 3 of April 22, 1947.

substituted by Lleras Restrepo (Colombia).[45] The *Third Committee* established a series of sub-committees that dealt with specific issues:

(a) *Sub-committee A* on internal taxation and regulation: it comprised delegates from Australia, Brazil, China, Colombia, Cuba, Denmark, France, Mexico, Netherlands, New Zealand, Peru, Turkey, the United Kingdom, the United States, and Uruguay. Lamsvelt (Netherlands) acted as Chair;[46]

(b) *Sub-committee B* on shipping and insurance services (new provision): it was decided that this issue should move to Chapter V of the ITO Charter (dealing with RBP), and thus removed from the negotiations regarding the GATT;[47]

(c) *Sub-committee C* on transit, antidumping, valuation, formalities, marks of origin, publication of laws, information, and boycotts. Delegates from Afghanistan, Argentina, Australia, Canada, Cuba, France, Lebanon, Mexico, Netherlands, Norway, Pakistan, Portugal, the United Kingdom, the United States, and Uruguay participated. The Norwegian seat was subsequently occupied by South Africa. Morton (Australia) acted as Chair.[48] This sub-committee appointed 6 *Working Parties* (Working Party I, Antidumping: Australia, Brazil, Cuba, Lebanon, Netherlands, United Kingdom, and United States; Working Party II, Customs Valuation: France, United Kingdom, United States, Uruguay; Working Party III, Customs Formalities: Australia, Haiti, Lebanon, Peru, United Kingdom, United States; Working Party IV, Improvement of transport facilities for goods in transit: Afghanistan, Australia, France, Lebanon, Pakistan, United Kingdom, United States; Working Party V, Geographical or regional origin: Australia, Cuba, France, United Kingdom, United States; Working Party VI, Information, and Statistics: Australia, Norway, United Kingdom, United States, and the UN Statistical Office.[49]

(d) *Sub-committee D* on safeguards, and general exceptions: Argentina, Belgium, Colombia, Denmark, France, Italy, Peru, Southern Rhodesia, the United Kingdom, and the United States. Shackle (United Kingdom) acted as Chair;[50]

(e) *Sub-committee E* on QR: Ceylon, Chile, China, Colombia, Egypt, France, Ireland, Mexico, Netherlands, New Zealand, Peru, South Africa, Sweden, the United Kingdom, and the United States. Holloway (South Africa) acted as Chair;[51]

(f) *Sub-committee F* on BoP: Argentina, Australia, Belgium, Brazil, Canada, Cuba, Czechoslovakia, France, Greece, India, Italy, Lebanon, Liberia,

---

[45] See CRH at p. 39.
[46] See CRH at p. 53.
[47] See CRH at p. 42.
[48] See CRH at p. 70.
[49] See CRH at p. 70.
[50] See CRH at pp. 81ff.
[51] See CRH at pp. 86–87.

5. The Review Session

Norway, the Philippines, the United Kingdom, and the United States. Melander (Norway) acted as Chair;[52]

(g) *Sub-committee G*, which discussed an ad hoc issue: following a Swiss proposal to this effect, this sub-committee dealt with the problems that countries which cannot invoke the BoP provision face when subjected to measures by those invoking it. The sub-committee was eager to discuss the problem but was unable to satisfy the Swiss request, in light of the spill-over that acquiescence to the Swiss request would have for other issues;[53]

(h) *Sub-committee H* on subsidies: Argentina, Australia, Brazil, Canada, Cuba, Denmark, France, Netherlands, Peru, Philippines, Sweden, Turkey, the United Kingdom, the United States, and Venezuela. McCarthy (Australia) first, and Mr. Warwick Smith (Australia) later, acted as Chair;

(i) *Sub-committee J* on state trading: Czechoslovakia, Ecuador, Egypt, Mexico, Netherlands, Pakistan, Switzerland, the United Kingdom, and the United States. Nash (New Zealand) acted as Chair;[54]

Of interest is also the *Joint sub-committee on Arts. 16 and 42* (MFN, and customs unions): delegates from Argentina, Belgium, Brazil, Canada, Chile, El Salvador, France, Haiti, Iran, Poland, Sweden, Syria, Turkey, the United Kingdom, and the United States participated therein. Sahlin (Sweden) acted as Chair. He was subsequently replaced by Royer (France).[55]

5. The Review Session

A *Steering Group* was established that was in charge of the organization of the negotiating process. Wilgress (Canada) acted as Chair, whereas Garcia Oldini (Chile), and Seidenfaden (Denmark), acted as vice-chairs.[56] Ahmad (Pakistan), Brown (United States), Phillip (France), and Sanders (United Kingdom) completed the composition of the group.[57] The *Steering Group* proposed that negotiations would take place in three stages: for the first two, plenary sessions were envisaged, and for stage three, a series of Working Parties would be established:[58]

9. Working Party I on Quantitative Restrictions;
10. Working Party II on Tariffs, Schedules, and Customs Administration;
11. Working Party III, on Other Barriers to Trade;
12. Working Party IV, on Organizational and Functional Questions.[59]

---

[52] See CRH at pp. 96–97.
[53] See CRH at pp. 102ff.
[54] See CRH at pp. 113.
[55] See CRH at p. 46.
[56] See SR.9/1 of October 29, 1954.
[57] See SR.9/3 of November 1, 1954 at p. 9.
[58] See W.9/2 of November 3, 1954.
[59] See W.9/10 of November 10, 1954.

Each of the Working Parties could establish ad hoc working groups to discuss specific issues.[60] A series of sub-groups were established that were mandated to review the work of Working Parties (they were named sub-groups A, B, C, and D).[61]

Finally, a *Legal and Drafting Committee* was established as well with a double mandate:

(c) to give expert advice on legal issues; and
(d) to remove drafting imperfections.[62]

Working Party I (Quantitative Restrictions)
Suetens (Belgium) was appointed Chair.[63]

Working Party II (Tariffs, Schedules, and Customs Administration)
Discussions in this group focused on two provisions: the current Arts. XXVIII and VIII GATT. Seidenfaden (Denmark) was appointed Chair.[64] Detailed proposals are included in Annex I of Doc. L/329, whereas various national proposals dealing with specific issues are included in various other documents.[65] Finally, this group also entertained a discussion on rules of origin, one of the thorniest issues in international trade. Negotiations were not successful, and they remain so 60 years later.[66]

Working Party III (Other Barriers to Trade)
This group dealt with what is often termed *fair trade*: subsidies, antidumping, state trading, but also other issues such as the list of general exceptions.[67] Garcia Oldini (Chile) acted as Chair.[68]

Working Party IV (Organizational and Functional Questions)
The mandate of this group was to study whether the mandate of the GATT should be expanded, and, also, what other institutional arrangements were necessary. Couillard (Canada) acted as Chair.[69] A number of delegations

---

[60] Such as, for example, the *Technical Group on Customs Administration* that Mr. Ashford (United Kingdom) chaired, see SR.9/26 of December 24, 1954 at p. 13.
[61] See W.9/64 of December 2, 1954.
[62] Perez Cisneros was appointed Chair, and the members were: Abramson (United Kingdom); von Bargen (Germany); Haguiwara (Japan); Hollis (United States); Monaco (Italy); de Saint-Légier (France); and Stuyck (Belgium), see SR.9/28 of January 10, 1955, its terms of reference are reproduced in detail in the same document. Germany eventually replaced von Bargen by Partsch, see SR.9/20 of January 21, 1955 at p. 1, and France replaced de Saint-Légier by Dubais, see SR.9/32 of February 2, 1955.
[63] See SR.9/25 at p. 5.
[64] See SR.9/25 of December 24, 1954.
[65] See notably, W.9/45 and 46 of November 29, 1954.
[66] See W.9/125 of December 20, 1954.
[67] See W.9/28 of November 23, 1954.
[68] See SR.9/23 at p. 7.
[69] See SR.9/23 of December 22, 1954.

(Australia, Canada, India, Indonesia, New Zealand, Norway, and the United Kingdom) were not opposed to institutionalized variable geometry: Australia, for example, would like to see some (if not all) of the GATT contracting parties negotiate intergovernmental commodity agreements;[70] New Zealand, on the other hand, argued in favor of introducing a new provision regarding the link between trade and employment (to be signed by some or all of the trading partners);[71] Norway, backed by Denmark and Sweden, wanted an extension of the GATT mandate to cover restrictive business practices (RBP) as well;[72] Canada, and India were moderately in favor of variable geometry, but definitely against multilateral expansion of the GATT's subject matter; Italy, South Africa, and the United States were clearly against any expansion.[73] The U.S. delegation on the other hand, was clearly in favor of making provisions for an adequate secretariat.[74]

The final report of this group with all proposals has been published as document L/327.

6. The Negotiation of Part IV of the GATT

The CONTRACTING PARTIES, the highest GATT organ, decided to establish a special group that would dedicate its work to the study of this issue: this was the Committee III (1958).[75] At first, Phillips (Australia), and then Donovan (Australia), acted as Chairmen. An *Action Committee*, operating under the chairmanship of Lall (India), was also established and dealt with the specific projects entrusted to it. The other institutions, relevant for the coming into being of Part IV, are the above-mentioned *Committee on Legal and Institutional Framework* (which had proposed a Charter on Trade and Development),[76] with Skak-Nielsen (Denmark) as Chair,[77] and the *Working Party on Preferences*, which had been created to discuss preferences by industrialized to developing countries, as well as between developing countries; Miyazaki (Japan) was appointed Chair.

---

[70] See W.9/57 of December 1, 1954.
[71] See W.9/79 of December 8, 1954.
[72] See W.9/84 of December 9, 1954.
[73] See W.9/27 of November 22, 1954.
[74] See SR.9/18 of November 23, 1954 at p. 2.
[75] To avoid confusing it with the Committee III that dealt with RBP, we will be referring to it as Committee III (1958) in the rest of the document.
[76] See 2SS/SR.2.
[77] See L/2195.

References

Abbreviations of Materials Frequently Referred to

DAFP   Department of Foreign Affairs. *Documents on Australian Foreign Policy, 1937–1949*. Edited by R. G. Neale. Canberra: Australian Government Publishing Service, 1975. *Australia in the Postwar World*, ed. W. J. Hudson and Wendy Way. Canberra: Australian Government Publishing Service, 1995.

DCER   Department of External Affairs. *Documents on Canadian External Relations*, edited by John F. Hilliker. Volume 9, 1942–1943. Volume 10, July-December 1946. Ottawa: Department of External Affairs, 1980.

DBPO   *Documents on British Policy Overseas*. Series I, Vol. 3. Britain and America: Negotiation of the United States Loan 3 August–7 December 1945. Edited by Roger Bullen and M. E. Pelly. London: HMSO, 1986. Series I, Vol. 4. Britain and America: Atomic Energy, Bases and Food, 12 December 1945–31 July 1946. Edited by Roger Bullen and M. E. Pelly. London: HMSO, 1987.

FRUS   U.S. Department of State. *Foreign Relations of the United States*. Washington, DC: Government Printing Office. Various volumes and years.

HM   Howson, Susan, and Donald Moggridge (eds.), *The Wartime Diaries of Lionel Robbins and James Meade, 1943–1945*. London and New York: Macmillan, 1990.

Aaronson, Susan Ariel. 1996. *Trade and the American Dream: A Social History of Postwar Trade Policy*. Lexington: University Press of Kentucky.

Aaronson, Susan Ariel. 1999. *Who Decides? Congress and the Debate over Trade Policy in 1934 and 1974*. New York: Council on Foreign Relations.

Acheson, Dean. 1944. *Post-War International Economic Problems*. Department of State Bulletin 11: 656–662.

Acheson, Dean. 1969. *Present at the Creation: My Years in the State Department*. New York: W. W. Norton.

Allen, William R. 1953. "The International Trade Philosophy of Cordell Hull, 1907–1933." *The American Economic Review*, 43: 101–116.

Amery, Leo. 1988. *The Empire at Bay: The Leo Amery Diaries, 1929–1945*. Edited by John Barnes and David Nicholson. London: Hutchinson.

Asbeek Brusse, Wendy. 1997. *Tariffs, Trade and European Integration, 1947–1957: From Study Group to Common Market.* New York: St. Martin's Press.

Bagwell, Kyle, and Robert W. Staiger. 2002. *The Economics of the World Trading System,* Cambridge, MA: MIT Press.

Bailey, Michael, Judith Goldstein, and Barry Weingast. 1997. "The Institutional Roots of American Trade Policy: Politics, Coalitions and International Trade." *World Politics* 49: 309–338.

Baldwin, Robert E. 1970. *Non-tariff Distortions in International Trade.* Washington, D.C: The Brookings Institution.

Baldwin, Robert E. 1980. *The Economics of the GATT, in Issues in International Economics,* edited by Peter Oppenheimer. Stocksfield, England and Boston: Oriel.

Barbieri, Katherine. 1996. "Economic Interdependence: A Path to Peace or a Source of Interstate Conflict?" *Journal of Peace Research* 33: 29–49.

Barbieri, Katherine. 2002. *The Liberal Illusion: Does Trade Promote Peace?* Ann Arbor: University of Michigan Press.

Brown, Jr., William A. 1950. *The United States and the Restoration of World Trade: An Analysis and Appraisal of the ITO Charter and the General Agreement on Tariffs and Trade.* Washington, DC: The Brookings Institution.

Butler, Michael A. 1998. *Cautious Visionary: Cordell Hull and Trade Reform, 1933–1937.* Kent, Ohio: The Kent State University Press.

Cairncross, Alec, and Nita Watts. 1989. *The Economic Section 1939–1961 : A Study in Economic Advising.* London and New York: Routledge.

Capling, Ann. 2000. "The 'Enfant Terrible': Australia and the Reconstruction of the Multilateral Trade System, 1946–48 ." *Australian Economic History Review* 40: 1–21.

Capling, Ann. 2001. *Australia and the Global Trade System: From Havana to Seattle.* Cambridge and New York: Cambridge University Press.

Chang, Won, and L. Alan Winters. 2002. "How Regional Blocs Affect Excluded Countries: The Price Effects of MERCOSUR." *American Economic Review* 92: 889–904.

Charnovitz, Steve. 1991. Exploring the Environmental Exceptions in GATT Article XX. *Journal of World Trade* 25: 37–55.

Charnovitz, Steve. 1995. "Promoting Higher Labor Standards." *The Washington Quarterly* 18: 167–190.

Chase, Kerry A. 2006. "Multilateralism Compromised: The Mysterious Origins of GATT Article XXIV." *World Trade Review* 5: 1–30.

Clayton, William L. 1963. "GATT, The Marshall Plan, and OECD." *Political Science Quarterly* 78: 493–503.

Conybeare, John A. C. 1984. "Public Goods, Prisoners' Dilemmas and the International Political Economy." *International Studies Quarterly* 28: 5–22.

Crawford, J. G. 1968. *Australian Trade Policy, 1942–1966: A Documentary History.* Canberra: ANU Press.

Culbert, Jay. 1987. "War-time Anglo-American Talks and the Making of the GATT." *The World Economy* 10: 381–399.

Curzon, Gerard. 1965. *Multilateral Commercial Diplomacy: The General Agreement on Tariffs and Trade and Its Impact on National Commercial Policies and Techniques.* London: Michael Joseph.

References

Dalton, Hugh. 1986. *The Second World War Diary of Hugh Dalton, 1940–45*, edited by Ben Pimlott. London: Jonathan Cape.

Dam, Kenneth W. 1970. *The GATT: Law and International Economic Organization.* Chicago: University of Chicago Press.

Dam, Kenneth W. 2004. "Cordell Hull, the Reciprocal Trade Agreement Act, and the WTO." Mimeo.

Diebold, William, Jr. 1952. *The End of the ITO*, Essays in International Finance, No. 16, Princeton International Finance Section. Princeton, NJ: Princeton University.

Dormael, Armand van. 1978. *Bretton Woods: Birth of a Monetary System.* New York: Holmes & Meier Publishers.

Drache, Daniel. 2003. "ITO: When Labour and Investment Standards Almost Mattered: A Putative History Lesson in Trade Politics That Ought Not to be Forgotten," pp. 9–28 in James Busumtwi-Sam et al. (eds.), *Global Instability: Uncertainty and New Visions in Political Economy.* Amsterdam: Kluwer.

Edwards, Corwin D. 1945. "The Possibilities of an International Policy Toward Cartels," in *A Cartel Policy for the United Nations*, edited by Corwin D. Edwards. New York: Columbia University Press.

Eichengreen, Barry, and Douglas A. Irwin. 1995. "Trade Blocs, Currency Blocs, and the Reorientation of World Trade in the 1930s." *Journal of International Economics* 38: 1–24.

Ethier, Wilfred J. 2004. "Political Externalities, Nondiscrimination, and a Multilateral World." *Review of International Economics* 12: 303–320.

Ethier, Wilfred J. 2007. "The Theory of Trade Policy and Trade Agreements: A Critique." *European Journal of Political Economy* 23: 605–623.

Finger, J. Michael, and Julio J. Nogués (eds.). 2006. *Safeguards and Antidumping in Latin American Trade Liberalization: Fighting Fire with Fire.* Washington, DC: The World Bank and Palgrave Macmillan.

Fordham, Benjamin O. 1998. "Economic Interests, Party, and Ideology in Early Cold War Era U.S. Foreign Policy." *International Organization* 52: 359–396.

Fossedal, Gregory A. 1993. *Our Finest Hour: Will Clayton, the Marshall Plan, and the Triumph of Democracy.* Stanford: Hoover Institution Press.

Gardner, Richard N. 1956. *Sterling-Dollar Diplomacy: Anglo-American Collaboration in the Reconstruction of Multilateral Trade.* Oxford: Clarendon Press.

Gardner, Richard N. 1980. *Sterling-Dollar Diplomacy in Current Perspective: The Origins and Prospects of Our International Economic Order.* New York: Columbia University Press.

Gelpi, Christopher, and Joseph Grieco. 2008. "Democracy, Trade and the Nature of the Liberal Peace." *Journal of Peace Research*, forthcoming.

General Agreement on Tariffs and Trade. 1949. "The Attack on Trade Barriers: A Progress Report on the Operation of the GATT, January 1948-August 1949." Geneva: GATT.

Gilligan, Michael J. 1997. *Empowering Exporters: Delegation, Reciprocity, and Collective Action in Twentieth Century American Trade Policy.* Ann Arbor: University of Michigan Press.

Gilpin, Robert. 1987. *The Political Economy of International Relations.* Princeton, NJ: Princeton University Press.

Glick, Reuven, and Alan M. Taylor. 2005. "Collateral Damage: Trade Disruption and the Economic Impact of War." NBER Working Paper No. 11565.

Gowa, Joanne. 1989. "Bipolarity, Multipolarity, and Free Trade." *American Political Science Review*, 83: 1245–1256.

Gowa, Joanne. 1994. *Allies, Adversaries, and International Trade*. Princeton, NJ: Princeton University Press.

Grossman, Gene M., and Elhanan Helpman. 1994. "Protection for Sale." *The American Economic Review* 84: 833–850.

Grossman, Gene M., and Elhanan Helpman. 1995. "The Politics of Free-Trade Agreements." *The American Economic Review* 85: 667–690. (a)

Grossman, Gene M., and Elhanan Helpman. 1995. "Trade Wars and Trade Talks." *Journal of Political Economy* 103: 675–708. (b)

Grossman, Gene M., and Alan Sykes. 2005. "A Preference for Development: the Law and Economics of GSP." *World Trade Review* 4: 41–68.

Harrod, Roy F. 1951. *The Life of John Maynard Keynes*. New York: Harcourt Brace.

Hart, Michael. 1989. "Almost But Not Quite: The 1947–48 Bilateral Canada-U.S. Negotiations." *American Review of Canadian Studies* 19: 25–58.

Hart, Michael (ed.). 1995. *Also Present at the Creation: Dana Wilgress and the United Nations Conference on Trade and Employment at Havana*. Ottawa: Centre for Trade Policy and Law, Carleton University and University of Ottawa.

Hart, Michael. 1998. *Fifty years of Canadian Statecraft: Canada at the GATT 1947–1997*. Ottawa: Centre for Trade Policy and Law.

Hart, Michael. 2002. *A Trading Nation: Canadian Trade Policy from Colonialism to Globalization*. Vancouver, BC: UBC Press.

Hawkins, Harry C. 1948. "Problems Raised by the International Trade Organization," in *Foreign Economic Policy for the United States*, edited by Seymour E. Harris. Cambridge, MA: Harvard University Press.

Hawkins, Harry C. 1951. *Commercial Treaties and Agreements: Principles and Practice*. New York: Rinehart & Co.

Hegre, Håvard. 2000. "Development and the Liberal Peace: What Does It Take to Be a Trading State?" *Journal of Peace Research* 37: 5–30.

Henderson, Hubert Douglas, Sir. 1955. "Great Britain's Postwar Commercial Policy," in *The Inter-War Years and Other Papers: A Selection from the Writings of Hubert Douglas Henderson*. Edited by Henry Clay. Oxford: Clarendon Press.

Hillman, Arye L., and Peter Moser. 1996. "Trade Liberalization as Politically Optimal Exchange of Market Access," in *The New Transatlantic Economy*, edited by Matthew B. Canzoneri, Wilfred J. Ethier, and Vittorio Grilli. Cambridge and New York: Cambridge University Press.

Hiscox, Michael J. 1999. "The Magic Bullet? The RTAA, Institutional Reform, and Trade Liberalization." *International Organization*, 53: 669–698.

Hoda, Anwarul. 2001. *Tariff Negotiations and Renegotiations under the GATT and the WTO: Procedures and Practices*. Cambridge and New York: Cambridge University Press.

Hoekman, Bernard M., and Petros C. Mavroidis. 1996. "Dumping, Antidumping and Antitrust." *Journal of World Trade* 30: 27–52.

Hoekman, Bernard M., and Michel Kostecki. 2001. *The Political Economy of the World Trading System*. Oxford and New York: Oxford University Press.

Howson, Susan, and Donald Moggridge (eds.). 1990. *The Wartime Diaries of Lionel Robbins and James Meade, 1943–45*. London and New York: Macmillan.

Hudec, Robert E. 1975. *The GATT Legal System and World Trade Diplomacy*. New York: Praeger.

Hudec, Robert E. 1987. *Developing Countries in the GATT Legal System*. Aldershot, UK: Gower.

Hull, Cordell. 1948. *The Memoirs of Cordell Hull*. 2 vols. London and New York: Macmillan.

Hussain, A. Imtiaz. 1993. *Politics of Compensation: Truman, the Wool Bill of 1947, and the Shaping of Postwar U.S. Trade Policy*. New York: Garland.

Ikenberry, G. John. 1989. "Rethinking the Origins of American Hegemony." *Political Science Quarterly* 104: 375–400.

Ikenberry, G. John. 1992. "A World Economy Restored: Expert Consensus and the Anglo-American Postwar Settlement." *International Organization* 46: 289–321.

Ikenberry, G. John. 2001. *After Victory: Institutions, Strategic Restraint, and the Rebuilding of Order After Major Wars*. Princeton, NJ: Princeton University Press.

Irwin, Douglas A. 1995. "The GATT in Historical Perspective." *The American Economic Review*, 85: 323–328. (a)

Irwin, Douglas A. 1995. "The GATT's Contribution to Economic Recovery in Post-War Europe," *in* Barry Eichengreen (ed.), *Europe's Postwar Growth*. Cambridge and New York: Cambridge University Press. (b)

Irwin, Douglas A. 1996. *Against the Tide: An Intellectual History of Free Trade*. Princeton, NJ: Princeton University Press.

Irwin, Douglas A. 1998. "Changes in U.S. Tariffs: The Role of Import Prices and Commercial Policies." *The American Economic Review* 88: 1015–1026. (a)

Irwin, Douglas A. 1998. "From Smoot-Hawley to Reciprocal Trade Agreements: Changing the Course of U.S. Trade Policy in the 1930s," *in* Michael D. Bordo, Claudia Goldin, and Eugene N. White (eds.), *The Defining Moment: The Great Depression and the American Economy in the Twentieth Century*. Chicago: University of Chicago Press. (b)

Irwin, Douglas A. 2005. *Free Trade Under Fire* (2nd edition). Princeton, NJ: Princeton University Press.

Irwin, Douglas A. and Randall S. Kroszner. 1999. "Interests, Institutions, and Ideology in Securing Policy Change: The Republican Conversion to Trade Liberalization after Smoot-Hawley." *Journal of Law and Economics* 42: 643–673.

Jackson, John H. 1967. "The General Agreement on Tariffs and Trade in United States Domestic Law." *Michigan Law Review*, 66: 249–332.

Jackson, John H. 1969. *World Trade and the Law of the GATT*. Indianapolis: Bobbs-Merrill.

James, Harold. 2001. *The End of Globalization: Lessons from the Great Depression*. Cambridge, MA: Harvard University Press.

Johnson, Harry G. 1953–1954. "Optimum Tariffs and Retaliation." *The Review of Economic Studies* 21: 142–153.

Johnson, Harry G. 1968. "U.S. Economic Policy toward the Developing Countries." *Economic Development and Cultural Change* 16: 357–384.

Jones, Ronald W. 1969. "Tariffs and Trade in General Equilibrium: Comment." *The American Economic Review* 59: 418–424.

Keynes, John Maynard. 1979. *The Collected Writings of John Maynard Keynes*, edited by Donald Moggridge. Vol. 24, *Activities 1944–1946, The Transition to Peace*. London: Macmillan, Cambridge University Press, for the Royal Economic Society.

Keynes, John Maynard. 1980. *The Collected Writings of John Maynard Keynes*, edited by Donald Moggridge. Vol. 26, *Activities 1941–1946 , Shaping the Post-War World: Bretton Woods and Reparations*. London: Macmillan, Cambridge University Press, for the Royal Economic Society.

Kim, Hyung Min, and David L. Rousseau. 2005. "The Classical Liberals Were Half Right (or Half Wrong): New Tests of the 'Liberal Peace', 1960–88." *Journal of Peace Research* 42: 523–543.

Kimball, Warren F. 1971. "Lend-Lease and the Open Door: The Temptation of British Opulence, 1937–1942 ." *Political Science Quarterly* 86: 232–259.

Kindleberger, Charles P. 1973. *The World in Depression, 1929–1939*. Berkeley: University of California Press.

Kindleberger, Charles P. 1981. "Dominance and Leadership in the International Economy: Exploitation, Public Goods, and Free Rides." *International Studies Quarterly* 25: 242–254.

Kindleberger, Charles P. 1986. *The World in Depression, 1929–1939*. Berkeley: University of California Press.

Kindleberger, Charles P. 1989. "Commercial Policy Between the Wars," *in The Cambridge Economic History of Europe*, vol. 8, edited by P. Mathias and S. Pollard. Cambridge and New York: Cambridge University Press.

Kock, Karin. 1969. *International Trade Policy and the GATT 1947–1967*. Stockholm: Almqvist & Wiksell.

Krugman, Paul R. 1997. "What Should Trade Negotiators Negotiate About?" *Journal of Economic Literature* 35: 113–120.

Lake, David A. 1993. "Leadership, Hegemony, and the International Economy: Naked Emperor or Tattered Monarch with Potential?" *International Studies Quarterly* 37: 459–489.

Leacy, F. H. 1983. *Historical Statistics of Canada*. 2nd edition. Ottawa: Statistics Canada. Available online at: http://www.statcan.ca/english/freepub/11-516-XIE/sectiona/toc.htm (last visited Jan. 17, 2008).

League of Nations. 1933. *World Economic Survey*. Geneva: League of Nations.

League of Nations. 1942. *Commercial Policy in the Interwar Period: International Proposals and National Policies*. Geneva: League of Nations.

MacDougall, Donald, and Rosemary Hutt. 1954. "Imperial Preference: A Quantitative Analysis." *The Economic Journal* 64: 233–257.

Maggi, Giovanni, and Andrés Rodríguez-Clare. 1998. "The Value of Trade Agreements in the Presence of Political Pressures." *Journal of Political Economy*, 106: 574–601.

Maggi, Giovanni, and Andrés Rodríguez-Clare. 2007. "A Political-Economy Theory of Trade Agreements." *American Economic Review*. 97: 1374–1406.

Mansfield, Edward D., and Brian M. Pollins. 2001. "The Study of Interdependence and Conflict: Recent Advances, Open Questions, and Directions for Future Research. *Journal of Conflict Resolution* 45: 834–859.

References

Mansfield, Edward D., and Brian M. Pollins (eds.). 2003. *Economic Interdependence and International Conflict: New Perspectives on an Enduring Debate*. Ann Arbor: University of Michigan Press.

Markwell, Donald. 2006. *John Maynard Keynes and International Relations: Economic Paths to War and Peace*. Oxford and New York: Oxford University Press.

Martin, Philippe, Thierry Mayer, and Mathias Thoenig. 2008. "Make Trade Not War?" *The Review of Economic Studies*, forthcoming.

Mason, Edward S. 1946. *Controlling World Trade: Cartels and Commodity Agreements*. New York: McGraw-Hill Book Co.

Matsushita, Mitsuo, Thomas J. Schoenbaum & Petros C. Mavroidis. 2006. *The World Trade Organization: Law, Practice, and Policy*, 2nd edition, Oxford and New York: Oxford University Press.

Mavroidis, Petros C. 2007. *Trade in Goods*. Oxford and New York: Oxford University Press.

Mayer, Wolfgang. 1981. "Theoretical Considerations on Negotiated Tariff Adjustments." *Oxford Economic Papers* 33: 135–153.

McDonald, Patrick J., and Kevin Sweeney. 2007. "The Achilles' Heel of Liberal IR Theory? Globalization and Conflict in the Pre-World War I Era." *World Politics* 59: 370–403.

McKenzie, Francine. 1998. "Renegotiating a Special Relationship: The Commonwealth and Anglo-American Economic Discussions, September-December 1945." *The Journal of Imperial and Commonwealth History* 26: 71–93.

McKenzie, Francine. 2002. *Redefining the Bonds of Commonwealth, 1939–1948: The Politics of Preference*. London and New York: Palgrave Macmillan.

McKeown, Timothy. 1983. "Hegemonic Stability Theory and 19th Century Tariff Levels in Europe." *International Organization*. 37: 73–91.

Meade, James E. 1940. *The Economic Basis of a Durable Peace*. London: Allen & Unwin.

Meade, James E. 1990. *The Collected Papers of James Meade*, edited by Susan Howson and Donald Moggridge. Volume IV: The Cabinet Office Diary 1944–1946 . London: Unwin Hyman.

Mill, John Stuart. 1848 [1909]. *Principles of Political Economy with Some of Their Applications to Social Philosophy*, edited by William J. Ashley. London: Longmans, Green and Co.

Miller, James N. 2000. "Origins of the GATT: British Resistance to American Multilateralism," *Cambridge University, Jerome Levy Economics Institute at Bard College, Working Paper No. 318*.

Miller, James N. 2003. *Wartime Origins of Multilateralism, 1939–1945: The Impact of the Anglo-American Trade Policy Negotiations*. Ph.D. thesis, Emmanuel College, University of Cambridge.

Mitchell, Brian R. 1988. *British Historical Statistics*. Cambridge and New York: Cambridge University Press.

Morrow, James D. 1999. "How Could Trade Affect Conflict?" *Journal of Peace Research* 36: 481–489.

Mundell, Robert A. 1964. "Tariff Preferences and the Terms of Trade." *Manchester School of Economic and Social Studies* 32: 1–13.

Newton, C. C. S. 1984. "The Sterling Crisis of 1947 and the British Response to the Marshall Plan." *The Economic History Review* 37: 391–408.

Norbom, J. O. H. 1962. *International Trade Statistics, 1900–1960*. Unpublished working paper, United Nations Statistical Office.
Notter, Harley A. n.d. *History of the Division of Commercial Policy*. National Archives. LF 59 – Harley Notter Papers.
Notter, Harley A. 1949. *Postwar Foreign Policy Preparation, 1939–1945*. Washington, DC: Government Printing Office.
O'Brien, Denis P. 1976. "Customs Unions: Trade Creation and Trade Diversion in Historical Perspective." *History of Political Economy* 8: 540–563.
Odell, John, and Barry Eichengreen. 1998. "The United States, the ITO, and the WTO: Exit Options, Agent Slack, and Presidential Leadership, pp. 181–209 *in* Anne O. Krueger (ed.), *The WTO as an International Organization*. Chicago: University of Chicago Press.
O'Halloran, Sharyn. 1994. *Politics, Process, and American Trade Policy*. Ann Arbor: University of Michigan Press.
Oneal, John R., and Bruce M. Russett. 1997. "The Classical Liberals Were Right: Democracy, Interdependence, and Conflict, 1950–1985." *International Studies Quarterly* 41: 267–294.
Oneal, John R., and Bruce M. Russett. 1999. "Assessing the Liberal Peace with Alternative Specifications: Trade Still Reduces Conflict." *Journal of Peace Research* 36: 423–442.
Palmeter, David N. and Petros C. Mavroidis. 2004. *Dispute Settlement in the World Trade Organization, Practice and Procedure*, 2nd edition. Cambridge and New York: Cambridge University Press.
Penrose, Ernest F. 1953. *Economic Planning for the Peace*. Princeton, NJ: Princeton University Press.
Pimlott, Ben. 1985. *Hugh Dalton*. London: J. Cape.
Polachek, Solomon W. 1980. "Conflict and Trade." *The Journal of Conflict Resolution* 24: 55–78.
Pressnell, L. S. 1986. *External Economic Policy Since the War: Volume I, The Post-War Financial Settlement*. London: HMSO.
Rassmussen, Kathleen B. 2001. *Canada and the Reconstruction of the International Economy, 1941–1947*. Ph. D. Thesis, Department of History. University of Toronto.
Regan, Donald H. 2006. "What Are Trade Agreements For? – Two Conflicting Stories Told by Economists, With a Lesson for Lawyers." *Journal of International Economic Law* 9: 951–988.
Reynolds, David. 1982. *The Creation of the Anglo-American Alliance 1937–41: A Study in Competitive Co-operation*. Chapel Hill: University of North Carolina Press.
Robbins, Lionel. 1971. *Autobiography of an Economist*. London and New York: Macmillan.
Rodrik, Dani. 1999. *Making Openness Work: The New Global Economy and the Developing Countries*. Washington, DC: Overseas Development Council.
Rubin, Seymour J. 1949. "The Judicial Review Problem in the International Trade Organization." *Harvard Law Review* 63: 78–98.
Schatz, Arthur W. 1970. "The Anglo-American Trade Agreement and Cordell Hull's Search for Peace 1936–1938." *Journal of American History* 57: 85–103.
Schnietz, Karen E. 2000. "The Institutional Foundations of U.S. Trade Policy: Revisiting Explanations for the 1934 Reciprocal Trade Agreements Act." *Journal of Policy History* 12: 417–444.
Skidelsky, Robert. 2000. *John Maynard Keynes: Fighting for Britain 1937–1946*. London and New York: Macmillan.

References

Skidelsky, Robert. 2005. *John Maynard Keynes: 1883–1946: Economist, Philosopher, Statesman.* London and New York: Penguin.

Staiger, Robert W., and Guido Tabellini. 1987. "Discretionary Trade Policy and Excessive Protection." *The American Economic Review* 77: 823–837.

Staiger, Robert W., and Guido Tabellini. 1999. "Do GATT Rules Help Governments Make Domestic Commitments?" *Economics and Politics* 11: 109–144.

Stein, Arthur A. 1984. "The Hegemon's Dilemma: Great Britain, the United States, and the International Economic Order." *International Organization*, 38: 355–386.

Toye, Richard. 2000. "The Labour Party's External Economic Policy in the 1940s." *The Historical Journal* 43: 189–215.

Toye, Richard. 2003. "Developing Multilateralism: The Havana Charter and the Fight for the International Trade Organization, 1947–1948 ." *The International History Review* 25: 282–305. (a)

Toye, Richard. 2003. "The Attlee Government, the Imperial Preference System, and the Creation of the GATT." *The English Historical Review* 118: 912–939. (b)

Toye, Richard. 2008. *Cripps versus Clayton.* Unpublished manuscript.

Trebilcock, Michael J. and Robert L. Howse. 2005. *The Regulation of International Trade*, 3rd edition, London and New York: Routledge.

Truman, Harry S. 1955. *Memoirs. Volume 1: Year of Decisions.* Garden City, N.Y.: Doubleday & Co.

Tumlir, Jan. 1985. *Protectionism: Trade Policy in Democratic Societies.* Washington, DC: American Enterprise Institute.

U.S. Bureau of the Census. 1975. *Historical Statistics of the United States, Colonial Times to 1970: Bicentennial Edition.* Washington, DC: Government Printing Office.

U.S. Tariff Commission. 1948. *Operation of the Trade Agreements Program, July 1934 to April 1948, Part 1. Summary.* Washington, DC: Government Printing Office.

Van den Bossche, Peter. 2005. *The Law and Policy of the World Trade Organization: Text, Cases and Materials.* Cambridge and New York: Cambridge University Press.

Verdier, Daniel. 1994. *Democracy and International Trade: Britain, France, and the United States, 1860–1990.* Princeton, NJ: Princeton University Press.

Wilcox, Clair. 1949. *A Charter for World Trade.* London and New York: Macmillan.

Wilgress, Leolyn Dana. 1967. *Memoirs.* Toronto: Ryerson Press.

Wilkinson, Rorden, and James Scott. 2008. "Developing Country Participation in the GATT: A reassessment." *World Trade Review* 7: forthcoming.

Wilson, Theodore A. 1991. *The First Summit: Roosevelt and Churchill at Placentia Bay, 1941.* Rev. ed. Lawrence, KS: University Press of Kansas.

Woods, Randall B. 1990. *A Changing of the Guard: Anglo-American Relations, 1941–1946.* Chapel Hill: University of North Carolina Press.

Worswick, David, and James Trevithick (eds.). 1983. *Keynes and the Modern World.* Cambridge and New York: Cambridge University Press.

Xiang, Jun, Xiaohong Xu, and George Keteku. 2007. "Power: The Missing Link in the Trade Conflict Relationship." *Journal of Conflict Resolution* 51: 646–663.

Zeiler, Thomas W. 1999. *Free Trade, Free World: The Advent of GATT.* Chapel Hill: University of North Carolina Press.

Index

Aaronson, S. A., 3, 50, 59, 95
Abramson, 123n, 294n
Abus de droit, 139
Accession, 169
Acheson, D., 13n–16n, 18, 27, 31n, 49, 51, 57–60, 62, 70n, 82, 84
Action Committee, 295
Actual value, 146, 147
AD. *See* Antidumping duties
Adarkar, 287, 288, 290
Advisory opinion, 165
AFL. *See* American Federation of Labor
Agricultural Adjustment Act, 158
Agriculture, 10, 53, 59, 77, 83, 245, 251
Ahmad, 293
Air traffic, 143
Alamilla, 288
Allen, W., 10n
Alvarez, 285
Amendment, 59, 85n, 152, 168, 169, 268, 282
American Federation of Labor, 107
Amery, L., 19, 24, 27, 33, 34, 43, 44, 47, 48, 53, 56
Anticircumvention, 135, 139n, 140, 147, 172
Antidumping duties, 132, 144–146
Arab League, 109n
Armstrong, 287
Article VII, 12–15, 17–22, 27, 28, 37, 39, 44, 48, 49, 53, 56, 57, 61, 69, 203, 213–215, 221, 226, 252, 254, 257, 276, 281
Ashford, 123n, 294n
Atlantic Charter in 1941, 12–21, 90, 252, 276

Attlee, C., 55, 56, 71, 86n, 91, 92
Augenthaler, 285
Australia, 3, 6, 35, 36, 39, 47, 48, 64, 71, 72, 76–80, 87, 96, 100, 101, 106, 117, 120, 121, 125–127, 129, 147, 153, 158, 162, 174, 186, 190, 266, 273, 279, 284–290, 292, 293, 295
Average level of duties, 167, 168

Balance of payments, 6, 26, 28, 32n–34n, 40, 43, 44, 46n, 64, 66, 71, 73n, 78n, 79, 86, 91, 101, 108, 110, 143, 151, 153–155, 172, 214, 215, 222, 228, 242, 252, 256–258, 281
Baldwin, R., 188, 189
Barcelona Convention of April 20, 1921, 143
Basic Instruments and Selected Documents, 121, 125n
Beaverbrook, Lord, 19, 24, 43, 45, 56
Benelux (Belgium, Netherlands, Luxembourg), 164, 279
BISD. *See* Basic Instruments and Selected Documents
Board of Trade (UK), 25, 26, 28–30, 33, 37, 41, 55, 61, 66, 71, 84, 88, 94
BOP. *See* Balance of payments
Boycott, 108, 113, 169–170, 248, 254, 286, 292
BrettonWoods, 43, 67
British Loan (1945), 2, 3, 65–72, 75, 89, 90
Brown, Jr., W. A., 95, 109, 133, 157, 158, 168
Brown, W. G., 84, 90, 280
Brussels Convention of December 29, 1913, 170

307

Brussels Convention on Nomenclature for the Classification of Goods in Customs Tariffs, 117n
Brussels Tariff Bureau, 150
BTN. *See* Brussels Convention on Nomenclature for the Classification of Goods in Customs Tariffs
Butler, M. A., 10
Butler, H., 81
Buy National, 134, 169, 170
Byrnes, J., 54, 71, 75

Camejo Argudin, 130
Canada, 3, 6, 10, 16, 34–36, 39, 42, 47, 49, 57, 58, 63, 64, 71, 72, 76–78, 80, 85, 86, 90, 93, 96, 97, 100, 101, 115–117, 120. 125, 133n, 145n, 152n, 162, 164, 168, 174, 180–183, 187, 192, 201, 266, 273, 279, 284, 286–295
Capling, A., 3, 78
Cartels, and restrictive business practices, 37, 40, 50, 79, 98, 99, 104, 107, 115, 144, 248, 251, 267, 285, 289, 295
Catudal, 291
CCC. *See* Customs Cooperation Council
CCCN. *See* Customs Cooperation Council Nomenclature
Chamberlain, J., 19
Charnovitz, S., 98, 163, 164
Chase, K. A., 167, 168
Chundrigar, 186
Churchill, W., 16, 18–22, 24, 25, 33, 34, 45, 55, 56, 68, 196
Clark, 183
Clayton, W., 23, 24, 27, 54, 55, 57, 58, 62, 64–67, 75, 80–82, 84, 86–92, 96, 196, 197, 245
Colban, 115, 287, 289
Collective action, 128, 190
Comisão de Similares, 141
Commercial considerations, 139, 159, 160, 234, 237, 259
Commercial Union (Meade), 27–36, 38, 201, 203
Commission A, 115, 289
Commission B, 115, 289
Committee I, 107, 285
Committee II, 99, 105, 107, 285–287
Committee III, 107, 125, 285
Committee III (1958), 125–127, 129, 295

Committee IV, 107, 285
Committee V, 107, 285
Committee on Chapters I, II, VIII, 289
Committee on Legal and Institutional Framework, 125, 126, 295
Commitment theory, 184–186, 198
Committee on Trade and Development, 132
Compensation, 12, 98, 128, 137, 205, 236
Conservative Party (UK), 19, 48, 55
Consular fees, 148n
Consultations, 2, 16, 21, 35–37, 61, 79, 104, 106, 108, 109, 149, 153, 155, 157, 161, 162, 165–166, 204, 212, 234, 241, 249, 250, 252, 253, 256–261, 286
Contracting parties, 96, 102, 103, 114, 119–122, 124–127, 130, 131, 133, 166, 168, 174, 283, 284, 295
Coombs, 96, 186, 273, 275, 285, 286, 290
Couillard, 294
Count de Liedekerke, 291
Countervailing duties, 101, 108, 144, 145, 225, 254, 281, 282, 285
CU. *See* Customs union
Cultural exception, 139
Customary international law, 111
Customs Cooperation Council, 136, 147
Customs Cooperation Council Nomenclature, 117
Customs formalities, 80, 108, 113, 147–148, 212, 254, 267, 282, 285, 292
Customs territory, 167, 227, 260
Customs union, 32, 68, 107, 109, 117, 121, 122, 167, 168, 186, 226, 227, 238, 243, 260, 261, 279, 293
CVD. *See* Countervailing duties

Dalton, H., 25, 27, 29, 30, 32–34, 47–49, 55, 56, 66, 68, 71, 84
Dam, K. W., 3, 10
DCS. *See* Directly competitive or substitutable products
de Saint-Légier, 123n, 294n
Devaluation, 153
de Vilhena Ferreira Braga, 115n, 289n
Developing countries, 50, 73, 78, 79, 85, 105, 121, 122n, 123–134, 153, 154, 158, 173, 174, 183, 186, 190, 202, 295
Diebold, Jr., William, 3, 95n
Dieterlen, 291

Index

Directly competitive or substitutable products, 138, 141, 142
Disposal of surpluses, 147
Dispute settlement, 29, 101, 125, 128, 165–166
Dispute Settlement Understanding, 165, 166, 186
Domestic quota, 151, 152
Dominions, UK consultations with, 6, 16, 18, 21, 24, 26, 34, 35, 37, 48, 53, 68, 69, 89
Donovan, 295
Dorn, 291n
Drache, D., 101
Drafting Committee, 2, 80, 81, 100, 101, 103, 105, 107, 108, 110–112, 114, 123, 268, 275, 286–288, 291, 294
Drafting Sub-committee on Quantitative Restrictions and Exchange Control, 286
DSU. See Dispute Settlement Understanding
Dubais, 123n, 294n
Dumping, 98, 122, 144–146, 218, 232

Economic and Social Council, 62, 73, 77, 106, 245, 251, 276
Economic Section, War Cabinet Secretariat (UK), 3, 25, 28
ECOSOC. See Economic and Social Council
ECSC. See European Coal and Steel Community
EEC. See European Economic Community
Effects doctrine, 173n
Eichengreen, B., 3, 95n, 183n
Elasticity pessimism, 127
Emergency, 6, 92, 109, 161, 162, 211, 229, 240, 245, 255, 286
Emergency conditions, 237
Employment, 6, 15, 21, 26, 31, 36, 38, 47, 51, 52, 54, 55, 61–63, 67, 71–73, 76–79, 81, 84, 85, 95, 98–101, 104–107, 114, 120, 169, 176, 186, 203, 239, 244–253, 261, 262, 266, 267, 270, 271, 275, 276, 280, 285, 295
Enabling clause, 128, 132, 133
Equitable share of world trade, 158
Equivalence propositions, 172
Ethier, W. J., 179
European Coal and Steel Community, 167
European Economic Community, 128
Evans, 126

Exchange rate, flexibility, 28
Exchange regulations, 148n
Exchange restrictions, 6, 31, 51, 108, 119, 155, 156, 230, 256, 260
Executive Board, 272, 275, 288
Executive Secretary, 118, 288
Exhaustible natural resources, 163
Export promotion, 128
Export subsidies, 40, 50, 64, 70, 77, 79, 85, 113, 114, 121, 133, 156–159, 173, 231, 232, 242, 258, 259
Export taxes, 69, 70, 136n, 179, 180, 230

Fair and equitable treatment, 159, 207
Fair trade, 122, 248, 294
FAO. See Food and Agriculture Organization
Fawcett, 291
Fees and formalities, 147, 174
Film hire tax, 140
Finger, J. M., 173
Fixed parities, 153
Fleming, J. M., 25, 26, 46, 61
Food and Agriculture Organization, 107, 111, 147, 247, 252, 272
Foreign Office (UK), 13, 19, 37, 47
France, 6, 12, 64, 65, 72, 75, 76, 78, 100, 101, 106, 115, 117, 120, 123, 125, 139, 147, 149, 152, 154, 156, 160, 164, 168, 174, 192, 266, 273, 276, 279, 281, 284, 286–294
Free trade area, 121, 122, 167, 168
Frontier traffic, 167, 211, 226, 260, 261
FTA. See Free trade area
Fumigation, 148

G4. See Group of 4
Ganguli, 163
Garcia Oldini, 122, 293, 294
Gardner, R., 3, 10
GATT. See General Agreement on Tariffs and Trade
GATT acquis, 198
GDP. See Gross Domestic Product
General Agreement on Tariffs and Trade, 1–6, 72, 74, 77, 80, 84–86, 91–108, 165, 277, 279, 280, 284
General exceptions, 101, 108, 162–164, 243, 260, 283, 286, 292, 294
General incidence of duties, 168

Generalized system of preferences, 130, 133, 135
Geneva Conference, 1, 4, 24, 27, 82, 83, 87–90, 94, 101, 103, 114–119, 135, 137, 141, 143, 145, 146, 148, 150, 152, 154, 155, 158, 160, 162, 164, 165, 167, 169–171, 183, 192, 196, 199, 201, 288–291
Geneva Convention of December 14, 1928, 170
Geneva Convention of November 3, 1923, 147
Geneva Final Act, 101, 114
Geneva Nomenclature, 117
Geographical or regional origin, 149, 292
GN. *See* Geneva Nomenclature
Government procurement, 109, 110, 134, 142, 159
Great Depression, 5, 180
Group of 4, 110
GSP. *See* Generalized system of preferences
Gunter, 286
Guttierez, 291

Haberler report (1958), 124
Hague Arrangement of November 6, 1925, 149
Haguiwara, 123n, 294n
Hart, M., 3, 77, 86, 88
Havana Charter, 98, 102, 103
Havana Conference (1947–1948), 95, 103, 120–122, 135, 137, 142, 143, 145, 146, 148, 150, 151, 153, 154, 156, 158, 161–165, 167–171, 283, 291–293
Hawkins, H. C., 16, 23, 26, 37–39, 42, 52–54, 56, 57, 60–62, 77, 78, 84, 109, 110
Hawley-Smoot tariff (1930), 6, 8, 24, 89
Heads of Delegations, 268, 289
Helmore, J. R. C., 25, 77, 84, 88
Henderson, H. D., 31–33
Hoekman, B. M., 173
Hollis, 123n, 294n
Holloway, 186, 290, 292
Horn, H., 131
Hudec, R. E., 3, 174, 185
Hudson, R. S., 24, 43
Hull, C., 9–14, 17, 18, 20, 22, 23, 25, 27, 31, 37, 39, 49, 50, 54, 55, 59, 83, 191, 192, 195, 196, 200

Hurst, A., 33
Huysmans, 192

ICA. *See* International Cooperative Alliance
ICC. *See* International Chamber of Commerce
ICJ. *See* International Court of Justice
IFAP. *See* International Federation of Agricultural Producers
ILO. *See* International Labour Organization
IMF. *See* International Monetary Fund
Imperial preferences, 10, 13–21, 23, 24, 26, 27, 29, 34, 35, 39, 43–45, 47, 48, 52, 55, 56, 62, 67, 68, 87, 88, 90, 91, 93, 95, 109, 133, 134, 171, 182, 183, 190, 196
Infant-industry protection, 174, 202
Information, statistics, and trade terminology, 108, 170–171, 286
Injury, 10, 50, 83, 101, 144, 145, 161, 209, 210, 240, 255, 258, 282
Inspection, 148, 189
Interim Tariff Committee, 105, 168
Interim Trade Committee, 168, 283
Internal taxation, 100, 254, 281, 285, 292
Internal taxes, 12, 86, 108, 109, 138–142, 204, 205, 208, 264, 282
International Chamber of Commerce, 107
International commodity agreement, 99, 115, 151, 163, 229, 230, 289
International Cooperative Alliance, 107
International Court of Justice, 165
International Federation of Agricultural Producers, 107n, 118n
International Labour Organization, 107n, 111
International Monetary Fund, 22n, 25n, 43, 99, 107, 111, 155, 156, 252, 256, 257, 260, 262, 286
International Trade Centre, 132
International Trade Organization, 2, 3, 23, 24, 28n, 51, 61, 62, 63, 64, 69, 73, 75, 77, 79, 84, 85, 87, 98–106, 108, 113–115, 120–122, 132, 136, 138, 139, 144, 147, 150, 152, 155, 156, 163, 165, 168, 171–174, 183, 186, 192, 201, 240, 241, 243, 245, 249, 251–253, 260, 262–264, 268, 269, 270, 272, 273, 275, 276, 280–283, 287, 289
Irwin, D. A., 8n, 94, 95, 118n, 183n
ITC. *See* International Trade Centre
ITO. *See* International Trade Organization

Index

Jackson, J. H., 3, 99–101, 119, 133, 136, 146, 173
Jenkins, T., 82
Johnson, H. G., 138, 144, 174, 178, 179, 287
Joint Committee on Industrial Development, 285
Joint Sub-committee on Arts 16 and 42, 293

Keynes, J. M., 13–16, 18–20, 25–28, 30–33, 37, 38, 41, 43, 45, 46, 54, 65–68, 70, 84, 110
King, 93
Kock, K., 174
Kojève, A., 110
Kojève, M., 287
Kostecki, M., 301

Labour Party (UK), 19, 25, 29, 55, 91
Lacarte, 125, 288n
Lake Success, NY, 2, 80, 81, 100, 111, 115
Lall, 127, 295
Lamsvelt, 292
Law, R., 37, 43, 44, 47, 207
Laws, regulations and requirements, 140
League of Nations, 5, 6, 25, 133, 136, 161, 163
Leddy, J., 23, 58, 59, 80, 81, 100, 107, 286
Legal and Drafting Committee, 23, 268, 294
Legal Drafting Sub-committee, 112, 287
Lend lease, 12, 13, 18, 20, 36, 65, 276
Letts, 129
Liability rules, 166
Licensing, 43, 119, 148, 227
Like products, 17, 127, 134, 138, 140–142, 145, 231, 247, 258
Lleras Restrepo, 292
London Conference, 99, 100, 103–105, 108, 110, 111, 113, 116, 118, 133–136, 138, 143–151, 153–157, 159, 161, 162, 165, 167–170, 172, 285, 287, 288
London Draft, 103–109, 113, 133–135, 138–140, 143–145, 147, 149–151, 153–157, 159–162, 164, 165, 167, 169, 287, 288n
Lovett, R. A., 92, 197, 277

Madrid Convention of April 14, 1891, 149
Margin of preference, 95, 129, 183
Marks of origin, 80, 108n, 133, 149–150, 170, 254, 267, 282, 285, 290, 292
Marshall Plan, 89, 92, 96, 121, 280

Mavroidis, P. C., 99, 122, 145, 173
McCarthy, 287, 293
McKinnon, R., 109
Meade, J., 3, 23n, 25–31, 33, 35–40, 46, 52–54, 61, 66, 68, 69, 71, 76, 77, 84, 110, 201, 203, 221, 286
Melander, 290, 293
MFN. *See* Most-favored-nation clause
Miller, J. N., 3, 11, 28, 44, 45, 55, 173
Mixing requirements, 139, 142
Miyazaki, 295
Moderow, 115
Monaco, 123n, 294n
Monteiro de Barros-Filho, 291
Morton, 138, 144, 292
Most-favored-nation clause, 5, 15, 40, 60, 204, 263, 284
Muller, 291

Nash, J., 293
National treatment, 80n, 100, 101, 107, 134, 135, 139–142, 264, 285
Naude, 289
New York Conference, 100, 105n, 107, 111–115, 134, 136, 139, 143, 145, 146, 148–152, 154, 155, 157, 159, 161, 164–170, 287, 288
New York Draft, 101, 103, 112–114, 119, 134, 139, 143, 145, 146, 148–151, 154, 155, 157, 158, 161, 164, 165, 167–170, 287, 291
New York Draft ITO Charter, 114, 134, 139n, 143, 145–151, 154, 155, 157, 158, 161, 164, 165, 167, 169, 170, 291
New York GATT Draft, 113, 114, 116, 134, 136, 139, 143, 145, 146, 148–151, 154, 155, 157, 159–161, 164, 165, 167, 168, 170, 290, 291
NGO. *See* Nongovernmental organization
Nogués, J. J., 173
Non adimpleti contractus, 136
Nongovernmental organization, 107, 118
Nontariff barrier, 50, 64, 119, 136, 140
NTB. *See* Nontariff barrier
Nullification and impairment, 98
NVC (nonviolation complaint), 113, 165, 172, 198

OCD. *See* Ordinary customs duty
ODC. *See* Other duties and charges
Odell, J., 3, 95

Ordinary customs duty, 147, 208
Other duties and charges, 109, 147
Ottawa Agreements. *See* Imperial preferences
Overton, A., 30–33, 35

Palmeter, D. N., 99
Panel, 122, 156, 166, 185, 186
Parangua, 108
Part IV, 103, 119, 124–127, 129–133, 173, 202, 295
Partsch, 123n, 294n
Penrose, E. F., 15, 26, 28, 41, 57, 61
Perez Cisneros, 123n, 294n
Philip, 192
Phillips, 290, 295
PPA. *See* Protocol of Provisional Application
Prebisch, R., 126
Predation, 173
Preferences, 3, 6, 10, 13–23, 25–27, 29. *See* Tariff preferences
Preferential arrangements, 108, 167–168
Preparatory Committee, 73, 77, 81, 94, 98, 100, 101, 103–108, 111, 112, 114–117, 186, 270, 274–276, 280, 283, 285, 286
Price dumping, 144
Price stabilization, 156
Principal supplier rule, 116, 174, 198
Prior commitments, 111, 175
Prison labor, 98
Property rules, 166
Protection, 9, 29, 36, 48, 55, 81, 82, 99, 110, 121, 131, 139, 141, 142, 147, 149, 163, 164, 171, 173, 174, 202, 207, 211, 212, 216–219, 222, 225, 234–237, 243, 247, 254, 260, 265, 281, 282
Protocol of Provisional Application, 96, 101, 119, 280, 282, 284
Provisional International Civil Air Organization, 143
Publication and administration of trade regulations, 108, 150, 286
Public order, 131, 164
Public safety, 164, 207, 218
Puig Arosemena, 291

QR (Quantitative restrictions), 79, 85, 121, 122n, 123, 152, 153, 162, 171, 292
Quarantine sanitation, 148

Rayburn, S., 57, 59
Reciprocal Trade Agreements Act (RTAA), renewal (1940, 1943, 1945), 8–10, 24, 36–39, 50, 57, 60, 62, 75, 81–83, 89, 96, 187, 188
Reciprocity, 58, 81n, 116, 130, 131, 178, 198, 199
Renegotiation, 109, 124, 136–138, 173, 185, 198, 268
Republican Party (U.S.), 8, 197
Reservation, 34, 164, 170
Restrictive business practices. *See* Cartels
Retaliation, 166
Review Session, 103, 119, 122–123, 135, 137, 142, 143, 146, 148, 150, 151, 153, 154, 156, 158, 161, 162, 164, 168–172, 293–295
Revision, 20, 75, 104, 121, 123, 135, 169, 222, 291
Rhydderch, 139
Robbins, L., 25–27, 37, 38, 45, 53, 61, 64, 66, 68, 70, 71, 88, 110
Robertson, N., 35, 36, 49, 58, 187
Rodrik, D., 131
Roux, 144
Royer, 115, 289n, 291n, 293
RTAA. *See* Reciprocal Trade Agreements Act (RTAA), renewal (1940, 1943, 1945)
Rubin, S. J., 165
Rules of origin, 294

Safeguards, 6, 34, 82, 99, 109, 113, 132, 145n, 154, 161, 162, 198, 204, 228, 251, 256, 264, 281
Sahlin, 293
Sanders, 293
Schuman, 167n
Schwenger, 287
Scott, J., 174
Secretariat, 25, 28, 30, 113, 118n, 143, 170, 295
Seidenfaden, 122, 293, 294
Serious injury, 50, 83, 144, 209, 240, 258, 282
Serious prejudice, 157
Shackle, R. J., 27, 28, 53, 64, 65, 287–290, 292
Shah, 127
Singer, H., 126
Situation complaint, 165
Skak-Nielsen, 295
Skidelsky, R., 70
Social dumping, 98n

Index

South Africa, 6, 35, 36, 47, 48, 64, 71, 72, 76, 100, 101, 106, 117, 120, 140, 141, 155, 162, 179, 186, 266, 287–290, 292, 295
Speekenbrink, 285, 286
State monopolies, 159
State trading, 159–161
State trading enterprises, 86, 109, 113, 159, 160, 259, 282, 289
Statistical evidence, 148, 194
STE. *See* State trading enterprises
Steering Group, 22, 293
Stettinius, E., 54, 56
Stuyck, 123n, 294n
Sub-committee A, 292
Sub-committee on Administration, 288
Sub-committee on Arts. 14, 15, and 24, 290
Sub-committee on Arts. 25 and 27, 290
Sub-committee on Arts. 26, 28, and 29, 290
Sub-committee B, 292
Sub-committee C, 292
Sub-committee D, 292
Sub-committee E, 292
Sub-committee F, 292
Sub-committee G, 293
Sub-committee H, 293
Sub-committee on Infant Industry, 290
Sub-committee J, 293
Sub-committee on Marketing Boards, 287
Sub-committee on Procedure, 286
Sub-committee on State Trading, 287
Sub-committee on Subsidies, 289
Sub-committee on Tariff Negotiations, 112, 157, 287, 288
Sub-committee on Tariff Procedures, 288n
Sub-committee on Voting and Executive Board Membership, 288
Subsidies
 domestic, 40, 105, 157, 158, 232, 243
 export, 40, 50, 64, 70, 77n, 79, 85n, 113, 114, 121n, 133n, 156, 157n, 158, 159, 173, 231, 232, 242, 243, 258, 259
Subsidies Code, 101
Substantial trade liberalization, 167
Suetens, 114, 115n, 285, 289n, 294
Suggested Charter, 77, 104, 105, 108–110, 138, 144, 156, 170, 171, 174, 272, 274, 276
Suzuki, 127

Tariff Commission (U.S.), 24, 38, 81–83, 94, 118
Tariff concession, 80, 83, 84, 86, 99–101, 113, 116, 117, 135, 140, 142, 172, 173, 263–265, 267, 269, 271, 277, 279, 281, 282, 284
Tariff escalation, 124, 131
Tariff Negotiations Working Party, 116, 291
Tariff nomenclature, 136, 265, 266
Tariff preference, 10, 17, 19, 35, 39, 50, 64, 69, 105, 125–129, 133, 134, 182, 227, 240, 247, 254, 255, 281, 286
Tariff reduction
 bilateral, 62, 221, 270, 280
 horizontal, 50, 57, 60, 62, 63
 multilateral, 30, 38, 49, 60, 198, 221, 222, 225
 selective, 50, 62, 64
Tariff Steering Committee, 117, 118, 291
Tariff valuation, 80, 113, 146–147, 223, 225, 226, 254, 267, 282, 285
Tax exemption, 157
Technical Group on Customs Administration, 123, 294
Technical Sub-committee, 107, 285, 286, 288
Termination, 17, 88, 169, 204, 244
Terms of trade, 2, 46, 99, 126, 127, 131, 177–185, 197–199, 201, 232, 240
Third Committee, 121, 291, 292
Tokyo Round, 101
Trade and development, 103, 122, 125, 126, 132, 295
Trade-related intellectual property rights, 149, 186
Transit, 80, 108, 143, 254, 282, 285, 292
TRIPs. *See* Trade-related intellectual property rights
Tumlir, J., 184

UN. *See* United Nations
UN Conference on Trade and Employment, 73, 95, 100, 101, 114, 120
UN Information Centre, 104n, 116n
UN Statistical Office, 292
Unfair practice, 144
Unforeseen developments, 82, 161, 209
Union Agreement of Paris/Brussels of December 14, 1900, 149

United Nations, 13, 73, 77, 80, 84, 86, 95, 98–101, 104, 106, 107, 114, 115n, 116n, 120n, 122n, 132, 144n, 192, 195, 245, 251, 252, 261, 262, 276, 280, 282
Uruguay Round, 119, 121, 132

van der Straten-Waillot, B., 192
van Tilchelen, 291
Vandenberg, A., 82, 83
Variable geometry, 295
VCLT. *See* Vienna Convention on the Law of Treaties
Videla, 109, 286
Vienna Convention on the Law of Treaties, 111
Violation complaint, 165
von Bargen, 123n, 294n

Warwick Smith, 293
Washington Arrangement of June 2, 1911, 149
WB. *See* World Bank
Weighted voting, 156, 272
Welles, S., 13, 16
White, H. D., 22, 37, 38, 41n
Wilcox, C., 24, 77–79, 81, 84–86, 89, 95, 96, 192, 270

Wilgress, D., 96, 115, 116, 121, 122, 192, 289, 291, 293
Wilkinson, R., 174
Winant, J., 18, 19, 45, 53, 57
Withdrawal, 12, 83, 88, 137, 166, 169, 204, 210
Wool, 87, 89, 278
Working Party I, 123, 292–294
Working Party II, 123, 292–294
Working Party III, 123, 292–294
Working Party IV, 123, 292–294
Working Party on Preferences, 125, 126, 295
Working Party on Tariff Negotiations, 116, 291
Working Party on Technical Articles, 289
World Bank, 43, 73, 99, 107, 111
World Economic Conference of 1927, 5, 147, 162n, 163n, 164
World Federation of Trade Unions, 107n, 118n
World War I, 5, 7, 9, 133, 191, 199
World War II, 1, 5, 11, 83, 99, 189, 192, 195
Wyndham-White, E., 118, 163

Young, 287

Zeiler, T. W., 3, 86, 91, 93, 95

Lightning Source UK Ltd.
Milton Keynes UK
UKOW04f0940180815

257109UK00001B/92/P